Mary Howitt, Fredrika Bremer

Life in the Old World

Or, Two years in Switzerland and Italy

Mary Howitt, Fredrika Bremer

Life in the Old World
Or, Two years in Switzerland and Italy

ISBN/EAN: 9783744726344

Printed in Europe, USA, Canada, Australia, Japan

Cover: Foto ©Andreas Hilbeck / pixelio.de

More available books at **www.hansebooks.com**

LIFE IN THE OLD WORLD;

OR,

TWO YEARS IN SWITZERLAND AND ITALY.

BY

FREDRIKA BREMER.

AUTHOR OF
"THE FATHER AND DAUGHTER," "THE NEIGHBORS," "THE FOUR SISTERS,"
"NINA," "THE HOME," "HOMES IN THE NEW WORLD," ETC., ETC.

TRANSLATED BY

MARY HOWITT.

Copyrighted American Edition, from the Translator's Manuscript.

IN TWO VOLUMES.
VOL. I.

PHILADELPHIA:
T. B. PETERSON AND BROTHERS,
306 CHESTNUT STREET.

TO MY READER.

It is a curious thing to keep a diary—for one's self only. I cannot conceive how it can be done. Once in my earliest youth I kept a diary, or rather a kind of moral account current, in which each day was entered with a short observation, of *good*, or *bad*, or *middling*. At the close of the year the days were added up; but when, after a few years' time, I discovered that the amount of the middling days was ever the greatest, I grew tired of the thing, and have never since kept a diary for—myself.

Besides, when one is happy enough to be surrounded, in one's home, by beloved brothers and sisters, one scarcely finds the necessity of keeping a written account of one's life for one's self. The heart's sighs, the questionings of the mind, the occurrences of the day, find immediate sympathy from the near and the dear who are at hand. When distant, one writes letters to them, and in these, one's diary. I had often done so, and latest in my letters from America. For I then possessed a mother and a sister in my home.

But a change came over my home; death entered; my home was made desolate, and I—solitary.

I felt it severely, when, two years afterwards, I again

found myself on a more extensive journey, for again feelings and thoughts became too much for me, and longed for utterance. To whom should I now write. I felt deeply the truth of a witty Frenchman's remark, "Oh how sweet is solitude! But one must however have somebody to whom one can say, 'Oh how sweet is solitude!'"

This somebody I had hitherto had, but now!—My first inquiring glance found empty space, but my second showed me, thee, my R——.

Thou hast often, for a long time, been a kind, encouraging friend to me, on my way, thou hast exercised no inconsiderable influence upon my life, by giving me an inclination to write and to learn, and to travel that I might yet learn something more—why then, why should I not write to thee the impressions of my travel? why not keep a diary for thee? let it become afterwards whatever it might, a printed book, diary, descriptions of travels, novel, or even—nothing at all. In any case, I felt that it would be a pleasure to me to communicate to thee the inspirations of the moment, to present thee with the flowers and the fruits of my life of travel.

This thought gave a new interest to my journeyings, and thou, my R——, becamest, in this manner, my traveling companion, often an encouraging, strengthening friend by the way, without thou thyself knowing any thing about it, and thou hast been such for now upwards of four years.

My journey is now concluded, and my diary complete. I herewith send thee my two years' travels in Switzerland and Italy.

It is not a romance, but a faithful description of reality—such as I comprehended it. I cannot help reality having at times something of the romantic in it.

I have imparted to thee my cheerful and my sorrowful impressions, as I went along; have made thee acquainted with the persons, the books, or the occurrences which made epochs in my inner life during my search after—that which I enjoin upon thee to seek as well as me. I have more frequently made thee participant of the pleasure than the fatigue of the day, and when I have become sleepy, or have feared that thou wast, so I have bade thee good-night.

I have thrice, during my residence in Italy, passed, with young friends, through romantic episodes of a deeply-exciting character. Of these I shall communicate to thee, as much as it is in my power to communicate without betraying their real heroines and heroes. I shall therefore allow myself to add to a good deal of truth a few grains of fiction, besides weaving up two of the romances into one. They will not essentially lose thereby, neither wilt thou.

It is a long journey to which I invite thee, in more than one respect, a pilgrimage, although its object merely dawned upon myself by slow degrees.

I shall conduct thee to places already frequently visited, and to subjects which have already been often written about; but we shall not be long detained by that which is familiar, but much more by the life of the present time in its various forms, its relationship to that of antiquity and—before every thing else—to the higher realm of humanity, the kingdom of God—the image of paradise, which we all, more clearly, or more darkly, bear in the depths of our souls—which it is the great business of human life to develop and establish on the earth.

And if, at the conclusion of this long journey, thou shouldst see this beautiful promised land present itself with a little more distinctness out of the mists of time, if thou shouldst feel thyself a little more courageous, a little more cheerful in thy labor for it, then, my R——, thou wilt not find this journey too long, nor repent having undertaken it.

This anticipation would seem like great pretension, but without it I should not have had the courage to undertake the journey, neither now, to have prepared this book.

I have, in its arrangement, divided it into chapters, which I have called STATIONS. They are intended to render a review of the contents easy, and Stations has seemed to me a good natural expression to indicate certain divisions of our traveling life. I say *our*, because—are we not all of us traveling through life!

FREDRIKA BREMER.

ATHENS, *October*, 1860.

CONTENTS.

FIRST STATION.

First day's journey—Entrance into Switzerland—Morning at Berne—Evening at Enghe—That which the Alps and the Sun said to me—Thun—The Titans when seen more nearly—A bath in the Aar—Queen Bertha—Arrival at Lausanne—Chilly days—New acquaintance—Picture of the Confederate States of Switzerland—"Des Terneaux" Chapel—The Free Church—Questions and Cogitations which led me to Switzerland—A Vinet—Sketch of Lausanne and its everyday life—"*A la Montagne!*"................33

SECOND STATION.

Rossinières—Our large Beehive—Life in the high valleys The footpath—The young girls and the Sunday-school—Chateau-d'Œx—My Chateau—The meeting at La Lechevette—Rambles in the Alpine valleys—La Comballez—Les Ormondes—Père Ansermez—The Folk-life of the high valleys—The Free Church—The Church of the future—The Idea of Protestantism..............................74

THIRD STATION.

Hasli valley and the Swedish emigrants—Rosenlaui—Grimsel—Gloomy scene—The source of the Rhone—The Forest Cantons—Grutli and its heroes—Life in Schwytz—Two types of Conservatism—Sunday on Rhigi—Nicholas de Flue—Life in Zürich—Einsiedeln, its pilgrims and teachers—Zwingli—My home in Zürich—Journey to Basle—Missionary Institution and Missionaries....................114

FOURTH STATION.

From Basle to Brussels—That which took me there—Le Congrès International de Bienfaisance—The New Exposition—Conversation with King Leopold—"The Little Sisters of the Poor."—Festivals and Ideas of the Future in Belgium—Ghent and the Beguines—Lace Making—Bruges—Flanders—A House in the Country—Ruysselede and Bernhem—Antwerp—Rubens' House—A Glance at Holland—A Statesman—Journey to Paris....................208

FIFTH STATION.

Paris at the present time, and Paris thirty years ago—Prado—Valentino—"La Salpétriére."—The Evangelical Church—The Deaconess-Institution—"Revue Chrétienne"—Statue of Joan d'Arc—An Attic and a Happy Couple—The Emperor and France....................238

SIXTH STATION.

Again in Switzerland—Railway Irregularities—Vintage at Montreux—Romantic Illusions—New Acquaintance—The First Prisoner of Uri—Winter Residence at Lausanne—War and Peace in Switzerland—Still Life—New Life and New Interests—Young Italy—Its Patriots and Poets—"Risorgimento d'Italia"—The Waldenses in Piedmont—New Plans for my Journey—I must see Italy—Spring Life at Lausanne—Educational Institute—A. Vinet....................253

SEVENTH STATION.

In Geneva—Countess de Gasparin—Merle d'Aubigné. The Arve and Rhone—Mont Salève—The Hero of the Scene—Visit to the Workshops of Watch-makers—Women's Work—A Female Worker—Churches and Ecclesiastical Affairs—Intellectual Life—Geneva, the Paradise of Unmarried Women — Calvin's "Institutions" — Jargonaut—"The Living Water"—Domestic Life—A New Flower—An Old Calvinist—Old and New Geneva....................287

EIGHTH STATION.

Neufchâtel—A Home upon the Heights—Charles Secretan—Flights—The Industrial High-valleys—La Chaux de

Fonds—Locle and Travers—The Island of St. Piérre—
Federal Festival at Berne—Again on Lake Leman—Chamouni and St. Bernard—Rest by "the living waters"—
Last days in Switzerland—Monte Rosa—To Italy!............324

NINTH STATION.

Journey over the Simplon—Domo d'Ossola—Bad Weather
—La Tosa—Unexpected Meeting—Lago Maggiore—"Stock-Fish"—Isola Bella and Isola Madre—The Valleys of the
Waldenses; their People, History, Latest Deliverance,
and Present Life—Rambles and New Friends—Turin—The
Po and Monte Viso—Carlo Alberto—Victor Emanuel—
Count de Cavour—Gioberti—Cesare Balbo—Primato d'Italia—Speranze d'Italia—What are the Wishes of Italy?.....379

LIFE IN THE OLD WORLD;

OR,

TWO YEARS IN SWITZERLAND AND ITALY.

FIRST STATION.

First day's journey—Entrance into Switzerland—Morning at Berne—Evening at Enghe—That which the Alps and the Sun said to me—Thun—The Titans when seen more nearly—A bath in the Aar—Queen Bertha—Arrival at Lausanne—Chilly days—New acquaintance—Picture of the Confederate States of Switzerland—"Des Terneaux" Chapel—The Free Church—Questions and cogitations which led me to Switzerland—A. Vinet—Sketch of Lausanne and its everyday life—"*A la montagne!*"

THERE is a small country situated, as you see, in the heart of Europe; its circumference is insignificant, and insignificant its population, compared with the powerful states which surround it—France, Germany, and Italy; but its mountains are the highest in Europe, and there the mightiest European rivers have their head-waters. Its people, a pastoral people, have stood foremost in battle for what constitute the most valuable treasures of all people — political freedom and freedom of conscience.

Separated by mountains and valleys, by dissimilarity of origin, language, and religious faith; divided into States and into families dissimilar in race—yet is this people, composed of many distinct peoples, united in love for freedom and for that common father-land —that little Switzerland. And over all the states, however dissimilar in manners, language, or religious opinion, a word prevails, with magical, cementing, binding power—a name alike availing to them all— it is *Sworn-Confederate*. If opposing elements separate them for a time, they are again united in this. Disseverance is dissolved in eternal unity.

I found myself in this little country in the beginning of the summer of 1856. The beautiful oak woods round Stockholm lay as if dreaming of spring when I left them at the end of May. A gray-green vail covered the northern landscape. Two days later, in Germany, I found summer, and the hay-harvest in progress. But much rain and the long railway journey had fatigued me so much that I could not but ask myself, whether I were not too old to undertake a long journey; whether, after a certain amount of years, it were not better for people to stop quietly at home.

At his house on the banks of the Neckar, I again saw Chevalier Bunsen. It was like a ray of sunshine. I had seen him a few years before as Prussian Minister in London, and then, depressed by the political embarrassments which were at hand, and forseeing the great and bloody war in the East, he was also suffering so much even in health, that I could not but think of him as one who had not long to live.

I now met with him again amongst the vineyards of Heidelberg, healthy, cheerful and overflowing with life and the enjoyment of labor. He seemed to me to have become younger by twenty years. He had now abandoned the diplomatic career and entered with unabated energy upon that scientific path of literature which combats for the freedom of thought and conscience both in religion and politics. He had begun great and important works. May he have time and strength given him for their completion! Every thing belonging to him, his countenance, his state of mind, his surroundings, nay even his study, had one expression, and that was—light.

Again I had cold weather and rain on my way to Basle. At Basle, the portal of the Rhine between Germany and Switzerland, the sun shone, and there was a lively gathering, as it were, of free, gay folk-life across the vast river in the moonlight evenings. Beneath the colossal wooden bridge flows the river, clear and calm, in a half circle embracing, the old gloomy city, which has a very learned look, like a professor in his chair. A short distance above the bridge plies a little ferry-boat, guided, as by a magic thread, from the one shore to the other; from the shore with its professor-like aspect and queer old houses, to the other with its green fields and trees. During the morning I allowed myself to be taken backwards and forwards by the little ferry-boat across the stream, and during the evening I wandered backwards and forwards on the wide bridge listening to the cheerful, fresh murmuring of out-door life. I also visited the Cathedral; and this was all which at that time I cared either to see or hear of Basle. It was my intention to return thither in the autumn—I would now merely go to the Lake of Geneva and forward to Lausanne, where I intended to rest.

There stands at a short distance from Basle, and not far from the road, a beautiful lime tree, at the foot of which is a stone of memorial. It is in commemoration of thirteen hundred Swiss from nine different cantons, who fought at St. Jacques with an army of thirty thousand French and Austrians, and perished on the field. But their brave defense excited such high esteem in the mind of the French Dauphin, who commanded the enemy's forces, that he did not venture further into the country, but soon afterwards made peace with its people at Einsisheim. The grateful fatherland raised this memorial to its heroic sons, with the following inscription:

"Our souls with God, our bodies with the enemy. Here fell, the 26th August, 1444, unconquered, wearied of conquering, 1300 Sworn Confederates and Companions in arms, against united France and Austria."

Magnanimous, affecting words! No one would be dear to me who could tread, without reverence, a soil where the stones thus cry out.

The memory of these brave men is still annually celebrated here by songs and orations.

I commenced my journey to Berne in a thick fog which made it all as one whether I had been traveling over the heaths of North Germany, or the most glorious Alpine region; there was nothing to be seen but mist. Thus I reached Berne. What I there experienced, as well as what you have just read, I noted down afterwards. It was in Lausanne that I commenced my Diary.

BERNE, *June.*—"To-day the mountains may be seen. It is clear," said the waiter at the Crown Hotel, as he handed me my morning coffee. I dispatched my breakfast in all haste and then went out. It had rained and been stormy during the night, but now it was bright and I could see the mountains.

I stood upon the lofty terrace of the Cathedral and looked around me. Yes, it was bright, indescribably bright and glorious. The splendor of heaven and earth seemed to me twofold. Far below my feet rushed the rapid Aar through verdant meadows, and there, encircling the distant horizon in their white draperies, stood the pyramids of the Alpine land, Schreckhorn, Doldenhorn, Finster-Aarhorn, Eiger, Monch, Yungfrau with its Silverhorn, and whatever other names they may bear, those primeval Titans, the beautiful and magnificent forms of Switzerland. They were quiet now, those ancient assaulters of Heaven. The Lord of Heaven had scattered over them a handful of snow and they were turned to stone. And now in helmet and armor of eternal ice they stand and reflect the glory of the sun. Oh, how white, how beautiful they looked, and how their majesty was enhanced by him. The storm of the preceding night had gathered itself into little islets of clouds which were collected in dark specks at their feet and there vanished, dissolved by the sunbeams and attracted by the concealed spirits of the mountains to the springs in their bosoms.

How my soul's eyes and ears drank in this sight, and listened to the voices which spoke to me from it!

"Have confidence in the sun! Let not thy courage

sink. Has not a natural storm but lately passed over thy life; did not heaven seem dark, and every prospect on earth closed? And did not the tempest, all at once, as by a magic stroke, become dispersed, and all was again bright? See the cloudlets yonder, below the mountains, how they melt away before the sun, which absorbs them, changes them into blue ether— or into fertilizing springs and rivers! Thus human sufferings and errors.—Ah! that which makes life so dark, and the heart so heavy, thus sink they into the deep; thus are they dissolved by the sun of the Divine Goodness. Have confidence in the sun! Sing, sing, O heart, and praise its power, as do the Alpine heights, the clouds and the verdant, ever youthful earth!"

Joyously rushed on the Aar with swelling waters; the birds sang, the acacia diffused its fragrance around, and the earth and the Alps shone brightly. Oh, this morning,—I can express but little of that which I experienced during it, of that which the sun and the Alps spoke to me!

I wandered for yet an hour in the ascending sunlight around Berne, that I might become better acquainted with its situation and physiognomy, shook paws with its bears, which, although turned to stone, parade the market, and stand round the fountains as large as life, and like friendly countrymen stretched out their paws to me. Berne, standing on its peninsular rock, around which rushes the lively Aar, reminded me vividly of the plain-featured but powerful Rochester, and the fascinating Jane Eyre in the charming novel of that name. Thus plain-featured but picturesque and stately is Berne, thus lively, full of the freshness of youth and individuality is the river which winds around its walls, a sportive naiad, and a strong, enlivening queen at the same time. Which possesses the greatest majestic power? It lies in the two combined. Without the Aar, Berne is barren and gloomy; without Berne, the Aar would lack its full significance.

In the evening I went to Enghe.

Enghe, one of the principal places of resort for the inhabitants of Berne, lies at about a quarter of an hour's distance from the town. It is a lofty headland formed by the Aar, and is planted with beautiful trees, forming a grand promenade, from which a still more splendid view, if possible, is obtained of the Oberland Alps than from the cathedral-terrace in the town. You seem here to be nearer to them; you obtain a deeper view into their mystical temple of nature. The clouds had again encamped above their peaks, but the descending sun shone amidst them with wonderful gradations of purple, gold, and pale rose-tint. How the mystical cloud-swathings throw the Alpine peaks, now into brighter, now darker relief; now elevated, now depressed them; according as the cloud draperies elevated themselves or dropped down, or the sunbeams caught upon them, presenting ever-changing pictures; for there was a soft movement in these Alpine regions, which was unfelt beneath the green trees of Enghe, where all was profound calm. At a little distance on the terrace, wind-instruments were playing soft and beautiful melodies.

That which I felt at this moment, I cannot describe,

neither do I myself rightly understand. A deep emotion overcame me, and caused my tears to flow, whilst a world of half-defined feelings, thoughts, presentiments, arose in my soul. I wept, but I was happy, astonished by a something new and wonderful, which resembled a revelation within myself.

I came to Berne merely to proceed thence to Lausanne. The object of my journey was a year's residence and quiet study on the shores of the Lake of Geneva. But at this moment the horizon extended itself, and it was as though I saw sun-cycle beyond sun-cycle shining above my path into a remote distance, and as it were gleaming out of the clouds, the towers of primeval and renowned cities, to which I, as yet, did not dare to give the name. The wonderful vision disappeared with the magical pomp of colors, and the melodies which called it forth. But that which remained, that which still remains in my soul, of this never-to-be-forgotten morning and evening, is the sense of inner, unimpaired health and strength, together with a presentiment of a larger purpose in my journey than I myself had given to it.

I was again free, after several gloomy, sorrowful years; free, not through my own individual endeavor, but released by God's mighty hand. I had before me an unlimited time which I might devote in freedom and peace to the solution of many long-cherished questions and investigations. Well, then! for these I will live, and endeavor to strengthen my half thoughts and my half light, and see if they cannot lead me to some great whole. And so may the Spirit of Truth, which alone I will follow, guide me whither and as it will!

Thus I said to myself, and calmed my excited feelings with a Vanilla ice—it was very delicious!—which I took sitting on a stone wall under the tree. The sun descended; the fantastic cloud-imagery among the Alps faded away; the music ceased, the few pleasure-seekers on the terrace departed either in groups or alone, but I returned happy in the evening twilight to Berne.

"I am solitary, but not alone!"

But the Titans of the Oberland had produced too great an effect on my mind for me to turn my back on them at once. No: I could not be satisfied without seeing them more closely; seeing their brilliant icy palaces, and hearing the roar of their waters. I could in a few hours reach Thun and Interlachen, the heart of the Oberland. I had been once before in Berne. Then I was young, but bound as a bird in a golden cage. Now I was old, but free, and——Divine freedom!

I went to Thun. Hast thou been to Thun and seen its lake and its shores? If thou hast not been there, then go, if thou possibly canst, for a scene of more enchanting beauty, on a large scale, is not to be met with on this beautiful earth. And the morning, how beautiful it was, when I rose with the young June sun and wandered along the shores of that mirror-smooth lake; first towards the little church, which, standing on a hill to the right of the town, looks so pretty amongst its leafy trees, and surrounded by its peaceful monuments. Every grave is indicated by flowering shrubs, mostly roses, and out of every flowering thicket rises a metal spire with a little gilded star at its point. The grave-stars shone like flames in the ascending sun. The dew lay in bright pearls upon the fragrant roses. How fresh, how peaceful was every thing!

I pursued my way along the lake, by the opposite shore, to the town. It led me through a natural path; the green-sward was covered with flowers, the tall grasses waved gayly in the morning breeze, and the little feather-adorned ladies looked forth from their dwellings. It was a great marriage-feast. A beautiful butterfly, just come out of its pupa state, sat with moist wings upon a leaf. I gathered it in my bouquet, and walked till I became hungry and weary. I then retraced my steps, and, so doing, met a young bridal couple, she with a garland of meadow-flowers on her brown hair, and he with one round his hat.

They were returning from the church, where they had been married this morning. They held each other by the hand, and thus walked side by side, healthy, handsome, gay, through the flowery scene, on their way to the Alpine hut, their home. But they were not happier than I was that morning; and their breakfast could scarcely taste more delicious to them than did mine after my early ramble.

I passed yet another enchanting morning at Thun, and wandered through its magnificent walnut and chestnut woods; after which I went on board the steamboat which goes to Interlachen. It was a beautiful afternoon; the heavens, clear and summer-blue, and the lake dimpled by playful winds. We left behind us the lovely idyllian scenery of the lake with its verdant park-like shores, and advanced rapidly towards the Titans, Eiger, Monch, and the fern-like Fru, or Blumlis Alp, and many others. The loftiest Alps of the Oberland stood before us in mingled magnificence. At length stepped out the twelve-thousand-eight-hundred-foot-high Jungfrau, and it seemed as if we were about to steam directly into her bosom. But the vessel swung abruptly to the left, and the snow-clad giants stood on our right; behind us the pyramidal Niesen: more distant, the new-old castle Schadow, which rises so picturesquely out of the waves; and we entered a bay between the mountains, in whose gloomy shadow we landed upon a verdant shore. We are at Neuhaus. Before us lies a plain, surrounded by immense mountain-heights. A friendly German lady and her daughter offered me a seat in their carriage, and thus we drove to Interlachen, a small town situated on a tongue of land between the lakes of Thun and Brienz, from which circumstance it probably derives its name: Inter-lacus.

The mountain air, the baths in the Aar which flows through the valley, the facility by which, from this place, the most celebrated scenes of the Oberland can be reached, have of late years made Interlachen a great resort of travelers in Switzerland, and large hotels have altogether driven away the shepherds' huts from the valley. As yet, the season for the baths has not commenced. The water of the Aar is quite too cold before midsummer, and the air of the valley too cold also. It is, therefore, now very quiet on the grand promenade, and the hotels are empty. Nothing now is to be heard in the valley but the ringing of cattle-bells, and this music is not of the most melodious description.

The valley is a plain between two lakes and the mountain-walls which follow them from shore to shore. Two rivers, the Aar and the Lutschine, flow through it with rapid course; but the general levelness of the ground, and the growing crops, prevent their being seen, except you are close upon their banks, and the immense heights on either side of the valley prevent you having an idea of its width. To me it appeared only as a moderate leap from one mountain-wall to the other, and on all sides the view is circumscribed, so that I confess to having felt myself considerably oppressed by the close neighborhood of the Titans, which, at this point, are more imposing by their mass than by their beauty, and which, morning and evening, cast their cold, dark shadows across the valley, so that it is there gloomier at the same hour than anywhere else in the neighborhood. The empress of the valley, the lofty Jungfrau, which is so magnificent when seen from a distance, is here a lofty, broad-shouldered Medusa, which seems ready to crush her worshipers. Ha! I would not live here!

But Hohbuhl's wood, opposite the giantess, is beautiful, and the view from its heights is celebrated. I set out on a morning walk and voyage of discovery there, and lost myself completely among its paths, which were covered with autumn leaves, so that I could not find a single elevation where I could obtain a general view, not even to ascertain whereabout I was. Nothing beautiful could I see, except a few green openings just at hand, where thousands of little butterflies were fluttering above the grassy sward, as if they were intoxicated by the sun, the morning air, and the perfume of the flowers. · Not so was I; captive in the labyrinths of the wood, I went round, and round, and round, hour after hour, seeking no longer for views, but merely an outlet, until, at length, after four hours' wandering, I emerged from the wood, and reached Interlachen, so wearied with walking, seeking about, the heat of the sun, and wood-snares, that I seemed to be at least sixty years old, and I began again to mistrust my strength for the journey I had undertaken.

I passed a bath-house on the banks of the Aar, on my way to the hotel—the Schweitzer-Hof. The door stood half open, and the thought suggested itself to me of a bath in the Aar. True, the season for bathing was not yet, and the Aar water was at all times icy cold. The Aar is a glacier river, and has its origin in the bosom of an ice-mountain not far from here; but the embrace of the Titans' daughter must be invigorating with a vengeance, and I would venture it! I enter the house; the kindly-mannered attendant says:—

"No one has yet bathed here; the water is still very cold, but you can make the trial."

Good; I will do so. But with the first attempt to step into the bath, I drew back with terror, for it felt like burning iron round my ankles. I bethought myself for a moment; summoned all my courage; the water was so clear and fresh, so smiling, so enticing;

I plunged down at once, and up again, and yet a second time; "hah, hah, hah, hah! ah! ah!"

What a wonderful sensation! what a change! I am, as it were, new born. I have left my old humanity in the bath. I feel strong, healthy, full of vigor, rejuvenated, scarcely five-and-twenty years old! The energetic life of the Aar was flowing in my veins. Thanks to the Titans' daughter.

Vitalized anew, soul and body, I wandered slowly along its verdant bank, reading in the "Album Swisse," which I bought at a book shop, with unspeakable pleasure, L. Vulleimin's sketch of the reign of Queen Bertha. It was my first acquaintance with this remarkable Swiss historian, and with the noble Queen, who is one of the most beautiful characters of old French Switzerland, and whom the people still honor as the good genius of the country. Whilst Rudolph, her husband, as King of Burgundy, carried war into Italy, and endeavored to conquer Lombardy, she remained at home, engaged in the benevolent works of peace. "She laid down roads," says her historian, "encouraged the cultivation of the soil, planted vineyards, and protected the poor serfs. At the same time that Queen Bertha founded convents, asylums for prayer and labor, she built fortresses in Gourse, in Moudon, in Neufchâtel, from the Alps as far as Jura; and, under the protection of these strongholds, the country, being defended from the ravages of the Huns and Saracens, was enabled to flourish. She rode on horseback through the land, visiting the peasant farmers, acquainting herself with their means of life, visiting their barns and hemp-spinneries, encouraging and rewarding the industrious. She made herself acquainted with every subject on which she gave commands; she even spun with her own hands her husband's clothing, and they treasure up to this day, in Payerne, the saddle upon which she sat and spun, as she rode through the country. She established many estates in the country (*metairies*), of which she herself was the mistress. She also built strong castles, which still remain and bear her name; and when Rudolph, tired of war, returned home, she induced him to unite with her in laboring for the culture of the country, and the administration of justice."

"The Princes in those days," continues Vulleimin, "had not as yet their fixed residences. They went from place to place, now dwelling in Lausanne, now in Payerne; now on the shores of the Lake of Thun, and they might be found, like the ancient judges of Israel, holding their seats of judgment in the open fields, beneath the shadow of a large oak. It is with reason that Queen Bertha is regarded as the origin of our earliest liberties (franchises); with reason that she is regarded as the mother of our population. A humble-minded woman, she still teaches to all future generations the virtues of the olden time. The people still believe that they see her upon the Vaud-Skaberg, holding in her hand an urn full of treasures, which she pours out over the country;" and the time in which Queen Bertha, at once motherly-mistress and Queen, spun the King's clothing, lives in the memory of the people as their country's golden age. "The good old time," is equivalent, in Swiss phraseology, with that in which Queen Bertha spun; "*ove la reina Bertha filava!*"

How excellent the women of a country should be when they have a Queen Bertha for their example!

The next morning, I took a ramble into the valley, and talked with the people who were making hay. The costume of the women is now more poetical than it was thirty years ago. The stiff black horse-hair gauze round the face, has now become soft lace, which falls gracefully. The more wealthy wear silver chains over the dark jackets. I also crossed the Lake of Brienz, the same morning, to Giessbach, met with two pretty little talkative girls, with wood-strawberries to sell, who told me about their goats. Each one had a goat which gave milk and butter—goats are the cows of the poor—and they joddled and sang so sweetly,—

"Auf die Alpen, auf die schönen Alpen,"

that they made me forget the flight of time, and the hour when the steamboat leaves. When, therefore, I reach the shore, it is gone. But no matter! I take, therefore, a little one-horse carriage, with a good tempered lad to drive, and go to the valley of Lauterbrunnen, which lies in the bosom of "*die Schönen Alpen.*" It is a beautiful day, and the first portion of the valley is like a lovely orchard, along which the two-armed river, Zwic-Lutschine, rushes down towards the plain of Interlachen. The road lies up the side of the river, with wonderful castellated masses of rock on the left hand, and on the right the white massive form of the Jungfrau.

After a leisurely drive of two hours up the valley, we reach the tavern at Steinbock. Here I order dinner for myself and the boy, and after having partaken of it set out alone up the valley, with the spirits of which I wished to hold silent converse. From Steinbock the valley becomes narrower, between ever higher mountain walls. Louder and louder roar the becks and the streams which, now swollen by the rains, are hurled from the glaciers down towards the valley and the river. Here falls the Steinbock, thrown like silver rain, driven hither and thither by the wind over the field which it keeps green below; here rushes down the strong Trimbelbach, foaming from the embrace of the cliffs; there the still stronger Rosenbach which the Jungfrau pours out of her silver horn. On all sides, near and afar off, there is a rushing and roaring and foaming, on the right hand and on the left, above me, below me, and before, out of a hundred hidden fountains, and ever wilder beside me rushes on the Lutschine, with still-increasing waters. It is too much, I cannot hear even my own thoughts. I am in the bosom of a wild Undine, who drowns her admirers whilst she embraces them; and the Titans are becoming ever loftier and broader, and the valley ever narrower, more gloomy and more desolate! I feel depressed, and, as it were, overwhelmed, but nevertheless I go forward. It is melancholy scenery, but at the same time grand and powerful! And scenery of this character exercises a strong attractive power, even when it astonishes. The shades of evening fell darkly over the valley, when I saw far before me, in its gloomy depth, a broad, gray-white, immense mass of rock, like dust, hurled thundering down from a lofty mountain. It seemed to shut up the valley. That is enough. I salute the giantess, the great Schmadribach, the mother of the Lutschine river, and turn back. Ha! no, it is not good to be here, and the society of the Titans is more agreeable for a simple mortal at a greater distance! I am glad to fall in with a little twelve-years-old girl, who is going the same way with me, and to have her company.

She lives in a cottage in the valley. During the winter she and her mother make lace; during the summer she goes to school on the Murrenberg. She was a pretty, sensible girl, and seemed contented with her world; she knew no other.

I was glad when I reached the good hotel at Steinbock, to be once more in civilized life; refreshed myself with a good cup of tea, after which I returned to Interlachen. But on my return, the Titans presented me with a glorious spectacle, and it was not without joyful admiration that I parted from their immediate neighborhood. The great spirits which terrify can also enchant. In the light of the descending sun the white peaks and fields of the Alps stood out in the most brilliant coloring; the lofty Jungfrau clothed herself in rose-tint, her blue glaciers shone transparently, and the lower the sun sank, the higher and clearer gleamed the Alpine pinnacles; thus they shone upon my return through the valley of Lauterbrunnen, which was delicious with the fresh mountain air in the calmness of evening.

Later still, in my Schweitzer-Hof, new astonishment awaited me from the camp of the giants. The head of the Jungfrau was surrounded with a soft glory of light, which increased in beauty and brightness—as did my curiosity—till at length the moon, shining in full splendor, slowly advancing above, crowned the Titaness with beauty, as it did also my day.

Two days afterwards, I was on my way to Lausanne. The whole road lies as through a magnificent park, and everywhere it is well cultivated, scattered with good houses, and presenting a prosperous aspect. Man and nature here live in happy association.

The sun was near its setting, when from a height and at a great distance still, I saw, deeply embedded in a circle of verdant shores and lofty Alps, the celebrated lake, which history at its commencement says, was wholly vailed by fogs, and surrounded by dense forests whence it took the name of the Lake of the Desert (Leman), and which afterwards, in the light of the sun and of civilization, has become a rendezvous for the whole refined travel-loving world of Europe.

My eye sought along its shore for Lausanne, because there it was that the noble, highly-gifted Vinet lived and taught only a few years back; and then I would gain intelligence of him from his friends and disciples, and from the Free Church, of which he was the originator and centre. It was for this purpose that I came to Switzerland.

"*Lausanne, la jolie,*" as it is called in an old song, and by many of its admirers, was brightly illumined by the sinking sun, which, however, set in thick cloud, as I reached my appointed home there in the *pension* of M. La Harpe, on the beautiful promenade, Montbenon. The gorgeous sunset coloring still continued whilst I walked on the terrace with my polite host and hostess, in admiration of the view which it afforded of the Alps and the lake, and listening to their descriptions of its beauty on calm summer and autumn evenings. I had the same view from my little chamber, and in particular from the stone terrace in front of it. There—that is to say, in my room—I wrote two days later.

LAUSANNE, *June 19th*.—Are there here Alps, a lake, enchanting shores, and a sunny life upon them? I see nothing but a thick fog. Lausanne "*la jolie*" has lain wrapped for the last three days in a dripping mantle of rain, which vails her and every thing in cloud and darkness. It is also as cold as with us in Sweden during October, and my little room, very charming in fine weather, is as gloomy as a cellar when the sun is hidden in cloud, and such a cloud! I believe that I never saw one so dense before. Soul and body seem as it were to shrink together in its cheerless surroundings. But, during this time, I was not without an inner sun. A couple of new acquaintances and ditto books, have lighted up my inner world, and enabled me meanwhile to forget the outer gloom.

The widow of A. Vinet is a fine middle-aged lady to whom one feels immediately attracted with cordial confidence. Hers is a beautiful, transparent nature. The Professor of History, L. Vulleimin, is a man of rare classical refinement, as well in person as in mind and character. Beneath his lofty forehead crowned with thin locks of silver hair, those dark eyes beam with all the fire of youth, and with a glance at once keenly penetrative and kind. The glance of his soul **is steadfastly** directed to the ideal of life, in society, in the church, and in the state. I have seldom met with a man whose mode of expression and manner have been so agreeable, seldom have experienced so much satisfaction and pleasure from any conversation as from his. Whilst, without, darkness and rain vailed the earth of Switzerland, his Introduction to the History of Switzerland—a continuation of J. Mucker's great work has raised to me the covering which hitherto concealed from my mind, the peculiarity of the Swiss Confederated States, and from it I select, as worthy of memory, the following characteristic traits of land and water:

"In the middle of Europe lies a country which in extent does not exceed some of the oldest provinces of France. - Its history loses itself too frequently in petty religious disputes. Its heroes are shepherds and peasants; yet kings have not failed to solicit union with the Swiss, who, however, on their part have very rarely returned the compliment.

"Helvetia has now submitted to, and now defied foreign powers. She sports without anxiety on the political ocean; and after every storm stands forth in renewed youth.

"The republics of Europe have died out one after another. Florence, Venice, Genoa! Switzerland alone, with her institutions, maintains, like an everlasting flower, her place in the light of the sun.

"This is a remarkable fact, especially for those who understand Switzerland. Diverse races, languages, manners, the most dissimilar interests—it would be thought impossible to form a body-politic out of these varied nationalities. In the heart of the Alps, the people are the old Goths and Rhetians; on the plains the Allemanni; in the west Burgundians mingled with Romans. On the banks of the Aar the German tongue prevails, around Lake Leman the Romande.

"A few miles only in Switzerland will divide life of the most primitive races from that of the most highly civilized cities; here herdsmen who often change their dwelling-place, there towns on the shores of the lakes, the Smyrna and Tyre of the Cantons. The old customs of the Sabines mingle with those of republicans, who live in daily intercourse with the two hemispheres. The extremes of time, climatized as it were, are drawn together. Two valleys bring into close proximity the most ancient institutions with those which are in the advance movement of the present time. Whilst more than one Canton endeavors with pious reverence to maintain its most ancient laws, the extreme opinions of modern freedom were advocated in Geneva long before they were adopted in France. Basle, in 1691, passed through a storm unobserved by Europe, which, exactly a hundred years afterwards, produced in France, the revolution. This Alpine valley speaks at this day the Romande language of the middle-ages; whilst from that Swiss town proceeded the movement which gave, in the sixteenth century, construction and rule to the French tongue, and from this other, that which prepared the way for Schiller and Goethe. Every thing approximates, every thing crowds together. A thousand colors are reflected as it were, in one Alpine lake. One contrast ceases merely to give place to another. When law is becoming universal, religion comes in and shelters it.

There was a time when all went to bow the knee before our Lady of Lausanne or Einsiedeln. Nothing then divided the Vaudois under the rule of Berne from those under the rule of Freyburg. How different is it now, both in custom and religion. Reform began in Switzerland at the same time as in Germany, and has given rise to her first as well as to her last war. Of a truth we know not either what crimes or what virtues, what old or new ideas, may not be met with at the foot of the Alps.

"It is in the midst of these contrasts that thirty sovereign states, all differing in interests and physiognomy, sit down to take counsel together for the common good. Cantons of twenty thousand souls take their place beside those of three hundred thousand. Monarchists, aristocrats, and the most dissimilar democrats sit together; all forms of government, with one exception only, the despotic. To which we must add, in order to complete the picture, the whole nation, armed, is always as one, upon the scene; that which is elsewhere accomplished by the will of some few, is in Switzerland accomplished by the voices of all; and that this people's modes of action as a sovereign people lead to perpetual agitation.

"Such has Switzerland been in all ages. It is this which characterizes Switzerland, that whilst it is a union of dissimilar races, languages, religions, natural circumstances, receiving every kind of culture, it yet remains the same.

"But what is the power that holds together these dissimilar elements? By what power, what art, is this confederate state still in existence, free and secure in itself?

"The soul, and vitalizing principle in our union is, love of freedom. Republicans anterior to Rome, our forefathers could not endure a monarchy. In later history they are the first-born of freedom.

"'We have seen,' says Bodin, in the sixteenth century, 'Athens change her form of government seven times in one century, and Florence also seven times under the government of their refined lords, whilst the Sworn-Confederates have maintained their popular institutions since A.D. 360.'

"Foreign powers, at the present time, are not ignorant that any attempt to overcome the Cantons would awaken the same resolute resistance as that of which Sempach and Grandson are the monuments. For others the festivities, gayeties, and splendid scenes of courts; for us the fraternal feeling which makes the heart throb in a nation fostered by equality on a free soil. We could not bear to live, if we had lost that which gives life its value.

"Behold, then, what the Swiss have in common, from the Rhine to the Rhone, from Geneva to the wild valleys of ———.

"The annals of Switzerland have shown their vocation for independence.

"'Helvetia,' said our fathers, 'is a confusion which God regulates.' They taught us not to doubt God; their history, never to despair of our native land. The great nations subsist by their masses,—we, by our faith and love.

"Our union is expressive of this. In what name

are we Sworn-Confederates, if not in those which are united in our banner.:

GOD AND THE FATHERLAND."

Vulleimin turns, after this, to the Swiss people, whom he admonishes to the development of a higher life in church and state. He encourages them to hold public meetings, and festivals, in the exercises and the sports of which, all the Cantons might give each other "*rendezvous.*"

"I would wish," says he, "that the arts, together with the sciences, should be represented there; they who cultivate the earth, as well as they who enlighten our steps upon it; the industrial arts, which multiply our means, as well as the fine arts, which beautify our everyday life. All are benefactors of the fatherland. All are the sons of freedom. As it attains to a new age, it will attain to a new worship. Its idea has extended itself—let us extend our hearts."

"But," continues this noble friend of freedom, "let us be careful not to confound freedom with that which often assumes her name. Few nations love her as we do; and few, also, have done her such bloody wrong.

" Here a people, proud of its poverty, believes itself to be the noblest on the earth, whilst it dreads slavery, and is the slave of blind prejudice. There a popular assembly believes it has conserved the public good when it has voted a sum for the purposes of higher education, or has humiliated some man, the honor of his country.

" When did jealous mediocrity believe itself free until it had dragged all down to its own medium stature!

"In this Alpine valley there are few laws, but also

little justice; no taxes, but neither are there any roads; a quiet life, but no noble endeavors in which man unites to conquer nature. I have seen freedom so enthusiastic that it resembled drunkenness; I have seen her so tardy and self-absorbed that it was the same thing as egotism.

"Do not imitate the old; even virtue imitated is virtue no longer; truth becomes prejudice. But since you are penetrated by the grandeur of the former ages, lift up your eyes to the heights on which the genius of humanity abides.. It is from him that you must derive your strength.

"Our most dangerous opponents live in the midst of us; our most fearful enemies are within our own bosoms. The most fearful of these are those which bring death into the soul, which sap the foundations of truth and justice, which trample upon the doctrines which are the guards of virtue, and the consolation of the sorrowful. · The man who will persuade us that Winkelried and the betrayer of the fatherland sleep the same sleep, is far more terrible than powder and shot to the peace of our domestic hearth. He endeavors to deprive us of that trust which is the sanctuary of freedom."

These are words which apply equally to all free people, and deserve to be considered by all. Whilst I read, I seemed to myself to be sitting by a fountain amongst the Alps, whose pure stream refreshes the waters of the river in its course through villages and towns.

Man, nation, humanity, eternal union! The day when I first understood this great concord, was that on which I first understood, with true emotions, myself and my own life.

June 24*th.*—Yesterday, all was enveloped in gloom and rain, and to-day, what a change! Yesterday masses of clouds were rolled from the Alps down upon the fields and valleys, threatening to deluge every thing! People talked of nothing but rain and gloomy prospects. The corn was in bloom; the vine ought to be just now in flower, but the rain and the cold!—nothing could ripen in the gardens; nobody could get even a few berries for dessert or preserving. It had rained ever since May. In the higher valleys, it had rained twenty-two days out of the thirty, and a family which had removed thither from Lausanne had been half drowned. It *might* rain the *whole* summer, as on some former occasions it had done. · In France, the rivers overflowed their banks. People prophesied "*une armée de calamités.*" (A beautiful prospect for summer pleasure.)

That was the case yesterday; but yesterday evening there seemed something like a faint smile upon the deluge-physiognomy of the firmament—something resembling a sunbeam penetrated the cloud-garment of the Jura, and to-day—what splendor! A brisk "*Bise*" (north wind) has chased, and still chases away, the dense clouds, piles them together on the peaks of the Alps, where they form triumphal arches, garlands, and diadems, which mount higher and ever higher, and Lausanne "*la jolie*" decks herself in sunshine, with bouquets of gleaming meadows, woods, and gardens, and mirrors herself in Lake Leman, which smiles in heavenly blue towards the deep blue heaven above.

The earth, covered with luxuriant promise, shines forth, with tearful eyes, it is true, as yet, but the sun kisses away the tears, and—oh, assuredly it is a midsummer festival, and hardly myself knew, during these last few days, how gloomy life was without sun, and I can well understand how the old heathen Thorgeir was willing to worship the God who made the sun. I would now have a May pole and a troop of a hundred children to dance round it, as formerly at Arsta! Here they celebrate Midsummer-day neither with divine service nor dance.

July 3rd. During these last wonderfully beautiful days and nights I have scarcely allowed myself to sleep, so intent have I been to enjoy, with my whole waking soul, the gorgeous coloring, the marvelous effects of light and shadow which morning and evening have presented in this glorious region; and the bright mysteries of the night; the singular splendor of the milky way, like a heavenly Staubbach, thrown in silvery cascades from invisible heights, down to the Alpine land of earth—it is a glorious show! I believe I never before saw the starry heavens so brilliant.

But my nocturnal flights out of my little chamber upon the terrace below, have caused me to take cold, so that for the present I am obliged to forego an excursion which I had intended to make to Chamouni, and, instead, to hasten my removal to one of the mountain valleys, (Rossinière or Chateau-d'Œx,) which Mme. Vinet recommends to me as a salubrious residence during the summer months. And to these and other **mountain valleys in the neighborhood of Leman, all** the people of Lausanne who are able to do so, betake themselves for some weeks, and there live in freedom, enjoying the mountain air, milk and fruit, in a word, all the luxuries which pastoral life affords in the neighborhood of the glaciers. For this purpose, the herdsmen give up their huts to the townspeople, who remove thither with their children and their households. One hears every day of individuals or families who had betaken themselves "*à la montagne*," or who are intending to do so.

I have in the mean time made some agreeable acquaintance, both in and out of Lausanne, which I hope on some future occasion to improve. First and foremost, two amiable persons, a married couple, intimate friends of M. Vinet, M. and Mme. F., at whose beautiful estate at St. Prex, near Morges, on the shore of Leman, it was very pleasant to me to converse with them of their deceased friend, who was alike remarkable as a man and a thinker. Mme. F. was at this time occupied in preparing for the press the notes which he left behind him, of the literature of France during the sixteenth century, a course of lectures which he had given in Lausanne. But my indisposition at this time prevented my full enjoyment either of the pleasures of society or the beauties of the country. And thus I merely saw at a distance "Wufflens" castle, with its many towers, a stately memory of Queen Bertha, the royal spinner, who held the sceptre and the distaff with the same hand, as the old song says, together with the trowel, building fortresses and towers which bear her name.

I was present at various evening parties in Lausanne,

where I greatly enjoyed myself, as, indeed, was the case with the social intercourse in Switzerland, from which I experienced only pleasure unmixed with the weariness which so generally oppresses me in parties assembled for the pleasures of conversation. The advantage here is, that it is so easy to enter both with gentlemen and ladies upon subjects of general interest, and to meet with persons who have thought on these subjects with more or less independence of mind. Even young girls can speak both sensibly and with interest of the various church establishments in the cantons, and their relationship to each other. Two pretty, young sisters told me, this evening, many things of interest relative to the Free Vaudois Church, in the high valleys (Pays d'en haut), which is asserted to be the most vitally illumined portion of this church. They vividly described the picturesque assemblies, and the divine worship in the open air, the beautiful singing, etc.

I spent last evening with M. and Mme. de G., at their beautiful country house, with its glorious view over the lake and mountains. But from every point around this lake are there lovely, magnificent views, and they contribute not a little to the peace and enjoyment of a social meeting. In the face of a beautiful evening sky, the thoughts become brighter and more cheerful. The people conversed together, and there was music. I noticed with pleasure the simple toilettes of the young ladies, and their agreeable, unpretending demeanor. There was no gossip nor idle talk. Health, and the peace of quiet thoughts, seem to rest upon these daughters of the Alpine land. Two married daughters of England's

Elizabeth Fry were of the party, handsome women, with that noble expression and bearing which distinguished their mother. They spoke with warmth of the great good which women may accomplish, even beyond their own house and home, if they will only with clearness and steadfastness work for that object which is the true bent of their powers. There was a great consciousness of womanly dignity in these ladies, beneath the gentlest, the most womanly exterior. All women ought to have the same.

The Blind Asylum is one of the most beautiful institutions of Lausanne, and M. Herzel, its superintendent, is, of a truth, one of its most interesting men. A fine instance of his skill is a young man who, from his earliest childhood, was perfectly blind, deaf and dumb, owing, I believe, to small-pox, but whom M. Herzel enabled to become an intelligent, thinking, useful, and happy human being. M. Herzel has employed, in his case, the same methods which the American philanthropist, Dr. Howe, employed for Laura Bridgeman, and his success has been equally perfect. Young F. is now a strong, healthy, perfectly intelligent, and unusually cheerful young man. His skill as a turner is wonderful.

I was shown a little letter and a pretty gift which the young American had sent to her unfortunate brother in Switzerland, who, in the first place, had written to her, and sent her a little present. Affecting intercourse this, across the ocean, between two beings whom misfortune doomed to spiritual life-long captivity, but whom human love and the spirit of science have liberated!

The principal founder and supporter of this institution is a M. Haldimand, who, although confined to his easy chair by lameness, is said to be the most active and benevolent citizen of Lausanne. To-day I paid a visit to the universally-beloved philosopher, at his country-seat, between Lausanne and Ouchy, and found him, a handsome, elderly gentleman, with great power and freshness of mind, although an attack of paralysis deprived him, two years ago, of the use of his limbs. He was seated in a circular room, with glass doors opening into the grounds, amongst the trees of which fountains were playing, and the view opened to the Alps. Two gentlemen were present, and the conversation turned upon the importance and prudence of as little as possible helping the poor, and by that means obliging them as much as possible to help themselves. Many anecdotes were told to prove that the ready help of the rich encouraged laziness, improvidence, dishonesty, etc. They maintained the great difficulty of doing any good, of meeting with any actually deserving objects of charity, and so on. I said a few words for children, for the sick and the aged. M. Haldimand commended the principles of Malthus's Political Economy, which he seemed wholly to approve.

I afterwards expressed my surprise to two of my acquaintances in Lausanne, at hearing this assertion of the utter inability to do good by outward relief, from a man who employed the greatest part of his time and his wealth in public or private benevolence.

"Oh!" replied they, with a smile, "this is a subject which is often brought forward by M. Haldimand, and the doctrine which he commonly preaches."

Certain men have certain favorite inconsequent modes of reasoning. The inhabitants of Lausanne say, that M. Haldimand ought never to die, and they trouble themselves beforehand with the thought of his decease.

Last Sunday I attended divine service at the chapel "des Terneaux," the principal place of meeting for the Vaudois Free Church at Lausanne. The chapel is a large hall, as simple as a school-room, without picture, without an altar, and without any proper pulpit for the preacher, who stands simply on an elevated stage at the end of the room, with a desk before him, as a lecturer in an ordinary lecture-room.

The chapel was full to overflowing. The assembly of this church was long forbidden, and its congregation even violently persecuted in the Pays de Vaud, and it is still inhibited there. But the respectability and courage of its members, together with the more liberal spirit of the times, has enabled it now to meet without opposition; and, after having for so long been compelled to hold their assemblies secretly and in private houses, now openly to congregate in a chapel which they have lately taken for that purpose, in the light of day, and on one of the most frequented promenades of Lausanne. The long-despised church has, from the great abilities of the preachers, now become the fashionable church of Lausanne, and is attended by the principal people. This was very evident on the Sunday I attended the chapel "des Terneaux." The sermon, by M. Bridet, a young man of great talent, both as an orator and a Christian thinker, from the text, "My soul thirsteth for God, for the living God," could not have been better or more awakening.

All this was very satisfactory to me. I missed, however, the liturgy and the public confession of faith. It seems as if the Free Church had not yet decided upon what this should be; but has satisfied itself, as yet, principally by zeal for a deeper earnestness amongst Christian professors in doctrine and in life, a perfect truth and consciousness in faith and in profession. It has declared itself independent of the established church in Switzerland, the national church, and dependent alone on God's word and Spirit, as foundation and guiding star. It is governed by synods, composed of clergy and laymen. But the priest is not, here, priest in the old significance of the term, but only a brother, who, by vocation and gift, is chosen to teach amongst brethren. The elders of the church stand by his side, as assistants, either in teaching or in any other work, and they also are chosen by the congregation. They can even perform divine service if it be needed.

In the afternoon a meeting for "mutual edification," was held in the same church, in which three or four persons spoke. One of these was a stranger passing through the place, who had joined himself to the Free Church from sympathy of feeling. His topic, as well as that of most of the other speakers, was, the Truth; the importance of being true before God and ourselves,—for we see ourselves as God also sees us— and before men. Earnestness in conviction, honesty and candor in profession, were insisted upon, which also was A. Vinet's great topic. Anecdotes of personal experience were related, to prove clearly what self-examination and what conviction really are.

Afterwards, various transactions of the synod during the past May were communicated. M. Schott admonished the congregation to make themselves acquainted with these, and particularly with all the affairs of the church, because this was the business of all good members. The details then followed, many of sufficient interest even for strangers. In the synod of one hundred persons, dissimilarity of views had been openly expressed, with the maintenance of the most perfect harmony, both as to individual temper and the business of the synod. Not a single word had been said which could cause regret. In the congregations of the Free Church, amounting to above forty, some deviated from others in sundry usages and institutions; but unity in the main object and intention had remained undisturbed. I was much pleased with a little man who seemed to be the finance minister of the Free Church, and who, with much tact and good humor, rendered an account of the not very brilliant state of the central fund, and admonished "the brethren and sisters" to a more liberal contribution.

The meeting closed by the singing, in an excellent style, the beautiful old hymn Agnus Dei. The chapel was, on this occasion also, very well filled, although not so numerously as in the morning.

The Free Church in the Canton Vaud originated in the revolution of 1845, when the new, self-constituted government required that the clergy of the national church should read from the pulpits, in the presence of their congregations, a long proclamation in vindication of its accession to power and its mode of action. A great number of the clergy refused to obey this command, because the new government had established itself by violence, and because the canons of the church required that the pulpit should be kept free from political questions and dissensions. On this, the new government gave the protesting clergy their choice between obedience to its commands or retirement from their several congregations, whereupon upwards of eight hundred ministers retired from their office, although the greater number did not know at the time how they should find bread or the shelter of a roof for themselves and their families. But this brave protest for the rights of conscience awoke sympathy in thousands of hearts. Abundant contributions of money poured into the fund which was immediately opened for the maintenance of the retiring clergy. A great many persons, and especially ladies, opened hospitals and provided lodgings for the homeless families, and strengthened them in their combat for truth and justice. In forty-three cases, a portion of the congregation seceded with their spiritual leader, and formed themselves into new churches by the side of the old—new also in this respect, that they dissevered themselves from the state, which had made its superior power to be felt merely by domination and arbitrary will. Such was the origin of the Free Church, which immediately became an object of open persecution to the government, and of enactments at once oppressive and ridiculous, which continued for several years. But, as is generally the case under such circumstances, the persecuted congregations became more firmly established, and organized with a higher consciousness of their great purpose.

What is it that lies beyond the mere outward protest? Is there here a higher, more vitalizing principle? And how does it stand with regard to the Bible and the principle which is the basis of Protestantism? Does this new Free Church contain the seed of a church of the future, one actually universal—like the sun and the gospel?

These are questions which I shall be better able to reflect upon, in the high valleys, where indeed the Free Church has its highest life, and where I shall have sufficient time and leisure. These are the questions which have brought me hither.

The political revolution of which I lately spoke, greatly resembled one of those which Voltaire called "*une tempête dans un verre d'eau.*" One fine day a crowd of people, some hundreds in number, assembled on the great terrace of Montbenon, with drums and flags, and a person in the crowd announced in a loud voice that the old government of the Pays de Vaud was at an end, and a new one, in conformity with the wishes of the people, was established, at the head of which was M. D. The good citizens of Lausanne were greatly astonished, and the city militia came forth immediately on behalf of the legal government, ready with armed hands to chase away that which had illegally taken its place. But these good men, averse to the shedding of blood, preferred rather to give way quietly to the usurping party, who had, in fact, a great portion of the working class on their side. These, and the adherents of the new government, upraided the old with being a "town-council" government, without sympathies for the people, or desire for their advancement; doing nothing for popular education in schools; never showing themselves amongst the people; opposing popular festivities, etc.: which charges were indeed not without grounds. The new government promised to be in a high degree popular, and began by removing from the universities the most deserving men and instructors, and replacing them by their own partisans. I hear it said, on all hands, that this revolution has thrown back the development of the country, and its culture, more than twenty years. In the mean time, the better general voice, and the spirit of the age, have compelled the new government, gradually to fill the offices of both city and State by men of ability and fitness; and for the last ten years, since this has been the case, it has continued steadily to advance, both in action and spirit, and now it is universally acknowledged, "not to work badly."

The government does much for the encouragement of schools—but rather, as it appears, by the increase of subjects of instruction than by the solidity of instruction itself—and of popular festivals there is no lack. Of these, shooting at a mark and dancing seem to be the principal. The day before yesterday, a great festival of the children of the national schools was held on the heights of "la Sauvabellin," a lofty plateau, an hour's distance from the town, where is a glorious primeval forest of oak and beech, which, it is said, dates back from the time of the Druids. Yesterday afternoon a still greater popular festival was held, at which I was present. People danced to thundering music on the turf which skirted the old forest. Many families were there with their children, and the children also danced. They were mostly of the artisan classes; all were well dressed and looked well to do; a certain gravity and calmness prevailed even in their enjoyment.

The view from the height of "la Sauvabellin," was very extensive over this glorious region, but who can attempt to describe its beauty as seen under a bright sunset? It is beyond all description. The festival of nature was to me more beautiful than the festival of the people, and the latter, it seemed to me, ought to have had a higher purpose than was the case. I could fancy that I saw the Druids come forth from the ancient wood, lifting to Heaven their venerable heads, gilded by the bright descending sun. Thus they took leave of each other, the sun and the beautiful wood, in silent solemnity. Below, was the buzz of the dancing crowd, altogether too thoughtless! But I will not be a member of the deposed government! I, too, was once young and full of thoughtless life!

July 6th.—In two days time, I leave Lausanne, to betake myself, like every body else, "*à la montagne,*" in the Pays d'en haute. But before I leave Lausanne, I will take a hasty sketch of the town and its life. Lausanne "*la jolie*" is, it must be candidly confessed, really an ugly little town, with narrow and winding streets, gray and dismal-looking houses. Picturesque it is, unquestionably, from situation, with its gray, irregular masses of houses, grouped round the foot of the stately old Cathedral "Notre Dame de Misericorde," one of the oldest and noblest Gothic churches in Switzerland. This, standing aloft in the middle of the town, with its tall tower, the bells of which are beautiful, with its terrace of thick-branched lime-trees, looks forth grandly and calmly above the tumult of human inhabitants, who seem to be clambering and climbing up and around its firm walls. Seen from Montbenon, it looks like a preacher in his pulpit, amidst his congregation. Around this stately Cathedral, around this kernel of gray-brown houses, which look as if they had stood from the times of the old Roman Laussaninum, extends in wider and ever wider circles a girdle of beauty and grace. This is composed of gardens, enchanting parks, and country houses, where the *élite* of the inhabitants, and wealthy families from the cultivated countries of the whole world reside—often the whole year through. These country houses are rarely remarkable for the splendid style of their building, or the luxury of their interior finishing. Their distinguishing beauty is that of their site, and the views which they command of the lake and the Alps—the heroine and heroes of the scene. These views are different in every separate situation, but the beauty of all are nearly equal. The larger residences have large gardens, beautiful pleasure-grounds and fountains; the smaller ones have, at all events, a terrace and a little grass plot, and all have an affluence of beautiful shrubs and flowers.

"How good," said Madame Vulleimin to me one day during a walk, glancing at a country-house, "how good it is that every one here can have in his dwelling a portion of the best and the most beautiful which life affords!" Every one here can have a small house, a garden, and—this view!

Few of the inhabitants of Lausanne are rich, but many are in easy circumstances, and life is simple. They meet at little tea-suppers, without luxury or pretension; they converse on the terraces, amongst flowers, with the Alps before them as their horizon, and the lovely lake at their feet. The more wealthy occupy themselves much with improving the condition of the poor, and especially with the education of the children. With these magnificent surroundings, it seems to me that human beings become more simple, true, and earnest. Life is calm, occupied, and full of kindly influences.

The grand time of Lausanne, the time when Voltaire—monarch of wits—held his court there, is past; but its good time seems to me to be the present. And especially the condition of the country, with its daily work, its conflict of parties, its institutions for the public advancement, its gay popular festivals, which unite all classes—the great Helvetian musical festival which attracts annually to Geneva persons from every Canton, not only for its enjoyment, but to take part in it—in one word, life here, in its rich and fresh manifold character, seems to me no poor continuation of the good time "when Queen Bertha spun."

There is yet another feature in Lausanne life which I must not overlook. More than once, on Sunday afternoons, and even on week-days, the melodious tones of choral singing have reached my terrace. These tones proceed from homes where parents and children celebrate together family worship. They testify to the work of the Spirit in the reform, which has taken the life of the Church into the innermost of life, and which has converted the domestic hearth to an altar. This is a peculiar trait in the reform movement, which, proceeding from Switzerland, has been planted in England, Holland, and France. But of this, more another time.

I will now go forth into nature, will live like the trees and the flowers there. Let me thank the good, great Father, for the beautiful weather which he has now given, for now they are making hay; now both the wheat and the vine is in blossom, and the whole face of the earth looks glorious and full of life. Now, however, it is very warm, and I exclaim, with all the people of Lausanne, "*à la montagne!*" "*à la montagne!*"

SECOND STATION.

Rossinières—Our large Beehive—Life in the high valleys—The footpath—The young girls and the Sunday-school—Chateau-d'Œx—My Chateau—The meeting at La Lechevette—Rambles in the Alpine valleys—La Comballez—Les Ormondes—Pére Ansermez—The Folk-life of the high valleys—The Free Church—The Church of the future—Idea of Protestantism.

ROSSINIÉRES, *July 3d.*—But lately, on the sunny heights of la Sauvabellin, at the gay folk's festival, with the vast and glorious view of Heaven and earth above and around me, now shut into a narrow, solitary valley of the Vaudois Alps, where one can see nothing but bare or wood-covered mountains, between which lie grass fields and low huts, and above which is seen a little stretch of sky, now dark with rain-clouds.

The journey thither, however, was beautiful and very queer. Imagine a labyrinthine road winding between lofty mountains, along which you are dragged, upwards, ever upwards, for several hours. So narrow were the mountain passes, sometimes, that you cannot conceive how you are to get through them; in other places so completely blocked up, that it seems as if you must drive right into the mountain, and if your carriage should get, as it were, a little shove on one side,—perhaps from the King of the mountain,—so that it is upset on the very brink of a precipice, you cannot see what should hinder you, and the horses, and the carriage, from tumbling down into the wild stream which thunders and foams below. It looks dangerous, and is not, indeed, wholly without danger, but both driver and horses are used to struggling up the steep roads of the mountain strongholds.

At the entrance of the narrow mountain pass, one comes upon the ruins of the castle of La Gruyères. In ancient times, it was the abode of the powerful Counts of that name; and they it was who first cultivated, and established inhabitants, in the high valleys which extend along the river Sarine—Rossinières, Chateau-d'Œx, Rougemont. One feels, whilst making this ascending journey, through these mountain passes, as if one were reading a romance of the middle age.

The sun was sending his last rays through the openings in the cliffs when I emerged to Rossinières. My abode is an immense chalet, or Swiss cottage—the largest amongst the Alps, it is asserted, in which a vast number of small windows, with their small panes, peep forth from beneath an enormous roof. The front and back of the house (the roof at the two ends reaches to the ground) are ornamented with a great number of painted figures; lions, deer, horses, flowers, flower-vases, birds, and other animals and figures, all more or less unnatural; scripture-texts remind the beholder of the shortness of life, of God's faithfulness and righteous judgment. The house was thus built, a century ago, by the grandfather of the present proprietor. The grandson, M. Henchey, has renewed the paintings and refitted the rooms in the spacious house, which is now opened to friends and strangers who desire to breathe the invigorating air of the high valleys. Higher up towards the mountains lies the village of Rossinières, with its lovely and finely-situated church and cluster of small houses. The whole valley is meadow and woodland. On every hand it is inclosed by mountains, the slopes of which are covered with pasturage. The loftiest of these, resembling in form a fortified castle, with five tall pinnacles, is called Rubli, and the tallest pinnacle Rubli-horn. The Sarine roars through the valley, along its stony bed, but lying so deep below its banks that the waters can only be seen when you stand close upon them.

The evening on which I arrived here was fine, but to-day one might fancy one's-self in Siberia! The black clouds rush along the mountain passes like avalanches, and pour down torrents of cold rain. Last night snow fell on the peaks and green pastures of Rubli.

The 10*th.*—Cold and rain still continue. I try to

forget them, by reading in my Swiss history, yet I freeze and am "in a dreadful temper." O, sun! sun! If one longs for thee on the plain, how much more here in the narrow valley, of which thou art the joy, and which without thee is only a hideous pit! Can the sun actually shine here? "Pays d'en haut" seems to me to be only a country up in the clouds, and such clouds! I never saw any thing like them. They hang like black crape over the heights; they roll in heavy masses down before them this—hu, hu, hu!

The 12*th.*—"Thou showest thyself once more, monarch of day, and joy of the earth, beloved, longed-for sun!" This commenced a sort of prose poem in which I this morning attempted to describe the combat between the sun and a huge gray cloud which would interrupt it, but which I shall not inflict on my reader. It is sufficient to say that the sun conquered the gray cloud; it fled away in scattered fragments over the mountains, and I, delighted, wandered in the sunshine, into the valley, saluted the flowers which raised their tear-drenched heads, and the trees which clapped their hands above them, and the heights which shone out in smaragdus green towards the blue heavens, and the castle whose bells rang jocundly from the mountains, and the country people, who were making hay along the banks of the rushing Sarine.

"There seems to be a heavy crop this year," I said, in passing by.

"Yes," replied they, "it has not been so good for these many years. And every thing else in the fields promises well!

And they tossed the mown grass aloft in the air,

with their great forks, that it might dry in the wind and the sun. That is the way here.

How the drops glittered in the sunshine! A glorious day!

The 18*th.*—Although the sun may be a rare guest in Rossinières valley, and seldom gives us its heart-cheering beams two days in succession, yet has it now afforded us, one day after another of indescribable beauty, when the wind has blown warm and yet fresh at the same time, the air been light, and when the whole of our little valley with its smaragdus-green pasture-fields and its fragrant hay-harvest, has been like a little abode of comfort and health. During this time our large bee-hive, as I call our chalet, with its many little rooms and windows, has filled with guests, who swarm forth into the valley. Two large tables are daily filled at noon and in the evening. There is an abundance of honey, milk, cream, butter, and cheese, in a word, of every kind of food belonging to pastoral life, and this of the very best—to say nothing of more substantial fare. People live here, for a season, simply and abundantly. I am perfectly amazed at the bowls of thick, whipped cream, which are carried every evening round the crowded tables and from which every guest can heap up his plate. Either with or without wood-strawberries, this prepared cream is really a heavenly kind of food. The crowning charm of the pastoral life of Rossinière is, that it is as cheap as it is excellent.

As in the mean time there is an incessant banging and slamming of doors in our bee-hive, I am as little within as possible, and as I do not like sitting long at table, and now yearn, above all things, for the quiet companionship of nature, I spend the greater part of my day in solitary rambles and little expeditions of discovery amongst the mountains.

Will you accompany me on one of these?—for one will serve as a sample of the whole. Our guide shall be the first good foot-path, because we cannot have a better; and if you would thoroughly enjoy the ramble, you must follow the path silently, and observe every thing with which it presents you. True it may be a little steep sometimes, but you will have secure footing and almost a flight of steps up the mountain. Here the path leads you over a noisy brook, there through a thick wood, mostly of pine trees. The tree-roots supply steps by which you climb ever higher and higher—for our path still ascends. Soon you see the valley behind you down below your feet, and you stand on equal height with the snow-veins which furrow the mountains on the other side of the Sarine; you see the clouds sailing below the mountain pinnacles. Now you are upon the height, and now the path winds round the shoulder of a cliff, and you find yourself upon a green meadow full of grassy hillocks, in which feeds a herd of variegated, well-conditioned cows, whose bells welcome you with a melodious chorus.* You still proceed, and the path winds round another mountain height, and a fresh view opens before you; another extent of valley with wood-crowned heights, the feet of which are scattered with

---

* Nor is this expression too strong. In the large herds of cattle the bells furnish a perfect choir, with base notes, soprano, and so on.

little cottages. In the hollows of the valleys roars the river; the clouds slowly roll along, dividing themselves amongst the immense rocky heights. In whatever direction you turn your sight, you behold Alps, valleys, deep woods, soft, waving pasture meadows, dark rifts of the mountain, whence, as you can see, flow streams in the spring season. Every thing is grand, wild, strong, but at the same time fresh and peaceful. Are you weary?—are you thirsty?—sit down upon that fragrant grass, beside this bank of wild strawberries, as large as those grown in gardens. More juicy, more beautiful ones cannot be found on earth; and this air—ah! do you feel it? It is impossible to describe its purity and freshness, its revivifying power, both of soul and body. Look around! Near you, and all around you, is a flower-world of old and new acquaintance. Here the sweetly-fragrant Alpine pink, with its spear-like leaf, *Dianthus superbus*, well deserving of its name; there, tall and erect, like a real king's candle, the stately yellow gentian, *Gentiana latea*, with thick clusters of gold-colored flowers; and there, the most ornamental of all umbels, the beautiful *Astransia major*. Pretty, bright-colored thistles shine out in crowds. Higher up come the Alpine roses, Rododendrons, and many another sweet-smelling plant which is only found there. But we will not go any further to-day.

We will descend and enter some of the little cottages at the feet of the mountains. We must not leave the foot-path without having become acquainted with the principal places to which it leads, the dwellings where human beings reside, spirits who love or hate, suffer and hope, worship and pray. Let us enter the first cottage on our way.

Within it is a young and pretty woman and four little boys. Three of them are platting straw. The youngest of these little workers is only three and a half years old. The little home, of one room and a kitchen, exhibits neatness and a certain degree of prosperity. We see well-supplied beds, and in the kitchen many shelves on which are ranged plates and well-scoured, nicely-kept wooden bowls. The young mother is kind and civil, and the boys, nice little fellows, but very pale. Straw-platting, which has now for some time become a branch of industrial labor in the valleys, and which brings a little money into the cottages, is not beneficial to the health of women, and least of all to that of children. It keeps the young ones too quiet, and their tendency to scrofula is increased by the straw-platting, which requires the finger to be always kept moist with water. This is not right, and even this young mother conceded the same. But what can people do? The children are many; they require food and clothing, and there is no other profitable labor in the valley for her and the children, and the father's earnings are not sufficient for them all!

The old, sorrowful story!

Let us look into this second lonely cottage, so small and so queer, that it might have been built by a hobgoblin as a home for himself. And there he comes out of the door. Nay, don't be afraid! It is true, he is as wild-looking and shaggy almost, as one of the aborigines of the country—at least as we fancy them—but he smiles very good-naturedly and mildly for all that, and he salutes us almost like a gentleman. And he is really a kind of Alpine gentleman; assists us politely across the mountain torrent; points out to us a better way amongst the labyrinthine paths, and accompanies us himself, talking whilst he does the honors of his little country estate. Yes, he really is a landed proprietor. The little hill yonder he has cultivated with his own hands, and planted with potatoes and beans, and even dug and sowed a little hay-field; and he will dig and cultivate till the whole circuit of little hills has become fertilized. He lives here alone; is already old, but contented with his lot. He has also his good qualities; he appears pious and peaceful—a happy man.

We now return home to our valley.

It is evening. See how the sun gilds the naked mountain tops in the east, Rubli-horn and the cupolas of the Mittags Mountain! Now it is gone, and how soon it becomes dark in the valley! The peace of evening drops down over man and beast; but still, on every hand, is heard the chorus of the cattle-bells amongst the mountains. When all else is gone to rest in the valley, this is still heard. Towards ten o'clock even that has become silent, and the chirp of the crickets and the soft murmuring Sarine are the only sounds audible in the quiet valley of Rossinières.

But if the valley goes to rest betimes, so is it also early in motion. Already before five in the morning, the goats and the cows come up for milking. Smoke rises from the cottages, and all the doors begin to slam in our great cottage. I live as the valley lives; rise early, and am early to bed; and it just suits me.

The people in the valley are peaceable and industrious; influenced by the calm and earnest spirit of the surrounding scenes to look into the depths of the soul and up to heaven, which rests above them. Their mental sphere of vision and their desires seem to be circumscribed, like their valley. They demand but little from life; are satisfied with the little they receive. Their longings do not extend beyond the narrow valley; and if they leave it for the plain, or for life in the town, they always return hither again. They read much during the long winters, either books of grave import or travel. Religion and the church are the topics most interesting to them, and in these they are well read. Merry-makings they have none. Religious gatherings form their principal social intercourse. Marriages are few, and in these, love is less the question than the means of living. The bride is often older than the bridegroom. Morals are so pure that during a hundred years there has not been a single illegitimate child born here. The health is good although straw-platting within the last few years has been found injurious, especially in the case of children.

I have seen several very pretty young girls, but the older women have hideous goitres. Yet it seems to incommodate them but little. The costume is not picturesque, and the women's black caps especially becoming. But a good-tempered kindliness, simplicity and earnestness render the expression agreeable, both in men and women.

"The people here are no better than elsewhere," said the good and thoughtful pastor of the valley, M. Becket, "but they have fewer temptations to evil and more inducement to a serious life."

The greater portion of the people of Rossinières belong to the national church, and merely some few of its population to the Free Church, the principal congregations of which are in the valleys of the Chateau-d'Œx and Les Ormondes. Good pastors of the old church have for a great number of years fallen to the lot of the people of Rossinières, and they have operated beneficially upon the moral condition of their flocks.

A lady, one of my English friends, amongst the inmates of the great bee-hive, and I, one day, during a ramble, passed a cottage from which proceeded the sweet singing of female voices. We stopped, and softly entered. We knew already that the proprietor of the cottage, Esther Marmilliere, was dying of a severe injury of the knee. She reclined in a half-sitting posture on a clean, comfortable bed. The whole room was neat and clean, although evidencing poverty. Two pretty and well-dressed young women sat, one at each window, at work, during which they sang a hymn in duet, in which the sick woman joined. They were her daughters, who lived in service at Lausanne and Vevay, and were now come over to see their aged, sick mother. At our request, they continued the hymn which we had interrupted. The expression of the old woman's wasted countenance, and the purity and strength of her voice, were wonderful; so also were her pious trust and peace in the prospect of a long and painful combat with mortal disease. Such flowers of spiritual life are not unfrequent in these valleys, and they testify nobly for the church which makes one of its missions the founding of a general priesthood in its congregation. What a sermon is this poor woman's sick bed!

Our large bee-hive becomes more and more populous with guests from many lands. Whole schools come hither, that the young girls may enjoy the fresh, country air for one or two weeks. Whilst the girls ramble through the valleys, the youths climb the ridges and summits of the mountains, making long and laborious excursions. And now and then, even a spirited young girl will accompany her father and brother on similar mountain rambles, and is in so doing as brave as the bravest.

A great number of the guests here are English families, mostly abounding in daughters. I regarded with somewhat melancholy foreboding, the future of a flock of six young sisters, between the ages of twelve and twenty, thinking how they would be able to find, each one for herself, space and a sphere of activity, without which no one can be happy in the world. One of these girls, my neighbor at the table, very tall, although still young, with a grave countenance, and wearing spectacles, and who blushed every time she spoke or was spoken to, seemed to me no unworthy candidate for a professor's chair,—but———

But the young girls practically replied to my "how" and my "but."

M. Becket, who had long wished to establish a Sunday-school in Rossinières, announced, the preceding Sunday, from the pulpit, that this would now be commenced. The primitive population, some so young that they could scarcely talk, flocked with great curiosity to the school-house, and here I saw, to my edification, my young girls, five of the six sisters, and two pretty young Americans, each taking her part, as teacher of a little troop of children. My bashful, blushing, and grave neighbor, with her spectacles, I saw surrounded by a dozen boys, whom she instructed with perfect self-possession, and at the same time with youthful delight and motherly sobriety.

After all, the better day dawns for the life of woman on earth; the narrow valley extends its bounds, and many paths are opened. There will be room, work, and life's gladness sufficient for all who sincerely seek and desire to find. Thus spake the conviction of my soul in the Sunday-school of Rossinières.

July 24th.—I have taken my last ramble amongst the mountains which surround this valley. The valleys of Chateau-d'Œx and Rossinières, are seen stretched out, from above, like verdant pasture-meadows, surrounded on every side by lofty mountain walls; and there below, have small two-legged creatures, called human beings, built little dwellings for themselves, no larger, apparently, than mole heaps, with openings on the sunny side.

These Alps are traversed in every direction by foot-paths. However high you may ascend, you always find a winding road between the mountains, and just when you fancy yourself at the top of the mountain, you see before you, a grassy plain, a Swiss cottage, children and flowers, sometimes the prettiest group of pines and deciduous trees, and before you, new heights, with pasture, fields, cattle, and cottages, and so on, everywhere, till at last wood and pasturage cease and the bare mountain alone rears towards heaven its bold peaks and horns. These rambles are sometimes fatiguing, but nevertheless indescribably refreshing, full of surprises and romantic natural scenery.

I have sketched "Rubli-horn;" and taken leave of my acquaintance in the bee-hive, amongst whom I shall miss an earnest, delightful young English couple, as fresh and full of the soul's life as the Alpine scenery itself, and whom I have occasionally taken with me on my mountain rambles. In a few hours I set off to Chateau-d'Œx, where I shall remain a couple of weeks, and shall study the life of the Free Church in conversation with one of its most pious and learned teachers, Pastor B.

CHATEAU-D'ŒX, *July 26th.*—My chateau is, for the present, a little Chaumière on the slope of a verdant mountain, at the southeastern end of Chateau-d'Œx Valley. The valley of Chateau-d'Œx is the largest and most important of these highland valleys, containing several villages and a wealthy population. It is considerably more open and of a more cheerful character than that of Rossinières. The pyramidal heights, which, of ever-varying form, inclose the large lower pastures, and within the recesses of which are many lesser valleys and heights, appear of a lower altitude. La Sarine here roars along a broader bed, with a greater wealth of water. In the middle of the valley, rises a large, round hill, where stood in ancient times the fortified tower which ruled it, and on which now stands the church, amid a garland of leafy trees. From my little room, which with its three windows is much more airy, more comfortable and agreeable than that I had in the great bee-hive, or in the elegant pension at Lausanne, I have a free view over the valley. My host and hostess are peasants. M. Favrodcour is one of the elders of the Free Church. After he has spent the day in the business of his small farm, he closes the evening with divine service in his own house. His wife—I wish you could see her, the pretty, kind-hearted woman, in the simple costume of the country people, but with the demeanor and conversation of the most educated lady. She is the daughter of the former surgeon of the valley,—with a benevolence so cordial, and an attention so delicate and so full of nice feeling, that one feels it a privilege to be the object of it. I only wish you could see how quietly and cheerfully she cares for husband and child, and the whole household, and the guest of the house, just as if it were a pleasure to her! She and her husband belong to a class which is constantly met with in Switzerland, but seldom in any other country, except in the United States of America, which, by education and natural refinement, resemble the higher classes of society, whilst they live simply, and labor like peasants.

My hostess has a great deal to do to-day, for she has to prepare and put up the food for the whole family, who are setting off in the morning to the annual meeting of the Free Church of the high valleys, which this year, is held at "La Lechevette," a lofty plain lying between the valleys of Chateau-d'Œx, Rougemont and Les Ormondes. It lies two heavy leagues from here, high up in the mountains. There all the members of the Free Church of the surrounding valleys are to assemble, and celebrate divine worship under the open sky.

Yes, but how does the sky look? It looks dark and threatening. Last evening, there was a magnificent thunder-storm; to day it has rained from morning to night. If it should be fine in the morning, I shall go on foot with the rest of the inhabitants of the valley, although the road is said to be tolerably fatiguing, for I have greatly desired to be present at one of these assemblies, of which I have heard so much, and which reminds one of the inspired times of the early reformers, when the new-born church sprang forth from Romish Catholicism, and sung its *Te Deum* in the open fields or in the depths of the forests, under the bright, free vault of heaven.

If my journey to La Lechevette be prosperous, and the weather favorable, I shall continue my pedestrian journey as far as the Valleys of Comballez and Les Ormondes, so celebrated for their beauty, after which, I shall return hither. But, it rains, and the heavens are full of clouds.

CHATEAU-D'ŒX, *August 2d.*—Again I am here, after—but I will relate every thing in due course. And first and foremost, I will speak of

THE MEETING AT LA LECHEVETTE.

At four o'clock in the morning, it was still cloudy, with mizzling rain, but by five the clouds had begun to disperse, and the sun faintly to illumine the mountain tops. It promised a fine day. The whole house was in motion; people were getting ready for the meeting. At six o'clock, I set out on my way thither, accompanied by the maidservant of the house, a certain strong and stout *Julie*, who carried my small traveling-bag, and who, except for her name, and a pair of lovely eyes, certainly bore as little resemblance as possible to Julie of "The New Heloise." My host and his family were to set out an hour later.

The little journey was glorious in the fresh morning air, and under the brightening sky. The clouds dispersed over the mountain tops, or sank into their clefts, and I gave them good-speed with my gaze. Here and there, people were seen leaving their dwellings in the valley, and setting out for the meeting. I seemed to speed along as if I had wings.

But now comes the climbing. Up! It is steep, and not to be done without labor, and pausing to take breath. My stout Julie puffs and pants under the burden of my little bag, to such a degree, that it goes to my heart. I perceive, with some surprise, that the poor, stout girl, labors under weakness of the chest. I hasten, therefore, to take a few small things out of the bag, which are absolutely necessary for me, and leave it at the post-house, which we are just now passing—and, in passing, it may be told that the postmistress is a peasant woman, who carries on the business with good management and skill, since the death of her husband.

With light hands and hearts we proceed after this, onward and upward, continually clambering among stones, and only now and then consoled by a little piece of good road. On one side of the road lies a precipice, at the bottom of which is a mountain torrent, on the other a perpendicular wall of rock, here and there covered with pine wood. The valley becomes ever narrower and wilder. There again comes an ascent, and, this time, of an hour's length, and very difficult into the bargain; after that, a second, but not so laborious. And now, after three hours, we are at our journey's end.

The narrow mountain pass at once emerges into an open, grassy plain, surrounded in the distance by pointed Alps, and thinly scattered with cottages. The morning wind blows cool over the fine, waving grass. This is "La Vallèe des Mosses," and the portion in which we find ourselves, La Lechevette. How delightful is it to rest myself here on soft couches of mown grass, which is drying in the sun, and to look around one on the extensive scene.

Troops of people are seen in long procession across the fields, hastening to the place of meeting; and as they meet from the various quarters, you see bright, kindly glances, and hear the cordial greetings and inquiries: "*Comment étes vous! Comment votre mère,*" and so on. "*Mais tres joliment! Mais pas mal!*" etc.

The people of the valleys are frequently related to each other, and they who now meet here have not seen one another since the last annual gathering.

In the mean time, you see the pastors and elders of the congregations busied in selecting the particular spot for the assembly, and afterwards preparing it for that purpose. The spot which they selected on this occasion, was a wood, the thick pine trees of which afforded a shelter from the heat of the sun. I was still busied looking around me on the scenery, and in watching the groups of people who had thrown themselves on the grass to converse, and to take breakfast, when a hymn, sung in quartette, was heard, strong and melodious, to proceed from the depth of the pine wood. Here, the little assembly of two or three hundred persons had grouped themselves, standing or sitting under the trees. In the midst, upon a somewhat open space, stood the pastors of the various congregations, and around them the elders, with their grave, honest countenances. The youngest of the teachers gave out, as the principal subject for meditation, the words of the Apostle Paul: "Rejoice always;" admonishing his hearers to examine what was the cause of a continued joy, even during the sins and sorrows of our earthly life. The cause of this, he declared to them, was the free grace of Christ.

The dark-eyed and dark-haired, but mild Penchaud, uttered a prayer full of ardent love. The elders, alternately with the clergy, took their turn in urging the importance of a more true, more perfect life in Christ. And thus the divine service was continued, with alternating prayer and the singing of hymns. All this was good, but I felt a want of a loving and elevating spirit, and felt in particular, the want of a mental communication of spiritual experience, which I had looked for from the numbers of this assembly, meeting together again after the interval of twelve months, and I was inclined to attribute these wants to the desire which the leaders of the meeting had, rather to instruct themselves than to induce those present to take part in its business. Long pauses intervened between the addresses.

About twelve o'clock, the forenoon service was ended, and the assembly broke up into parties and family groups for dinner. This partaking of the contents of the various provision baskets, was a time of joyous conversation. Such as had not brought victuals with them, were invited to partake with those who had abundance. Nobody was overlooked or uncared for; all were regarded as guests by a good housewife.

During the dinner, it was communicated from group to group, that a celebrated spiritual preacher from Geneva had arrived quite unexpectedly at the meeting. During the singing of one of the hymns in the forenoon service, I had heard a voice at a distance exclaim, "Look! there is the assembly!"—"*Voilà la réunion!*"

And soon after, the congregation was increased by the arrival of a great number of strangers, to whom, at the time, but little attention was paid.

Soon after the close of the simple meal, divine service again commenced. When the first hymn had been sung, I heard a voice, the energy of which greatly struck me. Under the aged pine trees, upon an elevation of the field, stood a tall, broad-shouldered man, whose whole exterior was remarkable. The forehead, beneath which a pair of deep-set eyes flashed lightning, the nose, the jaw, the whole features, stood forth powerful and irregular as the block of an Alp; whilst a tempest seemed to have passed through his wild, bushy hair. John the Baptist might have appeared such as he. It was the celebrated preacher from Geneva,—M. Berthollet. From the moment that he first rose, he ruled the assembly, and the assembly acknowledged in him its centre.

He began by stating that whilst on a visit to his native place in the neighborhood, he heard of the proposed meeting at La Lechevette, and had come thither without really knowing the exact point of meeting; but the singing of the hymn in the pine wood suddenly revealed this to him, and he now must say how happy he felt in finding himself here, in this assembly, amongst the Alps, beneath God's open heaven, and that he would avail himself of the occasion to address a few words to them from the depths of his heart. And with a powerful voice, full of ever-varying expression, and with arms outstretched, now towards the heights, now towards the assembly, he conjured his hearers "to think of the last hour, of the dark flood to which all must come, and to hold themselves in readiness for the last journey; because, as in the old time, no one could pass over Jordan who could not properly pronounce the word *Shibboleth*, so, on the day of judgment, no one could enter the kingdom of heaven who could not pronounce the name *Jesus*." After which, a discourse followed, so rich in anecdote and narrative from England, Switzerland, Hindostan, Nova Zembla, Canada, the Cape, and, in fact, from all parts of the world, of the miracles of Christianity, histories of conversion, of Christian death-beds, of souls saved out of mortal anguish, and all this interspersed with ardent prayers and beseechings to them "to reflect, to lay these things to heart, to come, come now at that moment to the Saviour," and all poured forth in a rushing torrent of spiritual eloquence, so that, altogether, it was—wonderful.

Here was a popular preacher of the right sort; one

really mighty to rouse souls out of a state of lethargy and dullness.

Amongst the various anecdotes, some striking, some affecting, which he poured forth out of his cornucopia over the assembly, I particularly remember the following, which he related in the most admirable manner:

"Some years ago, one of the most remarkable of the so-called street preachers in London, was a man named Rowland Hill. One day, the rich and worldly Lady Erskine came driving in her carriage across the very market-place where he was preaching. Seeing the crowd assembled round him, she ordered her carriage to stop, and inquired what was going forward, and was told that it was Rowland Hill, who was preaching to the people. She had heard speak of him, and curious to hear him herself, she alighted from her carriage, and accompanied by her servants, made her way into the crowd, which immediately opened for the elegant lady; and at once, without suffering himself to be disturbed by her presence, Rowland exclaimed:

"'My friends, here comes a soul which is to be put up for auction!'

"The people were startled, and some laughed. This rich, grand lady, to be sold by auction! Lady Erskine advanced nearer, and Rowland Hill continued:

"'I see three buyers about to bid for her. The first is called *The World*. Well, what wilt thou give, oh World, for this soul?' The World replies, 'Pleasures, ornaments, flatteries, festivities, for every day of her life!' 'All pleasures, and flatteries, and festivities, will come to an end, whilst this soul will last on, because it is immortal! It is too little which thou offerest, O World, and thou canst not have her! Now comes the second bidder; it is *The Devil*. How much, Satan, wilt thou bid for this soul?' 'All the power of the world, and the glory thereof.' 'But all the power of the world, and its glory, will pass away, whilst this soul wilt last on. Thou canst not have her, Satan, for thou offerest too little! The third bidder presents himself. Ah, that is the Lord Jesus! I expected no less of thee, O Lord! What, then, dost thou bid for this soul?' 'My peace in this life, and after it eternal bliss!' 'Take her, Lord, take her! She is thine, for a higher price no one can offer!'"

Berthollet added, that Lady Erskine was so affected by these words, that she made them a prophecy of the truth; she abandoned her worldly life of vanity, and became one of the principal supporters of the English church.

The assembly in the pine wood had, by degrees, gathered closely around Berthollet. Women sat in a half circle at his feet, their gentle countenances raised to him in a kind of astonishment, or bowed down in silent tears. The men stood around, with heads advanced, among the trees; as far as the eye could penetrate the woods, you could see listening, grave countenances, over whose powerful features passed again and again the expression of deep emotion. When the preacher ceased, they sang with life and ardor,—

"How beautiful upon the mountains are the feet of him who announced to sinners thy grace, O Lord!" etc.

Berthollet seated himself, bowing his forehead to his hands. Twice after this he arose, and again addressed the assembly. After the beautiful hymn of praise,—

"When time shall be no longer; when the finite shall have given place to the infinite,"

he drew a picture from these words of the time when all created beings, united in the kingdom of God's glory, should unite in singing praises to the Redeemer of the world.

During the pauses between the singing and the speaking, you could hear the low whisper of the wood, and the murmuring of thousands of small insects, which also, in their way, joined in the solemn worship. The clear, mild sky, gleamed through the waving branches of the pine trees; it was a moment of perfect, peaceful beauty and harmony, and a moment of unspeakable inward emotion,—a foretaste of the condition of the completed being! But, turned from the assembly, and with his powerful brow pressed against the trunk of a pine tree which he had embraced, stood the preacher, himself almost overpowered by the words with which he had shaken his audience; the veins swollen on the temples, and the beating of the pulsation visible!

Still one more hymn, still one more prayer of thanksgiving, and the pastors dismissed the assembly. The people took a quiet and cordial leave, one of another, and all hastened, each his own way, whilst the sun was yet high, that there might be time, before dark, to reach their distant valleys and homes.

Accompanied by a young peasant, who was appointed to me as my guide, I continued my way through " La Vallée des Mosses" to Comballez, where an enterprising man has opened a small hotel, and where I intended to pass the night.

The road conducted us over soft, and, at times, swampy, meadow-ground, and I had good opportunity for conversing with my guide, a handsome, friendly youth, from Ormondes Valley, by name Emanuel Isabel. He was a member of the Free Church, and talked cheerfully and sensibly of its spirit and importance. During the preceding winter, Ormondes Valley had been for several months without a pastor—from what cause I do not remember; but the congregation had, nevertheless, kept up divine service with undeviating exactness, and attended to all the affairs of the church by means of the elders, and those who were chosen as their assistants. One of the elders read a portion of Scripture every Sunday, and spoke from it to the congregation, instead of the pastor. Occasionally, even some one of the younger members was deputed to read something from the word, as well as to speak upon it. He, Emanuel Isabel, had more than once been called to this office.

"It is evident," continued he, with a beaming glance, "that the church is really a church, when she can thus, through God's word and Spirit be left to herself!"

He acknowledged, in the mean time, the necessity of study and knowledge in the highest leaders of the congregation, in order that they might be preserved from false doctrine, and be led forward into light and activity, and so on.

"La dent du Midi," and several of the Savoy Alps, reared their snowy and glittering peaks along the horizon before us, as we reached Comballez, and the sun was near his setting. Here I took leave of my friendly guide, who would not on any account receive payment for his services.

I obtained, in the pretty wooden hotel, a little room with a splendid view of the Alps, and an hour afterwards I was seated at a large table, with an elegant company, enjoying a good cup of tea, and that deliciously prepared cream, which is one of the greatest of the world's delicacies, and one of the most wholesome at the same time.

I had intended to have continued my ramble on the following day to Les Ormondes. But the view of "Dent du Midi," which shone forth in the early morning with all its dentated splendor into a cloudless sky, and the peculiar beauty of La Comballez valley, kept me there through the day. There I wandered early, and there I wandered late; visited the cottages; rested on the fragrant beds of thyme and mint at the feet of the mountains; contemplated the magnificent views, drank in the air, the freshness and beauty of life and thought, as I had done many a time before:

> Oh wunderschön ist Gottes Erde,
> Und schön auf ihr ein Mensch zu seyn;

The day was glorious. La Comballez valley consists of two verdant mountain feet, between which roars the mountain torrent, La Ruvaletta, deeply embedded between wild, riven rocks. The valley itself is embedded between lofty mountain walls, but the view opens both to the north and the south, and that to the south is of the most grand description. During the walk round a wood-crowned hill, at the end of the valley, you see, all at once, the glaciers, "Les Diablerets," which elevate themselves above Les Ormondes valley, the Savoy Alps to the south, in a magnificent amphitheatre, and below, in the distance, the Rhone valley, of which the dwellings and villages can be distinguished. La Comballez is said to be the highest of the inhabited valleys of this region. And even in this glorious July weather, the air was so cold, both morning and evening, that one was actually frozen.

Early the following morning, leaving my shawl and umbrella in the care of the host of the little hotel, I set out on an excursion, carrying with me merely my parasol and a little bag containing a couple of pears and a few light and indispensable articles of the toilet. Not a cloud was in the sky, and the air was so pure and invigorating, that it seemed, as it were, to support me. I did not feel my body. For a part of the way, I was accompanied by pastor L., with whom I had become acquainted the preceding evening. Conversation on the subject of the church had attracted us to each other, and it was now continued during our morning's walk. He was born in France, and had the Frenchman's ease and pleasure in talking; he belonged to the Swiss national church, and he contended for the individualism of the church, yet with moderation and judgment, and I listened to him with pleasure. I always listen to opinions which may differ from my own, if they be propounded by sensible persons, because I can say, with the Princess in Goethe's Tasso: "Ich freue mich, wenn kluge Manner reden, dass ich verstehen kann wie sie es meinen!" And I am also glad that sometimes I can by this means, come to a better understanding of things than they themselves.

The views of the Alps were magnificent beyond description this bright morning. When we came from the shady side of the mountain into the brilliant sunshine, just opposite Les Diablerets, my polite companion turned back to La Comballez, and with a light heart, I continued my solitary way, which now began to descend, the views ever expanding before me down to the green, shadowy valley of Les Ormondes.

Thirty years ago I traveled, in a close carriage, through Switzerland. How happy, I then thought, was the little ragged Savoyard, who, barefoot and free, went wandering at will among the mountains! How I then wished to be in his place! And now I wandered—not barefooted—but as lightly and as free as he!

It required two good hours of walking in the heat of the ascending sun, by which time I was considerably weary, before I reached the newly-built parsonage in Ormondes valley, and in the cool porch of which I rested, with the young pastor Lerèsche and his amiable young wife, who refreshed me with cool, sparkling water, wine, cherries, and other good things, and who made me most heartily welcome. Nor was the least refreshing part of the entertainment to me, the sight of this young, handsome couple, before whom the early "morning dew lay still upon life," and to whom the reality of life was now the most beautiful idyl. They had only been married fourteen days, and had been living here ten. They were young, good, handsome, in easy circumstances; they loved each other; they would live and labor together in the bosom of this fresh, grand, and pleasant country. Oh, say not that life is only a valley of tears! Amongst its dark shadows, what bright, lovely pictures present themselves!

I wandered on for about an hour before I reached "Le Creux," a hollow in the valley, where lies a little peasant farm, surrounded by trees and hilly crofts, in the very midst of an actual colosseum of primeval rocks, crowned by two ice-towers, Les Diablerets. From these icy walls, two hundred feet high, fall the torrents which form "La Grande Eau," which roar through the valley and, lower down, swell the waters of the Rhone. The owner of the peasant farm, generally called Père Ansermey, is one of the most esteemed and valued elders of the Free Church. He has fitted up a few rooms in his chalet, for the reception of strangers, who wish to spend the hot summer months in the cool valleys, and here a room was also prepared for me. Several ladies were residing here for the summer from various countries—Switzerland, Germany, England, Scotland—but all of such amiable and well-trained characters that they lived together as an actual band of sisters. They received me as a sister. They gratified my wishes in the most kind manner, gave me the best room in the house, the best of every thing. I cannot describe how good and kind they were. And much excellent and earnest conversation had we together under the shadow of our cottage roof, or during our walks in the valley. I was much interested also, in becoming better acquainted with Père Ansermey, who is a splendid example of the Christian peasant. He was now confined at home, in consequence of an injury received, a couple of months since, during the repair of his house, when he fell from the roof. He had, therefore, given up to his wife and son the care of the cattle in the higher pasturages of the mountains, whilst he remained down in the valley with his daughter—a good, managing, and pretty girl, our hostess,—to look after the place and a cow which had broken its leg. Père Ansermey waited till his cow was better, in order to go with her up into the mountains. He is a tall and powerful man, between fifty and sixty, with a splendid countenance and the most beautiful and expressive eyes I ever saw in a man.

During a short time that I was left alone with him, he asked me, in a half-dubious way, but with a gentle and most heartfelt voice, "whether I loved Jesus?" and when I replied, "Yes," how his countenance beamed, how his eyes brightened!

After this he related to me the history of his own conversion, which was that of a silent, inward struggle between an outer, not particularly edifying life, and an ideal of perfection, which became ever stronger and stronger in his soul. This inward combat attained to its height, when one evening at a dancing party, a bloody quarrel having arisen, Père Ansermey felt himself all at once compelled to say, "Think if the Lord Jesus were to come in just now!"

That thought and that moment became decisive to Ansermey. He hung upon a hook the violin on which he used to play for the dancing, and never touched it again for such a purpose. He was not averse, however, to innocent pleasures—which I now took upon me to defend—but thought that young people, after all, could employ their precious time in something better.

In the evening Père Ansermey performed family worship in our little circle. So doing, he read a chapter in the Scriptures and prayed, after which, he led, accompanied by his daughter, in the singing of such a hymn or hymns, as any of those present might desire. They were sung in quartette by the little assembly, and, frequently, extremely well. The music and words of one hymn, especially pleased me, which also A. Vinet is said to have loved before any other; it beg

"Great God of Truth, thou whom only I worship."

One day when I expressed my admiration of Père Ansermey's voice, which is of unusual strength and purity, he joyfully exclaimed,

"Yes, that is true; I have a beautiful voice!"

In the evening when he has closed his reading, he will repeat one or two verses of what he has read, adding; "These are lovely (or important) words; may God give us grace rightly to comprehend them!" Sometimes he will remain for a little while **perfectly silent after the reading**, as if in quiet devotion.

What a living answer is a man of this kind, to the assertion of the Romish church, that people of the uneducated class cannot understand the Scriptures, nor guide themselves by their light.

The valleys of Les Ormondes, the upper and lower, are said to be the most beautiful of the high valleys of the Vaud, and they are so from the number of grassy hills and fresh mountain streams; from the numerous verdant terraces and extent of pasturage. The people are handsome and more cheerful than in any other of the valleys. They are celebrated for their lively wit, and their disposition to look at life, and every thing, from its most amusing side. But here more than in any other valley, you find the want of many of the conveniences of life, not to say its necessaries. Bread (if not of the very coarsest kind) and meat, etc., must be fetched from a distance of two hours. Under these circumstances one could not but be astonished at the manner in which our table was furnished, as well as at our living here, which cost only three francs a day.

I spent three days here, one evening of which I passed with the ideally happy, and amiable young couple in the new parsonage. Interesting traits from the innermost of human life, furnished topics of conversation, with the sun, the Alps and the careering clouds before our gaze, one of those glorious spectacles which man sometimes will purchase at almost any price, and which nature exhibits here gratis every evening.

On the morning of the fourth day, Père Ansermey set off before dawn with his cow up into the mountains, and before the sun had illumined the spires of Les

Diablerets, I took my pilgrim-staff, otherwise, my little parasol, in hand, and, accompanied by my new lady friends, took my way to La Comballez. There we parted; but the grateful remembrance of two of those amiable ladies will never leave me.

In company of a pretty, but impish, ten-year-old, countrified Sylvie, I continued my way to Chateau-d'Œx, the whole way being on the soft grass of the high plain "Des Mosses;" and nowhere have I seen so beautiful and fine a species of grass, playing and waving in the wind like a thin gauze of smoke. The plain looked both rich and gay.

I still could see, behind me, the Savoyard Alps, and their cool shadows stretching refreshingly across the sun-lit plain.

After walking over the plain for more than two hours, I was both hungry and weary, and I imagined that my little Sylvie was the same. And see, just here, close to the road, stands a cottage, from which some men, who have been carrying hay, are coming, whilst a woman, with a good housewifely countenance, stands at the door. I ask her if she can give me something for dinner. She does not know, she replies, whether she has any thing that I can eat. "Have you eggs?" "No." "Potatoes?" "Yes, but not cooked." "Milk?" "Yes." "Bread and butter?" "Yes." Excellent! Then we have all that we need.

We go into the neat, cool cottage, where a fat little lad is asleep in his cradle, watched over by a pretty little Julie. The young mother spreads a snow-white cloth upon the table, and brings forth good bread, remarkably good milk, and other things, excellent pastoral fare, which Sylvie and I devour with right good appetites. In the mean time, the young mother takes up her fat little boy, to whom she talks in motherly fashion. He was her fifth child. The kind and handsome woman seemed pious and happy, and did not desire any thing for the meal which she had given me, but received gratefully, the small payment which I insisted upon.

The descent during the hot day, was fatiguing. Coal-black clouds were gathering in dense masses over the mountains behind us, and rumbling thunder began. Terrified at this prospect, my little Sylvie deserted me when only half way. The remainder was made under the most threatening sky, nor was it till about five o'clock, that I reached my valley and my home, having walked that day upwards of six leagues, and that without any excessive weariness.

My kind hostess provided for me in the best manner, gave me tea and a foot-bath; and now how good it is to be here in my comfortable dwelling, whilst the thunder-storm bursts over the mountains and valley, and the rain pours down. The thunder-claps are terrific, but the lightning very rarely does any damage in the valley.

11th.—It has struck, however, this time. The lightning has burned down house and home, barns and barn-yard, of a young couple and their aged parents. This misfortune has awakened general sympathy, and one of the elders of the Church made an excellent discourse to the congregation last evening on the subject. One of the most beautiful institutions of the Free Church is certainly that of the office of its elders, and the active part which it gives them in its affairs. They are real supporters and helpers of the pastor in his labors for the congregation. In my conversation with them, I have derived both pleasure and edification. These peasants have a freshness of thought and expression, frequently an originality, which carries with it an unction, and seems to go to the very fountain-head of the subject under discussion. Their wives and daughters also, are active in looking after the needy and sick of the congregation. They have besides, separate assemblies for prayer and work.

13*th.*—After somewhat more than two weeks' residence in this quiet valley, I am about to take my leave of it, in order to make a journey in company with M. Penchaud, to the Bernese Oberland, and to the Waldstetter Cantons, where the people are said still to retain their primitive manners and character. It is Schwytz, the cradle of the Sworn-Confederacy, to which my journey has especial reference. I will there visit Grutli, and revive in my mind the memory of the heroic deeds of the Swiss. In Hasli-valley, will I also inquire after the traces of the Swedish race, who, according to tradition, emigrated there, and gave to the Swiss people their temperament and their name.

Three weeks have passed like a calm summer day. I have enjoyed freedom and peace, made long excursions in the neighborhood, contemplated the people in their quiet life, and have even taken part in its occupations. The women are admirable for their industry, order, and domesticity, to which must be added, their gentle and kind demeanor. Each one of these high valleys has its separate branch of female industry. In that of Rossinières they plat straw, in Chateau-d'Œx, make lace, embroider, and make dresses. The principal occupation of the valleys, in the mean time, is the care of cattle and cheese-making. At this season, you meet horses continually laden with immense cheeses, coming down from the mountain pastures. So they travel on to the towns, where under the name of "frommages de Gruyères," they are purchased, and thence go forth into the world.

I have so far, spoken only of the bright side, of the life of these valleys. I must now also say something of its shadow sides. To these belong the moody quarrels and grudges, which when they once have begun between individuals or families, live on like gnats in stagnant water, and continue sometimes till death. To these belong, also, that depression of mind which not unfrequently overpowers the soul, and which usually takes the form of religious melancholy, terrors of the judgment, etc., and which sometimes even leads to suicide. More frequently, however, this unhappy condition of mind yields to the consolatory conversation of the pastor and the brethren, and the assurance of free grace in Christ. The necessity of labor is here, also, a continual friend at hand, which draws the depressed mind away from its moody thoughts, for none are here sufficiently wealthy not to be compelled to labor. The earliest cultivator of these valleys, the pious Monk Columbau, and his brethren seem to have given the stamp and example to a life of prayer and labor.

I have seen and heard here sufficient of the Free Church, to make me value it highly as a platform for the formation of congregations, "for a universal priesthood," in which every individual becomes a self-couscious and self-responsible organ of the vitality of the church. And this is good, very good. But it has also become clear to me at the same time, that its stand-point is higher and more correct, merely in so far as the established church is concerned, and that it has not as yet comprehended, in its deeper sense, the fundamental principle of Protestantism and the future, nay, that it even rejects all questions of a higher knowledge and excludes from the church, much and many things which an actual *Universal Church*, could not exclude, but would accept and sanctify.

It is not *my* Free Church, my church of the future. It is too exclusive for that, too stagnant, adheres too much still to the letter. My church, that in which I believe, that which I seek for, that in which I already, in the depth of my soul, live and worship, is one in which certain dogmas and forms would not separate those who are united in the same highest love. My church is that in whose lofty choir Fenelon and Channing, François de Salis and Herman Franke, Hildebrand and Luther, Washington and Vinet, St. Brigitta and Elizabeth Fry, may offer prayer and sing praises together; nay, from the broad temple-courts of which none are excluded who earnestly seek and love the supreme good, be its name Lao-tscu, Zoroaster, Buddha, Socrates, or Spinosa!—Have separate compartments or chapels in the church, if you like; nay, there ought to be dissimilar limbs, as it were, more remote and nearer organs in one great organism, but let it have a Holy of holies, where all united in love to

God and His Kingdom may assemble around "an Eternal Gospel which is proclaimed to all who dwell on the face of the earth." All other churches are too narrow for me, and do not answer the idea of Protestantism. The idea of Protestantism, the fundamental thought of Protestantism!—has the Protestant Church fully comprehended and embraced this? And that which is its highest and simplest expression? This has long been a question to myself and others. I have received for reply, when people have replied at all, the fundamental tenets of Protestantism are, "Righteousness, through faith alone on the free grace of Christ," and "the soul's immediate communion, with God through the Holy Scriptures, the fountain of all truth, of which God is the source."

By these two principal tenets of Protestantism, are combated the doctrines of the Roman Catholic Church, of righteousness through outward works, and of the church as an outward ordination and authority between God and man, with the divine right of binding and releasing, and at the same time, powerful to lead souls to God.

But has Protestantism even in these tenets expressed its innermost fundamental tenet, its *primeval Word!*

What is it that gave Protestantism the right to protest? It is answered: "God's word in the Holy Scriptures." But what was it that gave to the Protestant Church the right to explain this word differently to the mother church?

It is to the eternal honor of Protestantism, to have combated the false and injurious doctrines of the Romish Church; it is to its immortal honor, that it plucked the Holy Scriptures from out of the heap of human inventions, under which they had been buried; to have made them available to every man, and so doing, to have anew opened to Christianity the fountain from which the first congregation derived its life and its inspiration. Christianity beheld now here again, the living, historical Saviour. She could now inquire, hear, learn, from Him Himself, and His Apostles. Human intervention, Popes, Priests, Councils, no longer thrust themselves between Him and them, all human beings could become immediately, his disciples, all could receive immediately from Him, the word of Eternal Life! Thus, rejoiced the young, protesting congregation, over the Romish Church, and with reason. This benefit was unspeakable! To have placed the Holy Scriptures in the hands of the people to have learned from them, that not on outward works, but by the faith of the heart alone, depended the highest weal or woe of man;—that it seems to me, is the greatest work of Luther and the Reformation. This was also its pure principle, and the source of an infinite development. But just at the commencement of this development, when the newly-born church should have formed itself into being, difficulties and contradictions arose, which split it up within itself. They knew very well, that God's word in the Holy Scriptures, must alone be the basis and canon of the church. And now, the new disciples start forward, each with the Holy Scriptures in his hand, but none understood and explained them as the others. The architects of the church could not agree about the building. Each one would build it in his own way. Thus, a variety of churches and sects arose, which, even when they were agreed on the chief topic, yet acknowledged differences sufficiently great, to make them then—and still at this day,—quarrel one with another, like enemies. The Romish Church exclaimed triumphantly, "Where is now your Church? Where is your unity, where your cementing central point?" And it exclaims so to this day. Protestantism replies, as we have already said; but has an internal conviction that the answer is not satisfactory, and seeks for one of greater completeness, looking around for it, certain that it will be found, but, am I wrong, when I say that as yet, it has neither found it nor comprehended it?

Alas! I have made many inquiries and investigations; I have traveled over land and sea; I have searched in books and amongst men, to come to some light on this subject, to find an answer at once true, full and sufficing: an answer with which scoffers could be silenced, skeptics enlightened, and which should carry with it conviction and satisfaction to the soul. For the question does not alone concern the basis of Protestanism, but is first and foremost, the basis of all human wisdom; it concerns the *right* of humanity, that is to say, the *ability* of humanity to comprehend the truth even to decide and determine upon any of the highest questions; upon those which bear reference in the profoundest manner to the soul, to eternal happiness or misery. And—I still am seeking and still inquiring. But no longer altogether as I did formerly. I have seen for some time, in the depth of my soul's innermost, a light becoming clear, and have perceived a word—I perceived them even from my earliest youth, powerful but indistinct, and although the fogs of life and the anguishes of the heart may have dimmed them, yet have I seen them again and again, like heavenly stars gleaming through earthly clouds, and now I have come to Switzerland to endeavor to attain to a clearer comprehension.

In the morning I shall set out on my long journey to the primeval home of Swiss liberty, and to the source of the Rhone. Perhaps they will aid me in finding the primal word of Protestanism!

Farewell, peaceful valleys! Good, simple, cordial human beings, farewell!

THIRD STATION.

Hasli valley and the Swedish emigrants—Rosenlaui—Grimsel—Gloomy scene—The source of the Rhone—The Forest Cantons—Grutli and its heroes—Life in Schwytz—Two types of Conservatism—Sunday on Rhigi—Nicholas de Flue—Life in Zurich—Einsiedeln, its pilgrims and teachers—Zwingli—My home in Zürich—Journey to Basle—Missionary Institution and Missionaries.

MEYRINGEN, OBER-HASLI, *August* 21*st*.—The nearer you approach the High Alps, the more is the soul penetrated with unusual emotions at the sight of the grandeur of nature. The thought of its creation untold ages before that of mankind, and the sense of its immovable stability, leads the mind to draw a melancholy comparison between it and the fleetingness of our physical being. But at the same moment the soul elevates itself, as if to place a higher nobility beside this majesty of the life of nature. It is with such feelings that you reach Ober-Hasli, and wandering on the edge of gloomy precipices, along broken, and, as it were, riven paths, continually ascending, continually astonished by the grand scene, you leave behind you the region of fruit trees, and passing through pine woods and yellow gentians, enter the region of the Alpine rose, the savine, the small aromatic flowers that grow on the pasturages, and so reach the steep slopes of the mountains, where a slippery and dangerous sward seems to mark the limits of grazing for the cattle, and of human curiosity. For, higher up, immense masses of snow crush down the life of nature, and the ice of many thousand years clothes the Jungfrau, Finsterhorn, Wetterhorn and Shoukhorn, the lonely pyramids of this Alpine chain. The clear waters of the Aar rush forth from beneath a vault of ice. To a great distance, as far as the eye can penetrate, all is ice; immense crystals glitter in the depths; seldom is a chamois seen to speed through the icy desert; seldom a lammer-geir circles over these crags; man has made a few tracks, but for the extent of many, many miles, not a foot-trace can be discerned. The wanderer is easily swallowed up in the crevices of the ice, and when this happens, he is sometimes found, after several ages, carried away by the perpetually advancing glacier, immovable in the midst of its accumulated ice. Thus the earth lies buried under La Gemmi. La Gemmi rears itself, naked and broken up by time. The poisonous* Aconitum napellus, or Christmas rose, gives an agreeable effect, for it is the announcement of vegetation. From the lofty region of the Daulear See of the Engsten Alps, the path descends, sometimes over rocks, sometimes through the beds of torrents, along a naked wall of rock as far as Adelboden. Between the long icy valleys of the lake of Thun, in the bosom of the mountain, which extends westward from Niesen to Stockhorn, descending the while to Leman, lies the Oberland, a labyrinth of innumerable valleys, through which the Sarine, Simmen, Kander, Engstetenbach, and the two Lutschine rivers, increased by innumerable streams, proceed along their wild and devious courses to the Aar, or to the lake of Thun.

"In the highest regions, however, where grass can grow, you meet with herdsmen and their herds, whilst the fertile heights of Asia are desolate, because Asia wants that which blesses the Oberland—freedom."

Thus far my R., both for your benefit and mine, have I followed J. von Muller's description of the Oberland, because I acknowledge myself totally bewildered in the labyrinths of the Alpine country, which the powerful Swiss wanders through with a safe, though it may be somewhat plodding step, and I was not able to give you, like a new Ariadne, a guiding thread through them. I can merely show you one and another picture from it, whilst I go on spinning the thread of my narrative. I look upon the

---

* Plants, when produced on the lofty mountains, have a totally different power to what they have when grown on the plain.—*Author's Note*.

various knots tied in, as memories, and by the help of these I shall be able to uphold both you and myself.

The first leads me to the very beginning of this my pedestrian excursion to the high valleys of the Vaud, to the valley of Jessonay, and an evening spent there in the comfortable little inn, with a kind young couple, who were here to part, the one to become, from this point, my traveling companion, the other to return to her highland home and her little ones. But the young wife and mother wished to accompany her husband so far; and this evening, therefore, we spent happily together, the young couple, and their elderly friend, happy, both heart and soul, in the society of each other, and——in the midst of Alps and ice-fields it did the old heart good to warm itself with such memories from the domestic hearth. But now: now we must proceed on our journey.

And early on the lovely summer morning we set forth through the valleys of Jessonay and Simmen, magnificent scenery opening out on every hand, with "mountains high and low, deep valleys," and waters of the Zweisimmen rushing along in their wild career by the side of our road, and sometimes precipitating themselves in foaming cascades. Human dwellings are small, and seem here even smaller than usual, in the bosom of the giant mother. But the Bernese cottages—for we are now in the Canton of Berne—are more elegant abodes, at least outwardly, than the cottages of the Canton of Vaud. They are adorned with exquisite carving, and with wooden galleries, often very peculiar; and upon the gallery are flower-pots, from which splendid red carnations tower upwards, or hang down in splendid bouquets, in the midst of which you may see, at times, the father in his nightcap, smoking his pipe, and the mother, in her elegant Bernese costume, busied about one thing or another. The people seem to be in good circumstances; and the Swiss cottage, with its great roof, resembles a large hen with bright-colored feathers, covering her brood with outstretched wings.

By degrees, the valley becomes narrower, and, as it were, tamer—more idyllian—but it resumes its magnificent proportions when it expands towards the region in which the lake of Thun lies, as amid a verdant garland, encompassed by the icy giants of the Oberland. Again I say, make a journey to Thun, if you can; and go thither from this side. I do not believe you can find any thing more magnificently beautiful in the world. The scene reminded me of one in Sweden, that of the Wetter-lake, with Jönköpping on its banks, as you descend down the forest-pass of Oestergöthland." Nay, but that has no showy Alps as a back-ground.

And never have I spent a more spiritually beautiful evening than the last, on the shores of the lake of Thun. "Föhn," the sirocco of Switzerland, rustled unceasingly in the lofty trees of "La Chartreuse," and a heavy storm which had collected, discharged itself in lightnings which blazed on all sides around us, without thunder, and with merely a few drops of rain. When we returned towards the town it had cleared; the bells were ringing, and the moon, like a harbinger of peace, ascended out of the huge cloud which now retired behind the Alps. We expected a storm tomorrow, and the physiognomy of the sky promised nothing agreeable; but, towards noon, the clouds vanished, and the sail across the lake of Thun was as lovely as a scene of enchantment. Standing on the deck, I closed my eyes, that I might, as it were, feel and enjoy, with a more intense inwardness, the inimitable delight of the air, through which I seemed to myself to be flying; and when I again opened them, behold, I then was actually flying through the bright ethereal space towards the glittering snow-white heights, which stood forth in their calm magnitude, and breathed freshness towards us. Every object shone, but as if through a thin, gauze vail, like that which the Indian summer spreads over the landscape of North America. It was like fairy-land; it was magically beautiful. One did not wish to speak, or to move, but only to see and to feel. My friend and traveling companion felt it just as I did, and so, I fancy, did every one on board, for a deep silence prevailed. The wind, too, was still; and the lake lay smooth as a mirror.

The hospitality of kind friends enhanced to me the pleasure of this second visit to the lake of Thun. Thou little lake—thou little town—thou magnificent scene—I shall never forget you!

It was the height of the season at Interlachen. All the hotels were full. The grand promenade was thronged with elegant ladies and gentlemen; one might have believed one's-self on a Parisian boulevard; but all around was heard the ringing of the cow-bells in chorus, reminding one that one was in a Swiss valley. The number of guests at this little Interlachen now amounted to about five hundred.

We crossed to Giessbach. The description of this beautiful cascade (a poem of many stanzas), another can give you better than I can. The steamer across the Brienz lake was crowded with passengers, and I could not find a seat, until a peasant, squeezing himself into as little compass as possible, made friendly signs to me to take a seat beside him. On the bench just opposite to him sat his wife. They were peasants from the Canton Wallis, poorly clad, and not over-clean in the outward; but they had something indescribably gentle and good-tempered in their expression, voice, and demeanor. They told me that they had just re-returned from a pilgrimage to Einsiedeln, which they undertook in consequence of a vow which they made some years ago, when their only son broke his leg. He had recovered, and the good parents had made their thanksgiving pilgrimage. They were now returning on foot to their home in Wallis. They had crossed over St. Gothard.

Whilst I was talking with the good, communicative people of Wallis, four young peasant girls, in the holiday costume of Berne, were singing various of their country's "*Ranz de Vaches*," such as "*Les Amallis de Collombette*," etc. They had fresh and pure voices, and their joddling rang like glass bells. After they had sung, the prettiest of the four went round with a plate, but looked all the while so shy and so sweetly-earnest, that one could not do other than thank her and her companions.

Again I visited Lauterbrunnen valley, again I saw the gigantic fall of Schmadribach, which nearly frightened me the first time I saw it, at a considerable distance in the evening twilight. Its foaming-dirty-white mass of waters is not more beautiful, and not less frightful, seen in the full light of day and from a nearer point of view, but I had now the sun, and the companionship of a friend, and I experienced from the Undine valley only a deep and quiet impression. And whilst numerous streams sung and murmured, and Schmadribach thundered in the distance, my friend and I held quiet divine service in the great temple of nature. Sitting on little green hillocks, we read Vinet's Sermon on the Transfiguration, and one of Monod's "Adieux." These parting words with which the noble martyr, when on his bed of suffering, took leave of his friends and the world, gave to them at the same time the impress of his memory and his christian faith more powerfully than he had done in any of his orations from the pulpit:—

"They speak great truths who breathe their words in pain."

When A. Monod found himself seized upon by the cruel malady which caused his death in the prime of life, he grieved that he must cease to labor just at the moment when he hoped to have accomplished something really good for the church. Could he now but see how his parting sighs have become his most beautiful, perhaps his actual work!

This was my birthday, this day spent in the Undine valley, and it could not have been celebrated better.

From the Lake of Brienz we proceeded to Meyringen, and here we are now sitting on a lofty and extensive plateau in the midst of a garland of Alps, from the nearest heights of which several cascades are hurled to the plain. Here Reichenbach, most abundant in water and romantic beauty; there the three-armed Alpenbach, which, in spring, becomes dangerous from its floods. We are in Ober-Hasli, in the district where, it is said, in ancient times, a Swedish Colony established itself. I this morning paid a visit to Pastor Immer, a learned and sensible man who has lived a long time in the valley, in order to obtain from him such information as he could communicate on this subject. I have seldom conversed with a more agreeable or sensible man, and seldom seen such kindly moonlight beam from a full-moon countenance. The tradition which furnished the subject of our conversation, and which has been handed down from the most ancient time, from one generation to another, is this:

Up in some old country which lay far away in the north, amongst the Swedes and Frieslanders, there was once upon a time a famine. In consequence of this, the whole community met together, and it was decided by vote that every tenth man of the people should leave the country. These men, so elected, besought of God to show them a country where, as in their fatherland, protected from the power of tyranny, they might keep their flocks and herds in peace. God led them therefore to the country Brockinburg, where they established Schwytz.* As the chronicles of the middle ages give to Sweden, as well as to Schwytz, the name *Sueeia*, therefore Sweden is considered to be the northern country from which the Swiss province

---

* See J. von Müller's History of Switzerland.—*Author's Note.*

became peopled. As, in the mean time, Pastor Immer strengthened what I had already heard, namely, that the popular song in which this tradition is especially preserved, and of which I obtained a copy, is founded upon written record,* which, in its present form, is certainly not older than the latter half of the sixteenth century, as well as that no other written document on the subject has been discovered, led me to seek for other traces. I therefore inquired after the baptismal and family names prevailing in the district, after peculiar manners, songs, and old usages, especially at marriages and such occasions.

The following is what Pastor Immer told me:

"There is in this district a usage at marriages, which I never met with in any other part of Switzerland, as for instance, at the marriage feast, both the parents and the guests make the bridal pair presents either of cattle or money. The people love music and violent bodily exercises. They are a cheerful, kind and useful people, fearing God, but at the same time believing in the existence of dwarfs and many other spirits of nature, and in conjuration and witchcraft. Above all things they love freedom.† They believe firmly and

---

* The land Urbahr.—*Author's Note.*

† How truly Swedish are all these traits of national character every one will acknowledge who is more intimately acquainted with the national Swedish temperament. I could not find, however, amongst the names in the church books, any Swedish ones. But the resemblance of the female costume, and especially the head-dress, to that prevailing in certain Swedish provinces, struck me. And it seems to me that it would be easy for any who are more favorably circumstanced than I was, to gather among the Hasli people such traces as would be furnished by

fully in their Swedish origin, and the more educated of them are interested in Sweden, and are glad to hear any news from that country."

So far Pastor Immer. In the songs of East Friesland, which are especially current in Ober-Hasli, "Schweden and Oestfriedland," are represented as a neighboring country, and it is an "Obrist Schwitzerns" who conducts the emigrants from Sweden, each one with his cattle passing over the Rhine, and coming to the good country, "Brockenburg," where they established themselves. During a visit which I paid the preceding summer to Gothland,* I heard speak of a

---

their manners, customs, and traditions. In doing this, particular reference should be had to domestic life and to the women, those most faithful conservators of popular tradition, whether in tradition itself or costume.—*Author's Note.*

* The Vaudois archeologist, M. Troyou, has requested me to make inquiries whether, in Sweden, and especially in Gothland, the children, in a certain game, express themselves any thing like the following, which prevails:—

In Schwytz, thus:
Einige, binige, pumperti,
Tiffi, Taffi, numen-n—i,
Hättibrod, ninder der Noth,
Zechigfange—zöll zatter—erst dusse si.

In the Canton Vaud, thus:
Enik, Benik, top, te
Triff, Traff, kom me
Akabrö, Sinknö
Fine fane, tousse house.

In Berne, thus:
Anige, Bäinge, doppelde
Trift, Traft, trummer me
Acherbrod zinternoth
Zinter dfanne dusse gstande.

tradition, current there from the most ancient times, of a migration thence in consequence of famine, when every tenth person left the country.

The Hasli people are handsome, and remind me of the peasantry of Blukingo. I have made a sketch of a good old woman, in her peculiar head-dress. I now take my leave of the Swedish colony, to betake myself to the "Waldstetten," but whether across Brunig or Furca, depends upon what the barometer and Pastor Immer shall advise. Both seem doubtful. It would not be desirable to go to Grimsel and the "Glacier du Rhone," in bad weather.

Before I leave Hasli valley, however, I must say a few words about Rosenlaui, the beautiful ice-palace in its neighborhood, to which M. P. and I took a walk yesterday, conversing the while, on—the conscience, which made our walk doubly interesting. P. is occupied in writing, on this inner judgment-seat, a treatise, the singular depth and value of which, only his own great modesty and severe self-criticism can underrate. This morning, in the sunshine, on our romantically wild but beautiful walk, we went still deeper into the question: "What is the conscience?" I see and feel it the soul's holy of holies, a deeper conception than

In Basle, thus:	Anige bünige doppel de, Dickel, Dackel, domine, Ankebrod, in der Noth Zinne, Psanne Dusse stoth.
And in Solothurn, thus:	Andi bändi, doppede, Divi, Davi, Domine, Ackenebro, Zinereno Dfanne, Tiller, dusse stoth.

Author's Note.

that of P., who wholly regards the conscience as a moral eye,—as "*conscience morale.*"

We were interrupted by Rosenlaui Glacier, which all at once stood in astonishing beauty before us, but sent forth at the same time, such a current of cold air, as was less agreeable.

Rosenlaui is called a "Glacier des donnes," partly for its beauty, and partly for its accessibility. It struck me by its human resemblance. Rosenhorn, the crag which rises highest in its midst, represents the head, and from the shoulders, down each side, falls an icy mantle in glittering whiteness. The tower-like crags, Wellhorn and Engelhorn, rise on the opposite side of the mountain throne on which the icy giantess has been seated these thousands of years, and between these, project her vast knees, richly draperied by her icy mantle, from below the deep folds of which, her immense foot is seen planted upon the smooth mountain. It is around this foot, that the human visitors circulate. In the full, deep drapery which falls around it, and which forms ice-closets, and passages, they peep in and out as if they were hiding from one another, and then gaze wondering up at the vast knee, which rises one hundred feet above their heads. The beautiful azure color of the ice in the deep folds or walls of the glacier, has not as yet been satisfactorily explained, though many have endeavored variously to account for it.

It was remarkably beautiful this afternoon, although the sky was cloudy and soon vailed both the glacier and its visitors in cold rain. Many strangers had come up with us hither from the little town. The ladies walked forward, took off their gloves, and laid their warm hands cautiously upon the icy walls, and peeped into the icy closets. The gentlemen did the same, and even ventured higher, whither the glacier's self-constituted watch and ward invited them, for he had cut steps in the ice, and by means of these, any one could climb up into the more profound regions of the icy mantle. Cascades fall from the depths of the glacier, the largest of these is hurled down from below the huge knee, as if out of an arch, and falls at a little distance, with a thundering din, into a chasm between the rocks, which the eye cannot measure, and which makes one dizzy to look down.

Most people pay their visit in a very off-hand kind of a way. They come, look, and—turn round. I felt myself, however, so little satisfied by this visit in the rain, that I proposed to my companion, to stay over the night at the little inn in the neighborhood of the glacier, in hope that the morrow would afford us sunshine, and with it, the opportunity of seeing the beauty of Rosenlaui in full daylight.

We were the only guests who remained over the night, and we were rewarded for so doing, by the brightest sunshine the following morning. Under these favorable circumstances, we again visited the glacier, which shone in dazzling splendor. It was fatiguing to the eye to look at the white snow-mantle, as it glittered in the sun, at the bright, thousand-year, crystal walls of the vaulted closets, at the beautiful, manifold icy formations. It was singular that the azure color of the deeper folds, now, in the clear blue heaven, seemed less rich and beautiful, than in the gray sky of the day preceding. But the ice-walls were clearer, and more transparent.

As we stood thus gazing, a grandly-attired lady arrived in a chair, carried by four men. She alighted; approached the glacier, laid her hand upon the ice, peeped in below the knee, and said, "Is that all?"

"Yes," replied her bearers.

"Oh!" said she, turned her back on the magnificent giant form, reseated herself in her chair and was carried away.

M. P. and I lingered by the glacier until we had clearly impressed its image upon mind and memory, then we returned to Meyringen, looking back as long as we could, to Rosenlaui, which, as it were, accompanied us on our way with its glittering icy glance.

GRIMSEL, *August* 23*d*.—Mist, rain, and snow surround us here, which is a bad prospect for our journey to the sources of the Aar, and the Rhone. But our courage does not fail us, and it was not without pleasure that I beheld in the morning, the new-fallen snow around us, because it reminded me of the Swedish winter, and of the fresh, invigorating sensations which I have experienced while walking or driving through murmuring pine-woods, or over glittering snow-fields. But here, in the stony desert of Grimsel, all is cold, hard, desolate, terrible. Not a tree within sight, nor even a bush; only rocks, stones, and amongst the snow, a few meagre patches of grass, where a withered dock seems to be a king. Herds of goats, which clamber amongst the stones and crags, are the only living objects in the scene.

Yesterday morning was splendid after a night of

violent storm, and splendid was the journey through the green fertile Alpine valleys from Meyringen, along the Aar, on the road to Handek. Earth and heaven, mountain and valley, shone out in the ascending sun, the air was clear as crystal, and as pure and fresh, as—Alpine air only can be. I enjoyed it sitting in a chair, for the first time in my life, borne by two young peasants, from Meyringen, who seemed to have more pleasure in running with me, than in walking, which gave me the agreeable feeling, that I was no great burden. My friend, M. Penchaud, went on foot, like a true mountaineer, with his knapsack on his back, enjoying the walk with his whole heart and soul. Before us, went the respectable Gaspard—an acquaintance of Meyringen, with our baggage in a large basket, on his back. Thus, the journey proceeded upwards, ever upwards, from terrace to terrace, from plain to plain, through extents of luxuriantly-verdant valley, where the cottages stand so snugly on the green-sward, at the foot of the rocks, amongst which the snowy giants glance forth. Roaring torrents, large and small, hurl themselves down from the heights, tributaries of the Aar, whose foaming course we constantly follow, now on the right bank, now on the left, crossing it by small bridges or planks, which hardly look safe. It is a succession of wild, picturesque scenes, without grand views, but rich in ever-varying features, near at hand, rocks, wood, and waterfall. And so on, to La Handek. Here, we partake of a very good dinner, at the hotel, in company with a number of other travelers, and afterwards go to see the celebrated "Chute de l'Aar."

Here it is, that the Aar, not far from its source in the glaciers above Grimsel, hurls itself down amongst the rocks, into an abyss of two hundred feet. In this fall, its wildly-agitated mass of waters meets the silver cascade of Arlenbach, from the glaciers of Arlenberg, and uniting, plunge with a deafening thunder into the gulf below, from which ascends a dense cloud of spray. At noon, just when we were there, the sun threw a beaming rainbow over the dark cleft between which the fall is precipitated, and then was thrown out in perfectly dazzling splendor from the dark background of rocks.

The wind was strong on the bridge above the fall, and drove the spray over us. Besprinkled with water, but delighted with the scene, we left the grand, beautifully wild spectacle to continue on our journey.

From Handek, the scenery becomes wilder and more desolate. Trees are no longer seen, vegetation decreases, the mountains become more rigid, blocks of stone cover the land, life seems, by degrees, to be dying out. The glacier rivers roar more loudly, swollen with the torrents from the ice-fields and lakes lying high amongst the mountains. The splendid Gelten fall, seems to plunge down as if out of the very sky. At all distances, the eye meets, on the heights, ice and pointed rocks. The wild falls of the Aar increase the nearer you approach to its source. In some places the bridges have been carried away by it. The people are very busy replacing them, assisting me in my chair across, and through the roaring waters, I don't rightly know how, and I was scarcely dizzy. Now and then, we meet troops of gentlemen and ladies, on foot, on horseback, or in chairs. And these processions, with the long Alpine staffs of pedestrians, and the fluttering dresses and vails of the ladies, look very picturesque, but are not so agreeable to meet when the road happens to be fearfully narrow. Notwithstanding my confidence in the skill of my bearers, I sometimes grow dizzy when they suddenly swing round the point of a cliff, on the edge of the precipice where the Aar rages below.

The weather which was so beautiful in the forenoon, became in the afternoon, windy, and cold; clouds gathered on the heights, and rain began to fall; whilst the surrounding scenery grew increasingly savage and stern. Human dwellings were no longer to be seen; there was no cultivated spot of earth; nay, indeed, there was scarcely any earth at all. A kind of dwarf pine stretched its ugly shapeless branches out of the stony ground. It seemed to me like a cry for help from vegetation. The rhododendron, nevertheless, grows abundantly by the rocky streams, but the season of its flowering was over. A delicate and beautiful fern, and some small yellow and white flowers, still accompany us. But the wind is colder and colder, and, I know not why, but the heart grows heavier and heavier, amid these surroundings, which bring to mind all that is most depressing in human life. And this stony desert has also its gloomy story of humanity.

We reach the place were the old Grimsel Inn used to stand, which was burned down a year ago, as was believed by accident, but as has since been discovered intentionally to conceal a terrible murder committed by the host and hostess upon an unfortunate traveler, who stayed there alone during a night in the autumn. A memory worthy of this melancholy region!

But my bearers go on cheerfully, and, as I could fancy, with still lighter steps. They know that the place of rest is at hand; and just as they swing round to the left, a large, gray, two-storied house comes in sight between the naked gray mountains. It is "l'Hospice du Grimsel," the goal of our day's journey, and we have arrived in good time. We find here a great number of travelers of all classes, but, luckily for us, we can obtain two small rooms, though of the homeliest kind, and in them the prospect of rest and shelter against the increasing storm.

Sitting at my window, I amuse myself during the evening by watching the milking of two hundred goats, which operation is performed by two men, who each bears, fastened round his middle by a strap, a little stool with one leg in the middle. With this they go round from goat to goat, and seat themselves upon it whilst they milk. It looks as if it were a part of their body, and produces the most comic effect. They say that an English lady quite seriously believed that this projecting wooden leg was a tail, and that they who carried it were the aborigines of the country. But —what do they not tell about English ladies?

This morning the greater number of the travelers have left the hotel in rain and mist. We still remain, in hope of a change. The bad weather, which continued the whole night and this forenoon, has just cleared off—at 12'o clock in the day—by a violent storm.

Perhaps it may chase away the mist, which is still so thick that one cannot see ten paces around one.

Grimsel is indeed the dreariest place in the world. Not far from the house lies, with the most melancholy aspect, a dark little lake in its stony bed. A little further off lies another, somewhat larger, called the Lake of the Dead, because the bodies of the French and Austrians who were slain in a skirmish in the mountain pass, during the summer of 1799, were thrown in there by way of burial. And it is still believed that the Lake of the Dead serves as a grave for the wanderers who are killed during the winter in this terrible region.

ANDERMATT, *August* 25*th*.—Shortly after I had written the above, my good friend Penchaud came to me, tired and out of patience with stopping at this place, which affected him physically very painfully, and besought me to continue our journey, let the weather be what it might. We could not be worse than here, and if we were now to set off we might reach "La Furca" before night. I consented, but, I confess, with a heavy heart. To continue our journey in this weather, was for me to give up the purpose for which I had come. It was merely to see the "Glacier du Rhone" that I had undertaken this difficult and expensive journey; but in this fog one could see nothing. In the mean time it began to look as if it would clear up. But scarcely were we on our way up the steep Grimsel mountain, when a storm of sleet and wind came on again with renewed violence. I could only dimly discern the dreary shores of the Lake of the Dead through the thick fog. A vail of fog enveloped the whole of nature. Under these circumstances, I must entirely give up the chance of beholding the source of the Aar, although my bearers offered to take me there. But an excursion to this icy region I dare not venture upon, on account of my friend; besides, what could one now see?

With such deplorable prospects and thoughts we clambered up the naked mountain, in somewhat more than an hour's time. I was sitting very out of sorts, with my little gray shawl over my head to defend me against the wind and the rain, when my bearers, all at once, exclaimed: " *Voila le Glacier !*"

I looked up and saw in the air before me something white and shapeless shining out through the mist. Upon this white apparition I riveted my glance immovably; for every moment it became clearer, and by degrees it stood forth out of the thick, misty vail; the sun-illumed, snow-covered peaks of Gelmerhorn and Gallenstock, between which the upper portion of the Rhone Gletscher, or Triften Gletscher, spread out like a frozen waterfall covered with driven snow. I have no words to describe the spectacle which was presented to my gaze, whilst cloud and mist disappeared before the lightning beams of the sun, which seemed to overcome them. The clear blue heaven arched itself all the more freely over the shining Alpine peaks and ice-fields; and these stood forth all the clearer in dazzling grandeur and splendor, as we accomplished the last steep mountain ascent, called "Majenwand," from the beautiful verdure and the multitude of flowers fostered by the warmth of the sun and the moisture of earth produced by the

Gletscher. But I do not notice these, and scarcely feel any uneasiness about the steep path, on the sharp turnings of which, now slippery with the rain, my bearers can hardly keep their footing. All my senses are fascinated by the astonishing scene. But every moment the air becomes warmer and the wind stiller. The Rhone Gletscher in all its grandeur lies before us, below us; we sink down into its bosom and only beauty and pleasantness meet us on every hand; summer air and splendor in the home of eternal winter! Behold the scene as I saw it, as I see it at this moment.

At the foot of the broad snow-fall, between Gallenstock, Gersthorn and Gelmerhorn, rises an immense cupola of ice, surrounded on three sides by Alps towering to the sky; and on the fourth, extending towards an open extent of valley, two buks flow from the two sides of the icy cupola; these, at a little distance, flow together into one stream, and soon afterwards uniting with the waters of two warm springs, the eye follows their course, far, far in the distance, through the valley which opens to the southeast. This is the RHONE —the eternal UNREST, born from the bosom of the eternal rest. The Rhone is here like a lively boy who springs, full of play, from his mother's lap. .Its course is brisk but calm; its color milky, and nothing in its being betokens its future fate and grandeur; nothing, the mighty river whose floods almost annually desolate countries and cities, but whose waters also form valleys of unequaled fertility, and which, far away from its Swiss cradle, feed the cheerful vines of France in the valley of Avignon.

We descended for about an hour from the "Majenwand," when we found ourselves down in the valley and stopped at a little inn, only at a few minutes' distance from the foot of the icy cupola. After we had here refreshed ourselves with tea and wine, as well as rested for some time, we proceeded to the Gletscher. The sun shone with full power, and every object was bright in its beams. My friend and I wandered for a full hour at the foot of the ice-cupola, through a regular park of sun-flowers and other flowers, which grew here above two ells high, in indescribable luxuriance, between the ice-vault and the mountain walls. The air was as warm as summer, and this ramble between icy-cold winter and blooming summer was wonderful, was enchantingly beautiful!

The snow-clad mountains, the watchers by the cradle of the Rhone, stood in eternal rest; nor in the frozen force between them could any unrest be observed,* but in the icy cupola the birth-struggle of the river was in progress. Within was a deafening thunder and commotion, a rushing sound of released waters, and here and there little cascades were seen to pour glittering from the icy walls. For in many places of the cupola there were deep chinks in the ice. These walls were of a clear, blue color, but the

---

* The Swiss naturalists, Agassiz, Desor, and others, have, after long and patient investigation, discovered that the quiet or immovability of these glaciers, is merely apparent; that under the pressure of the snow-masses which annually accumulate upon their heights, they slide incessantly and softly downwards. In this way coming under the influence of the sun and the temperature of the earth, their ice is melted and the rivers are released.—*Author's Note.*

cupola, as a whole, is rather of a dirty gray than white, and in this respect forms a contrast with the dazzling beauty of the Triften Gletscher. In the highest parts of this Gletscher, where travelers rarely venture, a bloody shirt and a plundered pocket-book have been lately found. But of the murdered man, or the murderer, nothing as yet is known. There are few of these solitary regions which have not their appropriate story of misfortune or crime. The bloody traces of man meet one every where—stain even the eternal snow!

The sun continued to shine brightly during the whole time of our stay at the glacier, and its beams seemed to recall the masses of cloud which gathered together on the ridge of the Grimsel mountain, and which continued restlessly to vault themselves there, as if they were ready to hurl themselves down over the valley. I cannot tell how thankful I felt for this kindness of the sun.

"I have now, however, perfectly seen this grand work of Nature!" I was able to say to myself, when I was again seated in my chair, to continue my journey. And I was able to enjoy yet for a long time the splendid sight as we advanced upwards toward Furca, the sun continuing to bless us with his beams as long as we had the Rhone cradle in view. But scarcely had we lost it, when down came the cloud-avalanches from the Grimsel mountain, and we were soon enveloped in a cold mist.

Yet we were able to give the Matten Gletscher our silent admiration, and to salute the birth of the rapid Reuss from the glacier which is its cradle, but which has neither the beauty nor the grandeur of the glacier of the Rhone. The Reuss, insignificant in comparison with the Rhone in its after career, has, at its source, a much more rapid and wilder character; and many little streams soon hasten down from the mountain to increase its waters. It grows rapidly by these means, and hurries along with still greater violence in a direction contrary to that of the Rhone. How similar are the life-career of rivers and heroes! I know not whether any one has ever worked out this idea more beautifully than Tegner, in his little poem, "The River."

Our road lay along the course of the Reuss; but our road was a narrow foot-path upon the slope of a steep mountain, so narrow and in such bad condition, that I often felt myself in danger of my life, and was in a continual state of amazement that a road in considerable use should be left in a condition which, from that very cause, must often lead to the occurrence of misfortunes.

Again and again, we met troops of travelers on horseback or on foot, and that this did not happen in the narrowest and most dangerous parts of the road, was prevented by the guides, who went with their long Alpine staffs at the head of the procession. More difficult, however, became the dilemma when, at one point of the road between the precipice and the mountain-wall, our advance was stopped by a cow. She stood there immovably, with her horn-decorated brows facing us, and seemed to think to herself, as I did, "What is to be done now? One of us must tumble down the precipice, because pass one another we cannot, that's clear!"

My bearers took a view of the case also, but soon made up their minds. With hands and feet they prevailed upon the sober cow to turn round on the narrow path at the risk of her life, and she now became my pioneer until a wider space allowed her to get out of the way, which she did with a couple of joyful leaps, which I seconded in my heart.

We are now in the Canton Wallis. Snow-fields gleam forth on every side, but also with these verdant and grassy pastures. On one of these, close beside the glacier, grazed a large herd of cattle, attended by a herdsman and his dog.

This day's journey appeared to me very long, in the cold and mist; and more than once I silently wondered that any one could be so thoughtless as to undertake it. Twilight had already commenced, when at length we reached "La Furca," in such a dense fog, that I could distinguish nothing but the lofty hill up which we ascended, and the snow-covered roof of the little inn, which affected me as the mariner on the stormy sea, at the sight of land.

How pleasant it seemed here to sit down in the warm *salle* of the snug little, almost comfortable, *herberge*, and refresh myself with a good supper of tea, potatoes, and fresh butter. We ate and drank, we played chess, check-mated each other, and, before we separated, thanked God together for the day. P. has the gift of prayer, which it seems to me the Reformed Protestants, in an especial manner, possess, perhaps because family worship is more practiced by them than by the Lutherans. The prayer comprehended much under few words, and its quiet, earnest feeling, went to the heart.

A restless night succeeded, for me, to the quiet, holy evening; for the extreme cold prevented my sleeping. Fortunately, the weather changed during the night. The fog was transformed to frost-crystals, and the morning arose beaming over a snow-covered landscape. The sun shone gloriously, from a lofty blue sky. It was delightful to go forth upon the pure snow, and gather small, dark-blue gentians, which came forth as the snow melted before the heat of the sun. There were neither trees, shrubs, nor birds to be seen. The Furca valley lies 7,419 feet above the level of the sea, and is scarcely ever free from snow. Snow-clad Alps close it in on every side, so that there is no open view. Finster-Aarhorn and St. Gothard, the highest Alpine heights, which can be seen far beyond the others, rise on the opposite sides of the narrow valley.

It was Sunday, and all was quiet in the little inn. We also had determined to remain quiet during the early hours of the forenoon, and whilst the sun removed the frosty vail of night from the grassy sward of the valley, and the little hills, we read A. Monod's sermon on "*le plan de Dieu.*" It is a good thing to place the futileness of human plans in opposition to the plan of God. But, do we really know so little of God's plan, in its chief features, as this preacher represents? Has not He told us something about it? Has not He written it in Divine characters on the earth? And can we really understand so little, whether we act in accordance with, or in opposition to this Divine plan?

Towards noon we were again in motion. The road, but which is indeed no road, now continually follows the ever more rapid and abundant Reuss. The miserable path seems less dangerous than that of yesterday, and we begin to descend. The tract through which we pass is a petrifaction, without beauty or vegetation, but lovely cascades roar and glitter in the mountain, and the sun passes joyously over the rigid heights. Our road lies across many mountain streams, the only enliveners of the desolate region.

At length we reach a few poor houses. It is the little inn "Realp," where a Capuchin monk finds the traveler room to rest and refresh himself. We also solicit the good father's hospitality, because there is no other shelter on the road to Andermatt, the goal of our day's journey. We halt here, but are somewhat astonished when, instead of a Capuchin monk, a rosy young girl, with a red bow of ribbon on her throat, comes to meet us at the door. Within the *salle*, we found the father, who was playing cards with two shabby-looking semi-gentlemen, and two, ditto, half-grown boys. He was a large, jovial-looking man, good-natured and kind, but bearing very little resemblance to the model hermit of these parts,—Nicholas de Flue. After he had welcomed us, and given orders about our dinner, he asked permission to continue his game, which we, of course, gave. The rosy maiden, in the mean time, laid the cloth, and served us up a very good little dinner, for which a reasonable charge was made. We thanked the father and the rosy maiden, and departed.

The road from Realp was a very rapid descent, so that I sometimes grew dizzy, looking at the depth down which I was carried, especially as my bearers now moved with less elasticity. But the air becomes ever milder. We look down into the extensive vale of Urseren, which, though still without trees, is splendidly verdant. Afar in the distance, upon the greensward, at the foot of a lofty wall of mountains, shines forth, white and cheerful, a little town. That is Andermatt. And in the midst of the immense mass of mountains, we soon see the broad road of St. Gothard, which, in pliant sinuosities, winds along the heights, down into the vale; and we see heavy diligences, and carriage after carriage, rolling along it. Our weary little train proceeds through the green carpeting, and miserable roads of the Urserenvale, out upon the great high-road which seems to us to be thronged with people, driving, riding, and walking. I am delighted, both for my own sake and my bearers, when we reach Andermatt, and find comfortable quarters in the hotel of St. Gothard. The most difficult part of my journey is now happily ended, and I have taken care that my good bearers are as well supplied here as I am. Better and more satisfactory people cannot be found!

ALTDORF, *August 27th.*—The memory of William Tell surrounds us here. They show the spot where Gessler placed the hat to which Tell would not bow; the place where Tell stood when he shot the apple from his little son's head, and where he afterwards addressed the threatening words to the cruel bailiff, who had compelled him to do it. A statue of Tell stands in the market-place, which represents him at the moment after the fortunate flight of the arrow, with his child pressed to his heart. The paintings, both within and without the houses, represent passages from his life. One of these gives Bürglen as the place of his birth, not far from Schächenbach, where he met his death, as tradition states, in an attempt to save the life of a child during a flood. In a word, every thing here teems with the memory of Tell, who, singularly enough, became in the popular mind, the peculiar hero of the contest for Swiss liberty, whilst, in fact, there is not any thing particularly great or noble in the actions which are related of him, and whilst the learned critic doubts whether he ever had an existence at all; but, with all due respect to his superior wisdom, it seems to me a little short-sighted and stupid; for a great smoke does not rise without any fire, and that which has taken such firm hold of the popular mind and feeling, must, of a certainty, have its root in reality, however poetry may, of late, have adorned or misstated it. Even if there be no mention of Tell in the chronicles or narratives of those times amongst the men who formed the Confederacy of Grutli; nay, if his name never appeared with these until long afterwards, that is no argument against his still being in direct connection with the Sworn-Confederates, through his actions, as a man of courage and lover of freedom, who fought for freedom in his own way, and in that manner which Providence and the occasion inspired. The picturesque and romantic elements of his fate have made him the hero of the popular imagination, because it loves the bold and the striking. That there existed among the Scandinavian traditions the story of a father who was compelled to shoot an apple from his son's head, long before the story existed in Switzerland, seems to me no argument against its truth in that country. True, or untrue, however, it ought to serve as one proof more of the Scandinavian emigration, of which I have spoken; because the emigrants would assuredly carry with them their manners and traditions. Perhaps it might be this very tradition which suggested to Gessler the trial of shooting at the mark to which he put the stiff-necked Switzer! Such repetitions of facts are not by any means new under the sun.

We had a proof how deeply the episode of Tell lives in the memory of the people, from a little incident near Andermatt. During the lovely evening of our arrival there, we went out, my friend and I, to see the wild fall of Reuss, at the Pont du Diable, one of those beautiful, terrible scenes, in which Switzerland, more than any other country, abounds. On our return, we saw an elderly woman standing before a little chapel, into the trellised windows of which she was peeping, with more of curiosity than devotion, as it seemed to us. As we approached, she turned round and saluted us in a friendly manner. She was a tall, handsome woman, with strong features, well dressed in the country costume, and with the white over the head which I had already observed to be general amongst the women of this vale, and which I had seen nowhere else so worn, except by the country women in Sweden.

Penchaud asked the good woman, in his broken German, whether she could tell us any thing about Wilhelm Tell? It required a little while before she understood the question, and then her whole countenance brightened at once, and she began to declaim a rude poem in rhyme, in which Tell's actions were related in very strong and peculiar language. And as she went on, the old woman became quite animated, and strengthened the words by her gesture. Tell's unbending obstinacy before the Austrian hat; his shooting at the apple, as the mark; his kicking over of the boat which was to have conveyed him to prison; and finally his taking aim and shooting the arrow at Gessler, all were represented in highly-dramatic action by the old woman, as she recited the poem, and that too, in the middle of the road, where, in her zeal, she never troubled herself that the passers-by cast upon us wondering and inquiring glances. At the end both we and the old woman laughed heartily, shook hands and departed.

Early the following morning we set off from Andermatt, along the splendidly constructed St. Gothard's road, on which every turn is so measured, that, however steep it may appear to the eye, yet its descent never exceeds that which is safe for horses and vehicles. We drove in an open carriage, through a region, the magnificent scenery of which, ever more and more assumed a delicious and beautiful character. As we rolled along in our descent, the air became ever warmer. Beautiful walnut trees, lovely groves, twittering birds, surrounded us. Luxuriant, green pasturages, with trees, bushes, and cattle, gleamed out high up among the mountains, above which glanced forth the glaciers. The lower we descend, the more we come into the region of summer. We are now in the Canton Uri, the smallest and the poorest of the Swiss Cantons, and at the same time one of the foremost in the history of Swiss liberty. We drive past the ruins of Gessler's castle, Zwing-Uri, where, with chains and cudgels, he endeavored to overawe the free sons of the country, and which thence derives its name. We salute Attinghausen, the castle and abode of Walter Fürst, the ruins of which are still shaded by a garland of beautiful trees.

We drive in close companionship with the Reuss, through the vale, and a more beautiful vale than this is watered by no river. It has also been bathed with blood in more than one bitter combat. The French, the Austrians, and Russians have fought with each other and the sons of the country, more than once, in this, and the vale of Urseren. Poor, little Switzerland! Long and severe has been the fight for the freedom and the peace which thou enjoyest; nowhere more severe than in the Forest Cantons, the primeval home of the Swiss people.

Yesterday afternoon we went to Bürglen, the birthplace of Tell. On the place where his house is said to have stood, now stands a little wooden chapel to his memory, very finely painted and adorned with patriotic inscriptions. The walk thither, along the valley of Schächenbach, is one of the loveliest conceivable, from its affluence of beautiful trees; and the Schächenbach now flows clear and calm, as a thanksgiving hymn for the heroic deeds of old.

I have this morning paid a visit to the nunnery of the Franciscan order here. I had seen above the lofty wall of its garden, two walnut trees stretching out, partly verdant and partly withered branches, and I felt a desire to see the women, who, in the midst of this grand and beautiful natural scenery, shut themselves in forever, (for these nuns are under a vow of perpetual seclusion,) behind walls which prevent them from even seeing any thing of it. This convent receives, as I was informed, only ladies of high family, and it requires a very considerable portion to enable them to enter.

In the "Frau Mutter," with whom one converses through a grated window, I found a very charming, middle-aged lady, of great refinement of features and manners. The loveliness of her hands, and the delicate tips of her fingers, showed her to be of aristocratic birth. She answered my questions with simplicity and frankness. This order belongs to the contemplative, and, pre-eminently, to the praying class. The nuns have many and severe fasts. They have divine service every night from eleven o'clock till two. Their prayers cease only when the hour commences at which another praying choir, in another convent, takes up the prayers and performs service for the living and the dead. For the whole twenty-four hours, the whole year round, must these continue, without interruption, in the Catholic Church. Good and beautiful in thought! But who can answer for the carrying of it out? And can any blessing, either for the living or the dead, be expected from these prescribed Latin prayers, uttered by half-sleepy bodies and souls, as a day's work? Only three of the sisters here occupy themselves with the instruction of children. The rest are employed in the convent. Their quiet life and severe fasts, render many of them sickly. "Frau Mutter," had evidently a weak chest. I asked her if she had not sometimes a desire to see the world, and beautiful natural scenery? She smiled cordially, and replied, that she "had not the slightest desire for any thing of the kind." And this was said with so much candor and cheerfulness, that I dismissed all anxiety about "Frau Mutter's" conventual life. Let us hope that other sisters participate in her taste!

"It requires a great many kinds of people to make a world!" is an American proverb, of which I often find the truth.

A Capuchin convent, on an elevation in the valley, is said to be the oldest in Switzerland. In front of the convent you see one of those "holy forests," which are often found upon the slopes of the mountains in Switzerland, and which no one may touch, because they form a defense for the inhabitants of the valley against the avalanches or snow-lavines, which roll down from the rocks. These are broken in their fall by the holy forest, which itself stands firm and green amidst their fury.

This district is full of memories of the oppression and deeds of violence of the former Austrian bailiffs. Gessler and Landenberg are especially the heroes of such histories.

Here it was that Gessler, who was angry that the peasants had such beautiful houses, built his castle, which he himself called Zwing-Uri, by the sweat and money of the people. There it was that Landenberg, who, after desiring to take the oxen from the plow of the young Arnold of Melchthal, put out his old father's eyes, and laid a heavy fine upon him for the imagined crime of his son. "This thing," says an old historian, "went so deep into the heart of many an honest man, that they resolved rather to die than to leave such a cruel action unrevenged."

But it was not alone men's hearts that rose against oppression and deeds of violence.

It was thus that Margaretta Herlobig, the wife of Werner Stauffacher, spoke to her husband: "In former times the men of Schwytz did not remain satisfied under, and patiently bear such treatment; and it will become worse yet if they have not courage enough to oppose it, and to meet force with force. At this rate there will soon be an end of our liberty and our peace!"

If they who guard the domestic hearth admonish their husbands to defy dangers which in a twofold measure must press upon the heart of the wife, then, —then a great combat is at hand, a combat of life and death.

Against the avalanche which threatens to overwhelm the life of the vale, is opposed the holy forest of Freedom's Sworn-Confederates, who will either break, or themselves perish in the fight. This holy forest is the people of the Swiss Forest Cantons.

BRUNNEN, *on the Lake of Lucerne, or the Vierwaldstädter See, Aug.* 28.—Never did nature adorn more beautifully the cradle of Freedom than in Sweden and in Switzerland. There is Dalecarlia, here the Forest

Cantons, which became its first home. And here, on the banks of the Lake of Lucerne, I seem to myself to be sitting beside one of the quiet, deep lakes of Dalecarlia. The resemblance is striking. The same earnest, lofty beauty; the same encircling band of mountain and woody shores around the lake; the same gay, sunny, grassy fields among the mountains; the same silence over the grand landscape, and in its bosom a people of simple manners, of pious and quiet disposition, but, at the same time, of powerful will and unconquerable love of popular right and popular freedom! There is also a similarity between the Swedish and Swiss struggle for freedom. There it was the oppression of the Danish bailiffs, here of the Austrian bailiffs, in the names of their respective masters, which armed the people and converted herdsmen into warriors. But here the resemblance ceases, without the history of either people becoming less noble or less remarkable. The Dalecarlians gave themselves a leader and Sweden a king, in Gustavus Wasa. The men of the Forest Cantons gave themselves unity and power in the Sworn-Confederacy. I now return to this.

Encouraged by his wife Margaretta, Werner Stauffacher crossed the lake into Uri, to visit his friend Waltur Fürst, of Attinghausen. With him he found young Arnold of Melchthal, who was here in concealment from the wrath of Gessler. The three imparted to each other their troubles, and resolved rather to die than tolerate any longer the humiliation of the fatherland under an unjust domination. Property and life, *every thing*, would they risk in order to regain the old freedom for people and fatherland. They desire for themselves neither power nor possessions. If their undertaking succeed, they will, on its completion, again withdraw themselves to their own quiet life, and let others reap that which they have sown. Thus the three engaged to each other; and into this compact they invited associates whom they regarded as likeminded with themselves. In order to carry this out, and to arrange their plans of action, they established nocturnal meetings at Grutli—a solitary, green meadow on the banks of the lake, between Unterwalden and Uri.

There, under the free vault of heaven, surrounded by forests and night, they could converse in freedom; there they mentioned to each other the new friends whom they had found for the general design; thither they conducted the new allies, and took counsel together for the accomplishment of their plan.

One starry night, at the beginning of November, 1307, thirty men from the Forest Cantons of Uri, Unterwalden, and Schwytz, assembled here, under the guidance of Walter Fürst, Werner Stauffacher, and Arnold of Melchthal. Here, after they had firmly resolved, each man took his friend's hand, and, at the moment when the beams of the morning sun first tinged the summits of the primeval mountains, the three leaders, and with them the thirty men, raised their hands and swore, "By God who created all men for the same freedom, and by all the saints," this oath:

"That all would hold together, and in friendship live and die, whilst by their united power **they would** help their innocent, oppressed people to regain their ancient liberty and rights, so that all the Swiss should have forever, the enjoyment of this friendship. The Counts of Hapsburg should not, however, lose, in consequence of it, the least of their property or their rights, their people or servants, or one drop of blood, but the freedom which the Swiss inherited from their forefathers, would they preserve to leave to their successors."

They agreed as to the manner and the time of carrying out their resolution. After this they returned home, kept their own counsel, and gathered in their cattle for the winter.

This was the confederacy of Grutli—the first Sworn-Confederacy. Nor has the sun ever risen upon a more beautiful or purer confederacy. At the moment when I write this, the lofty meadow of Grutli shines out just opposite the lake, splendidly green in the morning sun, which seems as if it would bless this spot, whilst the Mythen-stone rises solitarily from the lake like an eternal monument, placed there by the hand of the Creator.

It was on New-Year's morning, 1308, when the fight for freedom was to commence. It began with the first hour, when, at the given signal of a horn, Landenberg's castle was stormed. The inhabitants of Uri demolished Zwing-Uri. Stauffacher, with his Schwytzers, took Schwanau and Küssnacht. The bailiffs fled, the castles were in flames, and the national tempest advanced from Alp to Alp. *But not a drop of blood was spilled on this day.* Freedom, not **revenge, was** the desire of the people of the Forest

Cantons. The love of justice and humanity led them to the battle against the tyrants. Their victory was perfect. God was with them.

The following Sunday the Confederates again met and renewed their oath for the defense of freedom and fatherland.

The murder of the covetous Duke Albrecht, by the hand of his nephew, and the slaughter of Gessler by William Tell, assisted at the same time the Swiss struggle for freedom. A pause ensued of astonishment and horror. But soon the house of Hapsburg armed itself afresh, that it might crush with all its force the young, free Switzerland. Duke Leopold, the brother of the murdered Albrecht, and the flower of Austrian chivalry, armed himself and took the field against the people of the Forest Cantons. But the herdsmen and peasants of the Forest Cantons also armed themselves. Hence occurred at Morgarten, on the 16th of March, 1315, that ever-memorable fight, in which a few hundred peasants of the three Forest Cantons, overcame, nay annihilated, a host of twenty thousand Austrians. And Duke Leopold, who swore to revenge upon the people of the Forest Cantons the death of his brother Albrecht, who threatened to trample the peasants under his foot, and who carried with him a wagon full of ropes to bind them with,—the proud, stately Duke Leopold was obliged to fly before the peasants. It was with difficulty that he saved his life. By lonely forest paths, and with but few followers, he reached Winterthur late in the evening, pale as death, and sorely dejected.

But the people of the Forest Cantons returned loud

thanksgiving to "the Lord Almighty who had given them the victory over their enemies."

It was in the mean time easy to see that this victory could not be conducive to their freedom. The men of the Forest Cantons foresaw clearly that new hosts would speedily be armed against them and their freedom. In order to overcome these and to permanently withstand their enemies, the Confederates saw no other means but by an Eternal Sworn-Confederacy with each other.

It was at the town of Brunnen, on the 9th of December, 1315, that the deputies from the Forest Cantons assembled and swore an eternal confederacy against "all warfare and all power, as well within as against themselves. A confederacy, unlike other federate unions at this period, which had trade-interests or the acquisition of power or honor for their object, this aimed only at the maintenance of the noblest prerogatives of humanity,—freedom, justice, peace, and happiness. Therefore it won by degrees the esteem and attention of princes and people, and became confirmed by them not long after its commencement. Therefore it extended its power by degrees from its home in the Forest Cantons over more and ever more Cantons and their people, whom it attracted with magnetic force into its freedom and peace-giving circle. Therefore, during the course of several centuries, it has been able to overcome enemies both within and without, been able to form a federal republic, which at this moment stands alone amongst the States of Europe, an example to many and esteemed of all.

The Forest Cantons, the kernel of the Confederacy,

whilst they developed for themselves the results of their contest and victory for freedom, assumed more and more a decided position against the rulers of other countries, and even against the ruler of their own church, the Pope. They stood steadfastly upon their ancient rights, freedom, usage, and even abuse. Like the primeval mountain of their own land, they stood opposed to the advance of the enemy, and even sometimes to the advance of the cultivator. They will not tolerate any law which they have not laid down for themselves, neither any thing new which has not grown up in their own soil. And hence it is that they have remained stationary, in a high degree, both as regards good and evil. But the good has developed itself in many excellent humane institutions, in trade-industry, in cultivation and general prosperity. Towns and convents have emulated each other in the cultivation of the land, even in the most savage districts, and every hut has become a home for industrial occupation, which has placed its inmates in connection with the trade of other lands.

I was told that in the Catholic Cantons, that is in the Forest Cantons, I should find a great difference as regarded order, cultivation, and comfort, between them and those who had embraced the reformed faith. But I did not find it so. On the contrary; wherever I turn my eyes I cannot but admire the excellent and respectable appearance of every thing that belongs to the country and its people. Every thing seems well-conditioned and prosperous. I have had this morning a better opportunity of judging, and with the same result, during a longer ramble than usual into the country by the side of a stream of the most crystalline water. The land seems to me to wear a holiday garb. Brunnen is the harbor for the Canton Schwytz, and the life and movement of the little town seem unceasing.

I might now speak somewhat less favorably of the conservatism of these Cantons, but defer doing so till I have seen more of them. They appear to me to look backward rather than forward, and that is injurious, in the long run. The old struggle for freedom and the rights they have acquired, seems to occupy the popular mind too exclusively, and to close it against higher spiritual development. The lately-ruptured Sonderbund is a bloody proof of this.

August 29th.—I visited Grutli during the morning, after crossing the lake in calm and beautiful weather. It is devoutly to be wished that the Swiss people may never take it into their heads to place upon this beautiful sun-lighted spot, a monument either of stone or marble, with inscriptions, etc. I cannot describe the peculiar charm there is, in finding here nothing besides the objects which surrounded the Sworn-Confederates during the nights when they assembled here, and upon the morning when the sun arose upon their solemn oath. This beautiful carpet of turf, these trees, this lovely pyramid, the Mythen Stone on the shore, this enchanting lake, with its garland wood and mountain, this image of Swiss scenery, and this memory,—are they not sufficient? And if people will still have any thing more, then nature and the popular poetical belief united, have provided it in the three springs from the crystalline waters of which people drink to the honor of the heroes of freedom, and which, it is said, sprung up in their footsteps.

Nor has Dalecarlia, the cradle of the Swedish champion of freedom, any other monument of its epic poem than the whispering forest, than the little hills, or the cottage, which served the hero as his stage of action or his asylum. And this is enough. Monuments of stone would be injustice to the popular memory.

I gathered some lovely grass on Grutli meadow, and sunned myself in its beautiful scenery and its ancient memories. After which, we rowed back to Brunnen, where we amused ourselves by contemplating two large inartistic works, in fresco, which are to be seen at the landing-place. The one is to commemorate the Sworn-Confederacy, which took place here between the Three Forest Cantons, on the 17th Dec., 1315, and represents these under the form of three men; the other represents two combatants, one of whom falls in a most dangerous and extraordinary manner. Below are the words—"Switer conquers Swen, and founds Schwytz."

I am told that the subject of the picture is a quarrel between two brothers, which occurred at the commencement of the Swedish colonization.

In the evening, my friend and I fell into conversation,—I know not rightly what led to it,—on the Calvinistic doctrine of predestination, which several of the ministers of the Reformed Church still adhere to, to this day; but not Peuchaud, who is too mild and too much enlightened. He observed, what a small space this doctrine occupies in the Holy Scriptures in comparison with the doctrine of free grace, its demands and consequences. This former dogma, originated by Augustin and Calvin, which it is easy for the natural sense of justice to refute, has its root in the difficulty, hitherto unsolved by the human mind, the uniting of God's omnipotence and man's free will. We talked on this subject, and then—we became silent. It had grown dusk, and, in the quiet evening, no sound was heard but the soft dashing of the waves against the shore on which our inn stood. The windows were open; I leaned against the window-frame, and looked out into the landscape. It was gloomy. Dark clouds hung over the heights, and threw black shadows in the mirror-bright lake. One shadow, in particular, lay there: so black, so profound, that even the brightness of the water was lost in it. And upon this dark object my eye was involuntarily riveted, whilst I listened with a melancholy feeling to waves striking upon the shore. They seemed as impelled by an inward unrest, of which the outward calm knew nothing; and I thought upon the questions always recurring, always dark, which from one century to another, hurl their waves with the same plunge, the same unsolved dissonances, against the human breast, causing its heart to throb with restless bitterness.

"Will it always remain the same, for me, for all?—the same in all times upon the earth?" I asked, dejectedly, and gazed at the dark shadow. All at once arose out of it, the most delicious music and wind-instruments. I could not see those who produced it—the dark shadow was as impenetrable as before—

neither did I inquire after it. I merely listened and drank in, with my whole soul, these heavenly tones, which ascended, like angelic voices, out of the deep. Eternal harmonies! are there such in the depths of the dark questionings of human life? And do we not hear a promise of the harmonious solution of these,— a promise of your harmonious concord, when we listen to our own soul's deepest anticipations and requirements?

In the far distance across the lake, a voice joddled so freshly, so joyously! Prophetic voices amid the shades of evening, receive my thanks!

Let us wait and hope! And having seen the sun rise, it would be pusillanimous not to wait and believe that it will penetrate with its light the shadows of earth—even those cast by the great mountain. Thank God, I can both wait and hope!

I proposed to Penchaud that, during the quiet evenings of our journey, we should read together the ninth chapter of St. Paul's Epistle to the Romans, which has so frequently occasioned me the bitterest anguish, and that he should help me to understand it in connection with the two following. For the right explanation of this lies infallibly in these.

SCHWYTZ, *August 29th.*—The town Schwytz lies at the foot of the lofty obelisk-like rocks, the Mythen, as quiet, as silent, as if it alone were occupied in collecting its memories. And that it is so, seemed proved by two acquaintances which I made to-day. The first in the morning, when we paid a visit to the Landamman Reding, one of the oldest and noblest families in the Canton. It was now represented by individuals of refined and elegant manners, living in a beautiful house, in rooms with silk hangings and antique splendor. They expressed themselves with displeasure against the Diet, which had lately met, and which, in its foolish democratism, had unanimously rejected a law which the government of the Cantons had conscientiously elaborated. Landamman R. occupied himself in collecting genealogies and records of the ancient noble families of the Cantons. He communicated to me a new variation of the old tradition of the immigration of the Swedes into Switzerland, and which strengthened it. The suggestion was interesting,—that they entered the country at eleven o'clock in the day, and that in memory thereof, it was ordained that every day, when the clock struck eleven, the people should pray a Pater Noster and three Aves,— a custom which is still held in reverence by the people of Schwytz. The high-born couple conducted themselves towards us politely, but with coldness. Not a breath of hospitality refreshed the visit. My friend, with his mildness and sensibility, was quite depressed by it.

In the evening of the same day, we paid a visit to a certain M. Kid, to whom we had a letter. We found in him a pale man, of gentle demeanor, and of an extremely interesting character. After a life of much labor and suffering, he had attained to a quiet independence, and could now wholly devote himself to those literary occupations which were dear to him above every thing. They consisted, principally, in collections having reference to his native town—Brunnen. His little abode was a museum of memories, appertaining thereto. In one work of twelve volumes (!) he had drawn up the history of every old house in the town, and of the families and trades occupying them. To this belonged portraits in the old-fashioned costumes, copied from those still existing in the churches and chapels of the place. Some of these were executed by good artists, and were really excellent. Amongst a collection of ancient documents, he possessed one which also had reference to the immigration of the Swedes.

Whilst M. K. himself lived with the greatest economy, he was still able to employ and remunerate several artists, who designed and painted pictures for him from the past, and even the present life, of his native town.

M. K. accompanied us home, and whilst on our way thither, he related to us some portions of his own life, which I wish I had space to repeat,—they are so pervaded by a spirit of noble pride, of faithful labor, and warm-heartedness. His earliest, bitter sufferings, as a child, when, his father being cruelly maltreated by the French soldiers, his mother had nothing for the wounded man but soup made of bread boiled in water with a piece of tallow-candle, and the son felt that he would rather die than complain; of his gradually struggling upward by making gunpowder; the payment of his debts; his purchasing of books; his earliest delineation of old houses; his courtship, marriage, and domestic felicity;—all these described so livingly, so evidently from the heart's faithful memory, were quite delicious! His good wife had now been dead some years. M. K. showed us her picture, extremely well executed, representing her at her spinning-wheel; and his life has, since then, been empty and overshadowed,—so he said, with an expression which showed how deeply he felt it to be so. He now lived merely in his collections of old memories.

There is a good and a bad conservatism. The former is a golden thread which links us to the past and makes us more thoroughly understand the present and the future; the latter is a block of wood which stands where it stands, understands in fact nothing, and goes no further.

We walked along the shore of Lake Lowertz. Rossberg, with its riven summit and gloomy tradition, lay just opposite. M. Kid related to us various incidents of the terrible occurrence when the summit of Rossberg was hurled down over the valley of Goldau and buried the villages of Goldau, Bussingen, and Rothen, together with four hundred and fifty-seven human beings. Amongst these was a wedding procession. It was the 22d of September, 1806, and the summer had been rainy. Early in the morning of the unfortunate day, dull, cracking sounds were heard in the mountain. Its fall occurred in a moment. Large herds of cattle had already taken flight. Many hundreds of animals, both large and small, together with human beings, were buried under the mountain ruins. Of these only two hundred were saved. There still lies the formerly fertile and rich valley buried under a mass of earth and rocks, presenting a very effective sermon to the worshipers of Nature, who see in nature nothing but harmony and the highest **revelation of the Creator's wisdom and goodness.**

But does not the Creator indeed permit destruction? Yes: and had he not a more beautiful Goldau valley beyond that, in which bride and bridegroom might complete their marriage procession, and enter into indestructible habitations, then the Creator would be—not a good, not a fatherly God. But what does Nature tell us about that other Goldau, about that realm beyond the fall of mountains, or any destruction whatever?

LUCERNE, 30*th August.*—Early this beautiful morning we set out in a little, open carriage, along the lake Lowertz, out of the Canton of Schwytz into that of Lucerne. The country resembled a vast orchard; in the meadows the people were busy with their second hay harvest. The people here have carried cultivation as high as possible up the mountains, combating with the mountain and the severity of the cold for a foot-breadth of cultivatable land. Amongst and by means of large stones, they collect and keep together the soil, and in it plant a few potatoes or flowering plants. It touches and it rejoices the heart to see this solicitude about the food-bearing earth. In the so-called "Hohle Gasse," or Hollow Way, by Küssnacht, a deep road which winds amongst trees and bush-covered, lofty headlands, we were shown the place where Tell concealed himself when he had shot Gessler—an action which was scarcely honorable—and a chapel has been erected on the shore, with images and paintings to his memory. The steamboat journey on the lake of Lucerne from Küssnacht was splendid between the vast mountains. Pilatus, Rhigi, and others, towards Lucerne, which, at the upper end of the lake, extends its quay, its handsome houses and church towers, with so much grandeur that one might fancy oneself approaching an important city.

But the importance of Lucerne consists not in its greatness, but in its glorious situation and its life. To the outward and grand features of this belongs the Reuss, which is hurled like a cascade out of the lake, and across the rapid smaragdus-green waters, pouring onward into the country, are thrown three bridges, one very peculiar with its number of paintings from Swiss history. To the outer life belongs also the number of steamboats which arrive here all the day through, and the multitude of travelers who transform the beautiful quay, with its hotels and *cafés*, into a Parisian boulevard. As belonging to the inner—but also to the outer—life at the same time, may be mentioned the trade expositions for the Cantons, which now attract visitors, and where we cannot but admire the great development of the little Cantons in every kind of trade and beautiful industrial occupation. The most peculiar seems to me a perfect choir of cowbells, from the largest to the least bell which is carried by the Swiss herds of horned cattle. When one approaches a herd, the whole being set in motion would produce—although the sound might be almost deafening—the melodious concert which often delighted me when I heard it up amongst the mountains.

Alone of its kind, is a work of art, called "the Lion of Lucerne," executed in memory of the Swiss guards, who were slaughtered in Paris, the 10th of August, 1792, whilst endeavoring to defend the unfortunate King, Louis XVI. I have visited the Lion this morning. The sun glanced through the trees as if to caress the beautiful monument. It is hewn in the rock—a colossal lion drooping in death over a broken column, which, though expiring, it still seeks to defend. The expression of sorrow and suffering in the countenance of the noble animal, is indescribable. One might say that it weeps. It made me weep. The design was by Thorwaldsen, that son of Iceland, who gave to all his works, the stamp of life, which genius alone can give. At the foot of the mountain-wall and the lion, lies a little sheet of water, deep and dark, reflecting the figure of the lion, the shadowy trees around it, and the sky which glances through them.

Alone of its kind also, is the panorama of Rhigi, which its artist, M. Meyer, now exhibits here. One sees the rosy dawn ascending, and the sun set above the magnificent scene, which is said to be painted with admirable fidelity. I shall soon perhaps be able to judge of this, as in the afternoon we ascend Rhigi. But without fine weather, nothing is to be seen. Mount Pilatus wears a nightcap of cloud which, people say, denotes rain. Perhaps, therefore, Mr. Meyer's panorama may be my only view from Rhigi. In order to accomplish this work, it is said that he ascended Rhigi one hundred and twenty times.

RHIGI CULM, *September 1st.*—There is undeniably, nothing like "weather-luck!" And without having something of this kind, people ought not to travel, because all the pleasure of the journey depends upon it. I am fortunate enough to have a little of this good luck, and that even now on the Rhigi.

The weather became calm and beautiful, yesterday afternoon, when we set off from Küssnacht, for the ascent of Rhigi; I, on a lazy Rosinante, which had much more desire to graze on the side of the road, than to go along it. Calm and blue, like heavenly mirrors, lay the lakes which we left below us, and which seemed to become ever smaller and smaller, as we clambered upwards. The road is broad, and in excellent condition, the whole way, and the views magnificent. After the ascent of three hours, we approached Rhigi. Reaching its lowest station or "Rhigi Scheideck," we were informed that the hotel at Rhigi Culm, was quite full; that it would be impossible for us to pass the night there, so many travelers having lately arrived on account of the fine weather. Nevertheless, I was determined to make the attempt. But when, half an hour afterwards, we approached the great hotel, at the summit, we saw on all sides, troops of travelers arriving on horseback, and in chairs. One fat gentleman was carried by eight men. Sighing, and yet jocundly, I told my friend that I foresaw what my fate would be; I should have to pass the night "*à la belle étoile*, under my umbrella."

Arrived at the hotel, we were met by the information, "that every place was full. A hundred guests had already secured rooms for themselves."

The kind, agreeable, hostess, however, added consolatorily for me;

"Wait, a little! Don't be uneasy! I will manage so that you shall have a little room. But you must be content with what you can get!"

"With any thing!" I assured her. "All I wanted,

was a roof over my head, and shelter from the night-cold!" My friend had already taken a room at Rhigi Scheideck.

Now, therefore, we calmly gave ourselves up to the contemplation of the grand scene. This is, as every body knows, the most extensive in the world, but not exactly in the sense which I call magnificent and beautiful. You behold the earth spread out like a map beneath your feet, and the gigantic Alps seem like small white sugar mountain summits, around the horizon.

But now commenced the grand spectacle of the sun's departure from earth; and here, it was a scene of wonderful pomp and beauty. The hundred guests stood in innumerable groups upon the wide plateau, and beheld with us the splendid show, but less silently than we did. The many-colored mass of people, their various physiognomies, their restlessness and noise, was a picture in itself, by no means without interest to the looker-on.

But now an Alpine horn sounds with trumpet-like clangor to announce that the sun has descended, that the scene is at an end, and that people can go to supper. The hundred, therefore, come into hasty movement, and stream down singly, or in groups, towards the hotel. Anon, the great table is occupied. People eat and drink, and chatter and laugh. A band of Tyrolese play "table-music," sing and joddle. I hastily swallowed some bread and butter, and a cup of tea, and then hurried forth again, and up the heights, knowing that I should now behold something unusually splendid in the "afterglow" of the setting sun. And so it was.

The western and southern horizon glowed like a ring of the clearest fire round the dark earth, the lower tracts of which now wholly disappeared from the eye; darkness resting upon the face of the deep. But in the north, dark, gigantic forms elevated themselves threateningly, from the home, as it were, of eternal night. These two half circles, these two embraces, of light and darkness, which here inclosed the earth,—the earth with all its desires and all its agonies, this tranquilizing day, this "Ginnunga-gap," this watchful, mysterious night, which inclosed these all in a ring—it was a sight, the effect of which is indescribable. It seemed to me that a brain not overstrong might become dizzy with this sight forever.

But I recommend all tourists, who love the forcible in color and effect, not to neglect, when on Rhigi, the scene after the sunset. I spent above half an hour totally alone, on the heights, and when I returned to the hotel, people were still sitting at table, eating and drinking and making a great noise, and the Tyrolese were still playing and singing.

After that, people went to bed. My room was a little attic, just large enough for a bed, a chair, and a table. There was also a large window, almost above my bed's head, and when I extinguished my candle, behold, a star beamed above me, so large and so bright, that it shone into my soul and I could not sleep. A starry heaven like that night on Rhigi, I never saw equaled. No wonder that it kept me awake, and allowed me to follow all its changes, till the blush of morning glowed, and it paled before sunrise.

And now again was heard the Alpine trumpet. It was the signal of sunrise. I hastened up and out. The one hundred streamed forth pell-mell to the plateau, in costumes and physiognomies which looked tolerably bewildered and only half-awake.

The earth seemed as yet altogether "without form and void," covered with the shades of night. But by degrees they became lighter, and you saw the little lakes down below vailed by thick clouds of mist, as of white cotton-wool. A gentleman stood on the summit with a couple of ladies.

"See," said he in French, pointing to the cloud-covered spots, "see, there is the eternal snow!"

And when the people round him laughed, he began,—exclaiming, in great amazement, "*Quoi?—Comment? —ce n'est pas?—Mais—Ah!*" etc,—to have a consciousness of, and an insight into his mistake, at which he himself laughed merrily.

And now people stand in silent waiting for whatever shall follow. The scene brightens by degrees, and an increasing glory is seen upon the white peaks of the Oberland Alps. Again the Alpine trumpet sounds, and immediately afterwards a dazzling ray flashes over the jagged mountains of the Canton Glarus. The giants of the Oberland gleam forth in its blaze, and soon the earth sphere grows clear in the sun's light. But the mist above the lakes seems to become denser, and to extend itself over the surrounding country. The morning spectacle is now at an end, and the hundred stream back again to the hotel to breakfast, and I follow in the stream.

It was Sunday. I had resolved to spend the whole day at Rhigi, in order to enjoy its scenes thoroughly. The greater part of the hundred guests left the mountain soon after breakfast. At Rhigi, at this season, there is a perpetual ebb and flow of human beings.

I seated myself on a rock on the lofty plateau. The mists had spread themselves from the lakes, over the whole earth, so that one could not in the slightest degree discern its dwellings, fields, or hills. A dense vail of cloud covered every object. Above this the white, jagged peaks of the Alps were alone visible, and above them arched itself a deep blue and perfectly cloudless heaven.

"If the people below there, under the vail of cloud, did but know how bright it is at the same time," thought I, grieved for those from whom this gray, cloudy heaven concealed the sun. Then the church bells began to ring down below. They rang for divine worship. It seemed to me as if the bright sound was dulled by the cloud-covering. But before long this was penetrated by the sunbeams, or riven asunder by a wind which was not felt on the heights where I sat; and from the river mist stood forth, one after another, towns and churches, villages, woods, cultivated fields, lakes and rivers. The first lake which stood out, blue and bright, was the little mountain-lake, Egeri, the lake of Lucerne, Zug, Sarnen, and others. By degrees, the whole region was unvailed, and it was an enchanting scene. But now, lying there in its whole extent, in the full blaze of daylight, the beautiful, affluent earth, it was no longer remarkable for the attractiveness of its beauty. Every object seemed so miserably small, and human beings as mere nothings. The landscape lay there, immovable and lifeless, like a map. It is true, that many places might be pointed out which were celebrated as the scenes of great battles and heroic achievements, but the greatness of these vanished, as it were, in the pettiness of the causes for which they were sometimes undertaken. The man athirst for conquest, should behold the earth from heights such as those of Rhigi. Methinks he would then ask himself whether it were worth while to steep it in blood for a few foot-breadths of land. It is only when war has reference to higher interests, that its exploits become great and important, even though achieved on a mere point of space.

During the forenoon, Penchaud and I read the Epistle to the Romans. The various chapters ought to be taken collectively, in relation to the whole epistle, of which they are a part. Thus only can they be rightly understood. We also read portions of P.'s treatise on the conscience. He regards this innermost principle in man, as the highest truth, in its development from the most elementary condition, to its full, concrete form, in the Christian consciousness. I stated my objections to various parts, but I cannot sufficiently express my opinion of the excellence and importance of the work in its purport and execution. Such works are of great value at the present time; but the author's conscientiousness prevents him from finishing "The Conscience."

We spent the afternoon in contemplating the Alpine

scene. The sky continued clear, and the air so calm, that the lakes appeared smooth as a mirror. A little fly, no larger than a point, skimmed backwards and forwards across the water,—it was a steamboat. At length I grew heartily tired of the immovable scene, and its map-like landscape. I longed for whispering trees, purling brooks, flowers and birds; for mankind—loving, suffering, laboring mankind. The morning was beautiful, but not equal to the last.

SARNEN, *September 3d.*—It is pleasant to rest here a couple of days after the fatiguing descent from Rhigi, which we made on foot. Passing through scenes of idyllian beauty and fertility, we arrived at Stanz, the capital of Unterwalden, and the smallest capital I ever saw. It lies embedded amongst mountains, in conventual quietness. It has been, nevertheless, the cradle of heroic souls. Arnold Winkelried was born there; and during the religious war, young girls fought there for their faith, and died with their arms in their hands. The greatest notability of the little city, at the present time, is the painter, Deschwanden, the most celebrated artist in German Switzerland. We visited him in the forenoon, and found him a small man, with large, soul-full eyes, and quiet demeanor. He stood, with his brushes and pallet in hand, surrounded by pictures of angels and saints, which he was painting for the churches and chapels of the Catholic Cantons. His angels seemed to me actually angelic; his Madonnas, with the child Christ, very lovely, but not deep in expression. His most important picture seemed to be one which he was **painting for the Cathedral of Corie, the capital of the**

Grisons. It is large, and represents the martydom of St. Stephen. Stephen is seen in the centre of the picture, sunk upon his knees, whilst his transported, beaming countenance is directed upwards. On the left, stand the people of the lowest grade, who are stoning him, frenzied, blood-thirsty, scarcely half-human, who, having tasted blood, are athirst for more, and rush blindly against the victim whose very purity irritates their savagery. On the right, you see a couple of Pharisees, who are turning away, with inexpressible scorn in their glance and on their lips. But Saul lingers, with a sense of reaction. You see, evidently, that thoughts and feelings are awakened in him which will afterwards make themselves acknowledged,—at the time when he hears the voice: " Saul, Saul, why persecutest thou me? It is hard for thee to kick against the pricks!" The expression in the countenance of the dying Stephen is the prick which, for the first time, has entered his heart. Deschwanden's picture has given me a better understanding of Paul's conversion.

Separated from the world in this convent-like quietness, Deschwanden seems to obtain, from the depths of his own soul, inspiration and the ideal. These have both purity and beauty, but hardly proportionable strength. Yet his Paul is grand, and he himself is one of the fortunate of the earth. We visited Winkelried's dwelling, or that which is said to be his,—a handsome but ruinous country-house, with its garden. The old-fashioned decorations of the rooms indicate an aristocratic condition. During the beautiful evening, we drove to Sarnen, the capital of Upper Unterwalden. The principal object of attention in this little city, seems to be the memory of Nicholas de Flue and his hermit-cell, in the neighborhood.

This man, the most celebrated saint of the Catholic Cantons, was born 1417. He was a wealthy man, and of the nobility of the country. At the age of fifty, he left house and home, and a large family, the youngest of which was still in the mother's arms, in order to devote himself to a life of poverty, fasting, and prayer, in a solitude far removed from mankind. Thus would he live, alone for God and heavenly things. He practised this mistaken service of God for more than five-and-twenty years, during which time, it is said, that he performed many miraculous works.

We have, during the day, made an excursion, under umbrellas, to the romantic Melchthal, where he lived his hermit-life, and where the whity-gray Melch roars wildly through the narrow valley. Its surroundings are, however, soft, shadowy trees, and green slopes. The dwelling of "Bruder Klaus," under which name Nicholas de Flue was known in his monastic life, is still standing on the rock near the river,—a miserable little hut, with small, four-paned windows. Here you find still, the wooden board, worn smooth with use, which served him for his bed, and also the stone, smooth also, which served him for pillow. The walls of the hut, and still more those of the little chapel in the neighborhood, are covered with votive tablets in his honor. The chapel contains, besides these, a series of paintings, representing scenes from his life, the greater number miraculous incidents, more or less absurd. His horse seems to have had its share in his saintly glory. In one picture, you see a remarkable white flower growing out of its mouth. The people in the surrounding districts seem to have a fanatical devotion for his memory, as well as faith in his power.

"Do you pray also to Brother Klaus, when you are in need of help?" I inquired from our young attendant, the daughter of the host of our hotel, the Golden Key, at Sarnen. "Yes, certainly!" replied she.

"But do you not think that God would hear your prayers, if you addressed them to Himself?" "Yes—but help comes more quickly if one prays to Brother Klaus."

It is an easy thing for the Protestant Christian to smile at the attributes with which the popular imagination, and the popular childishness of Catholic countries, deck out their saint; and the thinking world, of the present day, has another and a higher ideal of the Christian life, than that which is represented by the life of the self-torturing, world-abandoning hermit. But yet it is certain, that this lonely, self-abnegation of all which the world gives, brings with it, powers of which the earthly great are destitute, and which govern the heart of princes and people. To fear nothing but God, gives alone, immeasurable strength.

When the cruel Queen Agnes, in order to revenge the death of her husband, King Albrecht, had a thousand innocent persons, men, women, and children, tortured and murdered, in whose blood, she said, "she bathed as in morning dew"—when she, with the property of her victims, built upon the spot of Albrecht's death, the splendid convent of Königsfelden, where she herself lived in an ostentatious sanctity, which attracted the admiration of the thoughtless; then it was, that a pious hermit, Berchtold Strobert, refused her the absolution which she desired, addressing to her these severe words:

"Lady, it is a miserable God's service, to shed innocent blood, and to build convents with the spoil! God has more delight in kindness and mercy!"

And when, at the close of the fifteenth century, many of the Swiss Cantons, after long dissensions, were on the eve of coming to a bloody quarrel with each other, it was Brother Klaus, who, by his appearance in the Diet at Stanz, and his affecting and wise address to the Sworn-Confederates, succeeded in uniting them afresh. Berne, Lucerne, and Zürich, gave up their "Sonderbund," all the Cantons made mutual concessions, and Freyburg and Soleure, came into the Confederacy. A few years after having rendered this important service to his native land, Nicholas de Flue died, at the age of seventy. During his hermit-life he was a general benefactor and good counselor for the whole country round. The pictures of him, represent him as a very meagre form, in a capuchin cloak, bare-headed, and bare-footed. He is thus painted in his entrance to the Diet-chamber at Stanz.

In these Cantons, Uri, Unterwalden, and Schwytz, the smallest and poorest in Switzerland, we have encountered very little poverty, and seen only one beggar, a proof that the government takes good care of the common-weal. The land is everywhere beautiful and well cultivated.

During our hours of rest in this city, we have read the conclusion of St. Paul's chapters on predestination. His meaning, taken as a whole, seems to us, to be this. The election between people and people, man and man, is relative. The one is called earlier, the other later, to enter into the kingdom of God. If the first called misuse the call, he is cast off, and another takes his place. But the first can be replaced, if he will, and if he seek to be so, and thus all Israel becomes blessed.

The reading of these passages has produced a good and tranquilizing effect upon me. St. Paul's doctrine here, is no other than that love will, and that conscience must, agree with the prophet in believing in a just God and Lord, who "hath wrought and done it, calling the generations, even from the beginning."

Zurich, *September 6th.*—We arrived two days since at Zürich, the cheerful city; known for its hospitality to strangers, its freedom, and science, the Athens of Switzerland, as it is often called. We traveled in the early morning from Lucerne over the Albis. The air was cold; snow had fallen during the night on the mountains. We traveled by omnibus. A couple of gentlemen, our fellow-travelers, spoke of a revolution which had broken out the preceding day in Neufchatel. "The mountain is said to have come down into the city (*les montagnes sont descendues sur la ville*), and seized it in the name of the King of Prussia." Every body expressed amazement at the occurrence. What if that should turn something more than the Swiss revolution, which Voltaire characterized as a tempest in a glass of water, or lead to a great war! Nobody dared to prognosticate any thing about it.

We drove through the little Canton Zug, the entire population of which does not exceed seventeen thousand and some hundred souls, the greater number Catholics, but which yet takes its place and has a voice in the Great Federal Council, by the side of Zürich and Berne. From the summit of Albis, the sun-lighted view of Zürich, with its lake and its richly cultivated and populous shores, was indescribably beautiful.

In Zürich two suns seemed to be shining, because every countenance seemed beaming as from an inner sun. As so it was. There was a great festival there, the greatest of its kind in Switzerland. Six thousand little boys from the German Cantons, and all bearing arms as soldiers, had been for a couple of days assembled in Zürich, upon the Champs de Mars, on which they enacted the battle which took place—I do not know in what year—between the Austrians and the French in the neighborhood of the city. All these children had been quartered with kind friends in the city, and every body seemed to participate with their whole hearts in this military children's festival.

This had brought a great concourse of strangers to the place, so that there was no more room in the great Hotel Baur, neither in any other hotel. But this embarrassment became my good fortune, and I found a home and the most amiable hospitality, in a private house on the banks of the Limmat.

In the afternoon the great Thalach Street was crowded with people; faces looked out from every window, and every countenance was gay; every eye was directed to a distance with a look of eager expectation. The loud beating of drums was heard afar off, and you might read in every countenance, "Now they are coming!"

They are the Boy-legions who are entering the city after their manœuvring and fighting before it. And now they march onward, the youthful, future defenders of the fatherland, in separate detachments, according to their Cantons, in full uniform, with colors flying and excellent military bearing, and in advance of all, a large troop of little drummers, who drum as if they had never done any thing else all their days. It was in truth a joyous sight to behold these six thousand boys, with the roses of childhood on their round cheeks, with a gravity of expression and demeanor, as if they knew that they had already entered into the service of their native land.

Two of the young heroes of the future were quartered in the house where I found my home. They were from St. Gall, handsome lads of nine or ten years of age. I could not understand them, neither was their St. Gall dialect very intelligible to my hostess, but the politeness and the propriety, at the same time, with which these children conducted themselves in their strange home and at supper-time, testified to their excellent breeding. They were most hopeful examples of the rising generation of the republic. In the evening there were fireworks in the city, in honor of the six thousand young ones.

Canton Zürich is, after Berne, the most populous, and beyond comparison the most wealthy of the Protestant Cantons of Switzerland; and the city of Zürich, one of its most beautiful and most flourishing cities. Since the walls of its fortifications have been removed by order of the Grand Council, it has extended and developed itself daily in every direction, like a vigorous tree in the spring. Science, industry, benevolent institutions increase, as if in emulation of each other; and gardens and plantations encircle the increasing city with beauty. Its situation and the views of the lake and the Alps, are among the most glorious in Switzerland.

The enlightenment and education of the people seem to take the lead. Every week, during the winter, each professor of the academy delivers a lecture on his own particular branch of science, in a popular manner, suitable for the public, at the Hotel de Ville. The taste for science and art is by no means a stranger among the artisan classes. Butchers are collectors of pictures, sometimes even painters; tobacco-dealers, botanists. The wealthy M. F. Ascher, who employs several thousand work-people, at his large mechanical works—whence steamboats are sent to every lake in the republic—employs himself also, by giving them opportunities for moral and intellectual culture. The silk-looms maintain many thousand families without the workers being crowded in factories. The people work at their own homes and in the country. The looms stand in the cottages scattered about the fields of the Alps. The country people fetch from the town their orders, and the raw material, and carry back thither their shining fabrics.

The well-to-do and cheerful people, who crowd to

Zürich on the market days, show very evidently what is their condition. The poor in the Canton Zürich, are in the proportion of one to thirty-five, whilst in Berne they are as one to ten. The Professor of Political Economy here, M. Cherbulliez, considers that this very different proportion is occasioned by the circumstance, that, in the Canton Berne the State is compelled to assist the poor, whilst here in Zürich, they are almost entirely aided by benevolent societies. The ladies of the city distinguish themselves by their judicious activity in these, devoting themselves especially to the children, to the old and the sick. Mathilda Ascher—the daughter of the great manufacturer—is spoken of by all the needy as an angel of goodness and mercy.

Amongst the benevolent institutions here, I have been especially interested with the lately-established Pfünd Institution, in which upwards of seventy men and women of the burger-class, receive a home and maintenance for their old age. I saw an aged couple here, who told me that this was now the happiest time of their life. Both were sixty-nine. She could scarcely speak for tears of joy. The fresh air, the beautiful view, the lovely grounds which surround the institution, all were evidences of the piety of the founder, and the good sense employed in the laying out of the place. I noticed that on the well-supplied dinner-table, a bottle of wine was placed for each person. The old folks are entertained three times a day with coffee. Long live the good who thus interest themselves in making old age happy!

I have seen amongst the scientific institutions, the

Antiquarian Museum, and those Celtic antiquities which have been found in the Swiss lakes. All these ancient articles, whether arms, domestic implements, or personal ornaments, belonging to the primeval inhabitants of the country, have been fished up from these lakes, thus strengthening the view which Swiss antiquarians began to entertain, that the most ancient inhabitants of Switzerland built their dwellings upon piles in the lakes. The librarian, M. Weise, who showed me these interesting antiquities, which, in many respects, resembled those of the primeval inhabitants of Sweden, showed me also a document regarding William Tell, which he had lately discovered in the so-called "White Books," in the archives of Unterwalden. In this ancient book, of the fifteenth century, William Tell's history is related simply and fully, and in all its main features, is identical with that of the popular tradition. The language and style of the narrative prove its age and its originality.

I must now leave the lively, and in many respects, very interesting Zürich, for the details of two days which I spent at Einsiedeln, the Delphi of Switzerland, whither annually a hundred thousand pilgrims proceed from every part of Catholic Switzerland, and even from Germany, and where, at this very time, a great festival is to be celebrated. I have a wish to see life in the Swiss republic, under all its various forms.

ZURICH, *September 10th.*—We were sitting, Penchaud and I, upon the steamer, on the shore of the lake of Zürich, waiting till it should set out and convey us to Rapperschwyl, on our way to Einsiedeln, when I saw a young man, of remarkably agreeable exterior, hastily come across the deck and approach us with joyful looks. He placed himself before my traveling companion, and exclaimed:

"Penchaud!"

Penchaud looked up, uttered an exclamation of joy, his whole countenance brightened, and the two men were clasped in each other's arms.

They had been fellow students in Lausanne, at the time when, according to M. Penchaud's expression, the young girls in the city envied the youths their happiness in being students under such teachers as Alexandre Vinet, Choroles Schritau, and others, and when, according to Penchaud's own account, these youths assembled for conversation on the highest subjects, and remained together discussing them till one or two o'clock in the morning, and then walked home, arm in arm, in a regular intoxication of friendship.

Eight years had passed since all this. Penchaud, after having traveled on foot through France, preaching the gospel and disseminating the Holy Scriptures, had married in Switzerland, and settled down in one of the high valleys. Young Vogel, his friend, had become a teacher in the Tecknological Institute, at Wurtemburg. They had not seen each other through the whole of this period. On Penchaud's arrival in Zürich, Vogel's mother had telegraphed the news to her son.

"And thou hast come all this way merely for my sake," exclaimed Penchaud, with emotion, "just at the moment when I am leaving!"

"But I am going with thee! I am here for that very purpose!"

"Nay, that is delightful!"

And now the steamer was put in motion and the two friends sat side by side, in the most cordial conversation, whilst I enjoyed the sight of their happiness, and views of the richly-populated banks of the Lake of Zürich. Charming villas and manufactories, with their tall, smoking chimneys, lay interspersed with groves and cultivated fields. Before us, arose in the distance, the snowy Alps of Glacis and Appenzell.

At Rapperschwyl, we took a carriage, and entered and ascended the Canton Schwytz. The weather had become stormy and wet. After a three hours' drive, we arrived in rain and gloom, at the little town of Einsiedeln, which for the greater part is a town of houses of entertainment for the pilgrims to the convent and its Holy Virgin. Lights shone from every window in the town. Ten thousand pilgrims are said to have arrived for the morrow's festival. A letter which I had brought with me procured us rooms, however, and a most kind reception at the inn to which it was addressed.

San Loretto in Italy, St. James of Compostella in Spain, and Einsiedeln, or "Notre Dames des Eremites," in Switzerland, are the most frequented places of pilgrimage in Europe.

It is now, according to the chronicle, many centuries since Meinrad, Count of Sulgen on the Danube, built for himself a hermit's cell on the heights of Etzel, together with a chapel for a miraculous image of the Virgin, which had been given to him by Hildegard, Abbess of Zürich. He was murdered in the year 861, and the murderers were discovered by ravens which the holy man had fed. After Meinrad's death, the fame of his sanctity spread far and wide, and the Benedictine Monastery was built on the spot where his cell had formerly stood. Legends and dreams announced the election and consecration of the new temple by the Lord himself. A Bull of Pope Pius VIII. confirmed these and gave plenary indulgence to all pilgrims to "Notre Dames des Eremites." The believing, or superstitious throng streamed thither, and the monastery became the richest in Switzerland, after that of St. Gall. Rudolph of Hapsburg elevated its abbot to the rank of prince. A court was formed around him, and he became lord of great territory. At the present time the Monastery of Einsiedeln is the most considerable in Switzerland, and its abbot is generally chosen from some of the principal families of the country, and is called in the Catholic Cantons "the Prince of Einsiedeln."

The number of pilgrims amount yearly to 150,000, and it is said that since 1848 it has been on the increase.

The monks and priests of the convent employ themselves in the education of the young. A hundred pupils are received into its seminary. It has its own printing establishment, a considerable library, physical and mineralogical collections, etc.

The festival which is now about to be celebrated—one of the greatest in the course of the year—commemorates the announcement of the angels at midnight to the Bishop of Constance, that the Saviour himself, surrounded by legions of the heavenly host, had already consecrated the church. This was on the 8th of September, 948; and on the 8th of September, 1856, I went in the earliest dawn, with my traveling companions, to the celebrated church. The morning was damp and cold, but the stars, gleaming through the clouds, seemed to divide them and to give us hope of a clear day.

The monastry is a large and palatial building. In the church itself it was so dark that we could see nothing of its celebrated beauty and pomp. Numerous groups of pilgrims stood, or had fallen on their knees in every part of the church, but more especially around the little chapel in the centre aisle, through the gilded grating of which a little image of the Virgin, of black wood, with the child Jesus, also black, may be seen by the light of small, yellow, wax candles which the devotees have lighted and placed there. Both images are adorned with golden crowns and precious stones. Their countenances are unusually pretty and agreeable, but it produced a most strange effect to see a jet-black Virgin and child. They were considerably smaller than life size. Not a hymn, not a note of the organ was heard at this early hour. Nothing was heard but the dull murmuring of the pilgrims' "Pater Nosters" and "Ave Marias!"

All around St. Meinrad's chapel—the chapel which contains the Virgin—the church became more and more thronged with devotees. As the day dawned we went out. In the square before the monastery stands a splendid fountain which pours forth its unceasing water from fourteen pipes. We noticed several pilgrims go round and drink from every separate jet. Tradition states that our Lord Christ drank on one occasion from one of these pipes, and in order not to miss drinking from the one which quenched his thirst, the pious pilgrims drink from them all. Water drunk from the right one, will, it is believed, give health both to soul and body.

At ten o'clock the grand processions began. A gilded image of the Virgin is carried round the great square in front of the monastery; then follows the priestly array with standards and banners; then come men and women and children, all in order, and walking two-and-two. One beautiful division was composed of young girls dressed in black, walking one-by-one, carrying urns with relics.

To this succeeded High Mass. A letter of introduction from a kind Dr. K., of Zürich, to the present abbot and prince, Henry IV., obtained for me a place in the lofty choir, and afterwards a conversation with the prince and his court; but of that anon.

High mass continued a long time, but its beautiful instrumental and vocal music afforded me enjoyment, as did also its excellent organ. The priests who officiated in the choir, bowed themselves alternately before the altar and the abbot, who was seated on his velvet throne, without apparently taking any part in the service.

After this, the multitude of pilgrims spread themselves about the great square, where a large market was being held, partly for the sale of red ribbon, and pictures of saints, and partly of small printed papers, issued from the printing presses of Einsiedeln. I purchased a couple of these on speculation. They promised forgiveness of sin for two hundred days, to those who made a pilgrimage to the Madonna of Einsiedeln, and who prayed, with their whole heart, the prayer there prescribed to the Holy Virgin.

Provided with these indulgences, I set out in the afternoon for my audience with the Prince of Einsiedeln. Brother, "Master of the Kitchen," a tall Benedictine monk, conducted me through the long and numerous passages of the convent, with distinguished politeness and complaisance of manner. With him, however, and two others of the convent's notabilities, Father Brandis and Father Gallmorell, I had already become acquainted, having been shown round the monastery by them. The former was a little, animated, and merry man, who understood my "sketches," and talked about them as kindly and as cheerfully as a layman. Father Gallmorell, a tall man, of Italian descent, and with a perfectly Italian physiognomy, was known as the genius of Einsiedeln, and as a poet of no inconsiderable merit. He seemed to me profound, but at the same time cunning and satirical.

I was conducted into a handsome room, more suitable for a castle than a convent, adorned with good portraits of the former abbots of Einsiedeln. Here I was received by its present abbot, Henry IV. He was a man of fifty, of singular personal beauty and dignity. In his mild countenance, and refined, complacent manner, a certain degree of embarrassment betrayed itself; he blushed continually. It occurred to me whether high birth, and an amiable character, had not elevated him to the rank of Prince of Einsiedeln, rather than erudition and other gifts. His little court, which, equally with himself, took part in the conversation, which I desired, had evidently no great respect for these. Father Brandis frequently replied for him; nay, in his vivacity, even interrupted him without any ceremony. Father Gallmorell made, without any regard to him, his profound, half-sarcastic remarks, which seemed sometimes to have reference to us altogether.

My first question concerned the indulgences which I had bought for a few pence.

"They are issued," said I, "from your printing-press. Do you approve of their promise of forgiveness for sin for two hundred days, for such as purchase here these writings, and offer the prescribed prayers?"

The abbot seemed at a loss to know how to answer.

"Observe, I pray you," said Father Gallmorell, pointing to the little paper, "that it here states, for such as shall, with their whole heart, pray this prayer. The indulgence is merely for those who pray with the heart."

"But why, then, only for two hundred days? or for any fixed number of days? We Evangelical Protestants believe that God forgives the sins of the whole life to those who, with their whole heart, pray for it."

The spiritual gentleman said that the forgiveness here referred to, applied only to temporal or ecclesiastical punishment. I could not understand their explanation, and I am not sure that they themselves were clear on the subject.

My second question was:—

"The pilgrims to Einsiedeln evidently believe in the miraculous power of the image of the Virgin. Is it also your opinion that the image possesses any such power?"

"No," replied they, unanimously. "We venerate it only because the holy Meinrad venerated it." And this they all corroborated.

"But the people here," I said, "evidently believe quite the contrary."

"Yes, the people, that is true," said the abbot, hesitatingly; "and they ought to be enlightened, but, but—" he paused, and Father Brandis went on to say how this must be done: "by degrees, slowly, by degrees!" and Father Gallmorell examined his sandals with a sarcastic expression.

I mentioned the faith which the people had in the mediation and prayers of the saint, and inquired "how they—they, the wise fathers—could explain this also, in conformity with the faith of their church, that God alone hears and answers the prayers of men?"

"We think," commenced Father Gallmorell, in explanation, "that probably, like as a good father of a family allows to his children as a reward, the privilege of dealing out alms and gifts to poor, beseeching beggars, so also does our Lord, with his faithful servants. All prayers are heard by God alone, that is true, but he sends his nearest friends or servants to convey the answers to them."

This explanation was very good, and may, it seems to me, be not without its truth. But the worthy father forgot that the prayers of the people are actually addressed directly to the saint himself, besides that, they have concern to outward things and donatives. I noticed this to him, as well as that the comprehension of the prayer, and the soul's connection with God, by means of it, are done away with.

They conceded this, said that " the people ought properly to be enlightened, but, but—the church had, in all ages, believed in the mediatorial prayers of the saints."

"We have," said Father Gallmorell, "proof in the catacombs, that the early Christian church believed on this subject as we do."

My last questions had reference to the worship of the Virgin. "Did the Catholics," I asked, "found this upon any passage in the Holy Scriptures?"

The abbot looked quite nonplussed; but the acute Father Gallmorell, who was never at a loss for an answer, interposed:

"Not precisely in the Scriptures, but in the catacombs, it is evident that from the earliest times, the first Christians prayed to the Virgin Mary, as the Queen of Heaven."

I now observed that Father Gallmorell must be particularly conversant with the catacombs, but that I could not follow him, as I had never been there, and knew but little about them. But I said, "something ought to have appeared in the Gospels regarding the high dignity of the Virgin, if it had its foundation there. But our Lord Christ had always appeared desirous of abrogating the placing of faith in his earthly relatives, as participators in his work," and I referred to the words in Matthew xii. 48–50.

The abbot in the meantime had recovered himself, and he said:

"We believe that the words which the Saviour uttered on the cross to his disciple, regarding his mother, "Behold thy mother," were not spoken alone for him, but for every one of his disciples in the world, for all mankind and for all time! Therefore we venerate Marie, as our mother, and the mother of all mankind."

This explanation was beautiful, and it was beautifully given, and I conceded that it might have its truth within certain limits, as—but I would not any longer detain the noble prelate, of whose politeness I did not wish to take undue advantage. I thanked the handsome and worthy gentleman for his kindness and took my leave. He asked if I should like to see his own private chapel, and the other gentlemen conducted me into a room as splendid as a boudoir; brilliant with crimson velvet and gold fringe. Above the altar was a Madonna, by Deschwanden, beautiful and lovable, but too human, a figure less to worship than to fall in love with. Henry IV., of Einsiedeln, was evidently one of the elegant and amiable prelates of the Catholic church, not one of its apostles and saints; he was neither a brother Klaus nor a St. Meinrad.

It was remarkable how all these gentleman seemed to consider themselves thinking and enlightened men, far above the prejudices and superstitious of the people. The poor people!——

But is it not the people's own fault if they remain in the dark? It was at Einsiedeln that Ulrich Zwingli, pastor of that place from 1515 to 1519, first commenced his powerful preaching against the sale of indulgences, the abuse of which he became well acquainted with at Einsiedeln. It was here that he began to preach the gospel, and the new life in Christ, in conformity with the Holy Scriptures. He preached at this very festival of the angels' consecration, so powerfully against indulgences, pilgrimages, and monastic vows, that the monks abandoned their cells and the convent was empty for a time. The mild and cheerful man became violent, and his language sometimes coarse, as indeed it usually was at this time, when he saw the failing of the church and the sins of the people.

"I know it," he said, in palliation of himself, "those great sinners kindle my wrath. But Christ, Peter, and Paul also, attacked them with violence. I am very far from finding any pleasure in abuse; I am generally of so gentle, conceding, and good-tempered a character, that it troubles me!"

It was at Einsiedeln, that Zwingli saw the same criminal persons return year after year, laden with the same and renewed crime, to seek for absolution by kissing the holy relics, or by the purchase of indulgences, and learned more deeply to comprehend the wants of the people and the age. "In truth," said he, "the greatest villains come hither merely to get fresh courage, and not one is ever reformed!"

The noble reformer, however, was obliged to leave Einsiedeln. On New Year's day, 1519, he made his appearance as preacher in the Cathedral of Zürich. Here he explained the Gospels in their due course, comparing at the same time, their dictates with the abuses of the Catholic Church, and the deviation of its teaching from the precepts of the Scriptures. And week after week he became better understood.

It was in Zürich that the reformatory activity of Zwingli became perfected and bore fruit; but it was in his solitary cell at Einsiedeln, when he knelt and cried to God for "an understanding of the word," that the first beams of the light of the new day arose for him. "God does not grow old!" was an expression which he often used.

The study of the Holy Scriptures in Greek produced the conversion of Zwingli. He did not in all respects take the same views as Luther. Both received from Heaven the truth which they published.

"I commenced," wrote Zwingli, in the year 1516, "to preach the gospel at a time when the name of Luther was unknown in our country. I have not learned the Christian truth from Luther, but from the word of God. When Luther preaches Christ, he does the same that I do.—That is all!" Zwingli required, at the same time, the study of science, literature, and the classics. His heaven had room enough in it for Plato, Aristides, Camillus, and Scipio.

But Zwingli was not the only reformer in Switzerland. Luther stood alone in Germany, high above every other, and face to the colossus of the Romish church, whose great opponent he became. Luther, so to speak, is the monarch of the spiritual revolution. But the light of the truth, and of the new life, did not proceed from Germany to Switzerland, and, from thence, to France, and from France to England and Holland. All these countries were visited at the same time by the warm, awakening, vernal wind of the same new, life-giving sun. One and-the same teaching found its way, during the sixteenth century, into home and church of the most diverse peoples; the same spirit awakened every where the same faith. Throughout Switzerland, a reformer arose in almost every canton. Many leaders were seen, but not one general commander. It is like a confederacy of reformers arising in the republic of the Sworn-Confederacy, each one with his peculiar physiognomy and different influence. There are Wittenbach, Zwingli, Capito, Heller, Œcolampadius, Oswald, Myconius, Leo Juda, Farel, Calvin, in Geneva, Zürich, Berne, Neufchatel, Glarus, Basle, Lucerne, Schaffhausen, Appenzell, Gall, Graubünden.

In the German reformation there is one chief man, and one place of honor; in Switzerland the new life divides itself according to the thousand mountains. Every valley has its awakening, every Alpine height its clearing away of cloud.*

The high valley of Einsiedeln had its, also. Its people might choose between light and darkness!—I now return to my enlightened Benedictine monks.

The valuable library of the monastery, which is strictly closed against strangers, was nevertheless

* See the History of the Reformation by Merle d'Aubigne, vol. ii., book 3.—*Author's Note.*

opened at my request, to my friend Penchaud, who wished to see the writings of some of the oldest fathers of the church in their original language.

"It is quite wrong," said the mild abbot, "that our library should not be open to all who may have an interest in its collections."

Father Brandis and Father Gallmorell gave me several books, partly with reference to Einsiedeln, and partly of a higher interest, amongst which was Möhler's celebrated work, his Apology for the Roman Catholic Doctrine. Father Gallmorell gave me a printed collection of his poems, in which there is really "*la scintella celesta.*" The learned father accompanied me to the grated door of the monastery; behind which they withdrew, taking leave with a chivalric politeness which would have perfectly become courtiers; and I fear that the pious brothers were that, rather than servants of the Gospel. If amiable kindness and courtesy, united to handsome exteriors, could have converted me to the Roman church, these monks would have converted me; but——

I spent the remainder of the afternoon partly within, and partly out of the splendid church, observing the same scene, and listening to the same Ave Marias and Pater Nosters incessantly repeated.

At vespers, a magnificent *Salve Regina* was sung in St. Meinrad's chapel, by fifty monks. The music and choristers are excellent, but the singing is without shading in its strength; it is one continued fortissimo. Late, in the twilight, I went alone to pay a farewell visit to the church. The state of things there was very peculiar. The prayers were much louder, much more violent; people shouted aloud; they were taking heaven, as it were, by storm; but the prayers were all in Latin; always the same five Pater Nosters, and three Ave Marias, in succession, repeated with a fervency and hurry, as if all power and strength consisted in the number of prayers. Bands of ten or twelve pilgrims proceeded from altar to altar, from chapel to chapel, throughout the church, kneeling and repeating at every one, a number of Pater Nosters and Aves. Many of these pilgrims, as I was assured, are deputies for others, and for a certain fee, undertake to repeat here certain prayers, and to do a little, so-called, holy business—purchase indulgences, masses, and so on. Whilst the voices of the pilgrims, amidst the increasing darkness of the church, rushed like the waves of an agitated sea, the organ peeled a tranquilizing, monotonous Amen—so sounded the accords above the prayers of the people. Such was the conclusion of the scene. It was not edifying.

Early on the following morning, we drove under a brightening sky, back to Rapperschwyl. On the road, the two friends fell into an earnest conversation on political subjects, on the Swiss Revolutions, popular education, and such like questions, which so easily lead to bitter words and coolness between friends who discover themselves to entertain different opinions. The former comrades and fellow-students of Lausanne, even they discovered that, during the long separation of eight years, they had each taken different paths on more than one topic. And each advocated his own views warmly, but with so much moderation in expression, so much friendly regard and esteem for the other, that it was a pleasure to hear. One could see that on neither side had a single shade of displeasure disturbed the cordial relationship between the friends. And more than once during this journey, it has been a pleasure to me to observe the cheerful candor, and yet delicacy at the same time, which prevailed in the intercourse between these two young men, and which I have seldom seen among men.

I have again spent two extremely interesting days in Zürich, during which I visited the beautiful promenades both in and on the outside of the town, the Botanic Gardens, and the "Weid," with its glorious amphitheatre of the Alps of Glarus and Appenzell.

I have also, during this time, made the acquaintance of several persons whom I shall gratefully remember, amongst whom, are Professor Cherbulliez, and his family; an intellectual young Mme. Lavater, who presented me with her father-in-law's works; and those four young sisters W———, handsome and highly cultivated, who came to talk to me about their father. He had educated them, and trained them to independence, freedom, and useful activity; imparting to them the treasures of his heart and mind, he had been to them, at once, a father and a brother. By the assistance of his daughters he had established an educational institute, which was one of the most flourishing in Zürich. The good father has now been dead a year, and the daughters continue the work which he began, but it seems to have lost its best pleasure for them in his removal. Bright tears filled, again and again, their beautiful eyes, as they spoke of him. There are the most beautiful flowers on his grave. One of the handsome sisters is about to be married.

"We hesitated long," they said, "before we gave our consent, but———&c." It seemed as if all the four sisters married in this one. Thus they were all one in sisterly love. Their father had taught them to be thus attached to each other. All that was good was the work of the father. Blessings on him, and on all fathers who resemble him!

Zürich has given Switzerland and the world many distinguished men, amongst whom, Gessner—a monument to whose honor, stands upon one of the tree-crowded peninsulas between the Sihl and the Limmat, which during his lifetime was his favorite promenade,—Zwingli, Pestalozzi, and Lavater, are the most generally known. Many distinguished Italian refugees also, during the period of the Reformation, added lustre to the hospitable city; amongst these, is the pious Tellicare, who, during his life of eighty years, "never experienced three days of sorrow, and not a single one of anger." A rare life!—Italian family names are borne at this day by many of the most esteemed families of Zürich.

Let me here make reference, and prefer a request to the authors of certain books which I value very highly, because no books seem to me more difficult to compile—I mean guide books. They show us the way to towns and places, and give us the names of hotels, *cafés*, and promenades. But they very seldom tell us what memorable persons, what benefactors of their country and mankind, have been born and lived in these cities. And yet, this it is, which would give to a town or locality, a higher rank, and a more enduring memory on earth, than cathedrals, and battles, and which are more interesting to travelers with hearts, and heads, than information about the best hotels, and places of amusement. We implore for a little space for the great men in these guide books, which now constitute a peculiar branch of literature, and which no traveler can dispense with! For the want of such a chapter in my "Bradshaw," I stumble about in uncertainty, regarding these the Swiss Cantons' highest ornaments, and am quite certain, in consequence, to commit more than one oversight, more than one mistake.

Few countries on the face of the earth, ought to be richer in these, the noblest product of public life, than little Switzerland; few have given to the world so many great citizens. Is not this principally the effect of its federative states culture?—of the many central points around which public life groups itself, at the same time that all possess a common unity and a common object, for which one and all work in freedom, conformably with their genius and their power? Thus every Canton and its chief town may produce its highest human fruit. The Cantons of the Confederation appear to me to be, in their constitution, a type of all other great nations and confederate states in the world.

I have felt myself happy in Zürich, from the spirit of fresh spring-life which I could there perceive permeating the realm of heart and mind. The Ygdrasil of human life (the world's tree) shoots out vigorously in every direction, and thus it grows towards heaven, nay, in heaven!

And now let me utter a thanksgiving and a blessing upon the home into which I was received as a sister and a friend; that home in which long and bitter sorrow was overcome by many prayers and much work, and where much daily work did not prevent the most noble and delicate hospitality being shown to the stranger, nor the amenities and attractive pleasures of life being obtained for her. Let me, from my heart, thank the mother and sisters Rohrdorf!

The bright river which flows past their handsome, old-fashioned dwelling, and the sunshine in its waters are faithful images of my life during those days and in that home!

BASLE, *September 12th.*—Arrived here at eleven o'clock at night, and was miserably accommodated at the "Wildman," where the young "wildmen," the waiters, seemed to think that people came thither for their sakes and to obey their laws.

I parted in Zürich with my good friend and traveling companion, Penchaud, who returned home, whilst I bent my steps towards Germany. I was accompanied on the railway by my young friend Louisa Rohrdorf, as far as Baden, in the warm sulphur baths of which place ten thousand persons annually bathe. Here I parted from the amiable and lovely young lady, one of the most beautiful examples amongst the many, confined by a life of material labor, who courageously and patiently battle through the long weeks of labor without a complaint, whilst they secretly lift tearful, longing glances towards a life of thought, of soul-enjoyment, and activity to which they believe they can never attain!

There are, even in Switzerland, many such sufferers. This ought not to be the case there.

It was at Baden that the former princes of Hapsburg had their residence; and the ruins of their stronghold still elevate themselves above the town. It was here that the cruel Queen Agnes committed her atrocities to revenge the murder of her husband, King Albrecht; here where the wife of the innocent Von Wart knelt and prayed the pitiless woman, " by God's mercy at the Last Day!" to forgive him. For three days and three nights Von der Wart lay upon the rack; for three days and three nights his wife stood by his side, enduring his torture with him. He died asserting his innocence, and she, barefooted, went to Basle, where she died of a broken heart. Not far from this place is the great Convent of Königsfelden which was erected by Queen Agnes, and where, after having committed her wholesale murders, she lived, making pretensions to the honor of sainthood. For such saints there must be a reward in—hell.

At the town of Brugg, the Aar, the Reuss, and the Limmat unite their waters. The district is beautiful, and abounds with historical memories. The road runs through the Canton Argovie. It was with a melancholy feeling that I followed the course of the Aar through the fields. It flows broad and heavy, with sandy islands and banks, through green valleys, no longer resembling the rushing, living stream which I had beheld in its childhood, near its glacier cradle, and from whose waves I derived new vigor; now it was aged and weary, and allowed itself to go carelessly onward towards its change. Had it any presentiment that it went on at the same time towards a higher change, a greater history? It did not appear as if it had. My eye followed it with regret upon its tedious last journey, till it was hidden from view by a mountain.

Towards evening, I was driving along the banks of a mighty river, the cheerful waters of which flowed calmly through a flourishing region. It was the Rhine, now enriched with the Aar, the Reuss, and the Limmat, forever renewed from their sources in the Alps and the Jura. A glowing evening crimson-flushed the distant country towards which the mighty stream was flowing, and towards which I was journeying by its side.

I saluted it again with joy at Basle.

Basle has many great memories, and amongst these various noble and distinguished individuals. Œcolampadius and Erasmus lived and taught here. The noble Italian refugees and friends of the Reformation, Olympia Morata, from Ferrara, distinguished by birth, learning, and the noblest character, Curione and his daughters, found here an asylum.

The chief honor to Basle at this moment, appeared to me to be the publisher of the monthly journal, "Protestantische Blätter," Dr. Heinrich Geltzer, and this periodical itself, with its liberal and comprehensive spirit, as well as the great Missionary Institute, which makes this city a centre of missionary activity, not alone in Switzerland, but in Protestant Germany. Here the men intending to become missionaries are prepared to preach the Gospel to "all people and to all creatures." Here, again, they are assembled at the great missionary festivals, and together with them the societies and persons who take part in the great work,—the former to render up their accounts, the latter to hear and advise.

Two years ago, there was a want of means for the institute and its labors. The difficulty was laid before the people of the Protestant Cantons. It was proposed that every man and woman should give a "sous" towards the good work. Sixty thousand francs were sent into the missionary fund that year, by these means, and the same sum has been continued annually, since.

In M. Josenhaus, the Superintendent of the institution, I became acquainted with a remarkable and very unusual person. Such ought the peaceful champion of the kingdom of God upon earth to appear; thus ought he to speak, and thus to be penetrated by the feeling of no more belonging to himself, but to the work to which he has been called. Thus decided, thus steadfast, yet at the same time mild and cheerful, ought the man to be who, with undeviating firmness, must prepare young men for the fight of life or death, which is the vocation of the missionary, especially in the regions whither they are generally sent from here. A row of black crosses stands already on the coast of Guinea, and testifies of the dangers which there meet the preacher of the gospel; and yet fresh candidates are continually offering themselves.

The best and most persevering disciples come from the agricultural classes. As soon as they have overcome the first difficulties in their studies, these sons of the soil advance steadily. Youth of a higher grade, accustomed to a more delicate mode of life, can seldom long stand the hardships which they have to endure, and the relinquishment of all the conveniences of life. M. Josenhaus believes that women would be of great service in missionary labor, especially for the women and children, and in the education of youth. But they ought, in that case, to be sent out in little companies, of from four to six, under a superintendent.

The period of instruction, in the Missionary Institute, is usually five or six years. Mr. Josenhaus was now occupied with the formation of an alphabet which should serve for the instruction of all races of heathen and savage people. The impression which my intercourse with him produced upon my mind, was peculiar and profound. I never before felt myself so humble, and so insignificant. I felt ready to weep because I was no longer young, and could not enter upon this path, under the guidance of this man! Otherwise, I would have done it. God did not will that it should be so!

Six young men were now ready to go hence, to the deathly coast of Africa. Three of these go as missionaries proper, the other three as their assistants. Their portmanteaus were packed; their knapsacks buckled; every thing was ready, and on this day they were to set out. They seemed thoroughly equipped, both soul and body. One of them, a young man of thirty, struck me by the deep earnestness, and at the same time the cheerfulness, of his expression. To him might have been applied the words of

THE MISSONARIE'S CALL.

"My soul is not at rest. There comes a strange and secret whisper to my spirit, like a dream of night, that tells me I am on enchanted ground.

"Why live I here? The vows of God are on me, and I may not stop to play with shadows, or pluck earthly flowers, till I my work have done, and rendered up account.

"And I will go. I may no longer doubt to give up friends, and idle hopes, and every tie that binds my heart to theé, my country.

"Henceforth, then, it matters not if storm or sunshine be my earthly lot. Bitter or sweet my cup. I only pray God make me holy, and my spirit nerve for the stern hour of strife.

"And when I come to stretch me for the last, in unattended agony, beneath the palm's green shade, it will be sweet that I have toiled for other worlds than this.

"And if one for whom Satan hath struggled, as he hath for me, should ever reach that blessed shore, oh, how my heart will glow with gratitude and love.

"The voice of my beloved Lord, 'Go teach all nations,' comes in the night, and awakes mine ear. Through ages of eternal years, my spirit never shall repent, that toil and suffering once were mine below."

(*Aside to the Reader.*)

They tell me, my R——, that at the present moment you do not care much about Switzerland; that all your interest is devoted to Italy, and that I must hasten to conduct you thither. I would gladly oblige you in this respect, for I myself long to go there; but I must beseech of you to have patience with me yet a moment, and to hear what I have to tell you about Switzerland, and you will then acknowledge that the contemplation of the life and condition of a Confederate State of high development, is not unnecessary for the forming a correct judgment on one which is strong, after such a state of development; in a word, the perfect knowledge of life in Switzerland affords an insight into the Italian question, in its deepest significance—*the human.*

And do not all the higher political questions of the present time—and a great and glorious time it is, nor would I willingly have lived during any other—tend in all their bearings to the question:

Under what form of government can human and social life attain to its noblest and fullest prosperity?

A state which approaches to this condition, may serve as a model for one which is endeavoring after it.

The highest well-being to the people is also the people's highest and most sacred right.

Therefore, my R———, if you love Italy, and its young, freedom-seeking life, do not object to spend yet a few moments with me in contemplating life in the country where its noblest refugees have, in bloody and dark times, found an asylum against persecution, where they last breathed the air of freedom and learned the laws of self-government.

For this purpose, I will henceforth contract my copious journal to the notice of a few essential data, and advance with seven-mile steps through countries and times till I shall have scaled the Alps and descended to the soil of Piedmont, rich in promise.

The sun-illumined heights of Monte Rosa are not alone the points of union for the eye to glance over the valleys of Switzerland and Piedmont. Higher interests, more elevated heights, illumined by a never-setting sun, unite them and—all peoples.

ALBENS, *January* 1860.

FOURTH STATION.

From Basle to Brussels—That which took me there—Le Congrès International de Bienfaisance—The New Exposition—Conversation with King Leopold—"The Little Sisters of the Poor"—Festivals and Ideas of the Future in Belgium—Ghent and the Beguines—Lace Making—Bruges—Flanders—A House in the Country—Ruysselede and Bernhem — Antwerp—Rubens' House—A Glance at Holland—A Statesman—Journey to Paris.

THE golden September sun shone gloriously over the fertile plain of the Rhinelands, and golden harvests and wealthy towns lay basking in its beams and as I flew upon the wings of steam, over land and water, from Basle to Brussels. For I wished to be at Brussels on the 14th of September, to be present at the opening of the International Congress de Bienfaisance on the day following. I had been invited to this peculiar congress, the first of its kind, by a letter from its prime mover and conductor, Edward Duepeteaux, Director-General of prisons and benevolent institutions in Belgium. This invitation had reached me, indeed, before I left Sweden, and I then determined to obey the call. I had never received a more agreeable, and more valuable invitation. I should thus, in Brussels, hear, from deputies sent from the christian kingdoms of every part of the world, what was doing, and had already been done for the prevention of crime and the alleviation of distress, hear them consulting together as to what ought to be done in the future for this purpose. No wonder, therefore, that the impulse of my mind emulated the power of steam, in attracting me to Brussels.

I arrived there punctually on the afternoon of the 14th. On the same evening I saw Edward Duepetiaux, a man who in manner and expression of countenance possesses the peculiar combination of energy and gentleness, of the lion and the lamb, which I have seen only in one other man—our great Geijer. From the first moment I felt confidence in him as a brother. We met for the first time as though we had known each other all our days.

On the 15th of September, the Congress de Bienfaisance was opened, the first Congress on earth in which human love and science stood, before all nations, hand in hand for the same openly declared object—the best interests of the poor, with especial reference to their earthly life; and which, therefore, deserved the foremost place in the annals of the human race. Because, whilst it may be important for the regulation of outward, temporal affairs, to divide and arrange realms and peoples under certain princes and rulers, all this signifies but little or nothing to the inner development, to the well-being of the community.

The sittings of the Congress continued nearly a week, during which time, you heard—England and France, Germany, Italy, Switzerland, Holland, the Scandinavian Kingdoms, the United States, Brazil, Algeria, and Poland, state their various experiments, and explain their various institutions for the elevation of the working classes, and the improvement of their condition.

A Congress very similar to this had, the preceding year, been held in Paris, to inquire into the same class of subjects, though principally in connection with the moral means of influence, as education, literature, benevolent societies, and such like. The Congress of the Brussels people had boldly confined itself to the material means. It occupied itself with the dwellings of the poorer classes, their clothing, food, prospects of worldly success, as well at the present time, as for the future; but above all, with the establishment of such an order of things as should enable every man and every woman, by good conduct, industry, and forethought, to enjoy and secure worldly prosperity for themselves and their families. The chief activity of the Congress was evidently employed in this direction, although, as it seemed to me, not with full consciousness.* Soup-kitchens, hospitals, and such institutions,

---

* As I gave a very full report of this Congress, at the time, in an article which was published in the Stockholm Aftonblad, during the autumn of 1856, which was translated into various languages, I shall, therefore, here only touch upon a few of its principal traits.—*Author's Note.*

fell into the background; whilst in the foreground, newer and more thoroughly comprehensive labors for the health of towns, for the improvement of the dwellings and workshops of the poor; Savings' Banks, and Societies, the members of which could provide and insure for themselves, an improvement in circumstances with others, which plans belonged to health and an ameliorated worldly condition.

In the first chapter England stood foremost; in the second, it seemed to me that France, and especially Alsace, set a great and beautiful example. Most highly interesting to me, were the accounts of the working towns round Mulhausen, as well as the institutions established by many great manufacturers for their working people. Among these, one in Lisle was remarkable. The so-called "Associations Alimentaires," which, commencing in Grenoble in France, have spread themselves through the towns, both of Switzerland and Holland, seem to be in the highest degree important, as well for the wholesome nourishment with which it supplies the poor, as in teaching them the advantage of union amongst men. Little Holland seemed to me rich in such seed for the future, whilst Italy boasted principally of her establishments for the care of the poor. Nor was Poland behindhand in labors for the good of the people, and proved—like her latest, noble poet—that the politically unenfranchised people, may yet, if they will, take a noble place in the development of the moral freedom of humanity.

The highest importance of a Congress like the present, ought to be the initiative which it gives to these great questions of human improvement amongst all nations, and the greater enlightenment and more perfectly organized activity which it must lead to, especially if, as Mr. Duepetiaux asserts, they will be of more frequent occurrence in different parts of Europe. And when, conformably with the resolution of this Congress, committees shall be established in all countries, the object of which will be these especial topics, and which will keep up a constant interchange of communication upon them from land to land, then, surely, popular progress in the right direction will be easy and sure.

In this Congress of representatives from so many various peoples, there was no lack of distinguished individuals, who represented nations as well as ideas. Englishmen, Frenchmen, Germans, Dutch and Brazilians, were in this respect interesting. The most remarkable for his beautiful individuality, was the Italian, Count Arrivabene, member of the Council of the Congress, and whose influence was especially valuable in the proceedings of the Congress. For this assembly, of about three hundred persons, was very vivacious; and conflicting opinions, misunderstandings, fermentations, and outbreaks, occurred not unfrequently, which the fatherly interference of the worthy president could not always pacify. On such occasions the Italian nobleman, whose dark eye shone brightly beneath locks growing gray, and whose furrowed cheek still preserved the glad glow of youth, stepped forth with peculiar delicacy and tact, and proposed a word, or some middle course in which the opponents could unite, or else gave some explanation which prevented the combat of words from becoming like a cockpit. Sometimes the contest between the hot-headed opponents assumed such a threatening character, that a challenge, a duel, bloodshed, and tragical ending was feared. But no! In the hour of need, Count Arrivabene stepped in with the right word or the right measure, which pacified the combatants, and his handsome person and refined manners contributed, in no small degree, to give weight to his talent for reconciliation. A Count Arrivabene ought to be found in every assembly of council. The assembly here was nevertheless composed of "gentlemen." This was proved by the fact, that a vote of thanks to the ladies, who were present at this assembly, was moved by the chivalric young representative from England. These ladies were few in number, but evidently deeply interested by the business of the meeting. I was the only lady-member of the Congress, and as some of the gentlemen of the council wished me to say something, I prepared a written address, recommending that a better education should be given to the daughters of the lower class, than had hitherto been the case. This was read by Mr. Vickier, one of the members of the Council,—well read, and attentively listened to also.

At the same time and for the same purpose as the Congress, an Exhibition was made in Brussels, of every article most necessary for the use and advantage of human life. They were here collected from many different countries, alike with reference to excellence of workmanship, and cheapness of price. From the completely-furnished dwelling of the artisan, to the smallest article which could be either useful or agreeable to its inmates, nothing was wanting. Every necessary for the kitchen, the workshop, the nursery, the sitting room, were abundantly supplied. The fine arts had contributed their share. The home of the artisan might enjoy the delights of music at a reasonable cost. Appliances were also provided for the cultivation and beautifying of the garden in one section of the Exhibition, devoted alone to every species of garden tools. For the Catholic Belgium is, as in many other respects, united to its sundered sister-state, the Protestant Holland, by its love of flowers, and the cultivation of gardens. Industry, art, and science, vied with each other in the production of whatever could ennoble the condition of the poor working man, and elevate his earthly life.

A similar display had been made at the Great Exhibition in Paris in 1855, but then merely as an adjunct to it, and in a building apart from the halls of the splendid Exhibition. Now the whole circumstances were changed. The building, separate from and inferior to the rest, had now taken the foremost place. Cinderella had become the princess. And now from all parts came hastening hither by railway, people of the working-class, to behold the new spectacle. In one day alone, it was visited by ten thousand working-people. The greater number of articles there exhibited were sold before the Exhibition was closed.

One circumstance I must mention. Amongst all the representatives from so many different countries to this Congress for the outward well-being of the poor, I did not see a single minister of the gospel.

Catholic and Protestant had here assembled for one common, great, human object, and so doing appeared to forget that any thing separated them from each other; but amongst all these Catholics and Protestants which a common love united, I did not see one of those who, in an especial manner, call themselves the servants of Christ and the gospel. They find time nevertheless to journey to all kinds of meetings which call themselves clerical and evangelical. Why do they thus altogether ignore this, as if it were not worthy of the attention of the church?

Is it not because the church—as well the Protestant as the Catholic—have an imperfect comprehension of the object, both of the gospel and the church—the kingdom of God? That it regards this principally as a condition of the individual soul, as a condition on the other side of the grave, not as that which is founded already upon the earth, a kingdom of justice, freedom, and peace, goodness and happiness for all peoples, and for which all the powers and gifts of life must unite to labor.

Happiness! I repeat and emphasize the word, in the name of the Divine Teacher, who, by word and deed, testified of God's will that all the pure fountains of earth's joy should pour forth for all men; who blessed its bread and its wine, not merely for the soul's but for the body's enjoyment and benefit. For His kingdom embraces all mankind!

But until the church comprehends this in its great significance, it must not wonder that millions of intelligent, thinking, human beings will not listen to its preaching, and that they sometimes fancy they hear a more Christian, a more evangelical doctrine in socialistic, nay, even in communistic teaching. It is only the right understanding of the true evangelical communion which can overcome the erroneous doctrines of communism.

At the Philanthropic Congress of Brussels, it was only laymen—physicians, men of science, the followers of industrial pursuits, and statesmen—who came forward as servants of the gospel, promoters of the kingdom of God! I would have wished to have seen there bishops and priests, nay, even the Pope himself. And why not: if they would be faithful to the traditions of the Christian church? At the commencement of the new community, it was the pious clergy who taught the people to cultivate the earth and to ennoble all the gifts of life. But that labor has now become considerably more difficult, and demands new studies.

One day, towards the end of the Congress, I received a written communication, purporting that King Leopold wished to make my acquaintance. I declared my readiness to obey the king's commands, and requested that his majesty would name the day and hour, which was done, and at two o'clock the following day I betook myself to the royal palace, glad to become better acquainted with a monarch who lived in profound peace with his subjects, whilst revolution shook lands and thrones around him. Besides which, King Leopold had long excited a pleasant interest in my home, where my good mother had conceived an especial affection for this prince, as well as for Queen Victoria's husband, and always liked to hear them spoken of, on which account her daughter used sometimes to teaze her a little about her "royal flames." I thought of her as I was conducted by a chamberlain into a large, light apartment, where the king came to meet me. He took my hand with friendly politeness, said that he had read all my writings, and conducted me to an arm-chair, where he bade me be seated, he himself taking a seat just opposite.

I saw in King Leopold a tall, elderly gentleman, with the bearing of a general and the manners of a gentleman, with regular features, refined and sensible expression. His majesty began the conversation by inquiries about my stay in Belgium, and my impressions of that country, but soon struck off into a statement of his system of government, which he himself characterized as that "of good sense." He considered it the highest duty of the ruler to require strict integrity in the ruling powers, as well as in all the organs of government. He was a friend of the "*laisser faire,*" the "*laisser aller,*" being convinced that a free, well-governed people can best manage its own affairs; nevertheless the ruler ought to give them also that close attention, which would enable him at any critical moment, to step in with a direct and paternal interference, even in opposition to the generally accepted principles of the "*laisser aller*" system. The king gave an example of this, when by his foresight and direct extraordinary intervention, he preserved the manufacturing world of Belgium from an extremely dangerous crisis. I could not but regard his majesty's principles as in this respect in the highest degree correct and excellent, that is to say, when the ruler is possessed of a great amount of "good sense," as well as of fatherly benevolence towards his people. But when King Leopold finally summed up the impelling motives to a life of truth and justice, to be this: "the hope of reward in heaven," I said what I thought, that it was better not to reason in this way; that virtue was depreciated by any consideration of *reward;* and in this I was right. The king smiled archly, and said good-humoredly, such reasoning was "quite too strict," and in this he was right, that is to say, if the reward be accepted in its highest sense. "You shall be where I am; you shall see my glory," says our Great Master and Teacher to his dearest disciples, in the hour of separation, as the highest consolation and the highest reward for their trouble and labor on earth. And must not also the poorest, the most unselfish of all the sons of earth live thankfully in the prospect of this highest reward; a life with the Lord and the beholding of His glory—a perfected and blessed world!——

I do not know whether King Leopold comprehended this reward in heaven in its highest significance; whether he comprehended the life of the state and of the human being according to its highest ideal; but it did not seem to me so. And where indeed is the ruler of the present day who is capable of it? To him I would bend the knee, even if he sat on the throne of Russia! It is, however, certain that the present King of Belgium is a ruler of integrity, tact and fatherly benevolence, who may be regarded by all people as a blessing, if not, in every respect, as an example.

The king, during this conversation of about three hours, which was carried on partly in French, partly in English, which he speaks with equal facility, endeavored to make me clearly understand the principles of his system of government, which I regard as a great honor to me. He recommended me to make myself acquainted with the Belgian towns, so remarkable for their strongly-marked individuality of character. He listened with kindness and attention to what I had to say. This king evidently has a quick ear, as well as a great deal of tact—important gifts these in a ruler.

The people of Belgium have shown at this time, that they know how to value their king. A great number of brilliant festivals have lately been held in all the cities of the realm, to celebrate the twenty-fifth year of his reign. One of the most beautiful and most important of these, was given a few days since, in Brussels. On the spot where it was held, the foundations are now being laid of an immense monument, in which four symbolic figures, representing Popular Freedom, Freedom of Conscience, Freedom of Law, and Freedom of Trade, are to be grouped round the statue of King Leopold. A throne defended by these liberties, is a great thought, peculiar to the present age.

During my stay at Brussels, all kinds of festivals and meetings of many kinds were going on, partly in connection with the royal jubilee, and partly with the Philanthropic Congress and the Exhibition. Again and again you heard the gay and lively national melody " *la Brabançonne* " which generally announced the arrival of the Duke of Brabant, King Leopold's eldest son, for he himself was very seldom present. But people were very glad to see his youthful son, whose ingenuous manners, and handsome and agreeable countenance, produced, when he spoke or smiled, a pleasant impression. The young duchess, his wife, is a pretty blonde, very fair, with a full figure and an expression of life-enjoyment. The younger of the king's sons was absent on a hunting party.

Brussels sits like a holiday-attired princess, proud and elegant, on the table-land of Brabant, gazing out freely, on all sides, over flourishing, fertile fields. The new portion of the city, with its royal palace, its beautiful park and tree-planted boulevards, broad streets, large market-place, handsome, well-built houses, produced the most cheerful effect. Cleanliness and elegance prevail everywhere. Wealth and elegance are united with a certain character of permanence and strength. We are in the head-quarters of Brussels lace. But, nevertheless, one dark trait pervades it— the pale, ragged, begging children! Why should this exist in a city, and in a nation which has so lately rejoiced exultantly in being one of the best-governed in the world? It is asserted that the burgomaster of Brussels favors beggary, as a privilege of a Catholic country! In the old city one admires the proud buildings of the ancient time, the Stadthouse, the Cathedral, the house of Egmont, in the market-place, where he and Horn were beheaded. These, and many private houses, are built in a peculiar and old-fashioned style, yet they scarcely appear old, because they are kept in such careful repair. The memory of the cruelty of Philip and of Alba, and of the tragical deaths of their victims, give a gloomy interest to this portion of the city. But one thinks with joy at the same time, that the murderous powers of Spain and of the Inquisition are at an end.

Und seine Albas sind nicht mehr !*

Little Netherland has, in its fight for freedom, destroyed their dominion, and although one portion, Belgium, still continues faithful to the Catholic church, yet has this portion maintained the most precious of its liberties, which her sister-state of Holland also acquired by a long and bloody war.

I will now say a few words about a sight in Brussels, which delighted me more than all its palaces and parks. I saw, one day, above a hundred old people of both sexes,—the men on their side, the women on theirs,—in a handsome and spacious building, cared for and waited upon by nice-looking young girls, like aged parents by their daughters. These young girls belong to an order which was established a few years ago, and which, at this moment, is greatly on the increase; it is called "*les petites sœurs des pauvres.*"

In a little seaport town of France, lived, some years ago, a good clergyman, who had deep sympathy with old seamen, and the widows of such, who, feeble and decrepit, obtained a wretched livelihood by begging, and so doing, fell into still deeper misery, both of soul and body. He communicated his feelings to two young girls, who, both orphans, maintained themselves by the labor of their hands, and prevailed upon them

---

* Schiller, in *Don Carlos.*

to adopt these poor, neglected, old people—first one, then two, then several, of the most forlorn. The blessing of God rested upon their work. The old people rewarded their young benefactors by a renewed life, as it were, both of soul and body, as well as by the most heart-felt gratitude. A larger room was obliged to be hired for the old people, who placed themselves under the protection of the young.

The next step which the good pastor induced his young disciples to take was, to go out themselves to beg for the old, from the fear that if these returned to their former life of beggary, they might relapse into their former life of sin. This step was the most difficult of all to the young. But they took even this courageously, when they were convinced of its necessity, to complete the good work. They went, with a basket on their arms, from door to door. They had to encounter, at first, derision, hard language, and petty ridicule; but when they endured all with great patience, and continued to persevere in the spirit of self-sacrificing love, the derision was changed into admiration, and the hard language into gifts, and a more and more liberal feeling towards the object of their labors.

The good clergyman now began to extend the sphere of these labors. The number of "the little sisters" had, in the mean time, considerably increased, and he now sent them into various of the French towns,—Rouen, Toulon, Lyons, Paris. They went by twos or fours, and always began by hiring a couple of poor rooms, and purchasing some bedding. They then went out into the streets and lanes, and gathered together the most miserable and neglected old people; after which, they went forth to beg for them. In almost every case, their experience was the same,— first derision, scorn, and opprobrium, then attention, admiration, and the most cheerful assistance. The huckster women in the markets considered it as a right that "the little sisters," who were out collecting, should come to their stands, and if they passed without so doing, felt themselves ill-used. In many large houses and hotels, "the little sisters" were ordered to call on certain days in the week, to receive such provision as had been put aside for their old *protegés*. And the number of these, and the excellent places for their reception, increased everywhere; so also did the numbers of the "little sisters." And there was need. The first had already broken down under the diseases which they had contracted in their life of fatigue and self-sacrifice. And the lives of "the little sisters" had unremitting and great trials, but neither money, nor rank, nor family circumstances, were required to give consequence to the order of "The Little Sisters of the Poor." All that was wanted, was merely warm hearts, pious minds, willing hands, and good health. Many, therefore, came out of the homes of the poor themselves, from the crowded work-rooms of the needle-women, from the slippery saloons of the ballet, and from scenes more dangerous still, and became "little sisters of the poor," and themselves began a new life, by assisting the aged to close their lives well. Young girls even came from the higher grades of society, to unite themselves to these other youthful servants of their Lord.

It is now two years since "the little sisters" first made their appearance in Brussels. They followed their usual system: provided, in the first place, a room for the old, and after that, one for themselves. And great were their sufferings, during the first year, in a couple of small attics, where they were baked in summer, and frozen in the winter. The city authorities, together with several kind-hearted citizens, who knew the excellence and generally beneficial effect of their labors, were filled with compassion for them, purchased a large house and garden, and made a present of them to "the little sisters," and their poor, old people. This they have now occupied for several months; the number of the aged inmates has increased to a hundred, and "the little sisters" to ten. Amongst these, there is now a young lady from one of the best families in Brussels. She had long hesitated about becoming one of "the little sisters," from the fear of being elected a *sœur guêteuse*, (a begging sister,) for whose labors she felt a great repugnance. She was able, however, to withstand the inward impulse: she entered into the order of "the little sisterhood," and became—that which she dreaded—nominated immediately as one of the begging sisters. Her pleasing appearance, her retiring and refined manners, peculiarly qualified her to excite general good-will, and now she went forth daily upon this, for her, difficult work. Soon, however, it ceased to be so very difficult. People knew her, and the object for which she appeared amongst them.

I had already been told all this by Madame Duepetiaux, when one day I saw from the window of my excellent hotel, "The Windsor," a little low carriage, drawn by a donkey, standing before the door, with the words *"petits sœurs des pauvres,"* printed upon the linen covering, which was stretched upon bows over the carriage. A young girl, dressed in a costume similar to that worn by the French Sisters of Charity, stepped lightly from the little vehicle, and entered the hotel. I hastened down, certain that she was precisely "the little sister" whose history I knew. I found her sitting silently, waiting by the door, in a large saloon. No one could imagine a more pleasing exterior, a more modest, or more attractive demeanor. Her call at the hotel that day was expected, and a subscription had been made there, preparatory to it. Her silent presence sufficed as prayer and admonition, and her little donkey went away, no doubt, heavily-laden for the aged.

The following day, I visited them in their new home, and during their hour of dinner. They were seated at a well-arranged table, clean in their own persons, and well-dressed. The meal consisted of substantial and savoury beef-soup, veal, and boiled rice; and each person had a good glass of beer. The little sisters waited upon them; and every thing was done with perfect order and quietness. I went round the old women's table, and asked various of them, how they were satisfied? "Tolerably," replied some, with an air of condescension; several, that they were very well content: "that they had not any thing to complain about," and so on. But when they spoke of the little sisters, their mode of expression became warmer and more heart-felt. The men seemed, upon the whole, to be more grateful. An old man is more forlorn in his loneliness than a woman in the same circumstances.

In the sick-room, which was remarkable for its order and excellent arrangement, I saw an old woman quietly expiring, whilst two little sisters, who reminded me of consoling angels, stood watchfully, the one at her head, the other at her feet.

The preceding day, they had celebrated the hundredth birthday of a good old woman, had decorated her arm-chair with flowers, and carried her with songs, round the garden. She had been honored like a beloved grandmother in a large family. Thus, do the amiable little sisters, "devote themselves to the forsaken old people." They make them happy, and if possible—good. They have to encounter many disagreeables and difficulties, from the tempers, peculiarities, and bad habits of the old-folks. But they are able to overcome all by patience, piety, and good-humor. For this, youth and Christianity, are needed. The little sisters are possessed of these, and they, as well as the good work itself, are the talismen of their progress. May it go onward into eternity, and whilst it lifts the aged out of the filth of life, may it also prevent many of the young from sinking into it. For in this new, daughterly calling, they are consecrated as servants of the Lord; the greatest calling in the world, under whatever circumstances it may be carried out.

After a week spent at the Hotel Windsor, I removed to the beautiful home of the Duepetiaux's. And when the Congress, the Exhibition, and the festivals which these led to, were over, I set off in company with these amiable friends, to visit some of the remarkable towns and places of Belgium.

First of Ghent.

In Ghent, it was so rainy, that I could see nothing of the exterior of this celebrated old city, excepting the many bridges and canals, over which we drove. Of the interior, I saw the library, as well as various orphanages, or educational institutions for fatherless and motherless children, as well as poor girls. These are under the care of nuns; the girls are employed in lace-making, in which they acquire great skill. I had visited such institutions also in Brussels, and there, as in Ghent, had seen their costly labors; had seen small pocket-handkerchiefs, which cost each from five to seven hundred francs—and which seemed to me more suitable for the noses of angels than for those of human beings—small collars, which cost from two to three hundred, and so on. However wondrously beautiful this work may be, yet I cannot feel glad that this branch of industry is so universal amongst the female population of Belgium, and I believe that it is neither beneficial nor healthy in any respect. I received in Brussels, a well-written anonymous letter, which warned me not to judge of these lace-making, educational institutions, according to their outward seeming, assuring me that "the greater number of the young girls brought up in them, gave themselves up, on leaving them, to an immoral and dissolute way of life." I have not much faith in anonymous letters, nor in those who write them; still it seems to me more than probable, that the long-continued sedentary employment of lace making, must be injurious to the development of the young girls, both of soul and body; and also that the Catholic mode of religious education, which holds the young in a perpetual custody, and destroys every sentiment of freedom and self responsibility, must, in many cases, lead to the abuse of their late-acquired freedom, and to that immorality, which, sad to say, is one of the distinguishing features of Belgium, and which threatens its future.

In the library of Ghent, I saw—besides the backs of about one hundred thousand volumes—a sight which always takes away my breath, as it were,—a very beautiful picture of Maria of Burgundy, representing her at the moment when she rushed down from her palace, into the market-place, and endeavored to save the lives of some of her councilors and friends. She arrived too late—at the very moment when their heads fell beneath the ax. The figure of the youthful princess is one of the most touching pathos and beauty. So is also her memory, "which," says an historian, "came after that of her father, Charles the Bold, as the gentle spring after a severe and stormy winter." She tasted abundantly of the hardness and bitterness of life, as she did also afterwards of its pleasantness in the bosom of affection, and under both circumstances she remained the same excellent, noble woman, beloved in all respects. And thus she died in the bloom of her age, after having given birth to a son, who was the father of the Emperor Charles V.

We paid a visit one day to "le Grand Bèguignage," an institution founded five hundred years ago, by an illustrious lady, who afterwards received canonization, under the name of "St. Bèque," and who was its first "*Grande Dame.*" Even to this day, the establishment is governed by a superintendent, who is called "*la Grande Dame.*" She was, at the present time, a lady of noble demeanor, of frank and agreeable manners. About three hundred unmarried ladies live in this institution. A vast number of separate houses are built together, like a castle-wall, around a very large court, which may be closed. Some beautiful trees grow in the court, in the centre of which stands the Bèguine church. According to the rule of St. Bèque, which "*la Grande Dame*" steadfastly maintains, the members of the institution must attend the church three times a day. They were there at the time we made our visit, and thither we also went.

A couple of hundred figures were seated in the large white-washed church, wrapped in large, white dresses, producing an effect as if they were made of ice. Immovable, and all, as it were, shaped in the same mould, they sate on their benches in rows,—all bowed towards the altar. The sight produced an icy effect upon me, which the singing of a remarkably pure and beautiful female voice (the only voice which was raised during this divine service,) was not able to melt. And perhaps this same feeling influenced my impression of the whole establishment, which, nevertheless, has many good points, and where we met with more than one educated and kindly-disposed person.

The private rooms and the common halls were all of the same character. Order and cleanliness prevailed; but of comfort and beauty, there seemed to be none—nothing of that which is so well expressed by the untranslatable German word "*gemüthlichkeit*," and which may be found even in the poorest cottage. In order to live happily in such rooms as these, one must have some great soul-vitalizing object out of them. But this exists not in the Bèguignage. Every one who enters them may, indeed, renounce all personal luxury, and all outward worldliness, but yet may, at the same time, live merely for themselves, or for their friends.

Many of the individuals now there worked together in warm rooms. Most of those with whom I conversed appeared to have no cause of complaint. But sunshine was wanting as much within as without the house.

It cannot be denied that a well-ordered, large establishment, in which people can live comfortably, although frugally, at a reasonable cost, and have retirement and intercourse, just as they like, supplies a want in social life for many lonely individuals. But, I could never become enthusiastic about this; and if ever I were tempted to enter into a Catholic society, it would not be the Bèguignage.

From Ghent we went to Bruges. Bruges stands like a falling monument of ancient greatness. The city,—the population of which amounted, in the time of Louis XI., to four hundred thousand persons, does not now exceed forty thousand; of which, one half are said to require support. There are handsome streets and palaces, but they are empty and desolate. Bruges, they say, is sick, Bruges is dying, because Bruges has no longer any staple branch of industry which can sustain her life. Its small lace-making trade scarcely pays its own labor. The Abbé Curtou's excellent institution for the blind, deaf and dumb, and this man's amiable individuality, were, together with some portraits of Charles the Bold, and his gentle daughter—in whose countenance one can yet recognize that of the father—were all that appeared to me most worthy of attention in Bruges.

We sped across the fields of Flanders towards our private home, and towards two large colonies of children, Ruysselede and Bernhem. These were the especial objects of this portion of our journey. The wind blew soft, yet fresh, from the sea-side, across the wide fields, now covered with succulent and verdant vegetation, (colza, turnips, and such-like,) and rustled in the bending tops of the poplar trees in the long avenues which extended themselves endlessly through the country. Small, prosperous farms rose here and there, with thatched roofs, upon the fertile land, like its most well-favored productions; and here and there, also, stood forth an old mansion, with moats and towers, and a look of the middle ages. A fresh minor key prevailed in the air and the landscape, which had for me a peculiar, foreign charm. I seemed to myself never to have been more agreeably affected by outward objects. The novelty of the scene, the open views, the softly-waving fields, were refreshing, after the lofty hills and deep valleys of the Alpine land. Earth and man seemed here to grow fat together in a great quietness. So, also, it seemed to me, in the beautiful mansion of Oestkamp, where I and my friends spent some days in the family of Baron de Peers, the brother-in-law of M. Duepetiaux.

I had here the pleasure of witnessing the higher

Flemish domestic life, in its rural beauty and grace. The excellent master of the house, the active agriculturist and patriot, at the same time; the clever and amiable lady of the house; the happy children, dividing their time between studies, rural labors, and pleasures; and the happy domestic animals, which grazed fearlessly in the green meadows around the mansion—an old castle of the ancient times;—daily life in the cheerful family circle, familiar intercourse, mealtimes, the beautiful prints,—all presented a picture of prosperity and happiness, more beautiful and more perfect, than any by the great Flemish masters.

The two families set out from Oestkamp one fine morning, to visit the agricultural colonies for neglected children—Ruysselede and Bernhem. As I have already described at large these institutions, in a separate article, I will not here go further into the subject, but merely express the wish that they should be visited by all persons who have an interest in establishments of this class, for the children there appear to me to be placed in the best possible circumstances, for the complete development both of soul and body, more especially at Ruysselede, the colony of boys. The peculiar part which is assigned to music at this place, deserves especial notice; for its enlivening notes do not alone give the signal for all the divisions of the day, and its several occupations, signals for the boys marching in and marching out, but it also constitutes a reward for their good behavior. Every boy who conducts himself well, is permitted to learn music, and besides that, to select the instrument on which he would like to play. We were regaled, during dinner, with table-music by these boys, which could scarcely have been better performed by a well-trained military band.

In the girl's colony at Bernhem, on the contrary, I lacked altogether the salutary encouragement to good behavior which the rich gifts of the fine arts introduce into it; and moreover, drawing seems to furnish a seed of intellectual culture especially suitable for girls, and calculated to develope them, in more than one respect, for a higher class of social life.

People have said, and still say, a great deal against asylums for the neglected rising generation; and certainly it would be well if they were not required, if the careful training of the child could be safely left to families, or to the private home; but are there not times, in most countries, where, through former neglect, the number of innocent, friendless children, becomes frightfully great? It was so in Belgium, when, immediately after the February revolution in Paris, Duepetiaux obtained the consent of the Belgian Chamber to the establishment of these two asylums, the design of which he had long entertained. The prisons and poor-houses of the country, at that period, contained about twenty thousand poor children. On occasions of this kind, the asylum stands forth like the "holy grove," on the mountains of Switzerland. It breaks the fall of the increasing avalanche, which, when scattered in many directions, and melted by the sunbeams, becomes transformed into fertilizing brooks and rivers.

The glowing sunset smiled, in the softest rosy light, over the landscape, as we drove home, whilst the mist spread its soft, white vail, around the bright green wood. Every thing promised us a beautiful morrow. It shone upon our journey to

ANTWERP, *October 9th.*—At Antwerp, I was entertained in the former house and home of Rubens,—the relatives of Madame Duepetiaux receiving us with the greatest hospitality. The life-enjoyable, artistic home, with all its wealth of color, and where still many well-preserved pictures and ornaments bear witness to his taste, is inhabited at the present time by a young couple, so handsome and so loveable, that Rubens, had he seen them, would have seized upon his pencil, or have—flung it away.

The Museum of Antwerp, which contains many of the greatest masterpieces of the Flemish school, deserves to be frequently visited by all lovers of art. It furnished me with some hours of rich enjoyment. One painting, "The Adoration of the Three Kings," of which I have never seen any engraving, has, more than any other picture of Rubens, given me an understanding of his genius.

The harbor of Antwerp, the river Scheldt, which here, near the sea, is broad, and brings up into the city ships from all parts of the world, now landing on the quays their manifold lading, and the great emigrant ships, carrying out the superabundant population of Europe, to the still unpeopled, and affluent plains, of the New World, present a scene full of animation. The most remarkable object in Antwerp, however, is its Cathedral-tower, which elevates itself above the ancient church, like a crown of crystallized lace, light and airy, rising to a dizzy height towards heaven. This is the highest triumph of lace-making.

Across the broad quays, alongside the harbor, you see low, green fields, extending on the other side of the river, far, far into the distance. The tall reeds bend before the winds, as if they were beckoning into Holland. My heart and my inclination attracts me thither, because no one of the newer states of Europe has a nobler history, and no one, perhaps, at the present day, has preserved more unchanged the peculiarity of its popular life, manners, and costume. Neither had friendly voices been wanting, at the Congress, which called me thither, and made me conscious that the friend of humanity might find there, now, much to learn. I must now, however, content myself with pausing upon the strand, and thence saluting the good little country, with a glance of esteem and heart-felt acknowledgment.

It was a long and bloody struggle for religion and liberty of conscience, against Spain, at that time in the height of her power, that Holland grew great and free. She won in the struggle at the same time that the mighty Spain lost her power and sunk—and has sunk ever since—whilst the little Netherland ascended from the waves, a new creation, a new revelation of beauty and power in the eye of day. She grew in dominion on the sea, in dominion in the realms of art and science; in outward power; in inward wealth. She planted with beautiful flowers her soil, lately bathed with the blood of battles, and in the peace of her flower-gardens, gave an asylum to foreigners from other lands persecuted for religion and freedom of thought. And profound labors of the human mind sprung up on its free soil, as its noblest flowers.

It was in the gardens of Haarlem, that Linnæus grew great, under the fatherly care of Boerhave. Sweden did not understand her great son. Boerhave recognized his genius. Upon his death-bed, when the grateful disciple kissed his hand with tears, Boerhave drew his to his lips and said; "My dear Linnæus, it is I who ought to kiss your hand, because you will do more for science than I; you will become a new light to it!"———

May heaven smile above thee, thou good, little country; nurse of great men; keeper, at the present time, of the noblest treasures of humanity. I am now not able to tread thy free, peace-illumined soil—perhaps another time!

Yet once again, I returned to Brussels and to the beautiful home of my friends. I left it, grateful to have made the acquaintance of a married pair who belong to the affectionate and happy of earth; as well as in M. Duepetiaux, a statesman deeply imbued with a grand human idea.

"Labor for the elevation of the poorer classes in every respect!" were his last words to me at the moment of parting. "Believe me, this is the most important of all our undertakings. I have thought much, I have experimented and attempted much, in questions for the well-being of society, but I have never found any thing more momentous than this. It is not alone the duty of the Christian, it is at the same time the highest state-wisdom!"

Words these, worthy of observation, as coming from

a man, who has been for many years, Director of Prisons, and Philanthropic Institutions, in one of the constitutional, self-governed realms of Europe.

The next Philanthropic Congress, is fixed for the autumn of next year, and is to be held at Frankfort.

On the 12th of October, I traveled by railway, in six hours, from Brussels to Paris.

Amongst the passengers in the carriage, in which I traveled, was a military-looking man, with a light-haired little girl of three years old, upon his knee. The little one seemed to like making excursions in the carriage. A lively young Frenchman, who sat opposite me, took possession of her, and decked her out fantastically with flowers, in which business I assisted; the little one submitting to it all, casting every now and then a glance at her father, as if to say, "What do you say, what do you think now?" to which he did not fail to reply with looks of the utmost amazement. Finally, we sent the little one, like an animated bush of flowers, to her father, who clasped her, delighted, flowers and all, to his bosom.—Ever young, ever delightful relationship!—Eternal spring-time of humanity!

FIFTH STATION.

Paris at the present time, and Paris thirty years ago—Prado—Valentino—"La Salpétriére."—The Evangelical Church—The Deaconess-Institution—"Revue Chrétienne"—Statue of Joan d'Arc—An Attic and a Happy Couple—The Emperor and France.

In Paris I will, first and foremost, pay my respects to a young, new-married couple, and there see a little of Parisian life. I shall first speak of the last.

It was now more than thirty years since I first saw Paris, and, with my family, spent half a year there. We were in company, father, mother, six children, and a Swedish servant; now, I was here alone. But how well I remember that time, our family circle like a little Scandinavian vessel tossed on the tempestuous sea of Parisian life, and half wrecked by it; remember our hired servant "Clair," an ultra Buonapartist, who piloted us through it, and who used, on every occasion of want or need, to say in a low but significant voice, "*du temps de l'Empereur !*" in whose time every thing was so different, and in his opinion so much better.

This time was then past, Louis XVIII. sat upon his father's throne, and it was then the epoch called "La Restauration."

The old Parisian life was, however, in its full bloom. The handsome and the ugly, luxury and wretchedness, showed themselves unvailed, side by side. Along the boulevards passed a splendid procession of carriages or people on horseback; spectators thronged the side alleys, whilst miserable wretches displayed there, their open sores and decrepit limbs; women lay on the ground covered with black clothing, and surrounded by pale, half-naked children. The young gentlemen of the boulevards leaped over them. Well-dressed young men followed the ladies begging; dissolute women laid hands upon the gentlemen. The streets swarmed in the evening with human night-butterflies; the Palais Royal blazed with lights, gambling houses, and splendid shops; but after four o'clock in the afternoon, it was dangerous for a young lady to go across its inner court, even by her mother's side. More than twenty theatres were open every evening, to crowded houses; the great French scenic artists, Talma, Duchenois, Mlle. Mars, were still alive; Pasta and Mainville Feodor, sang at the opera; every theatre had its stars, and all had their passionate worshipers. Laughing pajazzas skipped along the promenades; jugglers and pickpockets swarmed; old women boiled their soup under the open sky, and educated their children by blows; every where there were outcries, noise, laughter, dancing. The fountains of the Tuileries played refreshingly in the stillness of the morning, and delighted children might be seen there at mid-day, skipping about and dancing in rings, whilst the gay world circled in splendid attire through the beautiful alleys. Paris was a grand melo-dramatic spectacle, which almost turned the head of the young beholder, and made him both laugh and cry at the same time.

That Paris of 1821 and 1822, I no longer recognized in the Paris of 1856. There were no beggars on the boulevards, no miserable, but at the same time no splendid display. There were few outcries and no laughter. The Palais Royal was dark. The police had interdicted gambling-houses, and taken the night-butterflies in hand. The new Emperor drove rapidly through the silent empty streets; but nobody took any notice of him, and he seemed to take notice of no one. His cheek exhibited more appearance of health and youthful vigor than I had expected to see; his profile may be called handsome; his eyes are disagreeable, dark, expressionless, without any glance—it may be said; in fact I did not see them.

In the Tuileries children still played amongst the heaps of withered leaves, which the wind of October whirled around. The theatres were closed, or had no longer any stars. Rachel was dying or dead. Parisian life appeared to me as if dead. Some inferior "*Café Chantant*," where there was singing without any regard to voice, alone assembled in the evening the promenaders of the boulevards.

I missed the melo-dramatic life of the former Paris, and I mistrusted the calm which the present exhibited. It was in itself a good thing that a strict police had compelled the discontinuance of any public display of its moral and physical wretchedness. But were they decreased by that means? Improvements had unquestionably taken place in the appearance and buildings of the city, but, as it appeared to me, in a way quite different to what I had seen in London a couple of years before.

In London, the most miserable quarter, the darkest streets of the city had been pulled down; its most wretched dens, dens of crime and poverty, had been broken into, and light and air poured into them, whilst at the same time dwellings of a better kind had been built for the laboring class and no expense spared to provide the artisan with a wholesome dwelling, good water, fresh air, light, and whatever else might aid in elevating him. In Paris the object had been first and foremost to beautify the principal quarters of the city. The avenue from the Tuileries across the "*Place de la Concorde*" to the *Barriere de l'Etoile*, is perhaps one of the most beautiful which any city can show; and more than one evening I sat delighted on the terrace of the Tuileries, in silent contemplation of its perspective, whilst the golden autumn sun went down calmly on the opposite bank of the Seine. *Rue de Rivoli*, with its handsome houses, stood like a regiment on full parade, and the walls of the Louvre covered with decorative sculpture. In the immediate suburbs of Paris, Louis Napoleon had constructed artificial lakes and mountains, to the great delight of the inhabitants of Paris. But *L'Isle de Seine* with its gloomy, mouldering masses, the Bureaus of Police and Justice looked like the most befitting haunt of all the gloomiest mysteries of Paris,* and on the first of October of the present year, there were found to be in

* Of the inner order there I have, however, reason to think favorably; for I obtained thence, without difficulty, an umbrella which I had forgotten in a hired vehicle.—*Author's Note.*

Paris ten thousand homeless artisans, who could only obtain accommodation by the direct and despotic interference of the Emperor and his police force. It is said that artisan-barracks are now being erected out of Paris, and within the city I saw that the poorer portions were pulled down and now in course of rebuilding. But would it not have been better to have begun with this, instead of adorning the Louvre and the wood of Boulogne?

And whither, in the meantime, had the night-butterflies which swarmed in the streets of 1822, now taken their flight? Whither, also, had the beggars and the miserable wretches betaken themselves?

I was told that the former now danced at Prado, on the *Quai aux fleurs*, whilst a better class of the same might be found at Valentino, and that the poor wretches who formerly begged on the promenades, now found shelter, and were provided for, at a great institution, called *La Salpêtriére*.

I visited these places, in company with the young couple, my friends, who, like myself, had a pleasure in becoming acquainted with the many sides and scenes of this world.

We drove, first, to Prado. We found, on our entrance, that the large, uncleanly saloon, contained nearly as many police as dancing guests. They stood in full uniform, glancing around them. By degrees, the hall became crowded; loud, thundering music, began to play, and people stood up for quadrilles. Each person danced according to his own pleasure; one sprawled out his legs, dancing "*can can*," as it is called; another took great leaps; men and women made tender grimaces to each other. The dancing was free and easy, though not offensively so.

I expected to have seen some ballet splendor, some beauty, as the attraction and apology for the low or loose morality of this assembly; but I was astonished at merely finding the ugly, the repulsive, in every respect. Strict police regulations require propriety in the style of dress and outward behaviour; all the women wore their dresses high in the neck; the greater number danced in bonnets; and seldom have I seen an assembly of plainer people, especially the women. It was *the ugly in its full bloom*, and besides that, painted, unabashed, without character, and without *esprit*. I thought of being a spectator of the scene for a couple of hours, but I was satisfied in twenty minutes. The repulsive figures, the disgusting physiognomies, the noisy music, the wild cries, which were sent forth every now and then, and those painted, unhappy women, who kept thronging in, ever more and more, the increasing fumes of punch and tobacco-smoke,—all this soon became intolerable to me, and we left the frightful assembly, just as it was beginning to arrive at its "*esse*."

Down on the *Quai aux fleurs*, the pure, pleasant night-air, and the starry heavens, met us in all their splendor. It was in striking contrast with the scene up above. I felt ready to weep over those poor night-butterflies and bats, which were not able to feel the beauty of this air and this heaven!

In the saloons of Valentino, was dancing, this evening the company which assembles, in the summer, in the *Jardin Mobille*. I went, in the quiet, beautiful night, with my young friends, to Valentino. I wished at once to see all I needed of this side of the *Mystères de Paris*.

The gas lamps shone dimly from the light arcades of the Valentino saloons. The apartment and the lighting, were very tasteful. The guests were not numerous, but these, evidently, of a higher social class in this grade of society. Many of the ladies were handsome, all wore silk, and were dressed with taste, as well as with more propriety than you often meet with among ladies in saloons of good ton. The orchestra was remarkably good; the supply of refreshments excellent; every thing was elegant, and no agent of the police was to be seen. Three or four quadrilles were arranged. A couple of female dancers soon attracted attention by their dancing, but most, one very lovely young woman, in a long brown, soft silk dress, high in the throat, extremely simple, but which did not prevent her slender, perfectly formed figure, from being seen. Cleopatra herself might have had such a head, with such freely-falling brown locks, a countenance as youthfully rounded, and as perfectly beautiful. She danced with the lightness of a bird, with swan-like motion, she stooped down and again raised herself from the waves of the dance, regardless of every thing but her own pleasure, and then went, with her hands lightly resting on the shoulder of her partner, back to her seat, with the bearing of a queen, whilst, with a half-vailed glance, she, as it were, biologized the bystanders, and seemed to say to them, "I do not trouble myself about you, but I know I can rule you all!"

Nothing, except the movements, and the changing expression, more than once repeated in the same manner, showed that they were studied. A crowd of gentlemen, elderly and young, gathered behind her, and seemed altogether bewitched by her beauty, her dancing, and peculiar manner; because, whilst her *vis-a-vis*, a handsome blondine, with full figure, was incessantly laughing and chattering, the Cleopatra like beauty stood perfectly quiet, proud, silent, and, as it seemed, indifferent to every thing but the dance. I neither saw her smile, nor speak with any one, but —she knew very well how she attracted eyes and hearts, and—woe to him who became her slave!—and yet she looked so young, so lovable, so—innocent! I felt inclined to exclaim, like Rowland Hill to Lady Erskine, "All this glory must pass away, but thy soul must still live on!"

The ball closed with a Malakoff polka, full of the roar of cannon effects in the music, but in which only a few couples trailed lazily along, in no condition to keep up with the music. They had called for champagne, but it would not foam: the pleasure, both of life and of dancing, was wanting. I was most amused by a couple, which, as I thought, looked like a country shoemaker and his wife, who danced with an enthusiasm and a gravity—and always together—which evidently showed that they were fully determined to have dancing and amusement enough for their money (three francs being paid for entrance), untroubled by the rest of the world—so might it be, the poor, honest couple! Of youth, beauty, or grace, they had none!

At midnight the ball closed, and we wandered home in the lovely moonlight night.

La Salpetriere.—I visited this place the following day. In this immense establishment, is contained, in classified order, the greater part of the unfortunates of the capital, who formerly used to expose their misery openly. The number of persons cared for here, amounts to about four thousand. Four hundred nurses attend to them, under the direction of physicians. Every particular species of disease is attended to in its own division; each peculiar division has its own peculiar house, its garden or grounds, and also its own physicians. I cannot sufficiently commend the order, cleanliness, the good air, nay, even comfort, which I found in this establishment, where, by wise centralization and administration, the municipal government of Paris assists a great portion of the wretchedness of its indigent population, and renders helplessness as bearable as possible, by the care which is extended to it.

I was least satisfied with the apartment in which the insane were kept—an immense attic, where they sat by hundreds; and the unfortunate raving maniacs, in their little rooms, which seemed too me quite too much like the cells in which wild beasts are kept—perhaps it cannot be otherwise! Yet cleanliness prevailed even here. But the powerful women who had the charge of these unfortunates of their own sex, gave me small confidence in their humane treatment.

The grounds in which these poor people were, at the time I was there, walking or sitting, are extensive.

Some of them were wildly leaping about under the beautiful trees, others were fighting. I was told that many of the women who dance at the *Quai aux fleurs*, come into this section of *La Salpêtrière*.

It did me good to see, in another section, the cheerful and kindly manner of the nurses.

"We think," said a young, handsome nurse, "that it does the sick good to see people cheerful about them. Poor things, they have trouble enough with their own sufferings!"

The visits of relatives and friends, is permitted only during a certain part of the day. A mother lay there in her bed, wringing her hands in despair, and calling for her son. The appointed, last hour was soon over, and he—was not come.

It is a pleasure to turn from these scenes of human misery, to others which awaken a hope of a better future.

Foremost amongst these at the present time, stands the evangelical church in Paris, on account of its school, its important Deaconess-institution, and its teachers. It is from this church, that, for several years, a number of sermons and spiritual orations have gone forth into all lands where the French language is spoken, with a new vitalization, for the heart and for domestic life. It was from the bosom of this assembly, that Adolphi Monad's "Dying-Sighs" lately breathed forth consolation and peace, for millions of hearts in the whole Christian world. It is there that, A. Vinet's most gifted disciple, the Swiss Edmond de Presancé, and his distinguished fellow-laborers in the *Revue Chrétienne*, open, at the present time, new prospects for Christian science and the church, by a liberal, true, evangelical Protestantism, which does not content itself with a negative stand-point against Catholicism, but opens itself to a full recognition of whatever truth and excellence it contains, and at the same time, following the example of A. Vinet, it takes up the most important productions of cotemporary literature and examines them, not from a narrow churchman's point of view, but from one of true, evangelical knowledge.

Time and space fail me to say more of the growing life of this congregation, but it appears to me to have a great future life before it. And if it be true that the present condition of France bears evidence of a secret, inward disease; and if it be true, as I have heard it wittily said, that this is the result of the reformation driven inwards, (*la reformation rentrée*,) then it may be predicted with certainty, that the re-establishment of its health depends upon this reformation again coming to the surface, with all its affluent result of vitality in domestic life, schools, the church, and the state.

I know that a great deal is done at the present time, even in the Catholic Church, at Paris, for the education and care of children; nay, indeed, we may have various things to say on this subject, at a later period. But no one can misjudge me when I have more hope of the education of a church which leads the child to Christ Jesus, and inculcates his own responsibility to God and his own conscience, than of that which, in the first place, leads him to the Virgin Mary, and **teaches a blind obedience** to the Catholic church, or to its priests. Obedience there must be, but not a blind obedience. In that case, a man knows not whether he obeys a God or an idol.

There is one feature of inner life in France, which I cannot avoid mentioning,—this is, the newly awakened enthusiasm for its female heroine and martyr, Joan of Arc. Michelet's excellent narrative of her history, after a most conscientiously careful examination of all sources of information, has brought forward, as it were, her figure, in its peculiar purity and beauty, as superior to the poet's Maid of Orleans, in Schiller's tragedy, as a noble reality is above even the noblest poem. This description seems to have turned anew the heart and mind, to this young, heroic saviour of France. Artists call forth again her form, both by pencil and chisel. I saw various of these representations, one of which had been lately executed for the church of Domremy; but not one of them comes near, in expression and truth, to the statue which the noble daughter of a king, herself an artist,—the young Princess Clementine, of Orleans,— executed of her, even before Michelet had perfected with the pen his masterly picture. Love and sympathy inspired the young royal sculptor in her work. This statue stands in the gallery of the Louvre. Its beauty and power consists in the expression of the head, and the clasped hands. It is simply Joan, the girl of Orleans, who sees nothing but her bleeding native land, listens to no other voices than those in her inner being, which command her to go and save it,—Joan, when she left her father's house; Joan, as she stood last on the pile at Rouen; when she, after the short season of darkness, again heard her inward voices, and heard only them, whilst the flames rose and rose.

Zouaves march in brilliant eastern costume, backwards and forwards, in the streets and markets of Paris, reminding the beholder of the last victorious movements of the West against the East, of victories in Algeria and at Sebastopol. It is the new picturesque outward trait which I recognized in Paris.

There were two scenes, however, which I beheld there, which will live in my heart's memory,—the one of a heavenly, the other of earthly happiness. Then I saw the dear old pictures which I saw thirty years ago, but which I have preserved in memory, as if I had first seen them only yesterday. There I now saw a new one, and stood riveted in enraptured contemplation of the Ascension of the Virgin, by Murillo. I wished that I could bring the fallen women of the saloons of Prado and Valentino to this madonna, that they might fall down before her as repentant Magdalenes. I wished that all human beings could see this picture, and beholding it, comprehend how the highest purity and love lead to a happiness so great that no human heart on earth can comprehend, no tongue can express it. This picture of the Virgin breathes life, beauty, bliss. One seems to see the crimson of the cheek grow pale before the light of heaven, as the flush of morning pales before that of the sun. Raphael's madonnas are soulless and lifeless, compared with this of Murillo.

The second scene, I saw in a little attic up five flights of stairs. There lived a young newly-married pair,—lived there by daily labor in the sweat of their brow. But the pure heart and the frank disposition, love, confidence in each other, health, hope, and the ability, like the sparrows on the roof, thankfully to enjoy every grain of corn which the hand of the Father scattered upon their path; all these were fully possessed by the young couple. They were Scandinavians, and had, by affection and industry, built for themselves a comfortable little abode, amidst the volcanic capital of France, the manifold spectacles of which gave variety and wealth even to their quiet life. They looked upon it all with undazzled eyes, with the purity and serenity of the northern temperament, without being either confounded or carried away by it.

"The volcanic capital of France!" Yes, spite of its quietness and emptiness for the moment, I could not but feel that this was like the pause of the volcano before its outbreak; and can it be otherwise? The present calmness of France is not based, like that of England, like that of Holland, and Sweden, and Switzerland, upon the consciousness of the nation, and its power of self-government. It hangs upon the life's-thread of one man,—on that of Louis Napoleon. And people have no confidence in this man. I heard thinking Frenchmen acknowledge it. He is the helmsman for the moment, but not for the future. No higher principle, no initiative to a new life, has ascended with him to the throne, collecting the restless aspirations* or endeavors of the age, and the people,

---

* At the moment when I prepare these lines for the press, Louis Napoleon appears to be on the way to acquire them in the

into a higher unity. He keeps together the old; he is a great police-master. The quiet people of France wish him life and success, because they know that to be the condition of the nation's order, and the calmness of life; but they acknowledge that the present state of things is one of uncertainty and unhealthiness. People live, as it were, provisionally, because they must, in any case, live as long as they can; but they see the sword of Damocles hanging above their heads. No large views, no fresh waft from hope in the future, refreshes the life of the day, and the future of France is as dark as the glance of its Emperor.

Yet still fortune favors him; yet still the French army keeps guard around his throne. But can the man who has broken his oath more than once, who has stolen from a noble royal family—whose place he occupies—the half of its property, and who has sent thousands of his countrymen to die in exile, worse than that of Siberia—can this man escape a Nemesis?

I know that in the theatre of the world, there are times and circumstances which can furnish an excuse for many things—many deeds of the acting personages; and that Providence at times gives even great criminals opportunity of atonement by great actions for former failings, opportunities to become the blessing of the people and to acquire the name of great men. But no such laurels as yet crown Louis Napoleon.

war for the liberation of Italy, and now lastly by his programme of peace; well worthy the attention both of princes and people!—*Author's Note. Athens, February* 1, 1860.

SIXTH STATION.

Again in Switzerland—Railway Irregularities—Vintage at Montreux—Romantic Illusions—New Acquaintance—The First Prisoner of Uri—Winter Residence at Lausanne—War and Peace in Switzerland—Still Life—New Life and New Interests—Young Italy—Its Patriots and Poets—"Risorgimento d'Italia"—The Waldenses in Piedmont—New Plans for my Journey—I must see Italy—Spring Life at Lausanne—Educational Institute—A. Vinet.

I FLEW by express train from Paris, to the foot of the Jura, and there took the diligence, which conveys the traveler across the mountain into Switzerland. It was late in the evening and quite dark when the train reached the Jura. And in darkness and storm the passengers removed from the railway carriages to diligences drawn by horses; a small hand-lantern being all the light afforded for this purpose. I requested that I might be placed in the same vehicle which contained my baggage; and I was assured that it should be so.

I know not what the case might be for the other passengers, but my luggage traveled to Geneva, whilst I, towards morning, found myself on the way to Lausanne. At Lausanne, I was obliged immediately to take the steamboat, which was going to Geneva, to look after my belongings. I was told at the diligence office, here, that such disorderly proceedings were not of unfrequent occurrence on the other side of Jura, and that it was willful on the part of the officials there that they might make a petty gain by the payment which they demanded from travelers for the restoration of their effects.

Whether this be true or not, I cannot say. Certain it is, that I spared neither care nor inquiries to ascertain that my luggage and myself traveled in company. That I should ascertain that it was so, was impossible in the general darkness of the station.

I had great difficulty in finding my luggage at Geneva, and, when I had done so, in gaining possession of it. And I must remark, once for all, and that with regret, upon the want of order, the want even of common courtesy and humanity, which I often met with at the railway offices in Switzerland, and which I never found greater in any other country whatever. Many travelers have experienced it as well as myself, and complained of it, and therefore I mention it here. On this occasion, at Geneva, I found this want in a more than ordinary degree. It is a very allowable thing that the gentlemen of the office should take their breakfast; but that they should go away for that purpose, at the very moment they had appointed for the traveler to find them at the office, in order to obtain his effects, and in the moment, also, in which he must continue his journey, seems to me unallowable, much less to be commended. In the present case, these gentlemen showed me my portmanteaux, at least, the locked door of the apartment which contained them, and—went their way. I waited some time: then asked a young man who alone remained behind the desk, why I could not have my property delivered to me?—that I was that morning to proceed, by steamboat, to Montreux, and heard already the signal given for its departure. I had been ordered to be at the office at eight o'clock that morning; it was now half-past eight; and—why would they not give me that which belonged to me?

The young man replied, with great indifference, that "the gentlemen were gone to breakfast: they would be back in time."

I still waited, standing,—for a seat was not offered me—very tired, and very much astonished at this behavior. Still more distressed than myself was a poor Savoyard, whose knapsack was locked in the same apartment with my portmanteau. He had to return this morning to Savoy, where he had got work; the steamer by which he had to go had given signal of departure, but the knapsack of the poor artisan was locked up, and the gentlemen, who had locked it up, had gone to breakfast. The young man at the desk repeated this information with admirable coolness, and occupied himself by whistling, whilst the poor Savoyard, almost beside himself with uneasiness and anxiety, walked rapidly up and down the office, tore his curling, dark hair, and, with his beautiful Italian eyes full of tears, uttered words of despair. And the gentlemen were still taking breakfast!—

It was now nearly nine o'clock. At the last moment, they came bustling in, drew forth the luggage, and told me what I had to pay before I could obtain possession of mine. It appeared to me unreasonable, and the whole conduct of the gentlemen more than suspicious. But there was now no time to dispute their demands; the steamer was on the point of leaving. There was nothing left for me but to pay, and take my property, or leave it in these thievish hands, and go away without it. I chose the latter, because this conduct appeared to me unjustifiable. How the poor Savoyard managed, I know not. Probably he was obliged to pay what they demanded, and whether or not he reached his vessel in time, I was not able to ascertain, for I was scarcely on board of mine when it was set in motion.

The scene, of which I here witness, really annoyed me. I love Swiss freedom, and the Swiss people; and it grieves me when I see its free men not taking the pains to be honest and humane men, in its best significance, "gentlemen!" The rude block may become an Apollo-statue, but it must not imagine that it is equally good in its first condition.

At Montreux I wished to see the vintage which was now in progress. In the neighborhood where Rousseau laid the scene of his "Nouvelle Heloise," at Montreux, just opposite the rocks of Meillerie, at Clarens, where people still wander in "*bosquets de Julie*," there, I thought, the most beautiful rural festival of the year would have an especially romantic character. But I deceived myself. Nothing could be more prosaic than the vintage in this district. Both men and women went gravely and silently into the vineyards, gathered the clusters from the vinestocks, bruised them in churns in the fields, loaded them in carts, and drove them away to the wine-presses. There was nothing about it to distinguish it from any other labor. In this harvesting of that which God gives to make glad the heart of man, there was no enjoyment of life.

And yet, this was the finest vintage that there had been for many years!

I experienced one agreeable impression—that produced by the kind manners and disposition of the country people towards strangers, to whom they most liberally presented the beautiful bunches, inviting them, also, to partake of the must which streamed from the wine-presses, and which is, indeed, the most delicious drink any one can imagine. And, in the evenings, you would meet on the roads, women returning home from the day's work, carrying a part of its wages on their heads, in large baskets full of grapes, the clusters and leaves of which sometimes garlanded them so beautifully, that no artist could have done it better, if he had wished to represent a Pomona.

But the air was cold: so cold, that it penetrated me both body and soul; which, perhaps, made me insensible to the celebrated beauty of the Montreux district. Its vast mountain chain seemed coldly to weigh me down, and the lofty rock-wall of Meillerie, Dent du Midi, and Dent d'Orche, closed up my view, and deprived me too easily of the little sunshine which the autumn still permitted. I grew regularly ill-tempered on these lofty mountains, and felt myself shut up in Montreux, as if within the walls of a fortress. I could not but remember the expression of a Dutch gentleman, "that Switzerland is a very pretty country, only it is a pity that the lofty mountains prevent one from seeing it!"

At Montreux I was obliged to climb high among the mountains to obtain any thing of an open view, and this, when gained, was nothing but the lake and its Alpine heights. A wide horizon is not to be found, and without that I never feel myself happy.

The little town of Montreux lies like an eagle's nest upon its mountain summit, and a rich fringe of golden stonecrop shines along the ridge of the house-roofs. In the house, you not unfrequently find comfort; and the view from the windows is great in height and depth, but the streets are winding and dark. Heaps of manure meet one everywhere. "The country-people," remarked an amiable Swiss lady, apologetically, "see in them the gold which makes the fields rich and the grapes juicy!"

I lamented that my eyes and my nose were too prosaic to take in this practical point of view.

The castle of Chillon rises out of the waves of Leman, on the shore of Montreux,—massive and gloomy, but infinitively picturesque. I visited it one gray, cold November day; visited its tower, its state-room, torture-chamber, *oubliettes*, and its deep, large dungeon-vault, resting upon the rock-foundations. Byron has inscribed his name at the foot of one of the massive pillars, his "Prisoner of Chillon" has inscribed it on the heart of mankind. But there is a more beautiful poem than that of Byron on the last political prisoner of Chillon, Bonivard; namely, the history of its first prisoner, the Count of Wala, which the Chronicler has preserved, and the noble historian, L. Vulleimin, has lately given to the reading world. Between the two prisoners lies the period of five hundred years.

One of the towers of Chillon elevates itself above

all the others: large, massive, square, and of a much older date; it is called, to this day, "Wala's Tower."

It stood solitary in the dreary region, an object of fear and horror, when, one day in the year 830, an armed troop approached the gloomy tower, and placed there a prisoner, with silence and deep mystery. But by degrees, it was whispered through the neighborhood who it was. It was the noble Count of Wala, the friend and general of Charlemagne, one of the chief men of the empire, lately Abbot of Corbie. Charlemagne's weak son, Louis, displeased by the severe censure which the honest Wala passed upon his mode of government, and the evil practices of Judith, his wife, caused him to be taken from his asylum of Corbie, and cast into the tower of Chillon.

"He continued a prisoner there for many years, without receiving any visitor," says his biographer, Pascase Rudbert, "except the angels, which in every place know how to find their way to the heart of the upright."

"Wala, like St. Augustine, believed in an eternal word, which continually communicates itself to the human soul; and his faith in God, the inexhaustible fountain of all consolation, preserved him from being cast down."

One day the doors of the prison were opened to this Rudbertus, the friend of Wala. He conveyed to the captive a message of peace from the emperor. Liberty, favor, and honor, were offered to Wala, if he would recall his severe expressions and confess that he had erred. Wala steadfastly refused. "How," said he, "would the Supreme Judge regard it, if I should pronounce on myself the sentence of a liar; if I should abandon the path of justice and truth? Believe me, my brother, that it is better that we continue on the way into which the grace of God has led us, and maintain our hearts firm in hope. We shall then at last enter into eternal life!"

"I was silent, I was abashed," writes Rudbertus, "when I heard Wala speak thus. I saw clearly that he, untroubled about his own interests, only thought upon the objects of his earnest love, God, his native land, the church, and the good of the people.

"During our conversation, we heard the waves of Leman breaking against the walls of the prison. Wala directed his gaze upon the unquiet waters, and accustomed to listen for God's voice in nature, as well as his own heart, he heard the foaming waves speak to him of God. Their ebb and flow told him of the same in human affairs; the immovability of the rock against which they broke, was an image to him of the stability of the soul which has its life in God.

"'Thus far may you come, and against these walls shall your proud waves be stayed!' said Wala, with a calm brow and a bright glance over the excited waters. Like the exiled seer in Patmos, he rent asunder the vail of futurity, and nourished by the divine mysteries, he seemed to have entered already within the portals of the kingdom of Heaven."

The doors of the dungeon opened some years afterwards to the noble captive, who was summoned to mediate between the sons of King Louis. He crossed the Alps between Switzerland and Italy, more than once upon the same errand. The last time, happy at the tidings of peace, of which he was the bearer to Tuscany, when he fell sick, and reaching the convent of Babbio—where he was elected abbot—he died amongst his brethren. His body was interred beside that of Columban.

Such was the first prisoner of Chillon. Chillon is a prison at the present time; but no longer for prisoners of state. It contains now many criminals, and amongst them a young murderer, of good family. There is a chapel within the castle, in which the prisoners attend divine service.

Several pleasant acquaintances, rendered the weeks spent at Montreux still more agreeable, and I enjoyed many beautiful and sunny hours in their handsome homes on the shore of Lake Leman. I frequently met in these circles, Professor Jules Bonnet, who has published excellent biographical sketches of Olympia Morata, the daughter of Curione, and who is now occupied with inquiries into the fate of the Protestants in Italy. He is young, and himself Provençal, he declaims the naïve songs of the Provençal poet, Jasmin, in the most charming manner.

But "*la Vandaine*" blew violently; the poplars before my windows became ever more scant of leaves; the waves hurled themselves, with heavy blows, against the shore. I seemed, in the night, to hear in them heavy sighs. The withered leaves fell in the beautiful groves, "*bosquets de Julie,*" and the autumn wind whistled—as it did everywhere else. I longed for repose in good winter quarters, and, towards the end of November, I returned to Lausanne.

In Lausanne, through the kind invitation of Madame Vinet, I obtained a friendly home with a kind and noble-minded widow lady. Two pretty young girls beautified it. My room was light and spacious; it faced the mid-day sun, and afforded a fine view across the deep valley, through which *le flou* cuts its foaming way, to the beautiful terrace of Montbenon, and thence to the lake and the mountains of Savoy, which here, at a distance, please me better than at Montreux.

The days passed on calmly and pleasantly. I lived in profound quietness, with my books, and my silent thoughts, receiving visits, and visiting the churches. In the evening, the little family of pensioners assembled around the evening lamps, and took it by turns to read aloud. By this means, I made acquaintance with the latest and most celebrated writers of Switzerland,—Töpfer and Bitzins.

Töpfer belongs to French Switzerland, and has written a number of novels, in which he describes its peculiar life with sportive, good-tempered humor; especially as it exists in the more cultivated middle class. Of peculiar characters, there are few; of peculiar ideas, none; but details certain states of the soul, scenery, natural appearances, and human dispositions, are often excellently given. The reader perceives an amiable good-nature, shining through all, like a golden background to his pictures. He is a good *genre* painter. Occasionally, he combats a popular prejudice, as in the novel of *Le Presbytère*,—the belief so prevalent among the peasants, of the goodness or reprobation of certain races, in consequence of the child's unavertable inheritance of the parents' vices or virtues. This Töpfer has refuted, with much feeling and earnestness. He has, in most of his smaller novels, merely endeavored blamelessly to amuse himself and others; and in this he has succeeded. I would defy the most sullen disposition to read *Le Col d'Anterne*, and many others of this class, without being betrayed by them into hearty peals of laughter.

Bitzins is an author of higher pretension. Although he, also, is a *genre* painter, yet his figures are more peculiar and living; they are drawn from reality; his earnestness is deeper; his humor more keen, often even bitter. He belongs to German Switzerland, and has written, under the pseudonym of "Jeremias Gotthelf," novels and romances in German, which wholly describe peasant life and manners, especially in the Canton Berne, where he holds a living. He is said not to be the best of spiritual shepherds; his descriptions, however, of popular life, are excellent. That which Fielding and Hogarth were in their own country, Bitzins is for Switzerland. He exhibits the low and laughable, rather than the good, in human nature; but when he does the latter, it takes a strong hold upon the heart. Besides, every one of his pictures is true to nature, naïve, living. He is a great artist, of the Flemish school.

Whilst we, in our little circle, were living on, in our quiet way, the whole of Switzerland was arming itself for war. The revolution of Neufchâtel, that "tempest in a glass of water," had produced its serious consequences, and far greater than many people expected. Prussia appeared in arms against Switzerland; Switzerland was up to defend herself and her own against Prussia. All differences, all contentions, whether small or great, were now forgotten, between the Swiss Cantons. They rose up like one family, like one man, for the defense of the common fatherland. The forest Cantons, as well as the Pays de Vaud, and Geneva, Zürich, and Freyburg, the isolated Granbundten, the Italian-speaking Tessin, each emulated the others in sending men and means for the same object; all armed themselves for the Sworn-Confederacy; and not they alone. The same spirit moved in the Swiss out of Switzerland. The electric-telegraphs worked day and night, bringing messages from the Swiss in Turin, Milan, Vienna, Paris, London; from wealthy bankers, who forwarded large sums of money for the expenses of the war; from young artisans, who were ready to leave their workshops, and place themselves under the banners of their native land. Nor were even young men of affluence behind them.

"My mother is herself packing my knapsack at this moment, and I hasten to join the army," wrote a wealthy young man from Vienna.

The enthusiasm was universal; it would even have seized upon me, if I had really believed that war would take place. But, I do not know how it was, I did not believe it, even when I saw mothers and wives weeping in the square, La Riporne, and taking leave of their sons and husbands, who were setting out to the camp; and from the moment when I knew that the Federal government had applied to the **Emperor of France**, requesting his mediation, I **felt** certain of the fortunate termination of the war for Switzerland, without a sword being drawn.

Louis Napoleon was a citizen of Switzerland; ever since his childhood, which was passed on the banks of Lake Constance, in the Castle of Arenaburg, has he been regarded as a son of the country. They had given him an asylum there at the time when his life and liberty were in danger; they had refused to surrender him to Louis Philippe, and now, in its hour of danger, Louis Napoleon could not disappoint the land which had been so faithful to him in his hour of need; and he, who was already in his childhood known for a kind of gentle self-willedness, by means of which he managed to carry out all his schemes, so that his mother Queen Hortense, used to call him *mon doux têta*,—would not he, now that he was a man, and seated on the throne of France, find or devise the means of accomplishing his will in so good a cause? Of this I was certain; and I therefore felt quite easy about Switzerland. It was, however, interesting to me, in the mean time, to see the general rising, the general spirit, in the Confederate States; the unity of feeling for the common native-land in these Cantons, most of which, however, knew very little of the rest, excepting that they were Sworn-Confederates.

"If this war should go forward," I wrote in my diary, in the month of December, "it will lead to a more inward union of the Swiss Cantons, than would fifty years of peace!"

In the Free Church, special meetings and prayers were held, for the averting of the threatened danger.

Neither did the ladies remain inactive. They established unions all over the country; they made collections, purchased materials, and made up warm garments for the defenders of the fatherland, who must go out to fight in the present bitter cold winter. I, too, set myself to knit a pair of mittens; but they were not finished before peace was established. Louis Napoleon mediated to the advantage of Switzerland. Switzerland was to retain Neufchâtel, which Canton was to become, in a still more intimate manner than formerly, a portion of the Swiss Confederacy. Ultra patriots, it is true, still cried out against the too great concession to Prussia, but the quieter and more prudent party throughout the country, were unanimous that the Federal government had done the wisest and best which was possible. The Swiss army was recalled from the frontiers, and the festivals of war were changed into festivals of peace. Te Deum was sung in the churches.

Thus began the new year of 1857. The Swiss Cantons resumed their life of tranquillity, the work of their railways, their common improvements, and— their petty quarrels.

By visits to the churches of different sects, by conversation with persons who were both in favor of and opposed to the established church, I endeavored to acquire an accurate knowledge of the relationship between the established church and the free churches, as well as of the relationship to the religious life in the heart of a people; and I came to the conclusion that both forms of ecclesiastical life are necessary in a state, if that life will attain to a condition of normal development and full consciousness. The established church, the old nursing mother, is the conservative power, which, while it faithfully preserves the great traditions and ancient forms, yet, with a liberal spirit, opens its embrace to receive the many half-matured, uncertain, or, as it were, still unsettled souls, which desire, indeed, but yet cannot bring themselves to a state of stability. She is not inquisitorial towards her own; she is tolerate with regard to inner emotion; she merely requires a certain obedience in the outward. It is only in countries where sects are forbidden by law, and the state-church alone rules, that she becomes despotic and dangerous to young souls, who are not seldom forcibly compelled, on the first occasion, to the Holy Communion, or thrust forth out of the pale of the church, which appears to them rather a police-institution, than a pathway to the kingdom of God. It is very different in countries where the Free Church and Christian sects have equal civil rights. These churches are exclusive, intolerant, but they are, at the same time, honest, and they have the life of conviction. They are frequently one-sided, but they require a fixed creed; they close their spiritual doors to those who will not accept it; they will neither recognize things done by halves, nor any secret reservation; they require decision and candor; they compel people to become keen questioners of their own state; they will not accept an acquaintance which is merely outward. No youthful soul is compelled by them to the Lord's table. If the young acknowledge themselves not ready, not sufficiently faithful as yet, the teachers defer the ecclesiastical ceremony, and advise the disciple to wait, and continue to learn and consider, until he can, with a full conviction, acknowledge himself as a Christian before the congregation. Such, at least, is the case in the Free Church of the Canton Vaud, that daughter of the spirit of Vinet. The Free Church requires that the course of life shall bear witness to the faith; she therefore becomes often enough inquisitorial towards her members. The pastor sometimes excludes from the Lord's table such as he considers unworthy to be present at it. Thus, for example, it has happened in the small church congregations, which, in Lausanne, have gathered themselves around certain preachers, remarkable for their gifts, as well as personal character, and have split off from the great ecclesiastical community. In these small congregations, the individual character and influence of the preacher is of great importance.

I sum up my statements thus: The state, or national church, is good, because it is the national nurse which preserves the old life, and nourishes the new, at the same time that it prevents its degenerating into licentiousness and individual fancies.

The Free Churches are good, because they incite and develop the spiritual life, the free thought, liberate the individual, compel him to self-decision, and they prevent "the mother" from falling to sleep; but both mother and child, both the old and the young, are needed for the people and for the state. They mutually incite each other, and work together, for the full development of the religious consciousness and life.

I now return to my own life in Switzerland. It

was good, tranquil, agreeable, but—not inspiring. There was good preaching, and good work, and a sufficiency of good society; but I felt the want of large views, of breadth, of horizon. The church spoke merely of the salvation of the individual soul. It turned away from science, and from the largeness of general life, as it did not concern "our city." Higher life and interests come to me from a distance; come from the country, on the other side of the Alps.

A Roman fugitive, who had lived in Lausanne since the unsuccessful revolution of 1848, and who was called Professor Arduini, commenced a course of lectures on the more modern Italian literature. He was an ardent patriot, had taken part in the Italian struggle for liberty, both in word and spirit. His lectures were, before every thing else, intended to exhibit the national party in the young, feeling, thinking, aspiring Italy.

In my far distant, northern land, I had, like many another, listened with sympathy to the exulting shout of Italy, on the ascension of Pio Nono to the Papal throne. Italy hailed him as her saviour from foreign oppression. The heart-rending biography of Silvio Pellico. "Le mie prigione," imprisonment in Spielburg, had found its way to our home and taught us to detest the power of Austria over Italy. We contemplated with joy, the handsome, benevolent features of the new liberator, in the portraits which were sent to us, of him. They seemed to promise a bright future for the beautiful, long-subjected country. But the tune soon changed. Delirious festivities and great words, and, soon after, bloody oppression darkened the bright scene. The flames of freedom seemed to ascend in smoke, and from the Italy lately so loftily ostentatious, but so soon again subjected, we turned away—too readily mistrusting her, too easily grown cold towards her. Other European nations had done the same. In Switzerland, the nearest neighboring country to Italy, I had lived for several months without once having heard its name mentioned. People had no knowledge of its literature; they never inquired about its life. It was only when some new nocturnal attempt of Mazzini's was related in the newspapers, that the public attention was turned thither for a moment, and people shrugged their shoulders and thought no more of the subject. The name of Mazzini, and his sly, bloody outbreaks, had become in the eyes of the rest of Europe, representative of the efforts for freedom in Italy, and these seemed to resemble the fever paroxysms of a sick man. No wonder that it had fallen into discredit.

Piedmont alone, stood amongst the Italian states, as an object of esteem and hope for a constitutionally free people. But it stood alone, a small state, at the foot of the Alps, and all the rest of Italy lay enchained by despotic princes, and its own imbecility!

I now learned for the first time, that this Italy had a national party advocating liberty, but in a spirit very different from that of Mazzini, and in opposition to its red flag; one which, with the power of ideas, with the word and with the spirit, openly combated for the liberty of Italy, both the inward as well as the outward. Around this white flag, I saw assembled the noblest patriots, poets, and statesmen, of young

Italy, from Alfieri to Uzo Foscolo, Gioberti, Guerazzi, Nicolino, Guiste, Lambruschini, Azeglio, and many others, who are living and laboring at this moment for the work of a peaceful liberation, the greater number in Piedmont, where alone, of all the Italian states, they can find shelter and safety. I learned that quite near to me, on the other side of the Alps, lived a noble people who were silently sighing after a freedom for which it fought and bled, but which did not possess strength enough to defend against powerful foes, both inward and outward; I learned that its heart beat and still burned, although silently, beneath the foot of the oppressor!

I sent for Signor Arduini to become my instructor; I read, with him, Dante, but soon laid him aside for the latest poets of Italy, Guist, so nobly bitter, so warm for his mother-land, (*Povera Madre!*) as he calls her; Nicolini, whose tragedy *Arnoldi da Brescia* advocates the rights of conscience in a style so noble, and beautiful; I became acquainted with the efforts of young Italy for a better education of her youth, for the freedom of thought, and the ennobling of life, and I heard the names of noble women mentioned as amongst the friends of the native land.

At the same time, I read the History of the Waldenses. I also now learned for the first time, that this little heroic flock of the oldest church, after centuries of persecutions, and of renewed combat for its faith and freedom, had, within a few years, won this liberty, and now lived happily in the valleys of Piedmont, protected by the King of Piedmont, and acknowledged by the laws, as a portion of its free people and participant of its rights. In my youth, I had read of the bloody persecutions of the Waldenses, those first protestants against the Romish Church. I supposed them to have been long since expelled, and to have vanished from the face of the earth; and behold, they lived, they flourished anew, flourished now as they have never done before, and that quite near to me! The little "light that shineth in darkness"—the device and type of the Waldenses,—had now come forth from the darkness and shone like the stars of the morning in the heaven of Italy.

Now all this affected and animated me! Italy, the celebrated museum of art; Italy, the home of beautiful ruins and palaces, of a singing, maccaroni-eating, *far-niente*-loving people, the admired land of the Pope, of artists, and tourists, had never so much interested me before.

But Italy—the Niobe of nations—defending with half-broken heart, the youngest child, hope, in her bosom; Italy, after long, dark centuries, awakened to new life, languishing after light, liberty, a higher humanity; longing to become herself, a pure harmonious note in the choir of free peoples—this Italy attracted me with irresistible power. I resolved to set out this very year to Italy, to search into its hidden life, to lay my hand testingly upon its heart.

"*Spiranze d'Italia; Risorgimento d'Italia*," were continually bright thoughts in my soul. These thoughts warmed me with an inner fire. There was need of it. The winter was very cold; I had never before suffered so much from the severity of the season. In Sweden, people have good rooms and fireplaces, and if they can purchase fuel for themselves they need not suffer from cold there. The mists and the snow-slush made heaven and earth so gloomy that Lake Leman seemed, as in the old times, a desert-lake, and the country around it "a region lost in cloud." Sometimes the air was dry and gray-cold, bitter, and biting, extremely disagreeable during a whole week's continuance. Ladies sat with their feet upon *chauffe-rettes* both at church and at home, but still suffered from cold hands.

The severe winter was not, however, of long duration, and sometimes, even whilst it lasted, days intervened so enchantingly beautiful, so filled with spring-sun and spring-intimations, that I was, as it were, intoxicated by them, and forgot the cold weather that was passed; but it soon returned. During one interval of this agreeable weather, I paid a visit to Morges, where I spent some beautiful days with my friends, the Alexis Forels. The conversation with them and the little circle of interesting persons who met at their house; together with a visit to the superior school for young girls, which is one of the distinguishing characteristics of that little town, made these days rich. I heard lectures delivered here by excellent teachers; such indeed as I had never heard before; and how happy, I thought, were the young girls, to be thus educated into thinking, discriminating, human beings! I longed to have been once more young, to have sat, as a pupil, upon these benches. Oh! my lost youth!—yet thou wast not lost, thou season of longing and suffering; thou taughtest me much, though I did not then understand it. I have understood it since; and that my desert wandering had its hidden meaning and purpose, God be praised!

Towards the close of February, spring commenced in real earnest, and then with a power and beauty which surpassed all my imaginings of what it would be, and which attuned my soul to a perpetual thanksgiving song. The fields became all at once verdant and covered with flowers, (for during the short winter the grass has not time to become yellow and die, as it does in the north,) and an indescribably living murmur of rushing streams, and cheerful children's voices, of singing birds and insects, arose in the calm, sunlit air, from earth towards heaven. The snowy diadem melted from the lofty Dôle, on the Jura chain, and the crimson glow of morning and evening shone with inimitable clearness and splendor above it. Leman lay tranquil as a mirror, and in the evenings, the fiery column of the setting sun sank into its clear bosom, seeming to penetrate far down into its depths— add to this, the air was as fresh, as pure, as light, as the breath of a child.

It seemed to me, as if earth were preparing itself for the visit of a god; and even I stood as if in a state of expectant waiting, as for something unusual which was about to happen. Nothing happened, however; nothing except *la bise* is entered in my diary, but not altogether conformably with truth, because the north-wind came indeed, and put an end to the enchanting scene, but this spring, nevertheless, was blessed to me from the quiet growth of my own spiritual life; and from the acquaintance of several interesting persons whom I met in social life, to which I now devoted myself more than I had hitherto done.

Lausanne no longer possesses any of that life which riveted Voltaire there, together with many intellectual travelers, and caused its social circle to receive the name of *société du printemps*, but it is still rich in good, cultivated, and very amiable individuals. I became acquainted with many thinking and agreeable men belonging to the teachers of the university; and the young, noble-hearted, truth-loving Professor Hornung became my friend. But above all, it did me good to see and to hear Professor Vulleimin. I never conversed with him without feeling my hope of the ultimate triumph of the good, more strong; without more clearly comprehending the development of human and political life into freedom and self-decision. Because the ideal of life is very clearly revealed to the mind of this thinker.

I found amongst the ladies also, many amiable characters; and I heard, many a time, words from their lips, worthy of remembrance for their depth and for the wisdom of life which they expressed. I saw the excellent Madame Vinet but seldom however, because she was confined to her home by the severe and incurable sickness of her only son; but every moment which I spent with her, remained as a point of light in my soul.

La société de la Rue de Bourg, is peculiarly that of the aristocracy of the city, and keeps itself tolerably exclusive to its own hill. It gives choice dinners, and is possessed of wit and worldly wisdom. Before all others, I bear in memory a young lady, with light blue eyes and golden hair; and an old lady, but so witty, so gay and good, that one became irresistibly animated, and, when with her, again young.

The other society of the place, which appeared to me to belong to the sphere of the University, was more grand, more genuine; a simple, unpretending family life. Very few social circles can boast of a female character like that of Clara Monneron, the daughter of Professor Monard, now in Bonn, so noble, so lovely, so gifted, and, at the same time, so perfectly modest. Our souls met one evening, when I was arguing with one of the most distinguished teachers of the Free Church, for the right of the truth-seeking heathen to an entrance into the Kingdom of Heaven: and when I found myself unexpectedly supported by young Mme. Monneron, who, with an expression of surprise in her gentle voice, said:

"What! Do you not believe that every soul which honestly seeks God will ultimately attain to him?"

I saw her but seldom, which I regretted. I went out in many directions; she seldom left home. But it was always a pleasure to me to converse with her. Her soul possessed the same ethereal beauty as her countenance. One recognized the author of the charming little book, "Augustin;" one seemed to hear an angel speak of earthly affairs.

I have also to thank a young lady in Lausanne for the following observation:

"What a number of important facts present themselves in life both with regard to soul and conscience, which are passed over by the historian. It belongs to us women to preserve and implant these sacred memories in the heart of childhood, and, so doing, to keep alive the sacred fire in the home!"

On Sunday afternoons, the population of Lausanne, of all classes, may be seen abroad, on the promenades around the lake, garlanded, as it is, with villas, grounds, and Alps. It is a tranquil life, but holiday-like and beautiful. Generally speaking, life is enjoyed here in a quiet manner, even by the artisan class of the population. Now and then there is an exception to this rule; but, then, it is owing to foreign influences.

One day in February was the fair. On one side of the square La Riporne, at the foot of La Cité, with its magnificent old cathedral, the country-people had set up their booths, and every thing was silent and and quiet. On the other side, however, of the square, stood the French traders in their carriages or their booths, keeping up an immense talking and merriment.

"Who'll have these handkerchiefs?" cried one. "I paid for them fifty francs a-piece; but I'll sell them to you for five-and-twenty—nay, for fifteen—twelve—seven—five—three—two—one franc and seventy-five centimes,—nay, for one and fifty, one and thirty,—one and twenty-five,—one and fifteen,—one and ten, one and five—*one franc a-piece!* Who has one franc in his pocket? What?—You have not even ninety centimes—not one? That is miserable!—you could never lay out your money better!" and so on.

Another cried, "See this trowsers-piece, direct from Paris. If you buy it you may be dressed like a **prince, a captain, an advocate, a syndic!** It cost me one hundred francs; but I'll sell it you for fifty—nay, for"—and then an abatement commenced on the same scale as before; "Now who will have it, lift up their hands! What?—Has nobody any money? Buy it all the same! That's nothing; there!"—and the trowser-piece flew into the embrace of a substantial old woman. "There, that is not merchandise which I sell you, but a present which I make you!"

A third commended a little flute, "an English flute, mounted with the purest silver." It had cost fifteen francs, but he would sell it for five—abatement then followed, as before—"Ah, well, you have not any money with you!—But for these handkerchiefs, however!—Buy them!—It is handsome, look you, to go out on a Sunday, with a corner of one hanging from each pocket, to show that you have money to spend on both sides!"

Each dealer shouts, and fights, as it were, with both arms, whilst he throws off, one after another, neckkerchief, coat, waistcoat, and stands there in his shirt-sleeves.

One, who appears to be more of a *Monsieur* than the others, because he wears a hat, and they only caps, stands in a cabriolet, and recommends, with pedantic loquacity, various razors, which he flourishes about and makes to glitter in the bright sunshine, before the eyes of the spectators.

Every shouting dealer collects around him a crowd of listeners; these, however, are circumspect purchasers, and don't permit themselves to be decoyed. Now and then, a handkerchief, a paper of buttons, a hunk of thread, flies into the embrace of a peasant woman or girl, and whilst they thoughtfully examine the wares, and slowly reach for their small coin, the dealer has turned himself to other customers, in perfect security that he will be paid. He who shouts the loudest, and makes the most violent gesticulations, attracts the greatest number of people around him. Here descends one who is wearied with shouting, and another steps up to his place, with fresh vigor, earrings in his ears, moustache over his lip, and the look of a Merry Andrew. He takes a couple of belts in his hand, and begins—not to shout, but to roar and bellow, so that he can be heard over the whole market, and the voices of all the other dealers are overpowered. This produces great effect. The people leave all the others to gather around this stentorian shouter, and evidently expect an uncommonly curious spectacle. And amusing and uncommon was the scene, assuredly, and entertaining, also, beheld at the foot of buildings bearing the date of centuries, and of the snow-covered Alps, which stood around like a magnificent Colosseum, beneath the clearest dark-blue heaven! The sun shone warmly; the bells of the Cathedral rung. It was a scene of southern life!

One evening, I paid a visit to the Darbyite congregation. The Darbyites are a kind of modern Quakers. Their community is governed by its elders; priests they have none. Any person can speak in the church, according to the inspiration of the spirit. I believe that the founder of the sect, Mr. Darby, an Englishman, is still living. Of late, the sect has found numerous adherents at Lausanne, and in other parts of the Canton Vaud. The Lausanne congregation was, this evening, especially large. Its principal leader is said to be now absent. Three or four men spoke feebly, and without talent. All spoke of the certainty of acceptance in Christ for every one who would believe in him. The hymns took up again the same theme, and compared the believers to "sheep which grazed in rich pasture-meadows, in the perpetual sunshine of grace."

I found the pasture-meadows, that is to say, within the congregation, very meagre of intelligence. I also became exceedingly sleepy, and many of the good sheep there were sleepy too.

The Darbyites are celebrated for the gravity and morality of their quiet life, as well as for the assistance which they mutually render each other.

The 13th of March was the election-day in the Canton Vaud, indeed, in the whole of the Swiss Cantons. I heard upright men, themselves electors, earnestly deplore the want of honesty and candor which is exhibited on these occasions, or which these occasions bring forth. Intrigues and hypocrisy abound.

A noble-minded man gave it as his opinion, that an absolute monarchy was a better form of government for mankind.

I did not agree with him. We must purchase, I said, that which is good in freedom—that which is noble in freedom—with the dangers of freedom; and these we must overcome by taking a higher moral stand. The Christian commonwealth and life are not a level plain, on which mankind can easily wander, like sheep in rich pasture-meadows, in the light of an earthly sun of grace. It is a Jacob's ladder to heaven, and every fresh step must be taken with labor and combat, until the crimson of its morning ascends. Civil liberty is, at the same time, an education for freedom; ought, at least, to be so. If the Canton Vaud, if the free life of Geneva, be still in its minority, it does not follow that they are always to remain so.

The aspiring life, in precisely these Cantons, is a pledge, that even here the good will overcome the evil; because, that which essentially grows, and is in the increase, especially in the Canton Vaud, is education, educational institutions of all kinds, and for all classes. Private schools and public lectures, especially calculated for the culture of the young, are continually on the increase. A great many excellent books are in circulation, whilst their low price renders them accessible to all parts of the country, and steamboats and railways make them so likewise.

I visited various of the higher schools for girls, and found everywhere much that was excellent in their arrangement, as well as in individual portions of the instruction given. That which, however, I lack in every case, and, indeed, which I have never yet found anywhere, is a clearly comprehended, and, for the pupils, a clearly expressed comprehension of the object of all education,—a view of life and instruction, which shows the latter as merely a means for the former, and which elevates life itself, from its local, circumscribed sphere, to a means towards the kingdom of God. That which I lack here, as everywhere, is a view of the individual relationship to society, which sanctifies every individual gift to its service, with a clear glance at the relationship of all gifts to the highest objects of society. Such a view ought to govern every educational institution,—to hover over it, like its good angel. If this be wanting in the education of young women, then the most essential is wanting.

Write above the cradle of every little girl: "Behold the handmaiden of the Lord!"

And inscribe the words in her heart, during the time of her education, and her life will then become good and noble, whatever her talents may be; and whatever her sphere of action may become, she will not live merely for a narrow and selfish aim.

And here let me say a few words about the man whom the education of young girls in the Canton Vaud, and for the whole of Switzerland, has to thank for its latest and highest development, which has caused young women in Switzerland to be sent for as teachers into all the countries of Europe,—the man who has given a new, more inward direction to the life of the Protestant church, and which it is only needful for it to follow out fully, in order to arrive at its fundamental principle,—its original source. My own individual gratitude also admonishes me to the same, because beyond any other living, interesting individuals and good friends in Switzerland, has been, and still is to me, the dead—undying

ALEXANDRE VINET.

Already in his earliest youth he was affected by his deep feeling for every thing noble and beautiful. One day he was reading aloud Corncille's Cid, in the family circle, and suddenly stopping, he rose up and left the room. His sister followed, a minute or two afterwards, and found him in his room greatly affected and bathed in tears.

His father was a just, but a severe man; nevertheless his son loved him with his entire warm heart. Long after the father's death, the son treasured up as a sacred relic, the peeling of an orange, which his father on one occasion had thrown to him.

It is now about twenty-five years, since a religious revival passed from England through the whole of Switzerland. It awakened souls to a consciousness of their inner condition, and produced an open acknowledgment of the same, as well before men as before God. It was an arousing—as in the early days of Protestantism—an arousing of the conscience against all hypocrisy, all sham Christianity, all mere thoughtless formalism. It flew like wild-fire through the country; it kindled all minds of a deeper character. People held meetings at which they openly avowed their faith, and their conviction. Skeptics, deists, nay even atheists, declared theirs, as well as the believing Christian. Men desired above all things to be honest to themselves and their neighbor. They protested against the tyranny over the conscience practiced by the state-church, and against the hypocrisy or the indifference which was the consequence thereof.

A. Vinet, at this time Professor of Literature, attached himself to the new movement, and soon became its leader, from his great eloquence both as a writer and speaker, and by means of which he conducted it beyond the protest, to the higher ground of the protest itself, and directed the mind to its highest object. Whilst he, like the great Pascal, asserted the power of the conscience to recognize the highest truth, and, in consequence thereof, the human right of self-decision in those questions which most nearly concern its eternal weal or woe, he placed before his hearers the relationship of Christianity to the human soul and life, with the inspiration of an evangelical genius.

His glorious work, "*De la Manifestation des Convictions Religieuses,*" became, to the general reader, the result of his earliest position. It received the prize from Guizot, in the name of the French Academy. I do not know any thing more beautiful or more elevating than the first chapter of this book, or any thing more deeply affecting than its last pages.

The result of Vinet's second and highest position; the relationship of Christianity to the human heart and life was read in his *Discours Evangeliques;* which are still read with rapture in the educated circles of Christendom, in all the larger cities from Paris to Petersburg. New *Discours Evangeliques* poured forth afresh, as from an ever-welling fountain, presented in ever-new pictures the word of Christian revelation, to the inquiring, truth-seeking, suffering, combating, human being. But Christianity was to Vinet, above all things, Christ, the living Saviour. He laid humanity anew upon the Saviour's breast. He himself reposed there, like another St. John, and derived thence his inspiration. In character and disposition, Vinet resembled the Master's most beloved disciple.

Vinet, by his assertion of the right of **conscience,**

and his profound criticism on the working of the state church, awoke innumerable minds. By his promulgation of the objective revelations of the Gospel to the human heart, and above all, of its divine leader, Vinet gave a new concentration to the Christian consciousness, which hitherto had too often understood Christianity as merely doctrine or morality whilst it overlooked its chief object—Jesus Christ, and God revealed in him.

The bringing of this livingly forward, was the aim of Vinet's later activity, both as a teacher and writer. His course of *Litterature Français*, so rich in noble metal, in beautiful flowers, and so instructive to the youthful mind—is an examination, from the Christian point of view, into the productions of French Literature during the last century. His University Lectures aimed at presenting, with an eloquence and ardor which, perhaps, never were surpassed, the relationship between the requirements of the human consciousness and the "glad tidings of revelation."

From his chair, as lecturer, where he still spoke with dying voice on these subjects, to his numerous pupils, he was carried one day home, never to stand up before them more.

"If I had lived longer," he was heard to say on his death-bed, "I might have been able—perhaps to accomplish something good!"

A more humble soul never existed.

Vinet died in the prime of life, but he had done more for humanity than most men.

Vinet has formed, as much by his own character as by his teaching, a school whence have already proceeded many of the young men who are at the present time, most full of promise for the future. Edmond de Presançe, Philippe Trottel, Penchaud, and many others, are amongst these. He was a true man; humble, and with bowed head, passing over the fields of earth, but his hand sowed fruit-bearing seed. Thousands of hearts have blessed it.

Mine is amongst these. For I stood solitary and depressed under many anxieties in my northern home, when a volume of Vinet's *Discours Evangeliques* was sent to me by his widow.

These strengthened and consoled me. A. Vinet became my friend, in certain questions my teacher. His spirit attracted me to Switzerland, and here have I, above all things, learned to love him still more. Seldom has a man been so universally beloved. And if I were tempted—and I am sometimes—to call for the assistance of some saint in my inner combat, I should lift beseeching eyes and hands to Alexandre Vinet.

When now about to leave Lausanne, and the Canton Vaud, it is very pleasant to me to place this humble thank-offering upon the grave-stone of its noblest teacher, the prophet of the New Church!

And now to Geneva, to the City of Calvin, to the Rome of Protestantism!

SEVENTH STATION.

In Geneva—Countess de Gasparin—Merle d'Aubigné. The Arve and Rhone—Mont Salève—The Hero of the Scene—Visit to the Workshops of Watch-makers—Women's Work—A Female Worker—Churches and Ecclesiastical Affairs—Intellectual Life—Geneva, the Paradise of Unmarried Women—Calvin's "Institutions"—Jargonaut—"The Living Water"—Domestic Life—A New Flower—An Old Calvinist—Old and New Geneva.

An old author writes; "Geneva had become the rendezvous of reform, its Rome, its Jerusalem. And when the pilgrims coming through the pass of the Alps or the Jura Mountains beheld 'the City of the Lord,' they united in singing the hymn of praise and victory.

"It is she, the little city, the new Bethlehem, where God has been pleased to let his Son be born anew, the city which he has prepared as a refuge for righteous men'!"

But of this I was not thinking, when, on the 15th of March, I hastened towards Geneva, across Lake Leman. The magnificence of the scene occupied both soul and mind. It was a glorious day, cold, but of inimitable brightness. Lausanne gave me the most friendly glance at parting, and I replied to it with all my heart as I saw its magnificent old cathedral, surrounded by masses of gray-brown houses and still leafless woods, vanish in the distance. I had been happy there.

After a journey of three hours, the steamboat approached Geneva; sweeping to the left into its broad bay. The lake shimmered as from millions of diamonds, and the great white lady—Mont Blanc—elevated herself on the northern shore, in shining white attire, in great state with all her court of ice-shapes, pyramids, walls, and towers, under the bright blue heaven, in the blazing sun—it was splendid!

An hour later I was sitting in a light and handsome room, up three flights of stairs, in the Bourg du Four, with a view of Mount Saleve and the Botanic Garden. A kind and educated lady, the widow of one of the distinguished teachers of the University, provided me there with a quiet and friendly home.

The Countess de Gasparin, known as a clever authoress, and especially for her work on marriage, paid me a visit the day after my arrival. This was amiable of her. She is an agreeable blondine, still young, with refined features—on the whole, a lovable person, with French ease of demeanor and facility of expression, very loquacious, and somewhat decided in manner. We were soon disputing on more subjects than people can discuss in many conversations. But it mattered not. One may like, and even become attached to, those with whom one cannot agree. And I liked the Countess of Gasparin for her candor and amiability, and I accepted with sincere pleasure her invitation to her country-house near Geneva. I was also rather curious to become acquainted with the Count de Gasparin, the man who had made her an enthusiast for marriage. For such she is; maintains that all women ought to be married, and asserts that statistics are wrong when they show that there are more women than men in the world. In the mean time, *la couple parfait*, as the married pair Gasparin are called, is always a beautiful sight on the earth.

I transcribe the following from my diary:

GENEVA, *March* 18*th*.—Yesterday I visited the celebrated historian, Merle d'Aubigné, at his country-house near Geneva, by "the living waters"—murmuring brooks—children of the river Arve, or of its Alpine spring—which never freeze or dry up, and which water this region in many directions. The historian of the Reformation, Merle d'Aubigné, is a man of a vigorous and splendid frame, with brilliant eyes under black, bushy eyebrows, a handsome and worthy representative of old Geneva, of the militant, Protestant city. His conversation is animated and rich in imagery, like a living chronicle. "The living waters" murmur cheerfully through his grounds—also the home of his childhood—watering its wonderfully beautiful trees. Death, however, has lately visited his house, robbing him of his wife, and, with her, of much of the cheerfulness of his life. But he has another wife in the Goddess of History, and he begins again to listen to her inspiration. He is now employed upon the fourth part of his History of French Reformation, in which he has a great work before him.

Over the door of his house is inscribed, *Tempus breve.*

Merle d'Aubigné is strictly orthodox as an historian, and adheres to the doctrine of literal inspiration. There may be a more profound theologian than he, but scarcely a more living narrator of history. His descriptions live. Persons, natural scenes, transactions—all are called forth plastically under his master hand.

The climate is almost as changeable here as in America. The day of my arrival at Geneva was cold but lovely; the next day, gray, windy, and disagreeable in the highest degree; and the day following that was a regular summer day, only too warm. In the evening, a little rain fell, then it became again clear, and the evening star, Venus, beamed forth in indescribable beauty. This is one of those periods which is said to recur every eighth year, when she receives and reflects the light of the sun, with an intensity which causes it to become to us, during some months, like a moon. Its most extreme splendor is said to occur in April and in June.

I make solitary excursions in and about the city, that I may make observations. This is a great enjoyment to me. Yesterday, the 22d of March, I took a glorious ramble along the banks of the Arve, to see its junction with the Rhone. Arve flows from the icy sea at Chamouni, and is here a tolerably broad, very cold stream, which winds, roaring with gray, turbid waters, now through sandy fields, now through fertile highlands, around which it forms for itself deep bays and curves. I followed the windings of the Arve for about an hour, from the handsome stone bridge at the little village of Carouge—formerly Savoyan, now a kind of suburb to Geneva—when, all at once, I saw standing up before me, in an oblique direction, the lofty ridge of a brown, precipitous earth-wall, on which stood beautiful trees and country-houses, and below which flowed the powerful Rhone, clear and of a metallic green-blue color; no longer like the little, milk-white stream, which I saw issuing from the cradle of the snow-field at Grimsel, neither like the furious river which comes down later from the highlands, bearing along their melting snows and masses of earth, rolling stones and timber, upon its agitated, turbid waters, down to Lake Leman at Villeneuve. For there, at the close of the Rhone valley, the clear lake receives the wild mountain wanderer into its deep bosom. An extraordinary combat then ensues; the waters of the Rhone and Lake Leman struggle together for mastery, but the earth-weighted waves are vanquished; they sink below the clear waters; the clear waters become uppermost and the Rhone disappears in the embrace of the victor. There he reposes long in the depths; is freed from the foreign elements which he has taken up during his wandering, which have disturbed his character and his life, and—who can tell what takes place down in the depths of the clear lake? The Rhone has vanished there; but he re-appears on the other side of the lake, at Geneva, and then so clear, so crystal-pure and beautiful! He has been born anew; baptized in a pure element. The coloring of the woods and the sky have melted together into his clear water.

This day was cloudy and heavy, yet at the same time the coloring of the Rhone was unspeakably translucent and lovely. When the rapid, gray waters of the Arve hurl themselves into the Rhone, the Rhone adopts the more rapid career of that river, but rarely changes its color and brightness. The Rhone does not become the Arve, but the Arve becomes the Rhone. The Rhone is the more powerful nature; besides which, he has passed through a purifying bath,—a new baptism. He is calm and clear. Thus he hastens on to meet the new destiny on the soil of France, and receives into his bosom the Leuth, the Saone, and the wild Durance, fertilizing vineyards along the French Rhone-valley, to Avignon, where he abruptly turns south, hastens on to the Mediterranean, and

> Speeds on, without tarriance, till he casteth
> Himself into his father's breast, and dies.*

March 24th.—A glorious day, after some clouds. Read, amongst other books, Père Girard's excellent "Methode Maternelle," and in the afternoon took a long ramble in the direction of Mont Salève and the highlands on the Arve. The whole of this side, between Geneva and Mont Salève—the boundary between Switzerland and Savoy—is cultivated like a garden, full of beautiful plantations, country-villas, and small farms. The air was warm, the sky deep blue, the larks sang, and many little flowers were out upon the verdant meadow-turf. Yellow auriculas are here common brookside flowers. Arve roared loudly, and numbers of little becks hastened along, singing, to increase his waters. It seemed to me that the earth was indeed beautiful!

And the hero of the scene—hast thou, my R——,

---

* The River, by **Tègner**.

ever heard speak of Mont Blanc? In that case, thou hast heard that it is a snow-covered mountain of Savoy, near fifteen thousand feet high, and thou hast in spirit, if thou hast not seen Mont Blanc in reality, beheld an icy giant raise his crown towards the stars. But from Geneva and the district around, from which the most beautiful view of the giant-mountain is obtained, it seems merely like an immense snow-hill, with many terraces. Its mass, its dazzling whiteness, its soft, rounded form, rivets the glance with an imposing power, which has, at the same time, a something tranquilizing and agreeable in it, especially when, in an evening, the giant is tinted by the light of the descending sun. The beautiful profile of Napoleon, which is seen portrayed in the highest outline of the mountain, and which it is impossible to avoid seeing, when you have once become aware of it, adds also to the grandeur of its physiognomy. From the Quai-Mont-Blanc, and from Rousseau's Island, one sees it, together with the whole chain of the Savoy Alps, very perfectly.

I spent yesterday afternoon and evening on Rousseau's Island, sitting in and wandering about the lovely groves around his statue, contemplating the Alps. They stood out splendidly, in the golden sunset, especially Napoleon's image, which was latest illumined by its beams. They seemed to me to shine, with the peace of God, upon the hero.

>He soundly sleeps on his bed of snow,—
>A calmer the world hath none—
>He will die no more; he hath struck his last blow;
>And his sentinel watch is the sun!

People talk a great deal about the rapid change which the sunset produces amongst the Alps. But this moment, their summits shone in gold and crimson; and the next, they pale, become ashy-gray, and stand, so to speak, a corpse. And this is true. But I have never heard any remark made about that which, however, is in the highest degree worthy of observation, namely: of the after-glow—the second brightness which lights up these snow-covered summits a short time after they have been observed,—a transfiguration which, during clear evenings, increases gradually, and illumines the heavens above them, to the very zenith, till one is sometimes ready to question whether the sun is not about to rise again; whether it is not the crimson of a new morning. The contemplation of this spectacle is a great enjoyment to me. I have sometimes seen this second brightness, such as to remind me of "that second light" of which our northern sages speak, which extends on to the midnight.

In order not to weary thee, my R ——, by talking about these eternal mountains, their height, and their beauty, I will, once for all, tell thee what they told me, that is to say, when I became well acquainted with them. Because, often enough, I have felt myself more oppressed than elevated by their immensity and immovability. But I am now on good terms with them, and have come to understand their silent language to mankind.

They stand in nature, like the prophets of the Old Testament, or more correctly speaking, like the old wise men and teachers of the Pagan world, and point us to a greatness high above that in which we, the children of the valleys and the plains, have our being.

For these pyramids are not the pleasant things of earth; they are not the fragrance of the flowers; not the singing of the birds, not the changing life of the seasons. Imperishable in their eternal peace, they are moved alone by the sun. The sun alone, causes them to glow or to become pale, and to paint for us images of life or of death. But they alone, receive its earliest beams in the morning, and retain its light in the evening long after it has departed from us. It is in their bosoms that spring feeds the great rivers, which fertilize the earth, foster the life of cities, and extend themselves, beautifying, benefiting, even to the smallest blade of grass.

I spent about two months in my lofty house in the Bourg-du Four, visited the watch-making work-shops for women; read Calvin's Institutions; made acquaintance with the latest great Swiss educators, Pestalozzi, Père Girard, Von Fellenberg, and Mme. Necker de Saussure, as well as with various of the thinking and amiable citizens, male and female, now living, of Geneva. My kind hostess and her children, all married, but who often meet at their mother's house, were amongst these. Her son, the young Pastor Bouvier, married to a daughter of Adolphe Monod, is one of the most beloved young preachers of Geneva, and, according to my opinion, the only man of genius amongst them.

I was introduced into the watch-maker's work-shops by M. Viande, one of the merchants of Geneva, a man of great humanity, and also of rare amiability of disposition and character. I could not have had a better guide, even with regard to the moral inquiries which I wished to make.

We began with the schools of pupils, where young girls learn, for a term of three years, to make every part of a watch. After this time, they select that particular part for which they have most inclination, or in the doing of which they are most expert. The perfected pupil may be sure, on leaving the school, of obtaining immediate employment amongst the watchmakers. Young girls from twelve to eighteen years of age appear very healthy and well cared for. Each one has her own little table and her own window-niche for her work.

The manufacture of pocket-watches is, at the present time, carried to a great extent at Geneva. An immense number are required for the Chinese market. A well-equipped China-man, I have been told, carries a watch on each side of his breast, that he may be able to regulate the one by the other. Wealthy Chinese cover the walls of their rooms with watches. These watches are of a more ornamental character, and have more filigree-work upon them, than those made for Europeans. Long live the Chinese!

At one of the greatest and best-conducted manufactories of Geneva, nothing but watch-faces are prepared, and elderly, well dressed, and well looking women, sat by twenties and thirties in clean, well-warmed rooms, working upon——watch-faces.

"Do you not get tired of always doing the same work?" I inquired from some of them.

"Oh, no!" replied they, and showed me that each little dial had to pass through fifty different operations before it was finished. This kept the attention awake, and prevented any sense of monotony. They work here from eight o'clock in the morning, till six or seven in the evening, and thus earn about fifty francs a month.

"Are you able to lay by any thing for old age, or in case of sickness?" I inquired from a mother who had worked there with her daughter, side by side, for ten years.

"Oh, no!" they replied, "we have no longer been able to do that, since provisions have been so dear."

"Nor yet for a little journey of pleasure, or holiday in the summer?"

"We never think of such a thing. We should by that means lose, not only money, but also our time, and possibly our place."

"Is not such a life as this heavy and void of interest?"

"We have Sundays for rest and refreshment, and the evenings for reading, or occupation of another kind. Besides which, we need not during our work be continually thinking about it!"

They seemed perfectly satisfied.

The workwomen who are able to execute certain more difficult parts of the watch, get higher wages, and can earn from five to ten francs a day.

In the mean time, this great division of labor causes

the great part of the women not to earn much more than their maintenance.

"My grand-mother made whole watches!" said an old woman, with a sigh, who was now sitting at home with her daughter, employed in one single operation in a little cog, for the great manufactory, "and at that time, women were much higher in the work than they are now, and also got higher payment. They were few in number, but extremely dexterous. Now they are innumerable, but their dexterity is employed upon a mere nothing—a very crumb."

And this was true, as far as the old woman was concerned, for the whole of her work consisted in drilling one little hole in a small steel plate, with a little machine which resembled a tiny spinning-wheel. Her daughter was seated at another little machine, and was merely making a little alteration in the hole which her mother had drilled; and six hundred of such holes must be made before they could earn three francs.

The old woman, who came of a race of watchmakers "from time immemorial," and whose grandmother had made whole watches, seemed to me, as she sat there, reduced to making one single little hole, a little portion of the watch, like a dethroned watchmaking queen. You saw plainly that her fate grieved her, but she bore it worthily, and with resignation, acknowledging that numbers now lived by that work, which, in her grandmother's days, belonged to a few privileged persons, and made them rich. Her daughters were both agreeable young girls, with fresh courage for life. The one had learned her mother's calling,—the other had prepared herself for the occupation of a teacher.

Enamel-painting is a kindred class of work, which, as well as watch-making, affords a good and safe means of support to a great part of the female population of Geneva, in more than one class. The work is done at home, or in work-shops; many well-educated young girls work for the manufactory at their parents' houses, and thus contribute to the prosperity of the family. The little watch-making shops, the little work-table, are to be met with in every village and small farm-house in the neighborhood of Geneva. The daughters of the peasants work at these.

I have seen and heard enough of the lives of these female workers, as well in their homes as in their work-shops, to thank God that so great a number of women here, are able, by means of a good and inexpensive branch of industry, to provide for themselves, and acquire an independence—which *may* lead to great good; and many beautiful examples can be given of these young female workers, applying their earnings to the support of their aged parents, or for the education of younger sisters or relatives.

For the greater part, they seem to become principally the means of the indulgences of vanity, or even of less allowable independence.

The female worker, in the full and highest meaning of her vocation, in the complete fullness of her life, is a character which I have not met with here, as I have done—in Sweden.

I remember there, a little work-table, at which is seated a woman, still young, working from early morning till late in the evening—sometimes even till late in the night—because work is her delight, and her perseverance and power of work are astonishing,—her eye continually fixed upon her work, even during conversation, whilst her skillful hand guides the graving-tool, and engraves letters, numbers, or tasteful ornaments, on articles of gold or silver—chronometers, pocket-watches, rings, &c. But the inner life is not occupied therewith; it gazes clearly around, and comprehends, with love, every work and every transaction which tends either to the advantage of the fatherland, or the honor of humanity. She is near-sighted at her work, but far-sighted as regards the great work in society; her heart beats warmly for this, and the little work-table has a place in its realm. How distinguished a place this is, her numerous friends know,—but not she herself,—the unpretending artist, the good citizen and friend, the noble worker—*Sophie Ahlbom!*

There is no want, here in Switzerland, as elsewhere, of female workers who are able to conceive of work as a means to a higher end, and who know the true place of the work-table in society. The sisters Rohrdorf, of Zürich, are noble laborers in this spirit; but that which is wanting in general, is an awakened sense, and an education for this higher view of labor and of life.

Another thing is also wanting,—a literature for the workshops, of an improving and entertaining character at the same time. Books are often read aloud during the silent, quiet work, but—not the best books. Good biography ought especially to be read in these rooms, where young men and young women prepare, as it were, their own future.

The remarks which I have made against the generality of female workers here, may be applied, with a still graver emphasis, to the male population of the work-shops. I know that, amongst these, honorable exceptions occur, but—I will allow a member of this class himself to make his naïve confession.

My good hostess, Madame Bouvier, related to me the following:

"I went," said she, "yesterday afternoon, up to the bastion, for a little fresh air, and seated myself upon one of the benches under the trees. A well-dressed and respectable-looking young man was sitting just by, and throwing bread-crumbs to the birds.

"After we had sat a little while in silence, I said, 'You are fond of birds, sir?'

"'Yes, very; but there are so few now, to what there used to be; people take their nests.'

"'You are from the country?'

"'No; I live in the city, but—the country is now very beautiful!'

"'Yes, and they say that there is an unusual promise of a good harvest.'

"'Yes; the prices of wine have already fallen.'

"'It is always a good thing when the prices of the means of life fall; but as far as wine is concerned, it is better when the price continues somewhat high, because, then, people drink less of it.'

"'Ah! what, indeed, could the workman do without wine! Believe me, he requires it; I know it.

He has not always a great deal to eat, and then a drop of wine gives him strength and courage.'

"'But it gives a false strength, which leaves him afterwards all the weaker. If, instead of wine, he bought good meat, would he not be the better for it?'

"'Yes, that is quite true. But you see, it is in this way;—things don't always go on pleasantly in life;—one has anxiety—sorrow,—and then one takes a drop of wine to cheer one's spirit.'

"'But—are you suffering from sorrow then, sir?'

"'Yes, madam; I have sorrow; I have had words with one of my acquaintance.'

"'And this is a young woman?'

"'Yes, madam.'

"'Oh, but that will soon be all over, and every thing will soon be right again between you!'

"'No, no—it will not be right again between us; because she will have me *mettre les pouces*,* and that is what I neither can nor will do! No, no, it is all over between us!'

"'But if you are in the wrong, you ought not to be unwilling to confess it.'

"'Yes, but you see all women are coquettes; they will have men to flatter them, make them fine speeches, tell lies—but that is what I never could do, nor would! Perhaps I may learn one of these days!'

"'But if she whom you love is unworthy, you must endeavor to forget her.'

---

* *Mettre les pouces*, an expression which implies taking the first step, giving one's self up.—*Author's Note.*

"'That's not so easy to do—not so easy! And I am now in that state of mind that I could throw myself into the trench yonder!'

"'All this comes because you of the working class—for I can see that you are one of them—are without religion.'

"'That is true, very true, madam. One does not think about such things. I have been shooting all day at a mark, to console myself.'

"'And that has not, certainly done you much good?'

"'Not the least! But this is what it is; one must divert, cheer one's self up;—that is what we call civilization. One must always have a pleasure before one as an object.'

"'But yet, you cannot always have pleasure as an object of life?'

"'Oh, yes, madam; it is really so; one must always think of the enjoyment; one styles it civilization. But after all, it has little enough to do with it; the girls put on fine clothes, and have a craving after pleasure; the men go to the clubs and amuse themselves, whilst their wives stay at home with the children, sometimes in trouble and want. But so it is—one thinks above every thing else about amusing one's self, and does not think upon much else.'

"'You are a journeyman?'

"'Yes, but I am well off; my earnings are good.'

"'You seem to me to be well off, and also to have good abilities; and I plainly perceive that you know how you ought to employ them. I wish with all my heart that you would act according to such knowledge, because then you would not seek for consolation and strength in vain. Fare you well!'

"'Adieu! I thank you, madame!'"

I read through Calvin's great work, *Institution Chrétienne*, during the present week, or rather I should say, fought my way through, because the reading of this work is an actual fight. And the work itself is a fight, an incessant engagement in phalanxes of twenty or thirty paragraphs and arguments, as many objections and still more answers with regard to all kinds of doctrines, dogmas, and sects. Manicheans, Arians, Servetus, (*ce mechant homme, cet èsprit impur!*) first and last the Pope, who is roughly handled. The strength of the book lies in the polemic against the doctrines of the Catholic Church from the doctrines of true Christianity. The style is everywhere powerful, clear, and excellent. There are beautiful thoughts and passages; in certain parts, great logical ability, as for example, in the dogma regarding the Trinity; equally great sophistical art in the treatment of the baptism of children, and as dark and strong a onesidedness in the treatment of "Grace;" a similar want of human conscience and human kindliness in his manner of stating the doctrine of predestination—which Calvin bases upon detached passages of Scripture—and such a self-complaisant absorbtion in his portraiture of the seemingly good cast into eternal perdition and eternal torment, that the leap from Calvin to Helvetius, Diderot, & Co., seems to me quite natural. Between these men and Calvin, Rousseau is a salutary shining beacon. And he well deserves his beautiful monument at Geneva, upon his verdant, solitary island.

After I had combated for a couple of hours with Calvin's flint-like logic and his contradictions in this absurd doctrine, I grew weary and melancholy, and went out to breathe the soft, fresh, vernal air, and God's goodness in it. To what frightful absurdities does not the blind worshiping of the letter of the Scriptures lead! The letter killeth, but the spirit maketh alive; was said by the Lord.

Calvin's letters, lately published by the young Professor, J. Bonnet, are equally indispensable for the right understanding of Calvin's character. They have, to a certain extent, reconciled me with him. One sees in them a soul actually possessed by one only thought and one object—the honor of God.* This gave to him the same calm, assured bearing in the presence of kings and queens, as before the meanest of the people. He acknowledged merely one worthiness in all, namely, that of being worthy to serve in God's work—which was, in Calvin's estimation, the progress of the reformation. All were reprimanded and admonished accordingly. The Prince of Condè was gravely rebuked, "because he made himself agreeable to the ladies, whereby he became ridiculous, and in consequence thereof, injured the interests of God." The noble and pious Duchess René of Ferrara, was obliged to hear, that she "must now suffer for the

* One proof of this is also Calvin's express prohibition, that any other monument should be raised to him after his death excepting a stone upon his grave. It is no longer known in Geneva what spot of ground contains his dust.—*Author's Note.*

pusillanimity which she showed in her youth towards her service of God."

As regards the bloody sentence of the unfortunate Servetus, Calvin is evidently not free from private malice. But so dark were those times and so much were people accustomed to the heretic perishing in the flames, that very few voices in Protestant Switzerland and Germany were raised in protest against the doom of Servetus. The greater number approved of it; even the mild Melancthon. So little was, even then, understood the sacredness of conscience and the right of honest opinion. Calvin has impressed his stamp on Geneva, both as regards good and evil, and the city which protested against Rome, is still intolerant, stern, and diplomatic, the Rome of Protestantism. But the strict Calvinists are now, however, few and—the age of Calvinism is past. Thank God!

Much dearer than my acquaintance with Calvin, has been the acquaintance which I have made with the great instructors of Switzerland, for the words of the past are true:

> "*Aux autres nations offrant un grand exemple;*
> *De l'education l'Helvetie est le temple!*"

And no people has given greater teachers of this class to humanity. Pestalozzi is known throughout Europe. His heart contained a heaven of kindness and love.

That which is peculiar in his method—with which I am too little acquainted—appears to me to consist in his manner of quickening the attention of the scholar, of developing his faculties of observation, and changing lessons learned by heart into lessons of objects. As for example. He used, in his Institution at Yverdun, to assemble the scholars round a little representation of the city, and let them tell him what they observed in it; then he would take them up one of the mountains round the city, and let them see the same image in its actual proportion and relationship to the surrounding country. Pestalozzi's Institute fell to pieces after a short success; his scholars were dispersed, and he himself, half insane with sorrow, ended his days in a cottage on the Jura. His method is no longer spoken of, but like the sap, which, though unseen, circulates through all the branches of the tree, his mode of instruction, and the devotion he gave to every branch of the work of education, still continue. Many a one has to thank the fact of having come in contact with him, for the good development of their whole lives. It was in a conversation with Pestalozzi, that C. F. Ritter received the impulse which determined his subsequently noble scientific activity—and which presented to us the earth and different parts of the world, in a plastically visible and conceivable form. In many respects, the spirit of Pestalozzi was obscure, impractical, simple, and even childish, but he had mother-thoughts—(*idées Mères*).

Such too had Père Girard, who desired to make the influence of the mother the principal means of the child's inner development, and the mother the child's principal instructor also.* No man, and no woman either, has more profoundly comprehended the voca-

* Pestalozzi desired to do the same, and has aimed at this object in his beautiful little book for the people, *Lienhardt and Gertrude.—Author's Note.*

tion of the mother, or has spoken more beautifully on the subject, than this monk of the Franciscans in Freyburg. It was owing to the fact that his own mother stood forever before the eyes, even of the gray-haired father, as an ideal of all excellence.

"I have seen her," wrote he, "surrounded by fifteen children, embracing all with the same love, the same care, and even in the midst of her domestic occupations finding time to give them instruction in so lovely a manner, and so productive of results, that the most learned educator might have taken a lesson therefrom. Her instruction became really education."

This type of the mother was so precious and so exalted in his mind, that he applied it to Providence, who was not spoken of by Père Girard as "*the fatherly*," but as "*the motherly.*" "*La Providence Maternelle* is a favorite expression of his.

It is this, his mother's natural method, which he considers himself to have merely developed and systematized in his "*Cours de langue Maternelle.*" His method of instruction he calls, "The motherly method." This work, which received the prize of the French Academy, deserves to be studied by all mothers. Girard's motto as educator, was

"Words for thoughts, thoughts for the heart and for life."

The most novel and important part of Père Girard's motherly method, seems to me to be the *Grammaire d'idées*, in which he enables the mother, or the teacher, to introduce the child into the realm of thought and social life, through an organized grouping of ideas, **and an explanation of the words which indicate them.**

This lesson of ideas, or the higher grammar, has not been so much perfected, as indicated by genial hints and examples; but, nevertheless, sufficiently so to encourage the more fundamental thinker to take up the thread. This, if properly handled, would afford young people, and even older ones also, an invaluable assistance in working their way through the labyrinth of the world, and appears to me to be a requisite in education.

His excellent method, his amiable manners, his love for children, in all of which he was another Pestalozzi, but with more beautiful plans, and a more lucid mind, attracted to him a great number of pupils. In a short time, his school numbered five hundred children. But Père Girard talked much about nature, and the "Maternal Providence," and not at all about the infallible Catholic church, and the holy father in Rome. The Jesuits got wind of all this, and—one fine day, Père Girard was removed from his convent, and his beloved, flourishing school at Freyburg, to another convent, in a remote Canton of Switzerland, where he could not busy himself with the education of children. His school in Freyburg was soon after broken up, and his pupils dispersed.

I have obtained a portrait of the fatherly monk. Heart and genius beam from those dear eyes, and from the honest, cheerful countenance. Père Girard lived till within the last two years, and was often visited by traveling strangers.

Von Fellenberg, the third in order in this triumvirate of the Swiss schoolmasters, was the founder of the great educational institution of Hofsvyl, near Berne.

His idea was an all-sided and harmonious development of the human being, yet with especial regard to each individual's particular disposition or talents. His institution is still in existence, carried on according to his principles, by one of his best pupils.

Madame Neckar de Saussure has written only on the education of women; a great work, universally read and esteemed, as well in Switzerland as France. She seems to me to base her doctrine of education upon a deeper and more general foundation, than any of the other spiritual architects. This is the *impulse towards perfection* which she finds in every human breast; and this impulse must be guided and satisfied by the means which it furnishes. It is affecting to observe how willingly she would open to women all the means which could satisfy this highest, noblest need, and how she secretly grieves because these cannot be conceded in their present circumscribed social condition. She does not say, nor yet does she see, how this can be otherwise; but she gives beautiful and noble hints to parents and educators, and she is the best and the pleasantest comforter of the life-wearied and aged. The last chapters of her work produce upon me the same effect as "the after-glow," on the peaks of the Alps. It is evening, and the sun has set, but nevertheless, one enters into "the second light," and looks for the flush of a new dawn.

They have now all departed into the silent unseen, those light-bearers on the path of the younger generation. But "good heads still talk after death," says the proverb, and it is true in the highest sense, as regards these genii of education. Publicly or privately, their labors for the young still go on, and instruction becomes, more and more, education. The large school of Professor Naville, in Geneva, is based upon the method of Père Girard; and who can calculate the homes in which Madame de Saussure's book has not awakened new life, and nobler views of life, and of the vocation of woman?

Many courses of lectures have been given this spring, in Geneva. Amongst these, I have been most interested by those delivered by the amiable and Christian archæologist, Troyon, on the remains of the dwellings and mode of life on the lakes, of the most eminent inhabitants of Switzerland. For the rest, it seems to me difficult to live in Geneva, without every day learning something new. The city is full of intellectual life, of many kinds,—ecclesiastical, political, and scientific, of interests and questions, of lectures, exhibitions, and sermons,—from which one can almost always learn something; and if it be true that Geneva is, as I have been told, the paradise of unmarried women, *le paradis des vieilles filles*, it is so, in fact, because they can there so easily satisfy that hungering after the food of intelligence, which is being awakened more and more in the women of the present time, and which the unmarried have more time to satisfy than they who have husband, and children, and housekeeping duties, to occupy them. Besides which, women, in this Canton, attain to a legal majority at the age of twenty, and by this means, whether in or out of the paternal house, to a certain degree of independence. This is also the case in other of the Swiss Cantons, and, indeed, as I believe, in all of them.

Yet have I never anywhere heard of such heart-felt, perfect relationship, between parents and daughters—especially between fathers and their daughters, as here. I have nowhere else seen daughters so fully devote their whole life to their fathers, and become their helpers, not merely in the home, but also in their work and scientific labors. Madame de Staël's eloquent pen has made the world acquainted with the reverence which she entertained for her father. Thus was the great Haller beloved by his daughter; thus the celebrated Saussure by his.

Amongst other beautiful instances of this relationship, at the present time, I have heard Professor Navillé and his daughter Rosa mentioned, who, being companions in life, have been also companions in death; and the author of La Theopneustie, M. Gaussin, and his daughter, at the same time his faithful companion and helper.

This does not surprise me. These relationships are, in a high degree, natural, and they would be more frequently met with, if fathers were more frequently really good, just, unselfish educators of their daughters, and if the laws of the country were equitable and promotive of freedom and independence. There are eternal laws, as well as eternal covenants.

I mentioned sermons in Geneva, and I must say a few words about these and the preachers. In many of the latter, I found talent, and good qualifications, but as combined with genius, only in one instance—the young Bouvier. In the Church, *la Polissêrie*, which is also called the Layman's Church, the preaching consists of free discourses by various of its members, partly clergy, and partly laymen. I once heard the text of the Canaanitish woman treated with a psychological profundity, and living power, which affected me in the highest degree. Each new speaker went deeper than his predecessor into the heart of the narrative. Amongst these, a Colonel Tronchisi distinguished himself. I listened and wept, as though I myself had been the woman of whom they were speaking. On other occasions the discourse and edification would be meagre enough. Too much latitude is given to the impulse of the moment.

I heard again, more than once, the gifted preacher to whom I had listened in the high-valley of La Lechevette, and always with great pleasure, though not so great as in the pine wood, under the open heavens. Count de Gasparin, also, gave religious discourses, and that to an immense number of hearers. I was present on one of these occasions, and I most heartily thanked the noble, gifted speaker, because he combated the Calvinistic doctrine of predestination. I cannot adopt his view of the mechanical inspiration of the Bible, nor believe the words of the Bible *quand meme*, according to his advice; neither do I find it edifying. But the man himself, I like.

The representative of the strict Calvinistic doctrine of predestination at the present time, in Geneva, is properly, the venerable C. Mallan, who built his own church there. His uncommon talents—his handsome person also, and his personal dignity, have gained for nim a not inconsiderable number of hearers and— blind adherents. I had heard so much about him that I wished to become acquainted with him, and went, one day, to his church. He spoke merely about grace in Christ. His discourse and his noble, dignified exterior affected me. I desired to hear him again, and see more of him. A day was fixed for this purpose, and M. Mallan sent me, as the "theme and preparation," a little treatise entitled, "*Le Libre Arbitre d'un Mort.*" By this, I found that neither I nor any human being had the slightest free-will. I was as *dead* as a stock, a corpse, but that I must be full of rejoicing at the same time, that without any merit of my own, I had been received into eternal bliss, whilst my brother, without any fault of his, had been thrust down into eternal perdition. After I had read this work, I declined the meeting with him.

I can, for many good reasons, excuse a person who holds narrow views on certain subjects, but I cannot forgive any one who rejoices in a doctrine which makes God the most unjust of fathers, and mankind as his blind, heartless instruments.

People here are coming, gradually, to perceive the one-sided doctrine of predestination is based upon such a view of the divine character. Mallan's church is now attended by but few; its condition is become dilapidated, and he, himself, is like Marius in the ruins of Carthage.

One topic, and one protest, occupies the whole of Protestant Geneva, at the present time, and that is against Catholicism and its encroachments. More and more Catholics are continually flying hither from Savoy, and are now building themselves here, a magnificent cathedral. The Catholic bishop attracts an ever-increasing audience to his sermons. All this is a great grief to the true Genevese, and they speak violently against the encroaching church, which they, in the mean time, assure themselves they need not fear. The polemics against it, either written or spoken, are really extraordinary. But I would first ask these learned, protesting gentlemen, whether it would not be better to inquire what it is in Catholicism which is the cause of its present progress, and which leads so many noble-minded, so many thinking, earnest individuals to be attracted to this church? Because, to attribute it merely to error and delusion is an injustice at once to probability and to human nature. Ought they not to inquire whether there are not doctrines in this church which the reformed church has too hastily abandoned, and which it must resume and elucidate, before it can overcome the Roman Catholic Church, by itself becoming Catholic, in the higher significance; that is, universal, all-embracing? I have long had a presentiment of there being such treasures to be found, both for the heart and mind, in the old church; but I will seek more decided knowledge on these subjects. I will inquire in Italy!

With the perfect married couple, Husband and Wife Gasparin, I have become earnestly well acquainted. They invited me to dinner-parties and soirées. I begged them to afford me "hospitality of the soul," which it is not in the power of all to give, but which was not difficult to them, if—they would. They most kindly understood my desires, and permitted me the enjoyment of quiet hours in their domestic circle—quiet, earnest conversation. We did not agree—it was not possible for us to agree—

upon many topics; but I learned from them the better to understand how much good there may be even in the view which faithfully attaches itself to the Divine inspiration of the letter of the Scriptures. I learned to have esteem, in this respect, for noble natures.

The Count de Gasparin is a nobleman, a *gentleman*, in the last and fullest meaning of the word, and is well worthy of the entire, devoted love of a gifted woman. In conversation and discussion, he is infinitely agreeable. Both husband and wife labor for the good of the people, partly as writers, partly as helpers and counselors in their temporal needs, especially on their own estate—for they are wealthy, and employ their wealth in a noble manner. Would that there were many who resembled them!

I must now say a few words about a citizeness of Geneva, who does not bear the slightest resemblance to Countess de Gasparin, nor yet to any other handsome Genevese lady, but who rules there with more arbitrary sway than any of these, namely, *La Bise noire*. Ha! a cold shudder goes through both soul and body when I merely think of her, and remember her severe government during the last fourteen days which I spent in Geneva. The heavens were leaden, the earth gray, the wind icy-cold; the air dry, like pulverized arsenic, and about as wholesome. The little, green buds on the trees stopped their growth. People kept in-doors, or went out with blue noses, and came in again with colds in their heads. The universal temper fell under the dominion of *la Bise*, and I became convinced that it is *la Bise noire*, to which must be ascribed that contentious, critical contrariness of temper which the Genevese themselves acknowledge to, which they comprehend in the word *Avener.* *Le Genevois est avener!* is an accepted expression. But it most certainly arises from the fact of *la Bise,* that hideous Xantippe, being a fellow-citizeness of Geneva.

The old Genevese has been more than ever *avener* during the last few years, because the government of the Canton, during this time, has been in the hands of a faction, which, under a show of working for the public good, labors to put an end to its old manners and usages, and vails an actual libertinism under the beautiful name of *liberalism.* The leader of the faction, and the present Governor of Geneva, James Fazy, keeps a public gambling-house, and enriches himself in various less reputable ways. The favor which he shows to the Catholic party, and the Catholic influence within the city, give him a majority at the election, which the honest Protestants of the city are not able to withstand; besides which, when they go up to the state-house to vote on questions of government, they are so violently attacked by a low rabble, brought together for the purpose, that the greater number decline to vote at all. In the mean time, the Philistines rule, and the truly loyal sigh over the humiliation of the city of Geneva. The handsome, new electoral palace has received a name indicative of the prevailing spirit, and the adherents of the government are called *libertines.*

In many outward measures, however, it seems to me that the immoral government has really the best interests of the people at heart; and that ought to be the reason why it maintains its hold. It is, at the present time, carrying out great works in the city, which find employment for a great number of persons, and will, in the end, essentially alter many portions of it.

"It provokes me," said an honest old Genevese to me, "but—I cannot bear to think, after all, that it will be—for the best interests of the city!"

If this spirit of improvement will but leave untouched the old Rhone island, with its picturesque buildings and memories from the time of Julius Cæsar! It presents a remarkable contrast with the adjacent, well-built, new quarter of the city.

Geneva is at the present time, together with Basle, the wealthiest city of the confederation. Millionaires are reckoned there by hundreds. I have, however, heard say that that the millionaires of Basle have ten times more millions than the millionaires of Geneva.

On the fourth of May the sun again acquired his power; the air became delicious, and I removed from my good home upon the heights in Geneva, to a country parsonage in the neighborhood, beside the "living waters," at Jargonaut.

EAUX VIVES DE JARGONAUT, *from May 6th to June.*—It was evening when I arrived here. A young girl, whose lovely eyes beamed with heartfelt kindness, silently conducted me to my room. I heard the plash of a fountain; the nightingale was pouring forth his clear, abruptly-varying song in the groves; the fragrant lilacs waving their leafy branches outside the window, and the great walnut-tree stretched up, towards the evening heaven, its young, red-brown leaf-buds upon its yet naked branches, whilst above the quiet, verdant grounds stood the new moon in the hour of twilight. It was wonderfully tranquil and fresh; wonderfully pleasing! It produced at once a soothing and solemn effect upon my mind. Home, sweet home!

Those "living waters," these fresh streams from the great ice-fountains in the bosom of the Alps, which murmur through the whole neighborhood of Jargonaut,* are now nearly dried up on this little property, but I feel the breath of the living waters in the atmosphere, in the domestic life, within which my own life is now flowing on quietly. The cheerful piety and affection, the silent activity, the inner life which prevails there, like a blooming spring-time, and united together all its members, the good, old parents, the young daughters, who are eyes to the half-blind mother and hands to the aged father, whose hands are crippled by rheumatic pains; the one servant of the family, so pleasant and so clever at the same time; the hours of worship, morning and evening, which assemble all; the cheerful meal-times—all were good!

How good it was for me to be there; how precious and agreeable to become acquainted with a family at once so excellent and so happy! For, as yet, no sorrow had approached this home; no adversity. The

---

* Naut signifies, in the old language of the country, a little stream, or beck.—*Author's Note*.

infirmities of the old people were not treated as sorrows. They were borne by them so cheerfully.

The aged pastor Coulin is a patriarch in appearance, as well as in life and disposition. The short periods which he consecrates to prayer morning and evening, are genuine pearls of their kind. A pearl of heavenly dew, which fructifies one and all.

I lived here for about a month; how peacefully the days passed! The weather was charming; I saw the trees come out into leaf, the lofty walnut-trees, unfolding by degrees their ruddy-brown, as it were, not yet awakened, leaf clusters; listened to the song of the nightingale in the thick lilac hedges under the blossoming fruit-trees. Every day I spent some time in a grove, upon a little hill in the grounds, and nearly always found the nightingale there, seated upon a bough, sometimes quite near to me, and singing so deliciously that it was a perfect joy to listen. For this enchanting little bird seems to love human beings, and its song is, as it were, a conversation with its hearers. Its separate sentences have each separate meanings, and one has time between each to have one's own thoughts. The nightingale replies to them; it encourages; it consoles; and its pearl-like trills are irresistibly refreshing; one drinks in with them the purest champagne of nature. I sometimes went thither, into the grove of the nightingale, when the visits of strangers had wearied me, and there is no weariness so great as that which human beings experience from their own kind—and the nightingale then came and sang peace and freshness into my spirit. There, too, I sat, more than once, with friends whose conversation made my life richer. I especially remember amongst these one man—Professor Amiel—and one woman, whose name I will not mention—but this, however, I will say, that more refreshing to me than the song of the nightingale, was my intercourse with that spirit which glanced around with such freshness and freedom, with that heart which devoted itself so entirely, so fully, to the work of the joy-giver and the comforter. It is this heart, rich in love, this soul with its clear power of organized activity, that Geneva has to thank for the new impulse which has been given of late years to her youthful female population of all classes, in the good work of progress and Christian activity.

We read aloud in the evenings,—Louise's and Mary's fresh, youthful voices, making the reading doubly agreeable. The two young sisters had each their own peculiar gifts, with which they beautified life for themselves and others. I read much with Louise, and we made long excursions together. I made acquaintance with the great Swiss naturalists, Haller and Bounet, through their writings and correspondence; for these two scientific men were friends, and were united, not merely by science, but by religious convictions. It is very interesting to notice, in their letters, during Haller's long, last sickness, the observations which both of them make on the power of prayer. They analyse it as it were a natural production.

"It allays my sufferings," writes Haller; "it gives me rest during my sleepless nights, and peace in the bosom of an infinitely loving Father."

Bounet's *Palingénésia* became a valuable treasure to me. I had hitherto never seen an explanation, according to natural philosophy, of those words, which have ever been so precious to my mind, the command "to preach the gospel to all creatures,"—not an interpretation thoroughly applicable to the animal races of the doctrine of St. Paul, in the Epistle to the Romans.

Bounet became early blind, in consequence of overstraining his sight in his observations on the mode by which the species of some of the minuter animal races were continued; but how much more insight did he not remain possessed of, than most persons, with their healthy eyes! His *Palingénésia* is an answer to many a deep, silent, anxious question of the soul.

Maine de Binan's biographical sketches, edited by Ernest Naville, were published during this time. I have seldom read a biograph which furnishes more material for thought, or a more edifying introduction, than the preface of the author. The young sisters and I read till midnight, in order to finish it. The aged parents always retired early to bed, and generally recommended us to do the same; but we were not always obedient.

Sometimes, the young son of the house, one of the most beloved preachers of Geneva, now pastor of Genthod, the former home of Bounet, the naturalist, came, with his handsome young wife, to the paternal abode, and, so doing, enhanced its cheerfulness. Sometimes, interesting acquaintances came from the city, or from some of the neighboring residences.

I have never, at any time, enjoyed more deeply instructive conversations, than here and at Geneva.

I value the women of Geneva, especially for their domestic and Christian virtues. They are indefatigable in good works. But these virtues belong, principally, to the Swiss reform.

One of the most beautiful blossoms of this country, and which I never met with anywhere else, are a kind of Homes of Health, *Maisons de Santé*, which persons of wealth have established in the country, near the city, partly for children, partly for aged persons of the poorer classes. I saw one of these children's homes, in which frequently may be found a dozen pale, sickly little ones, under the care of a young teacher; and also one of those intended for elderly people. This latter had been established by Colonel Trouchin, on his estate. These homes are open merely for the summer months. The little children played amongst the flowers; the elder invalids sat or walked about, under shady trees, in beautiful grounds. How good it was to see them, and to hear them say that since they had been here, they found themselves much, very much, better. The fresh air, good nursing, proper and wholesome food, the unanxious life which they spent for several weeks—because they enjoy all this free of cost, or at a very trifling expense, if they can afford it—gives to many a one life and new courage.

One peculiar gift possessed by the women of Geneva, is their talent for drawing, and especially for sketching, which is done by them with great firmness and accuracy. With good schools for drawing, Geneva ought to produce distinguished female artists. But of these, there is an utter deficiency. Geneva possesses some male artists of note, especially landscape painters; and Swiss scenery has no better painter than her own sons. M. Calame occupies the first place, at the present time, amongst the Swiss landscape painters.

In the beginning of June, I left my beautiful, hospitable home, near Geneva, for my last great flight into Switzerland; but I must yet once more return to my home, and my young sisters, by "the living waters," before I cross the Alps and enter Italy.

EIGHTH STATION.

Neufchâtel—A Home upon the Heights—Charles Secretan—Flights—The Industrial High-valleys—La Chaux de Fonds—Locle and Travers—The Island of St. Piérre—Federal Festival at Berne—Again on Lake Leman—Chamouni and St. Bernard—Rest by "the living waters"—Last days in Switzerland—Monte Rosa—To Italy!

It was a deep interest of the soul which drew me to Neufchâtel. I was there to pay a visit to Charles Secretan, the youngest friend and cotemporary of Alexandre Vinet. The doctrine which Vinet enunciated in his *Discours Evangeliques*, Charles Secretan had independently developed in his *Philosophie de la Liberté*, and and afterwards in his Method for the Discovering of Truth, in that which concerns our higher interests.

I had derived too much good, and too much pleasure, too many rays of light, from these books, not to desire the acquaintance of their source—the author. I wished to become acquainted with him, that I might thank him, and that I might learn more about him; for I was still seeking for a lost word—for a masterkey to certain trains of thought—to certain innermost questions of life—innermost chambers; and Secretan's works, beyond any others that I had met with of late years, had led me to the way where I had a presentiment—where I was certain—that this masterkey was to be found; but I would now seek it with the help of his eyes.

I had been invited to his house ever since my first arrival in Switzerland. To see him there, to see the sun shine in the work-room of his mind, as I had seen it on the peaks of the Alps, and to be able to read its primeval word, was one of the objects of my visit to Switzerland—and without attaining to this, I was unwilling to leave the country.

Upon a height covered with trees, above the lake of Neufchâtel, and not far from the city, on its banks, stands a little house, which shines white against the blue back-ground of sky. A garland of green encircles it. Below it lies the clear lake, and behind this, a vast half-circle, an immense panorama of Alps, from the Jungfrau to Mont Blanc.

There, in that little white house upon the heights, dwells the author of *Philosophie de la Liberté*, with his wife and their children. But—he is ill, suffering from one of those bad, enigmatical nervous complaints which attack the soul, still more than the body, and darken its world. The athletic soul in the athletic body rises up against it; but the Nessus-garment adheres to the frame as by the power of an evil magic; the strength of Hercules does not suffice to rend it away.

But, happier than Hercules, the Christian philosopher in this case has still hope left, and in any case the unwavering certainty of God's mercy and fatherly providence.

It was very precious to me to spend a little time with Secretan, even though in a different manner to what either he or I had thought of. More than once I heard him painfully lament that, in consequence of his suffering, he could not make my visit what he would have desired, nor yet converse with me as he should have wished.

But, noble, generous friend! If thou hast not been able to say to me what thou wouldst have said, yet hast thou said that which God willed thee to say to me. What philosophy, indeed, could have had the value for me of those words which thy candor and thy suffering called forth from the depths of thy soul? What teaching could have been more instructive than that which thou gavest me with such rare and perfect candor?

For this I thank thee more than for all besides. And yet at the same time it is so infinitely much which thou hast given me in thy beautiful and richly-spiritual works!

In these, as also in the periodical, *Revue Suisse*, of

which Charles Secretan is the editor, he stands as a mediator between two opposite parties, which are incessantly in combat, the one against the other, and whose representatives in Switzerland are, on the one side, Merle d'Aubigné, M. Gaussin, in his Theopneustie, and Count de Gasparin, in his periodical *Archives du Christianisme,* and the other Genevese, Edmund Scherer and his fellow-laborers in the Strasburg publication *Revue de Theologie.* The former maintain the literal inspiration of the Scriptures; the latter reject it, and—both parties go too far. Science, however, and the thinking public, are gainers in the mean time by the contention, because it is carried on with fairness by fair and learned men. Edmund Scherer, as an individual, is noble and amiable; but the unreasonable and intolerant conduct which he has met with in Switzerland, in many quarters, may well have tended to make his own behavior more unyielding and his opinions more one-sided. Between these combatant camps—in the east and west of Switzerland—stand Vinet and Secretan, and the school which they have founded. They say but little about the husk and the mere forms, but they study to preserve the kernel and the spiritual meaning, as well in life as in books. An independent thinker, M. de Rougemont, a Swiss of the Canton of Neufchâtel, has lately joined this party. I had often heard him spoken of, but it was in the house of Secretan that I first became well acquainted with him by his book, *Christ et ses Temoins,* a work which takes an important place in the theological literature of the present time. It has benefitted and interested me by its honest examination into points which less vigorous or less honest minds would willingly have turned aside from, and by the importance which he ascribes to the part of the Holy Spirit in the creation of the new time, and particularly of the church of the future. He is neither a perfectly lucid nor yet logical thinker, but he introduced much light into many questions by his honest and deep investigations, and the real geniality of his mind. Finally, M. Geltzer, in Basle, and Edmund de Pressancé, in Paris, are the Swiss minds which, whilst they ally themselves to this centre, open their monthly publications, *Protestantische Blätter and Revue Chretienne*, for discussion on every important topic in the realm of mind, on a high, true, liberal, evangelical basis. Such is the position of little Switzerland in the region of spirit and thought, between the great neighboring countries of Germany and France, and in the power of the Word active in both.

At the present moment Neufchâtel does not promise much in this department for the future. At the great annual examination of the schools generally, at which I was present, the male portion of the youth was severely blamed for their want of earnestness and perseverance in their various studies, for their deficiency in the *feu sacre*.

All the children of the home which was now my own—remarkably well endowed by mother nature—obtained each one a prize in their class. The eldest daughter carried away the highest prize which a female pupil could obtain.

"We have all got something!" said the little ones

exultingly to me, "and Sophie, our dear Sophie, has got the highest prize!"

The happy mother contemplated her children with beaming eyes.

From Neufchâtel I made visits to two neighboring institutions, both celebrated in Switzerland, *Mont Mirail* and Prefargis.

Mont Mirail is an educational institution belonging to the Moravians, which has been established above a century, but which is still in a beautifully flourishing condition, under the protection of the United Brethren. All familes, both in German and French Switzerland, who place a high value on the religious tendency of education, desire to send their daughters thither. The life of the United Brethren is educational, inasmuch as it places the Christian life as the highest in its tendency, and a continued career in deeds of love as the true imitation of Christ. Hence it arises that they flourish peacefully in dissimilar countries, and amongst all Christian sects; hence their activity in the education of youth, and for missionary labor, and their success in both. They do not despise Christian science, but they lay the greatest weight upon prayer and the course of life.

"Pray and labor," seems to me to be their motto. The faith which they have in a special providence (*providentia specialissima*) over every believer, and in His immediate guidance in all, even in the smallest event of their lives, gives to the members of this body a peace, which is not unfrequently perceptible in their demeanor, and which gives even to plain countenances a ray of beauty.

Prefarges is an institution for the insane, which is rendered by its beautiful situation and fine air, together with the affectionate zeal of its superintendents, a Bethesda for many of these unfortunates. The greater number of the female cases of mental suffering here, were, I was told, derived from the class of governesses! A fact well worthy of consideration in a country where so many young girls devote themselves to the vocation of teachers, without being led to do so by the highest motives, or by any decided capability for it.

Accompanied by Charles Secretan, and his wife—one of the noblest and most amiable women with whom I became acquainted in Switzerland—I set off to Chaux de Fonds. The road thither, was one continual wearisome ascent, but the grand views which it presented of Alpine scenery, made it a continual source of interest. Thus we ascended to La Fête de Rang, into the region of the pine and the north-wind, and beheld from its summit, the wooded district of Lorraine, on the soil of France, with the mountain-chain of the Vosges, in the blue distance. The early morning walk, on the day following, across the flowery, dewy meadows, amongst mountain lakes, and wooded hills, amongst herds of well-fed cattle, whose bells rang in a melodious chorus, whilst the larks sang their jubilant songs in the sunny air, and those Alpine views around us which ever increased in grandeur as we ascended—I cannot describe how glorious it was! Even Secretan was enlivened thereby.

Like a little town of Nuremberg toy-houses, which one takes out of a box, and places in stiff formality upon a table, lies the town of Chaux de Fonds upon its elevated plain, without trees, and without beauty, surrounded by bald, and not very lofty hills. One can hardly find a more unlovely situation. Nevertheless, a flourishing, well-to-do population of fifteen thousand souls lives within the town. Watch-making is the soul of its activity. Even the unpleasing character of the scenery and the severity of the climate contribute, I was told, to the success of the life of labor there. It is cold; it often rains; the people have nothing to divert them out of doors; they prefer rather to be in their houses at their work-tables.

I had intended to have paid the town merely a passing visit, but it turned out otherwise, owing to the hospitality which was shown me by the young couple, M. and Mme. Gerdt. I remained with them eight days, during which time I received from them, and several other cultivated persons of the place, a degree of cordial kindness, the memory of which I retain with a grateful heart.

My impression of the life of the industrial population may be thus summed up:

Fresh life, fresh labor. Amongst the working classes a considerable degree of self-confidence and no want of levity. Too little thought for the morrow, and none for eternity; but good dispositions as fellow-citizens, mutual good-will and helpfulness. Marriages are numerous, and, mostly, early in life; divorces are very rare. Husband and wife work at the same occupation, and get good earnings, which makes living easy. The skillful workman soon builds his own house.* The women can earn from three to fifteen francs a day; the greater number, however, less than five. They like their work, but become, in consequence, less clever as housewives; give themselves no time to attend to cooking, and their clothes, and often not even to take care of the child which is ill, which cannot be compensated for by any amount of pecuniary gains. This working-life is assuredly not altogether good for married women. For the unmarried, it

---

* The High-valleys of Neufchâtel have produced several remarkable tradesmen and citizens. One of these, M. David Pury, whose statue stands in one of the principal market-places of the city of Neufchâtel, was a poor, fatherless, and motherless boy, supported by some of the towns-people, yet by industry and genius, he became one of its wealthiest men. Grateful for past kindness, he bequeathed by will, the whole of his large, self-acquired fortune, amounting to four and a half millions of francs, to the town. One little trait of this man's life has appeared to me so beautiful and instructive, that I cannot avoid here mentioning it. A young man in M. Pury's office, one day, cut up a pen with his pen-knife, and then threw it away, carelessly, from him.

"Why do you throw that pen away?" inquired his principal, mildly; "I will show you that it will still serve for some good purpose."

He took up the pen, mended it carefully, and then wrote with it a check for a large sum, which he immediately handed to the young man, for the benefit of his indigent family.

"Osterwald," is a name which the inhabitants of Neufchâtel reckon amongst their great names, "perhaps, because we, ourselves, are small!" pleasantly, said one of the representatives of the Canton to the Federal Council.—*Author's Note.*

appears to me a great blessing. But on this subject I will let my young and lovely hostess, Mme. Gerdt, speak:

"During my stay in some of the large cities of Germany, I often saw young girls in indigent circumstances, driven to miserable marriages for the sake of a living, and many even driven to an evil life, from the insufficiency of honest earnings. When I saw these unfortunate girls, whose appearance plainly testified of their wretched calling, I longed to arrest them, and say to them: 'Oh, why do you not adopt some honest trade, and gain for yourselves a comfortable independence, and a respectable position in life? If you only knew how good, how beautiful, this would be!'

"The sight of this misery amongst the young women, actually affected my health. I no longer took pleasure in any enjoyment; I saw everywhere this secret cancer, and knew not how it was to be remedied! When I returned hither, people believed that I was seriously ill.

"Here I was not afflicted by this sight. Here every young woman can, without difficulty, acquire, by her own labor, an honorable living. She need not marry merely for the sake of a secure position in life. She can wait till the husband comes whom she can highly esteem and love; and if such a one does not offer, she can live actively and happily in her own home. Her labor maintains her. She is not a burden, but an assistance, to her family. If she falls into error, the cause lies in herself, but not in her circumstances; not in the bitter temptation—want!"

I had, during this time, the pleasure of reading, in my quiet chamber, the diary of Lavater, and thus making acquaintance with this spirit, which was vitalized and inspired by the light and love of God. He is not a strong, logical thinker, but a soul which, at one bound, embraces the central point of the Christian revelation, and presses it to his warm, deeply sensitive heart. Hence his ardent comprehension of the personality of Christ, as eternal life, eternal love, and eternal operative power; hence his rejoicing life in that divine love, even under the deepest consciousness of his own deficiency.

"Fear not!" he exclaims to the repentant; "fear not! You are already forgiven. Your sins are already swallowed up; God's Holy Spirit is already in your heart! You are more dear to God than you know of. God cannot hate the being he has created; he hates only that which destroys his most beautiful work. To eradicate this destructive element from human nature, is the work of Christ. Let us have faith and rejoice, even when we are compelled to despise ourselves a thousand and ten thousand times! This feeling of repentance is wholesome; but you must not stand still there. Have faith! have faith! A human being—for whom the Son of God has uttered a word of prayer, has permitted himself to be nailed to the cross—is of more value, in the sight of God, than ten thousand worlds without souls; and of what consequence is the whole world, in his sight, who numbers every hair of man's head, who takes heed of the sparrows which fall? Fear not, then; only have faith!"

I wish I could impart this rising up into God above the wants and shortcomings of our humanity, to some of my Swiss friends, who sink themselves too much into the consciousness of sin. This they must have, that they may all the more inwardly, all the more lovingly, comprehend the Saviour.

From Chaux de Fonds, I went, with my kind entertainers, to Le Saut du Doubs, saw its beautiful cascade, and its wonderful natural basins, in the bosom of the rocks, which appear as if hewn, by the hand of man, into circular Colosseums—a glorious trip, on the loveliest of days. I then proceeded to Locle, where the inhabitants work and live as they do at Chaux de Fonds, and thence to the most beautiful of valleys,— Val Travers; the inhabitants of which are wealthy, by the manufacture of machinery for watch-making, but are said to be quarrelsome and disagreeable.

In Val Travers, however, I became acquainted with an amiable mother and daughter, my kind hostesses, ultra-Calvinists, who maintained that we, one and all of us, were "vipers;" and also with the work of Jean Reynaud, *Terre et Ciel*, which I shall add to my small library at home.

From the highlands of the Jura, I proceeded down to Sommerhause, a beautiful champaign, on a terrace, by the Lake of Neufchâtel, of which a young lady was the proprietor and mistress. Women, in the Canton Neufchâtel, attain to legal majority at the age of nineteen. There are several single women, of various ages, settled on their own fine properties, around the lake. Friendship, the beauties of nature, reading, and active benevolence, occupy their life, and make it good and happy. My young hostess was a rich heiress, but not on that account any the less humble and amicable. She, as yet, lives alone at her beautiful "Sommerhause." Here I met a Swiss lady, who has become a Swede, by marriage. I cannot say how agreeable it was to me to become better acquainted with Baroness Raumel, *née* Dardel, now on a visit to her native country, and to spend a few days in her society.

My young hostess drove me to the island of St. Pierre. Hundreds of islands, larger and more beautiful than this, lie in the Mäler Lake, but none so celebrated. Its unequaled environment of lofty Alps, and Rousseau's memory, have made it a place of pilgrimage to tourists. It resembles a smaragdus, set in gray-stone, for the Bernese government has allowed a low stone wall to be built, upon which people can walk round the island. Beautiful ancient trees crown its lofty plateau. The only building on the island, the old convent, erected a thousand years ago, and dedicated to St. Peter and St. Paul, is now a farm-house, where strangers are also entertained, and where, at the present time, one could be splendidly regaled with strawberries and cream. Here it was that Rousseau dwelt; his room is held sacred,—that is to say, is not inhabited. It has four bare walls, quite covered with the names and inscriptions of visitors. There is said to be one line, under which appears the name Pitt, as follows:—

"Conquer—no matter how!"

And not far off, another, signed Emanuel Kant, consisting of these words:

"Pure means for a pure object!"

The confessions of faith of the head of a political party, and of the moral philosopher!

The visitor to Rousseau's room—which, however, is very uncomfortable, and has only one window without any view—must not forget to lift up the trap-door, and see the little, secret stairs by which Rousseau escaped from his numerous visitors. An institution which might be very valuable!

In itself, the little island is enchanting, from its luxuriant vegetation and its simple natural beauty. Its northern slopes are covered with vineyards. The people were at work in them, pruning the vine-shoots, so that they might bear more fruit.

I spent two days there, reading, botanizing, and enjoying the air—pure and delicious, as if of heaven,—the solitude, and the view of the Alpine chain during the magnificent evening-spectacle of death and resurrection—the "after-glow" dyeing the snow-clad summits with a transparent crimson brightness which seems not to be of the light of this world. I could very well understand how happy Rousseau must have felt himself here.

Hence I proceeded to Berne.

There was then holden in Berne—those first days in July—the great Federal festival, with Olympian games, in the spirit of the newer time. Shooting societies from nearly every Canton of the confederacy had hastened hither to compete with each other for prizes of from one thousand to three thousand francs. Exhibitions, deputations, toasts, songs, speeches, entertainments, waving flags, and everywhere scenes, partly of pleasure, partly of solemnity, were to be found.

An immense barracks, capable of entertaining four thousand persons, was used as a refreshment hall. Each Canton had its own division of table and seats; and each division its own appointed entertainers. The place for the great shooting matches was Enghe. The prizes were contained in a temple, around which waved the flags of all the Cantons. Omnibuses, crowded with people nodding to their friends, hurrahing, and waving hats and handkerchief, ran upon the road between Berne and Enghe through clouds of dust; but every body in the very best humor.

Every Canton had contributed its share to the great Industrial Exhibition in the city. The beautiful articles produced in asphaltum, from the Canton Neufchâtel, and the embroidery from St. Gall and Appenzell, were the most remarkable to me. It approaches almost to the incredible, to see what art can produce in these respects. The least cheering circumstance of which appears to me to be, that these beautiful productions of art foster the taste for personal luxury in dress and furniture. This cannot be good. It belongs to heathenism. Immense draperies of stuffs beautifully arranged, show what this industrious little Switzerland exports, in this branch, to other countries, to the East and West Indies!

That which especially pleased me at this Federal festival, was its spirit and temper. One could have fancied one's self to be at an immense, joyful family-feast. All was cordiality, kindness, and thorough enjoyment. The pleasurable gave its hand to the useful. All the Cantons met as brethren, as children of the same Liberty, of the same beloved mother-country, and here, united in sportive and earnest intercourse, learned to know each other better, and the better to understand the meaning of their Confederation.

The new palace of the Federal government, at Berne, is nearly completed, and is a magnificent building. The government evidently is endeavoring still more to develop a central life in the confederated states, and, by so doing, to lead them to a higher unity and harmony. And is as it should be.

I returned by way of Freyburg from the great family feast to the shores of Lake Leman. In Freyburg I paid a visit to the grave of Père Girard, which a dirty Franciscan monk of Père Girard's convent, and who smelt strongly of brandy, showed to me. A snow-white marble stone, with a simple inscription, covers the resting-place of the friend of children. I heard in the Cathedral of Freyburg the remarkable organ which, like that at Rome, gives a perfect imitation of the crash of thunder, and the roaring of the wind, and choruses of beseeching human voices. The organist played "*La Promenade sur Mer.*"

Whilst on the shores of Lake Leman I again visited Montreux and Clarens, saw the Rhone valley at Bex, visited old and new friends in their summer home— the Alpine cottages on the glaciers, from the icy fountains of which the good housewives themselves fetched the snow to cool our refreshing beverages. The summer was in its prime, the Swiss scenery in its full splendor; and I thought to myself, there is yet Paradise upon earth!

Nevertheless, there passed even now through this Paradise—"the ruins of the lost Paradise," say the pious Swiss—sounds of dissevering discord, misfortunes, the result of want of prudence, or of fool-hardiness, which were dividing loving hearts, and led to death and sorrow in families where life appeared till then in its purest bloom. People make their "*reflexions chretiennes et morales,*" but for such griefs as these I know of but one consolation, and that lies in the courageous exclamation, "Fear not them who can only kill the body!"

At the close of July I returned to Geneva, in order from that place to commence my last mountain journey in Switzerland, to Chamouni, St. Bernard, and Monte Rosa.

But first to Chamouni!

Chamouni has been so frequently visited, and so frequently described, that I shall say but little about it, and that little principally for the purpose of endeavoring to deter others from going thither—like me.

The kind parents Coulin intrusted to me their eldest daughter, my young friend Louise, as my companion on this journey; for she, no more than myself, had as yet seen the celebrated Mer de Glace.

Early in the morning of the 31st of July, we left Geneva. The sleepy little maid-servants, the morning winds, were up late, but at length, however, they came to sweep aside the masses of cloud, and pile them on the mountain-tops; but the dust of their so doing did not settle for a long time, and obscured our view.

"We shall not see Mont Blanc to-day, that is certain, and that is a pity!" thought I as we drove in the diligence through an atmosphere darkened with dust and mist, along the ever-narrowing mountain pass.

But suddenly an icy pyramid shot forth to the left of our path, then another and another, and finally Mont Blanc stood forth in his own lofty person with a night-cap on his summit. When, however, we arrived at Sallenches, the giant doffed his cloudy night-cap, for the sake of Louise's lovely eyes, as I averred, and the whole of the brilliant chain, in the midst of which Mont Blanc was enthroned, stood forth in full sun-splendor against the blue sky-background.

We hailed the sight with rejoicing eyes, ate a good little dinner at Sallenches, and journeyed onward.

In a cloud of dust, between five and six in the evening, we arrived at Chamouni, and obtained rooms at the Hotel de l'Union, on the brink of the roaring Arve, which rushes through the whole length of the narrow Chamouni valley—and with a view of Mont Blanc. But the Alps had again vailed themselves in cloud. However, at sunset, first one Alpine sphinx and then another, unvailed itself, and stood forth free from cloud, as if under the enchantment of the sun. And now indeed it was beautiful to behold the forms which by degrees presented themselves, the portals and the perspectives which opened, the fantastic forms which came and disappeared whilst sunbeams and clouds gamboled or strove together aloft, and one Alpine spire after another shot up above the region of clouds, shining as if of pure gold, till the whole mountain chain lay before us distinctly with its deep glaciers, its acute pyramids, even to the rounded colossus of Mont Blanc. Louise and I stood in a green meadow of the valley, contemplating this scene with uplifted eyes and hearts, which rose still higher—till the sun had set, and the after-glow had succeeded!

It would have been impossible for us to have had a lovelier evening at Chamouni.

But the initiation into the mysteries of the ice regions has other scenes than this, and I will now speak of one of them.

It was the following day. We ascended through pine-forest to Le Montanvert. It is here that one sees before one the so-called *Mer de Glace*, a broad stream of ice and snow, the offspring of the highest Alps, which pours itself between lofty mountain-ridges, down into the valley of Chamouni, where, from beneath its icy gates, issues the river of Arveron. I say "pours itself," because the frozen river slides from the heights down into the valley, and these icy masses, are besides, as one knows, in a state of continual advance.

From the height of Montanvert we saw the *Mer de Glace*, also called *Le Mont Blanc des dames*, splendidly shining in the morning sun, and a party of gentlemen and ladies crossing to the opposite side. It looked quite calm and agreeable. Why should not we do the same? Our guides encouraged us to do so, yet with a certain cautiousness of expression.

In half an hour we could cross the Mer de Glace; afterwards we should have about an hour "somewhat difficult road," in the mountain to *Le Chapeau,* but once there, we should see a grand sight, and then also, every danger and difficulty would be over, "and—the guides would have earned a double day's wages!" Of this last consideration, however, they said nothing, but the knowledge of it was the reason of their encouraging words.

I was tempted, by the thought of becoming acquainted with the beauties and dangers of the Mer de Glace, and determined to undertake the hazardous journey; but how I repented of doing so, when, in its midst, I discovered what the nature of it was! For one did not merely run the continual danger of slipping and falling whilst climbing over the icy billows, but one found one's self perpetually on the brink of wide crevices in the ice-mass, of two or three hundred feet deep, and across which one must leap, without any other foot-hold than a smooth icy-wave or hillock. I was now in a state of silent despair at having undertaken this enterprise, particularly as I had Louise Coulin with me. If any thing should happen to this young girl! if I should not be able to restore her in safety to her parents! then—I could not live myself! I thought about turning back, but my guide assured me that we had already accomplished the worst part of the way; that what yet remained was, in comparison, without danger. Even he himself fell, more than once, on our slippery career.

With an anxiety which cannot be described, my eyes followed Louise, who went before me, with her guide, as lightly and nimbly as though they were dancing a minuet. This guide was a young man, who had only, within the last half year, become incorporated into the guild of Chamouni guides, and I, therefore, felt all the less dependence upon him; but he was light-footed and agile, and, in reality, better than my old, safe, but very heavy-footed, conductor. My guide was a peasant,—Louise's was a cavalier; but Louise's was not only young, strong, and safe upon his feet, but he enjoyed the undertaking, and never thought about danger. But as for me!——

And when we found ourselves midway on the Mer de Glace, and I was desired to notice the splendid walls of a broad ice-fissure, in the abyss of which the thundering roar of waters is heard, and was called upon to admire the brightness and width of the Mer de Glace, which is even from this point, up to the very top of the mountains, where it is born—I felt myself like one doomed to death, with the rope already round his neck, who is desired to notice "the beautiful prospect!" But I said nothing, and as Louise gayly recommended me to do, I broke off little pieces of ice, and let them melt in my mouth. This, and the beaming glances of my young friend, refreshed me.

The sun shone with great heat, melting the ice, and through the latter part of the road, we went sliding and splashing through a regular ice-slush. How delighted I was when I had once more firm footing on the earth, and I saw Louise there in safety. I gathered and kissed a little common crimson flower, which grew on the borders of the ice, like a kind salutation of welcome.

But the joy was of short duration; for, in order to reach Le Chapeau—the only way, on this side, down to Chamouni—one must clamber along the side of a perpendicular rock, without any thing to hold by but a rope, fastened by iron nails, as a hand-rail on the mountain wall. One walks along a narrow pathway cut in the rock, midway between two perpendicular mountain-walls,—the one above, the other below. At the depth of many hundred feet below this again, is the Mer de Glace, with its sheer descent. A moment's dizziness, and all would be over! The guides now began to advise us to hasten, "because stones are frequently precipitated from the rocks above."

I glance up, and see that masses of stone are hanging above our heads, as it appeared, just ready to fall. But how is one to hasten here, where one must give heed to every step, and hold fast by the rope? And now even this ceases, and the path goes before me steep up hill. I have merely the guide's hand, who pulls me up.

"We shall go quite safely!" he says, consolingly.

"Nay, on, on, go on still faster!" I replied, whilst I see stones and debris giving way under each heavy step he takes, and I pray silently, "Deliver us from evil!"

Louise, with her light-footed guide, is already up and out of danger, upon firm ground, and now—I am so too,—and now the danger, and all the difficulties of the journey, are overcome. We are very near the

Chapeau, and may quietly rest there, before we go further. I feel ready to cry.

But a few minutes later, when we had reached the Chapeau, and little Alpine cottage, sheltered by a rock in the shape of a hat-crown, and seated upon a wooden bench, in the cheerful sunshine, with my young friend's hand clasped in mine, I felt so unspeakably thankful to have overcome all the perils of the way, that I could not do other than share Louise's delight over the extraordinary spectacle which the Mer de Glace presented from this place; for at this place, the pressure from above has caused the ice to mass itself together, and to assume the most remarkable forms. Imagine to yourself a stream of ice-witches and hobgoblins, with their children, and bag and baggage, on their journey to—the lowest pit! Here a gray giantess, with three daughters, in hoods, shawls, and crinolines, are advancing majestically forward; there a whole procession of gray nuns; here monks without heads; there giants in berserker-mood; and yonder a castle of ice, with many towers, like an immense artichoke, with its points somewhat turning inwards. In general, it seemed to me that the figures of the Mer de Glace resemble the forms and peaks of the circumjacent mountains. Saussure saw, from the heights of Mont Blanc, groups of its pyramids and needles, like the leaves of an artichoke, turning inwards towards the middle;—imagine to yourself all this crowd of dirty-gray ice-witches, little and big hobgoblins, now in fantastical groups, now a solitary, lofty figure, amongst towers, columns, ruins, as of a demolished city;—imagine all this immovable, and yet advancing downwards, on a slope of from two to three leagues! Sometimes a witch loses her head, which, set at liberty by the sun, is precipitated into the depths below, and one hears it roaring down, like the sound of subterranean thunder.

My lively young friend was delighted with the strange scene. As for myself, with the impression of the excursion into this region of witchcraft fresh upon me, I felt, spite of the irresistibly comic character of the scene, grave and almost depressed in spirit. We partook of a poor, little, but expensive dinner, at "The Hat," whilst we contemplated the witch-stream.

When, after this journey of eight hours, which I had made on foot, we returned to Chamouni, I felt myself "knocked up," both soul and body; but I and my young friend took each a warm bath, drank a cup of refreshing tea, and went to bed, and instead of a restless night with dreams about witches and abysses, I had pleasant dreams, and in my waking intervals, clear, good thoughts; felt the witchcraft leave my limbs, and fresh vigor infused—delightful!

Afterwards I found these words in my "Bradshaw," with regard to the journey across the Mer de Glace, and to the Chapeau, "This journey is so hazardous, that we will not advise any one to undertake it." And I seriously would dissuade one and all from it, who may have weak knees, and an old heavy-footed guide, and a dear young friend, whether male or female, in company, and also, one and all, who may have the least inclination to dizziness.

But one and all may have entire pleasure in a journey to the source of the Arveron. The river issues from the foot of the Mer de Glace. We now see it from the green meadow below, where the icy sea abruptly terminates. Here, as on the precipitous descent, its fantastic icy-figures group themselves still more wildly, and seem to twine their arms round one another, as if to support themselves on the precipice—but in vain! They must be hurled down into the abyss and swell the roaring waters of the Arveron. One fancies that one sees an icy city and its inhabitants paralysed with horror, hurried onward to the gulf. Within the rigid, dead mass, life is yet roaring, but for them with a dissolving, destroying power. The river is born and emancipates itself in its subterranean vault.

One of the icy shapes towered above all the rest, and this was a form of beauty. The figure, the position, the clear, icy-draperies, every thing had a wonderful resemblance to the Sistine Madonna with the child. But this beautiful figure even, sped on towards the sheer descent.

On the evening of this day, the firing of a cannon announced that another ascent of Mont Blanc had been accomplished by some adventurous travelers. My guide blamed these adventurous people, and declared that it was a piece of pure "*betise*" of *Messieurs et Dames*, to risk their own lives and the lives of others, to climb up there to see—most frequently—nothing. He himself, had been more than once on these Mont Blanc journeys, and more than once had fallen into the crevices, up to his arms, and had been only saved by means of the rope by which the whole procession of ice-travelers are attached the one to the other, for no person undertakes the ascent of Mont Blanc attended by less than six guides. One of these gentlemen may still be seen in the valley of Chamouni with green gauze before his eyes, owing to the severe injury which they received from the ascent of Mont Blanc. The skin of most people peels off after this visit to the summit, and they suffer more or less in health. Three ladies only, and all three unmarried, have hitherto accomplished this journey—Mlle. Paradis, Mlle. d'Angeville, a lively, energetic French woman, whom I saw in Geneva, and an English woman whose name has escaped my memory. The two latter ladies, when they had attained the highest summit, had themselves lifted upon the shoulders of their guides, that they might rise to a greater height than any of their predecessors.

Mlle. d'Angeville was, however, accompanied upon this journey by a skillful draughtsman, who took views and sketches by the way, so that her undertaking was not without its results for the benefit of others. I know, however, that I have no desire to become the fourth of these aspiring ladies.

Horace Benedict de Saussure has connected his name for all time with that of Mont Blanc, because he was the first scientific man who penetrated its mysteries. But he was not the first who ascended it; this was a peasant from the Vale of Chamouni of the name of Balmat. He it was who discovered the path to the summit; but not possessing scientific culture he could not make scientific observations. Without Balmat, however, perhaps De Saussure might not have been able to reach the summit of Mont Blanc.

From childhood, De Saussure had a singularly deep love for mountains, and for wanderings amongst them. He had spent several years in ascending, for the purpose of scientific examinations, the greater number of the most considerable mountain-chains of Europe. But Mont Blanc still stood vailing itself and its Alpine chain in mystery, in defiance of the young mountain-explorer's longings and endeavors.

"It had become with me," he writes, "a kind of disease. My eyes never beheld this mountain, which can be seen from so many places in our district, without my experiencing a painful feeling."

At length, after twenty-seven years of longing and fruitless endeavor, Saussure succeeded in August, 1787, in achieving the longed-for ascent, and from the summit, was able to survey the Alpine chain in all directions.

"The arrival on the summit," he writes, "did not give me, immediately, all the pleasure which might have been expected;—because the length of the struggle, and the sense of the trouble which it had cost me to reach it, seemed, as it were, to have irritated me. And it was with a kind of wrath, that I trampled the snow upon its highest point. Besides, I feared not being able to make the observations which I desired, so greatly was I troubled by the rarity of the atmosphere, and the difficulty I found in breathing, and in working at this height. We all suffered from fever."

Every thing, however, succeeded to Saussure, beyond his expectations, he saw every thing, and was able to make all the observations which he had so long, and so ardently desired to do.

"I scarcely believed my own eyes," he says; "I seemed to myself to be dreaming, when I saw beneath my feet the terrific, majestic peaks, the acute summits of Midi, Argentiere, and Le Geant, the very bases of which it had been to me so difficult and hazardous to climb. I understood their connection and their form, and at one single glance was able to clear up the uncertainty which years of labor alone could not have done."

Amongst the lesser observations which De Saussure made on the ascent, the following have interested me. "We saw," says he, "near the summit, only two butterflies; the one was a little gray night-butterfly (phaline), which flew across the first snow; the second, a day-butterfly, which appeared to me to be *le myrtil*. The flower, belonging to the perfect class, which I found at the greatest altitude, was a *silene acaulis*. Small mosses were, however, growing upon the very highest rocks."

Saussure, when in shadow, saw from the summit of Mont Blanc, the stars in the light of day; and the color of the sky was almost black.

He was able only to remain four hours and a half on the summit of the mountain, when he was obliged to return. But in the stillness of the night, when he recalled all that he had actually seen, and felt the grand picture of the mountains clearly imprinted upon his brain, then he experienced an unmingled satisfaction. And well, indeed, might he! He had accomplished a great undertaking for science. Even science has its heroes and noble martyrs.

But how any body can desire—for no other purpose than to be able to say, "I have done it"———but enough on this subject."

On the 4th of August, Louise and I set off, through the *Tete Noire*, to Martigny, one of the most beautiful journeys which any one can take on a summer's day. Good roads, magnificent scenery, both behind and before, and through the whole valley, bold forms of wooded rocks, fresh rushing waters, the purest mountain atmosphere;—I seemed to myself to be reading one of Sir Walter Scott's Highland novels. The moon rose above the beautiful chestnut woods as we reached Martigny, in the Rhone valley, where we found the air oppressively warm.

The following day, we took a little carriage, and proceeded to the Great St. Bernard. The road is good, but narrow, and the turns are everywhere so precipitous on the one side, that it is impossible to avoid feeling dizzy at the thought of being upset. And such misadventures do happen at times.

We are now in the Canton Valais. At one point of the road we met a procession of monks, together with men and women, who were murmuring prayers to the ringing of bells, dressed in white, and on their way to some shrine of the Virgin in the neighborhood, to pray for rain. The procession came from villages in the mountains where the drought was fearful, and harvests burned up in consequence.

As far as Cautine du Praz, the road is passable for

a carriage, afterwards you must either ride or walk. Louise chose to walk with me, and our guide went before us with the mules and our traveling bags.

The sun was still burning hot, but the pilgrims who had been praying for rain appeared not to have put up their prayers in vain. Clouds were gathering; thunder was heard, and very soon it began to rain. We toiled wearily onward with our Alpine staves in our hands; but now it grew dark, ever thicker clouds gathered above us and the ground was wet with snow. And the Hospice, the so-much-longed-for Hospice, would not come into sight! At length, however, we beheld a large, regular, gray mass of buildings arise from the gray rocks around it; and seldom has the hospitable *herberge* been greeted with greater joy. The sympathizing salutation of the monks "*Pauvres dames!*" sounded to us like delicious music. The latter part of the way we had to walk through deep snow, and were wet through, both by it and the rain.

But we changed our clothes, and were then taken into a large room where a good fire rejoiced both soul and body, and were now seated at table with many other travelers, partaking of tea and bread and butter And as she regaled herself with the oriental nectar, Louise turned her beaming glasses upon me, whispering "*c'est bon!*"

We then lay down to rest, on very massive beds, under whole avalanches of sheets and feather-beds About one hundred and fifty persons, mostly poor travelers, were lodged at the Hospice this night.

I was awaked in the morning by the pealing roar of the organ. It was morning mass; at the latter part of which, I was present, but not much edified, owing to the incongruous mixture of spiritual and worldly music.

You are shown, in the little church, the grave of General Dessaix.

"I will give you the Alps for your monument!" said Napoleon to his dying general, after the battle of Marengo; "you shall rest on their loftiest inhabited point,—in the church of St. Bernard!"

I had some conversation on the life in the convent, with Père Clavendier, a very kind and well-informed man, who appears to have the especial charge of travelers of the more cultivated class.

"I should not remain here long by myself," said he, "but we are many, and so I stay. We often witness sorrowful occurrences. Two years ago, two of our brethren went out, with a couple of servants, to seek for a man who was supposed to have lost himself in the mountains; they were scarcely fifty paces from the house, when we saw an immense avalanche fall and bury our poor friends under eighteen feet of snow. When we recovered them, they were dead! We often find poor travelers, whose feet are frozen, and here we nurse them till they are sufficiently recovered to continue their journey."

It is now an unfrequent occurrence for travelers to perish in this region; the cases of being frozen to death usually do not exceed two in the course of the year.

"We ourselves," said Père Clavendier, "may hold out twelve or fifteen years, but our dogs not above seven or eight years; they then become rheumatic and die. Is it not so, Mors?" continued he, as he patted one of the large, pious dogs; "thou wilt hold out for another year, and then thou wilt die!"

Mors wagged his tail assentingly, and I thought of Luther's words to his dog:

"Don't grumble, little Hans; thou, too, shalt have a golden tail some day!"

The Hospice of St. Bernard was founded about a thousand years ago, by the pious Count Bernard, of Menthone. From eighteen to twenty thousand travelers, passing between Italy and Switzerland, are annually entertained here, without the good Augustine monks exacting the smallest payment. The more wealthy travelers generally leave a donation in the alms' box of the church, and the country people carry thither, sometimes, gifts of butter, cheese, &c. But this does not amount to much. The convent supports itself, and also its thousands of pilgrims, by its own funds. During the revolution of 1847, these funds were seized upon, and the fathers removed from the convent. But the travelers across the mountain loudly demanded the accustomed fathers, and the old hospitality. The government was obliged to reinstate both; and thus St. Bernard's Hospice remains at the present day, a monument of Christian love, and an honor to the Catholic church.

But its time will soon be over. The Sardinian minister, Cavour, has obtained the consent of government to the construction of a railway, which will run right through the Alps—Mont Cenis being even now tunneled for that purpose—uniting Piedmont with Switzerland and the rest of Europe. In about ten years, it is said, that this great work will be accomplished, and then St. Bernard, the *herberge* of ten centuries, will be deserted; for no one will take a difficult journey of four or five days, when they can, without fatigue, and at small cost, accomplish the same in twelve hours.

A separate building, near the Hospice, contains the bodies of those who have perished on their journey across the mountain. They are arranged along the walls, and present a fearful sight. By degrees, they fall to pieces, and the floor is strewn with skulls and bones.

Why do they not allow the earth to cover these remains? They cannot teach any thing, and they inspire a horror which does not belong to the death, which is the cause of their being here.

"Death by freezing," said the young guide, on our way, "is not painful. One goes to sleep, and does not wake any more. And when one is poor, without any thing to look forward to on earth, a little sooner, or a later, what does it matter? All must go the same road. It is a good thing to die without suffering!"

A melancholy little mountain lake lies at a short distance from the gloomy tenement; and just below, the road begins to descend on the Italian side, into Piedmont, and the lovely valley of Aosta.

Not far from the Hospice, stood, in former times, a temple of Jupiter, to which, probably, the same merciful duties were attached, as belong to the Christian refuge for Alpine travelers; in proof of which, we may accept a small, but very remarkable collection of antiquities, which have been found on the spot where the temple stood, and which are now preserved within the convent. Several bronze plates are amongst these, inscribed with thanksgivings to *Jovis Pœninus*, for his protection, and a number of delicately-worked bronze figures of heathen divinities, appear, like the others, to be *ex votos*, consecrated to his temple by grateful travelers across the mountain. There is also, in this collection, a beautiful female hand, also in bronze, around wrist and fingers of which, a snake twines itself.

"This represents the hand of Eve," said the good monk who showed us these things.

"But—Eve's hand in the temple of Jupiter?"

"Oh!" replied he, "they had also, amongst the heathen, the traditions of the fall!"

The air was damp and cold, this morning, and heavy hailstorms made the ground white around the Hospice; the sky was heavy and cloudy,—every thing was gray and gloomy. Nature is here eternally vailed; it knows neither the life nor the flowers of summer.

With a grateful heart, and a sense of high esteem, I took my leave of the pious men who live here to rescue their fellows; caressed the large, good-tempered dogs, who participate in their work of love, and availing ourselves of a break in the clouds, I and my young friend set forth on our return. We reached La Cautine happily before the rain began, and made the remaining descent of the mountain amidst storms of rain.

At seven o'clock in the evening we were again at Martigny, where we found it very hot. We had in this day passed from the climate of Spitzbergen to that of northern Italy.

We should now have undertaken the journey to Monte Rosa, but that sun and fine weather were necessary, which at the present time we did not enjoy. The heavens were clothed in rain-clouds, and the barometer had fallen; we therefore determined to defer the journey, and return at once to Geneva.

In the early dusk of morning, we drove through the Rhone valley, from the swampy, sterile district around Martigny, to the woody and fertile neighborhood of Bex, magnificently embraced, both on the right and the left, by the mountain chains of Vaud and Valais.

We enjoyed the fresh air, freed from dust, which the rain had laid, the fantastic cloud-imagery which gathered around the mountains, and the ever-varying play of light and shadow. Thus we sped along, on the wings of steam, from Bex to Villeneuve, and thence, by the steamer *L'Hirondelle*, across the waters of Lake Leman, and so to Geneva. And there, by lantern-light, I was able, thanks be to our Lord, to restore my beloved young companion safe and sound to her parents and relatives, who were waiting for her on the shore. And again I spent a few days with her in the good home which I am able to call mine, and where they would scarcely receive thanks for all the kindness which I enjoyed there.

"The home of the pastor of souls ought to be hospitable!" said the good Pastor Coulin, when I thanked him for the beautiful hospitality which he and his family had shown to me.

And now let me linger somewhat upon these last days in my Swiss home, where, for the last time, I was able to partake of the refreshment of repose, such as can only be enjoyed in a home like this!

Do not let it, dear R——, appear too tedious for thee to linger yet a few moments with me. Soon, very soon, we shall cross the Alps, and then—proceed far out into the wide world; now, however, let us linger and rest a moment in the home beside the living waters!

I transcribe the following from my diary:

JARGONAUT, *August 15th.*—A still summer rain has been falling ever since morning; it seems to us all like pleasant music, because, for the last two months there has been no rain here, and the earth thirsts and languishes for it. The nightingales sing no longer in the wood, and the great walnut tree is now bearing fruit, and pears and plums are ripening around my quiet home, where every thing is alike good, pleasant, and peaceful.

I have spent the morning in reading, and in the comparison of the ancient classical ideal of man and life with that of more modern times; that is to say, of Christianity. The differences are, in many respects, great, but in none greater and more striking than in the doctrine of the aim and purport of life, and of the immortality of the human soul. The former, amongst the wise of antiquity, is confined merely to the perfecting of the individual as regards his relationship to the state. They know nothing of a life devoted to the service of humanity. And as regards the latter, there is always in the minds of the most enlightened, a constantly recurring doubt, like a cloud over their brightest yearnings. They stand hesitating over the question, "to be or not to be!" Such are Cicero, Seneca, Marcus Aurelius. Socrates believed more and hoped more, but still how feeble and dreamy, even in Phædon, are the images of a future life! How differently do Peter, Paul, and all the Christian prophets speak! New revelation—new inspiration!

Comparisons of this kind are the enjoyment of my soul. They are Alpine journeys, which invigorate instead of wearying. And I rejoice far more than De Saussure did, when from the newly attained summit I can survey the various branches and scope of the Alpine chain, which is denominated by me, the Education of the Human Soul.

Sunday, August 16*th.*—Morning family worship is already over. After breakfast, Nancy carried, as usual, the Bible to her father, who read from its pages the fourth Psalm of David, and at its conclusion made the following observations:

"Parents can love their children with an equal affection, and yet at the same time have for each separate child a separate tenderness and care with reference to the child's character, or talents—sometimes even faults. Thus is God in relationship to mankind. He loves them all equally, but yet every separate individual with an especial care, so that every one may regard himself as standing in a separate relationship, as it were apart with Him. We see in this the relationship of Christ Jesus to his disciples. Every one of us can then severally say with David, that he is loved of God. Every one of us has from Him an especial ray of His light and grace. Therefore, Father, we pray for ourselves and for all, 'Lift thou up the light of thy countenance upon us!'"

The observations of the excellent Pastor Coulin seldom extend beyond five minutes; but there is more matter in them than is generally found in longer discourses. We conversed afterwards, for a short time, of persons who, even under the most severe trials, have yet possessed within their souls this sense of the Divine Fatherly care and guidance.

August 17th.—My birthday. I have not mentioned it to any one in my kind home. No beloved sisters have, as on so many a former occasion, greeted me on this anniversary with flowers, presents, and little amusing devices. But pleasant and strengthening thoughts have visited me, and made this day to me like a festival. Partly by conversation, partly by reading, partly, and above all, by the soul's centring itself into its own depth, meditating upon its highest phenomena, have I been, during my residence, carried forward in the inquiry which, beyond every thing else, drew me hither. This summer has been especially favorable to me. The flower which had long been in bud within me, has here blown—I know not how. Probably like other flowers, by God's light in connection with the impelling force of natural growth. How can it be otherwise?—that which I sought to know I have now found; and of this I will speak more particularly another time. But that which I would here exclaim to all seeking and thirsting souls, is:

Have no mistrust! Brother, sister, thy thirst, thy seeking, are prophetic. They testify of the fountain; and they will, sooner or later, lead thee on to it, and give refreshment and peace to thy soul.

Whilst yet very young, I wrote, on one of the few occasions when I gave vent in words to an overflowing but as yet unenlightened soul:

"O thou consuming flame of my silent nights and restless days! what wouldst thou with me? There are moments in which thou illuminest eternities, others in which thou merely burnest and tormentest me."

I am now become old, and I still feel the flame there, as formerly, but it no longer burns and torments me. God first kindled it. It has been fed by Him and He has allowed it to become for me a silent, guiding light,—an eye for His sun. He has changed my unrest into rest. I have thanked God for the gift of life.

In the shelter of the peaceful home, which is one of the most beautiful flowers of the Swiss soil, I will cast a last glance upon the state of the Confederacy, and ask:

What fruit has its tree of freedom borne?

That the confederate people, spite of their being split into small states, with dissimilar laws, languages, religious creeds, manners, and usages, feel themselves nevertheless, brethren, by a common mother-country and a common freedom, and that they feel this mother-country and this freedom to be their most precious possession, and will defend them with life and blood, is proved by the last general rising on the threatened war with Russia, during the foregoing winter. That the Cantons during the times of peace squabble one with another, is no less one of their everyday customs, as it is amongst not very good brothers and sisters in many homes. And sometimes even bloody quarrels have grown out of squabbles, as in the war of the Sonderbund. The sentiment of freedom has hitherto been more Cantonal than Federal.

Many people upbraid the present government with endeavoring to obliterate local interests and local considerations in order to effect a greater centralization, a common feeling for the Confederate state. But this is, after all, evidently a great step towards a higher union. And the common festivals and exhibitions, by means of which the government is endeavoring to awaken in the individual Cantons the mind to the common unity and the common home, as well as to call forth brotherly love, are beautiful and estimable in themselves, and especially calculated for the purpose intended. Yet they have not succeeded in assembling all the children of the land. Neither Graubündten, Valais, nor Tessin, were to be met with at these gay national festivals. However, railroads extend out their arms more and more into all parts of the country, and before long, Graubündten,* Valais, and Tessin, will no longer sit solitarily behind their mountains remote from Berne, Geneva, and Zürich, as they do at present.

As regards political freedom in the Cantons, I have heard more evil spoken than good. Party feeling is often carried to an unprincipled length. The better class of citizens are set aside to give place to the worse; the bold, unprincipled man is the conqueror, and the ignorant set themselves in the place of the wise. The later revolutions in the Cantons have nearly always taken this direction. These facts have led me to the conviction that the Constitutional Monarchy must be, perhaps, of all forms of government, the safest and the best for the freedom and prosperity of the people. In the mean time it is clear that amidst these agitations, the Swiss people are receiving a political education, and that the new governments, compelled by the pressure of public opinion, are adopting a course

---

* And Graubundten ought to be the last of all to absent herself from the union-feast of all the Cantons, because she constitutes the great *Schweitsari* of the Confederate states. She is the Canton which produces the most delicious tarts and pasties, and many other kinds of confection, and which sends out to every country in Europe, artistes of this class, who are known under the name of *Schweitsari*. This art is said to have been introduced into Graubündt by emigrants from the Roman states during the gastronomic period of the Empire, and has there established itself, together with a number of Latin words, which make the dialect of Graubundten very peculiar and prove its Roman origin; Graubundten deserves, therefore, a place of honor at the table of Sworn-Confederates.—*Author's Note.*

favorable to the education of the people, and consequently salutary. And until this general political education is completed, no one can judge with any certainty of the republican form of government. Switzerland is as yet young in her public life. It is only a few years since its union established its form of government on that of the North American States. Is it not under the shelter of its republican freedom that Switzerland has already produced so many men remarkable for their influence on the development of mankind in almost every branch of human culture?* Is it not under the shelter of this tree of freedom that so many excellent educational institutions have sprung up and daily increase for the younger generation, so many beautiful asylums for the aged, and for those who have suffered shipwreck in life? Is it not in its shelter that every home, and every private individual has the opportunity of enjoying independence of conscience and the noblest culture? Let us not fail in the due estimation of such fruits of popular freedom!

There exists in Switzerland—whether it be the result of the political institutions of the country, or from any other influences—a certain high-toned opinion with regard to that which is right, moral, and

* Geneva alone has given to the world several of the most celebrated amongst these; Jean Jaques Rousseau, the social reformer and friend of mankind; the naturalists Bounet, De Saussure, and De Candolle; the teacher of Political Economy, Say; the historians, Sismondi, and Merle d'Aubigné, and many another celebrated name; besides the most intellectual, most gifted with genius, and at the same time most warm-hearted of female writers, the daughter of Neckar, the noble-minded Mme. de Staël.—*Author's Note.*

of general utility; and as regards the duty of every man to labor for that end, which operates beneficially, and in the spirit of the highest education, upon its youth, and even upon strangers who have remained in the country any length of time. The mind of many a thoughtless young man, from other lands, has here taken a more serious direction, and he has learned to live for higher interests than hitherto. And if the governments of the different cantons would be willing to give higher salaries, and improve the outward circumstances of persons who devote themselves to the education of youth, then Switzerland would soon stand, amongst its Alps, as a high-school for the young of all nations of the Christian world, for both women and men have the most decided gifts for this noble calling.

That of which I found the want in Switzerland, even in education, is the free, and, in its highest sense, universal spirit, which I felt to be so vitalizing, so regenerative, in the United States of America; and amongst the multitudes of lectures and sermons of this country, I should have wished to hear something which extended the political and social horizon sufficiently to embrace other nations also, and the universal human interests, the great confederation of mankind! That the Swiss republic is not altogether indifferent to these, is proved, in the mean time, by its sympathy with the struggle for liberty in Greece, and its zeal for missionary labors.

The women of the educated classes stand high in religious earnestness and activity in works of human love. They are truth-loving, industrious, maternal, full of an educational spirit. It is customary in the Cantons Vaud and Geneva, for every young girl, after her first communion, to take upon herself the instruction and charge of a poor child. I have rarely met with peculiarity of character among the ladies; the requirement and aspiration of higher intelligence, more rarely still. Domestic life, the religious life, and nature, seem to be all suffering for the generality. The woman in Switzerland, who enjoys, at the present time, the largest mental horizon, and who, with the most ardent heart, embraces the highest interests of social life, and who regards the Swiss Confederation from its highest point of view, is not a woman of Switzerland at all, but a daughter our unenfranchised country, of the people of Roumelia, Countess Dora d'Istria.

The men appear to me to be of sterling character, prudent and energetic, but many of them have, as regards the other sex, a good deal to learn from the French, and even from Englishmen. The Swiss man, it appears to me, does not often regard his wife, according to the requirement of the beautiful Swedish term, *Maka*, or equal; and not unfrequently, an otherwise good and distinguished man, deserves the satire which the little son of one of my acquaintance, on one occasion, unconsciously expressed, when he said to his little sister:

"Now, thou shalt be my wife. Go and stand in the corner!"

SHE.—"But why must I be thy wife?"

HE.—"That I may have somebody to scold!"

But this behavior is perhaps an exception to the rule.

The position of the young woman of the educated classes, in the house of her parents, appears to me, on the contrary, near to perfection; at all events, it is so in French Switzerland. The daughters are there educated to the right use of freedom, and they obtain this freedom in their best years. Every young girl, whether she marries or not, receives a settlement from her parents, and the means for an independent life before she attains to her five and twentieth year. In the good home, which is for the present mine, the two daughters were each allotted their portion equally with their brother, when he entered upon his office, and commenced life for himself. Nevertheless they know not a better home than that of their parents. And I do not believe that any country can exhibit more beautiful relationships between parents and children, and especially between daughters and their fathers. I have already spoken on this subject. But it is scarcely possible to say too much on these beautiful, perfect relationships. In them lie noble seeds of the future. For good, well-educated daughters, become good mothers, and it is upon the mother that the future of the child, and of the nation, more essentially depends.

In a few days I shall leave Switzerland, probably forever. Monte Rosa is the last point which I visit within its realm, and I am to be accompanied to Monte Rosa by both my young sisters, Louise and Nancy, from my beloved home beside the Living-waters.

ZERMATT, *September 3d.*—We are seated in the valley, at the foot of Monte Rosa; and whilst we are resting here, so that in the morning we may be able to ascend to the celebrated rock-rose, we are writing, the youthful sisters to their parents, and I to thee, my R——.

On the 1st of September we left Geneva. The morning was warm, the lake like a mirror; but the old "Helvetia," soon made its waters foam and roar. The sun had not yet risen; dark, purple-tinted clouds hung above the heights in the direction in which it would rise; it looked like a chamber-alcove, behind the curtains of which the glimmer of the night-lamp, contended with the light of day, and where all is silent and mysterious.

But not for long. The sun came forth "like a bridegroom out of his chamber; and like a giant who rejoices to run his course." The day was beautiful, although not perfectly clear. A soft, misty vail rested upon the heights; not a breath of wind stirred. But Lake Leman had never been more animated; steamers came and steamers went, saluting one another in passing by lowering their great red flags, with the white cross of the Confederation, down to the blue waves, which they seemed to kiss. Life upon Lake Leman and its banks, at this moment is a daily festival. The numbers of travelers either of great celebrity or high rank greatly increase it; the King of the Belgians, the Grand Dukes of Russia, Marshal Pellissier (the conqueror of Sebastopol) the French philosopher Cousin, and I know not how many other celebrities from foreign lands. The region where formerly the people contended together in bloody strife, has become that in which they, by preference, assemble for the cheerful and amiable enjoyment of life. Everywhere people are in movement to look about and to amuse themselves. On every hand flags are waving and salutes are given. And besides all this, these rich banks are at this moment infinitely beautiful. They are clothed again in new verdure after the late rain. The fruit-harvest is almost as abundant as the corn-harvest has been, and for many a year the vineyards have not displayed such a wealth of clusters. There is a universal blessing over the earth!

In passing by, I cast grateful, leave-taking glances, at the various places where I enjoyed life with nature and with man, and where I sometimes experienced the most amiable hospitality,—St. Prix, Lausanne, Clarens, Montreux! They lay peacefully surrounded by their splendid grounds and walnut trees,—the loveliest trees on the banks of Lake Leman.

So farewell, thou beautiful, richly blessed land! Mayst thou bear thy beauty, and thy harvests, for the joy of millions, and bless and benefit many a stranger, as thou hast benefited and blessed me!

At Bex, we were met by the kind Pastor Secretan, who conducted us to his hospitable table. At Bex, our little party was joined by a kind young girl, who wished to see Monte Rosa, and I am now the mother of three young daughters, whom I shall introduce to the regions of the new-world. Increased responsibility, and with it increased anxiety as to the event of the journey, for the sky is becoming cloudy.

We roll along, by diligence, to Sion, the chief town of Canton Valais, between the mountain-walls of the Rhone valley, which look down gloomily upon us. We stop at Sion, and set off early the next morning to Viege. The clouds travel with us, or rather rush on after us, till finally they drop down upon us in downright rain. A dismal prospect for Monte Rosa; but my young friends are in the highest spirits, form one droll impossible scheme after another, to accompany me to Italy, and laugh heartily at their own fancies. I cannot but laugh with them, but yet am myself any thing but merry.

We have dinner at Viege,—an excellent little dinner, and are waited upon by a handsome, clever Rosa. Viege lies at the entrance of the Zermatt valley, and here the mountain-river, the Viege, throws itself into the Rhone.

At Viege, we must decide either for or against the journey to Monte Rosa. We inquire from all weather-oracles, and behold, the sky grows clearer, and seems to promise favorably. We determine to venture the attempt. This evening we shall reach St. Nicholas. It is two short days' journey, through the Zermatt valley, which is celebrated for its grand scenery.

We set off. Two of us ride, two of us walk with long Alpine staffs in our hands, two guides accompanying us. We see, in Viege, many traces of the earthquake which occurred, last year, in the Canton Valais. The church roof has fallen in; many houses are in ruins. Our journey is beautiful; the valley infinitely picturesque. Both on the right hand, and on the left, shine out glaciers and cascades, from the woods and the mountains; amongst the former, the glacier Balferni stands out like a giant. It was not till dark that we arrived at St. Nicholas, where we obtained good quarters. The next morning looked likely for rain; nevertheless, we are up early, and when we come abroad, behold! yonder gleam forth the eternal mountains,—the snow-clad summits of Monte Rosa, in clear sunshine, directly before us, at the end of the long valley. It was heart-stirring, and so was the morning air,—fresh and pure. One did not feel either one's body or one's feet; one seemed to have wings.

And our journey was beautiful, this day, between the lofty mountains, from amongst which gleamed forth snow and fields of ice, whilst the pleasantest woods of melize-trees come down from the mountains, to the banks of the foaming Viege, which roars through the valley. Our road lies along the riverside, by a good footpath. Little villages, with their white churches, lie in picturesque disorder, upon the mountain plains. Even amongst these, has the earthquake left traces of its desolating power.

The weather becomes more and more hopeful. We pursue our journey cheerfully, botanizing and talking by the way; and the higher we ascend, the more am I at home among the vegetation. I am able to present my young friends with Swedish whortleberries and mosses. The light, agile forms of the young girls, the gay effect of the fluttering ribbons of their broad hats, gladdened me during our ramble; and both they and I agreed that we had never enjoyed a more agreeable journey. They will now, all of them, go on foot with me. One of the mules goes along unencumbered, and the other carries our small amount of baggage.

The valley becomes narrower by degrees, and assumes a more gloomy character, but the grand object, at its further end, stands forth, vast and elevating to the soul. We are now within view of the glacier of Matterhorn, which comes down from the rock in a serpent-like sweep; and now of Matterhorn himself,—a colossal snow-giant, of indescribably defiant aspect, and which seems to lift up his proud neck towards heaven, as if he would defy both God and man.

The valley is shut in, at Zermatt, by the Riffelberg, a plateau of 7,000 feet above the level of the sea; and this plateau is the footstool, as it were, of the giant-forms of Matterhorn and Monte Rosa. Matterhorn (*in French, Mont Cervin,*) looks out over Switzerland; Monte Rosa towards Italy,—which beautiful land one seems to behold, as in a grand panorama, from its snowy summit.

We reach Zermatt in good time, in the day, and in the evening ramble on the foot of the Riffelberg, along green meadows, where the cattle are grazing on the edge of the glaciers. In the morning, we would ascend the mountain, but the sky is again becoming cloudy, and the spaces of blue growing ever less and less !

RIFFEL, *September 15th, at an altitude of 7,500 feet.*—Whilst thick mist and cold surrounds us here, in the midst of the region of ice, and prevents our seeing any thing of its wondrous forms, I will, with sunshine in my heart, give some account of our ascent hither during yesterday.

The night before, at Zermatt, I had been awaked by the rain beating against my chamber-window.

"That is pleasant!" thought I; "and think of all the young girls who have accompanied me hither, on purpose to see Monte Rosa!"

In an hour's time, however, the rain had ceased, the moon shone through my window, consolingly, and I —went to sleep.

In the morning, I was awoke by Nancy's joyful exclamation:

"*Mont Cervin est tout découvert!*"

I hastened up, and assuredly, there stood the defiant ice-clad giant,—or, more properly, giantess, for it is in the form of a woman, with an immense crinoline,—in glittering splendor, raising her proud head towards the clear blue heavens. Not a cloud was to be seen. How happy we were over our breakfast; and after breakfast, we began the ascent.

We were soon, all of us, either on horse or on foot, clambering up Riffelberg,—now under the leadership of Ignace Biner, the best guide in this Alpine region. And ever, as we climb, we behold the Alp-horizon become more extensive; one ice-peak after another rises up, and immense ice-fields spread out their white, shining table-cloths, between them, until the whole northern chain of Swiss Alps stands in a vast semicircle around the horizon. We halt upon gum plains on the mountain, to contemplate the glorious spectacle, whilst we rest in the sunshine. I felt indescribably grateful to be able to see this in company with my

young friends, because I saw through all their eyes,
—and how those eyes beamed!

Monte Rosa and its world were, as yet, concealed from us, by the heights of the Riffelberg. Matterhorn alone enthroned, without a rival, from the east to the south. But the ascent begins to be very difficult for me; I never felt it more so. I am obliged to stop every five minutes, to recover my breath. Is it owing to the increasing rarity of the air, or is it old age? But Louise maintains that it is the air.

We have left behind us the last Alpine huts, and now even the last trees,—the delicate melize-trees, which look as if they, too, like me, had a difficulty in climbing the ascent. The last tree reached a little higher than the others, and stands bowing to the mountain, as if it said, "We can now go no further!"

The shrubs of the Alpine rose, and every other larger kind of plant and shrub, have ceased. There are now only little mountain-flowers—Nancy's little favorites—low grass, as well as mosses and lichens, accompany us still. The wind has become cold, and the piled-up mass of the Riffelberg comes ever nearer to us. At length, after three hours' ascent, we have reached the first great plain of the Riffelberg,—bare, save for a little yellowish grass,—but where *La Maison du Riffel*, the ugliest and most inconvenient of all Swiss hostels, was welcomed by us with great satisfaction.

A large fire was burning in the saloon, where we rested and had dinner. We had now Matterhorn, so to speak, exactly before our eyes, but Monte Rosa was altogether hidden from sight, by the loftiest summit of the Riffelberg,—Gornergratt.

The height of Gornergratt is 2,000 feet above the *herberge* of Riffel, and Ignace Biner dissuades us from undertaking the ascent to-day, because "it is already late," and we might now, at all events, see Monte Rosa from the plateau of Gugli. It is best to defer the ascent of Gornergratt till the morrow. Good,—so said and so done.

In the afternoon, when we had dined, we all turn out, as merry as can be, to botanize on the heights of the Riffelberg, because the weather is enchanting, and a breath of ill-humor on the part of Matterhorn, with cloud and cold wind, has vanished again. The sun shines, and the air has the amenity of summer.

We climb, without difficulty, up some of the little hills, where a flock of sheep still find pasturage. We leave the mass of the Riffelberg on the right, we make a circuit round the Gornergratt, to the left, and now, almost all at once, a spectacle presents itself, so grand, so extraordinary, and at the same time so beautiful, that it is overpowering.

It is a world of snow and ice,—towers, mountains, valleys, streams, fields, waves,—but not harsh, not terrible,—a fantastic world, in which the large in mass unites itself to softness and beauty in form; and there, —there to the left, southward, towards Italy,—lies, upon shining white hills, the immense snow rose,— Monte Rosa,—round and soft in all its outlines, like a Provence rose, although its projecting petals are blocks of granite. Clouds sink caressingly into its soft, half opened, chalice, and throw its southern edge somewhat into shadow; but the sunbeams caress it at the same time, as if to take leave, lighting up, continually, new regions of its inner world. Far below our feet, creeps the Gorner glacier,—an immense icy path, nine leagues in length. It requires an hour to go straight across it from the point where we sit. On the opposite side rise the giant mountains, Castor and Pollux, Breithorn, St. Theodule's Horn, with many other horns and waving icy summits, on to the Matterhorn, which bounds the view to the north. Every one of these giants is from twelve to thirteen thousand feet in height, above the level of the sea. Monte Rosa is upwards of fourteen thousand; and this is second only to Mont Blanc, amongst the Alpine heights of Switzerland; but its soft, rounded form, does not give the full idea of its altitude, whilst the Matterhorn, which is upwards of one thousand feet lower, rising up boldly, as it does, in its crinoline, appears considerably higher and more mighty.

We sat, for a whole hour, on the summit of Gugli, contemplating the wonderful world of snow, and listening, now to the thundering din which was heard at times, proceeding from it, telling of the fall of an avalanche, which we, with our eyes, could only discern by a little white smoke arising here and there; and now to the echoes, like silvery voices, which Ignace awoke by his laughter, in the mountains. Louise fancied she heard little enchanted princes laughing in the ice-palaces.

The sun, in his descent, cast the brightest beams over the soft peaks of Cima di Jazi, which shone white towards the heaven of Italy,—as white, as pure, and as soft, as if they had belonged to some snow paradise. We were never tired of watching the struggle of the sunbeams in the chalice of Monte Rosa, with the clouds, which seemed as if they would imbed themselves there; but suddenly a violent wind arose from the side of Matterhorn, and we saw the wicked giantess, as if jealous of the attention we bestowed upon Monte Rosa, encircled with a girdle of dark cloud, and assembling a whole host of the same above her head. They were evidently not to be trifled with, and we were obliged to make the best of our way to the inn. And there we have been obliged to remain ever since, enveloped in mist and cloud, which Matterhorn, the wicked witch, has gathered around us. We console ourselves with good books and good humor, but as regards the journey up Gornergratt, and its view of the Alp-panorama, both southward and northward, there is but little hope. It is as cold as in the middle of our Swedish winter, and probably we must soon relinquish our lofty abode.

We have, however, seen Monte Rosa, and its ice realm. Chamouni is nothing in comparison with it!

VIEGE, *September 7th.*—Fear for the continuance of the mist and the cold up in the snow-region, caused us to descend to Zermatt, without reaching the summit of Gornergratt. I am sorry for it, on account of my young friends, who, in the mean time, are amiable and contented with what they have seen. And very cheerful was the return with them, on foot, through the beautiful Zermatt valley, and in good weather. We spread out our dinner on the edge of the spring, and drank of their refreshing waters; we thought our mode of traveling was the most agreeable in the world.

Query: Could we not also in Sweden contrive short pedestrian journeys of this kind for our young girls?

I am now alone. I have separated from my amiable young Swiss sisters, who have returned to the homes of their parents. If I am right in my conjectures, there will soon be a great change for one of them—Louise. May it tend to her own happiness, and to that of her family! She and they have become cordially dear to me! They will constitute my family bond with Switzerland.

And now Italy, to thee, to thee! This very night I shall cross the Simplon.

NINTH STATION.

Journey over the Simplon—Domo d'Ossola—Bad Weather—La Tosa—Unexpected Meeting—Lago Maggiore—"Stock-Fish"—Isola Bella and Isola Madre—The Valleys of the Waldenses; their People, History, Latest Deliverance, and Present Life—Rambles and New Friends—Turin—The Po and Monte Viso—Carlo Alberto—Victor Emanuel—Count de Cavour—Gioberti-Cesare Balbo—Primato d'Italia—Speranze d'Italia—What are the Wishes of Italy?

DOMO D'OSSOLA, *September 10th.*—Switzerland, its mountains and valleys are now, for me, on the other side of the Alps, and I am in Italy, the much-sung-about, the greatly-praised Italy! But the heaven of

Italy looks cloudily down upon me, and it rains. Whilst I rest here a day, at the foot of Simplon, I will say a few words about the journey across the mountain.

I waited at Viege for the diligence, which passes through that place in the night from Lausanne. It arrived at three o'clock, but quite full. They gave me, however, a little carriage with one horse; a brisk, active young woman at the public house, helped me in, together with my luggage, in the dark, and away we went up the hill. My carriage, very rickety from the beginning, grew more out of condition with every jolt. But the peculiar and grand character of the journey occupied my attention. From Birisal to the heights of the Simplon, I went on foot. The scenery was wild, and of an imposing grandeur. The sun shone upon the mass of cloud, and wind chased the misty shadows amongst the mountains. All around, in an immense circle, glaciers and snow-covered mountain peaks gleamed forth from amongst the clouds. Before me rose a lofty mountain, shaped like a cupola, the top of which was covered with black cloud, whilst the lower part was lighted up by bright sunshine. It was the peak of the Simplon. Troops of misty shapes were chased round it by the wind, as in a wild sweep, while they strove to reach the top, which seemed, in its turn, to reject them. The black cloud lay threateningly above, and the white misty spectres careered around, like the unhappy and unsettled souls in the hell of Dante. Still increasing in number, they ascended from the depths below; still more and more wildly were they chased round the ice-clad mountain—clad as in tatters of ice—into the dazzling sunshine beneath the black, forbidding cloud. Masses of water were hurled down from the neighboring glaciers with thundering din. There is danger here from avalanches during spring and autumn, and for that reason strong stone galleries are built on many parts of road, to serve as a shelter for people and for carriages. Avalanches and torrents are hurled down over the arched roofs, and down into the abyss on the other side. Even now, masses of ice hang threatningly upon the heights to the left, along the road, but these will dissolve in foaming rivers which will find their outlet in deep clefts of the mountain, over which the road is carried, or they are conveyed away by means of strongly conducted gutters over the roofs of the stone galleries. One of these streams is hurled down with a force and a din which is deafening. The whole of this scene was so wild and so magnificent that it thrilled me at once with terror and joy. The sun gleamed through all as with lightning flashes, and as if in combat with the demons of nature.

I wandered along the Napoleonic road in security nevertheless, between precipices and the raging sport of waters. Many *maisons de refuge* are erected at short distances along this part of the road, to afford asylums to the traveler in case of misfortunes or snowstorms.

The wind became still colder, and the sky still more cloudy as we began to descend through the dark mountain pass. The road along its whole extent, is laid down, or rather constructed with most admirable skill. Napoleon had it calculated for heavy artillery. "But can cannon pass the Simplon?" inquired he, impatiently, from General Dessaix, whilst this titanic work was in progress. Peaceful diligences, laden with peaceable tourists, now pass along it daily. Of the beauties of the descent, I shall not say much. I saw deep. wooded mountain clefts, and beautiful waterfalls, but I had seen so many ravines and waterfalls, latterly, that I could scarcely distinguish between them. Besides, the weather was rainy, and I was sleepy, both from being awake all night, and from the cold. I enjoyed the consciousness of a warmer atmosphere and of no longer being perished with cold, as on the heights.

My traveling companion in my little carriage, was a young Englishman of the verdant species. He was continually asking me, "What is this?" "Where are we coming to, now?" and so on; although I assured him that I knew no more than he did, and that I was here for the first time, myself. It was of no use; and in five minutes I heard again, "What is the name of this place?" "Where are we now?" At the place where we changed our horse and equipage, a very small carriage was given us, so small indeed that there seemed to be no space between us and the horse.

"Now where is our driver to sit?" inquired my young traveling companion from me.

"On our knees," I replied calmly.

"Good Heavens!" exclaimed he, horror-stricken, "I shall sit behind!"

And so he did, spite of the pouring rain. Our

driver, in the mean time, actually found room for himself on the foot-board at my feet.

The heights had now begun to clothe themselves with rich verdure and beautiful trees, when a stone pillar near the road showed itself, with these words:

ITALIA.
STATO SARDO.

And anon, the beautiful valley of Domo d'Ossola, revealed itself with immense chestnut-forests, laden with fruit, and amidst which gleamed forth white houses, chapels, and churches. Cheerful colors, bright yellow, and red, shone upon the houses, gates, and towers, and produced a pleasant effect.

At Isella, we undergo a visitation from the customhouse officers, but without much trouble or annoyance. The countenances, expression, language, are here, all Italian. There is an agreeable, smiling expression in their dark eyes, and in their expressive mouths.

Amidst pouring rain we entered into beautiful Italy, driving along the fields of Piedmont, between wooded heights, and over the sandy plain, where the river La Tosa rolls its turbid waters. Thus we arrived at Domo d'Ossola. Here every thing has an Italian character, and looks gay and beautiful, spite of the rain. Broad streets; fresco-painted houses; young men, who go along singing, arm-in-arm, with garlands of vine-leaves round their heads, in the midst of the rain. It produces a sunny effect.

It rained so hard at the time of our arrival, that I was glad to get under the shelter of a roof, as soon as possible, which I did at the post-house, where we stopped. I was conducted into two or three large, naked rooms, the floors of which looked as if they were rubbed with tobacco-saliva. But I was assured that it is *un bello nero,* and the place very clean; I endeavored to believe so, though I could not see it. Neither have I ever seen it yet. The hotel is full of empty, cold, rooms, with doors which will not shut, bells which will not ring, and every thing at sixes and sevens—not as in Switzerland! But the bed is good; the table very good; the attendants obliging; and in the morning I hope to reach Lago Maggiore, and the Borromean Islands.

PALANZA, *on Lago Maggiore, Sept.* 12*th.*—When did any one ever think of Italy, Lago Maggiore, Isola Bella, otherwise than in connection with a clear sky, brilliant sun, and every thing under the most bright and agreeable aspect? But I had the experience that when it is bad weather in beautiful Italy, it is so with a vengeance, and when it rains here, it does not soon leave off.

At Domo d'Ossola, I found only a moment to go out, to look round me a little, and read over the door of a church, the great words:—"Indulgenza quotidiana, perpetua et plenaria;" the full meaning of which I leave to another time. In the evening, all the elements were in convulsion, and there was a thunder-storm, such as I never heard before; flash upon flash, peal upon peal, and such flashes of lightning! They lit up the whole heaven and earth, which looked black as the grave!—and so on till midnight. Nevertheless, the tempest was magnificent, and I enjoyed the wild spectacle, in my desolate hotel.

Next day, I was seated in a kind of omnibus with a dozen other persons. Three horses trotted on heavily with us along the drenched roads. The rain had now ceased, but the sky was cloudy.

At the station, the conductor came round to the carriage, and, laughing heartily, announced to the travelers that they would not be able to proceed further that day than Vogogna!

Voices from the omnibus.—What? What? Vogogna? Why? Why not forward to Palanza?"

Reply.—"The Tosa is flooded; it cannot be crossed!"

Long faces in the omnibus, and gloomy silence.

We again trot forward, and it begins again to rain, with low thunder.

Towards noon we arrived at Vogogna, a small and not an ugly town, picturesque in situation, and without any fault, it seems to me, except that of not being the place at which we thought of passing the night.

In the middle of the road stands, with a very melancholy look, as it has stood since last night, the great diligence from Simplon, without horses, waiting till "La Tosa" permits it to cross.

Now arrives a large private post-carriage; draws up, and the people begin to ask what it means?

"*Halte là!* It is not possible to cross!" says La Tosa. The horses are taken out. Now comes a large, handsome landau. The same question; the same answer, and the same fate. Now come three large carriages in train, Grand-Seigneur-like; and so are the gentlemen who are seated within them, all in gray over-coats. They are the King of the Belgians and his suite.

"Nobody can go any further!" says La Tosa, who has no respect to persons. King Leopold looks around him for a moment on Vogogna, with disparaging glances, and returns to Domo d'Ossola.

A portion of his suite and we others console ourselves by dining. I ask for a chicken and a cup of *boulli;* both are remarkably good, but I have so dreadful a headache from the thunderous state of the atmosphere, that I am quite reconciled to the thought of passing the night at Vogogna. In the mean time, the clouds clear off, the sun shines, and I set out on a little ramble of discovery along the ravines by the side of a little mountain stream.

In the mean time, some of the gentlemen of our traveling party set about to ascertain the state of La Tosa. The river is somewhat above an hour's distance from Vogogna. They find that the ferry is now passable, and returning with these tidings, require that the conductor should put to his horses, and continue the journey. But one lady, who has a place in the coupée, does not appear to the general summons. She has, on the assurance of the conductor that the journey will not be continued that day, gone up into the hills. The omnibus-gentlemen send a couple of persons to bid her return, and, at the same time, compel the conductor to begin his journey. The foreign lady may come after when and how she can. The foreign lady has little idea of the fate that awaits her, when she hears voices shouting after her among the hills, and sees people beckoning her back to the inn.

Arrived there, she finds the omnibus gone, within "*un quarto d'ora*," as she is assured. But a traveling party, who have a private carriage, wait kindly to take the lost one with them as far as the ferry on La Tosa.

The lady pays at once her bill at the hotel, gives *la buona mano* to all who desire it, and takes her place, with thanks, in the four-seated open carriage. Here she finds herself opposite an elderly gentleman, evidently an Englishman, who is very much absorbed in the pages of a thick book, and a much younger lady of remarkably lovely and attractive exterior, with lady-like manners; on the back seat sits a young person with the appearance of a lady's maid, and the stranger takes the seat beside her. The lovely lady accepts very graciously her apologies and thanks, and unites warmly with her in astonishment over the behavior of the omnibus. For the rest not many words are exchanged on the road to La Tosa; the gentleman merely remarking, with humorous gravity, as he just glanced up from his book:

"The diligences shall first cross, and if they are drowned, we will not go after them; that's all. We are on the safe side of the affair!"

And again he was absorbed in his book.

We now approached La Tosa, and heard its dull roar; and see! Here, upon this side of the river, stand the diligence and omnibus, and all the other carriages waiting, because there is yet a large procession of carriages and carts, which have first to be brought over, and the ferry is actively employed for this purpose. This is what my omnibus companions have got with all their manœuvring.

On alighting from the stranger's carriage, the guest whom they had taken in, said to the polite proprietor:

"If ever you should come to Sweden, to Stockholm, I beg you will inquire for Miss Bremer, who will be glad to thank you in her own home for your kindness to her!"

"Miss Bremer!" exclaimed the lady—"what a singular meeting! Miss Bremer, allow me to introduce my husband to you, Sir Thomas Lyell, of whom you must have heard during your travels in America!"

"Sir Thomas Lyell! Oh, certainly!"

And now we are deep in an infinity of topics, of people, and occurrences in America. Immediately we must part. The carriages are in motion for crossing the river. Sir Thomas himself carries my little traveling-bag to the omnibus, to which we struggle through deep sand and miry clay, talking the while on slavery. The handsome lady waves me a friendly farewell—we have agreed to meet again in Rome—and now I am on the ferry-boat, where the carriages and passengers stand in order, the carriages in one place, and the passengers in another, because the passage looks dangerous. La Tosa rolls along rapidly and broad, with its dark, agitated waters; it has again retreated to its banks, but it has left evident traces on the shore how high it was only a few hours since.

The deep mud of these shores, the number of carriages and carts, asses and other animals, which had to be conveyed across; the screaming and shouting of the drivers, and the merciless flogging of the poor beasts, which are ready to sink in the clay and sand, make the passage across in the highest degree difficult and noisy—and La Tosa the while rolls along so heavily and dark! But the broad ferry-boat glides safely by its strong rope, across the swollen river, and carriages, animals, and men arrive happily on the other side. The omnibus passengers creep up again into their places, I in mine, in the coupée, between the two gentleman, who do not seem to have easy consciences in the presence of the traveling lady, who has been so unexpectedly conveyed hither by an English baronet. She felt somewhat inclined to pray them for the future to bear in mind the command, "Thou shalt love thy neighbor as thyself," but she did not, satisfying herself merely by a reproach to the conductor. He threw the blame on the gentlemen; "You should have heard how they went on with me!"

The gentlemen said nothing, but looked a little ashamed of themselves; and again we trotted on.

But the clouds cleared off; then the stars shone out, and in their light we caught glimpses of Lago Maggiore, along the banks of which we drove for a full hour before we arrived at the "Hotel de l'Univers," at Palanza.

The whole traveling world seems to have streamed this evening into the Hotel de l'Univers, which is full to overflowing, and the waiters have so many calling voices to attend upon, that the traveler who is bashful must wait to the last. That is my lot; but what does it matter? I have, after all, obtained some refreshment, and towards midnight a little chamber also, in a house or magazine out of the hotel. It is true, the chamber is like a prison cell, with cobwebs in every corner and at all heights; iron bars before the dirty window, and so on; but it contains, nevertheless, a bed, a chair, and a table. A little active "Nina" assists me to prepare my bed, and then I rest deliciously, whilst I listen, at intervals, to the loud claps of thunder, and the torrents of rain which again pour down through the livelong night.

In the morning the sun shines, and the sky is bright to the south, over Lago Maggiore, but above the heights of Simplon and Monte Rosa it looks—as it must have looked at the time of the deluge. Violet-black cloud envelops the Alpine region. After breakfast I go out on the road by the lake, and am there witness to a great fishing for wood.

The lake is covered with drift-timber, which the rivers Tosa, Ticino, and others, swollen by the violent rains, have carried hither from the mountain valleys. There is timber of all sizes, large trees and small— mostly beech, as it seems to me—branches and twigs, portions of trees, planks innumerable; and boys and girls, old men and women, young men and women, are busy along the shores fishing up the timber and the branches that are borne thither by the force of the waves. The young ones leap exultingly with their bare legs into the water; the old people drag the more precious waifs and strays towards them with rakes. A great number of larger and smaller boats are out on the lake, which are catching the same kind of fish with hooks and lines.

"This is actually *buona fortuna*," said a poor working-man to me, as he sat resting on a piece of timber on the bank, "because all wood which is not marked, belongs to him who fishes it up; and now every poor family round the lake can lay up enough for his winter-supply. Look what I have caught!" and he pointed, with beaming eyes, to a little pile of wood and boughs, which he had laid together on the shore.

The timber-fishing continued the whole day, spite of the rain, which again began. As the day wore on, the Piedmontese soldiery appeared on the shore, to defend the property of the great timber-owners. The soldiers behaved extremely well, and did not prevent the fishing. Boys and girls ran into the water, snatching at the large fish; they are all bare legged, and all are gay, and chatter and shout and laugh; the girls are even handsome, with a sunny light in their dark eyes; but there is a sunny light in the whole of this scene, as if it were some kind of folk's festival. Even the little children have their part in it. The fathers take up their little ones, who are sitting on the banks, and kiss and caress them, as I never before saw fathers caress their infants, and as if they would say, "Now we shall have fire under the pot to boil the potatoes, thou jewel!" And the *bambinos* are charming little things, as they sit or lie there, half-naked and merry. I did not see a single one crying. In the mean time a violent quarrel arises amongst the fishing men about a piece of timber, and they scream, and threaten, and gesticulate, as if they were ready to murder one another, but they do not come to blows, the quarrel evaporates in fierce words and gestures.

On one large pile of wood, three women are standing, of a handsome, Italian type, and with classical forms—evidently grandmother, mother and daughter, for all have the same features,—and down below the pile stands a meagre, little, ugly fellow, like a dried skin, in a yellow-gray nankeen spencer with flaps, and pantaloons of no color, who shrieks and gesticulates, and with a violent torrent of words, accuses the women of something—I don't rightly understand what—probably of having taken some of the wood which he had collected. A well-dressed, elderly man, with the appearance of a gentleman, seemed to be the judge between the two parties. The women on the pile of wood, contented themselves with few words and great gesticulations, extending their arms and hands, as if accusing the little fellow, who seemed out of his senses, and darted about them like a bat. Spite of their proud bearing and handsome persons, and the extremely ridiculous figure he cut, it appeared to me that the right was not on their side. The peace-maker ended the quarrel, by taking the little yellow-gray man away with him, probably to draw up for him a formal accusation against the women. The youngest of these, a handsome, dark girl, with long, hanging plaits of hair, sent a contemptuous gesture after the two, as they retired from the scene.

Twilight came down, and one and all prepared to turn homeward with a part of their booty. The men dragged beams and boughs after them; the old women carried the smaller pieces which they had collected in baskets on their backs. Every body had something.

"Life is heavy for poor folks here in Piedmont,"

said one of the old wood-fishermen to me. "It is not here as it is in France, where every body can get about as much as he needs for himself and his family. In Piedmont there are some very rich, and many very poor!"

"I must hear more about that before I believe you, my little old man!" thought I.

I have now obtained a better room, in the great world's hotel, with a free view over the lake, and I shall not depart hence until I have seen it and its islands, in full sunshine.

Monday Evening, September 14th.—I have now done so! Yesterday was a most lovely day; the calm lake reflected the bright blue heaven.

At nine o'clock in the morning the steamboat from Lucmagno conveyed me to Isola Bella.

The Borromean palace and its gardens occupy nearly the whole of the little island, upon which they are raised high above the lake on the terraces. It is a kind of fairy-palace, where art has done every thing and has even constrained nature. Every thing is symmetrical, even in the gardens; trees, flowers, statues, every thing stands in state. There are many magnificent, large rooms in the palace, and pictures which I believe are valuable, but of these, it was not possible to form any just idea, from the haste with which strangers are hurried through. Magnificent furniture, mosaic tables, and a number of curiosities abound. I observed amongst these curiosities, a marble bust of Carlo Borromeo, with the inscription *Humilitas*, above which hovered a golden crown.

The lower story of the palace, which almost entirely

consists of mosaic halls, seemed to me to be the most original portion. In the upper marble halls, I caught a glimpse of some figures which excited my curiosity more than their articles of luxury. These were a tall, elderly gentleman, with a bald head; a young ditto, with a handsome, dark Italian countenance, and two quite young girls, with white aprons, dark eyes, and dark, long plaits of hair. The young girls seemed a little curious to see the crowd of strangers, who were conducted by a servant in livery, through the state apartments, but were prevented doing so by the gentlemen, and consoled themselves instead, by waltzing over the marble floor, and every time they passed the open doors, casting merry, inquiring glances into the gallery where the strangers were standing. I saw also, through a half-open door, a table spread for a few persons—as simply as in any well-to-do country clergyman's family; but this side of the palace was forbidden to the curious, and in these few moments, I could only obtain a glimpse of the present Borromean family, the proprietor of these celebrated islands. The old Count, his son, and these two daughters, reside for present on Isola Bella.

It is said that the palace and grounds of Isola Bella cost annually thirty thousand francs to keep them up. The family which owns them, is still, as formerly, immensely rich. Nothing in these costly designs astonishes me so much, as that any body will go to such a vast expense and so much trouble for a great child's play. For in reality this little, great piece of work is nothing more. It seems infinitely small amidst its grand surroundings of lake and mountains. There is not a single view from the highest terrace which is grand, because the island lies too near the mountainous shore on the one side, and the eye sees all round nothing except the lake,—which does not appear large,—and its garland of mountains.

On the part of the island which is not occupied by the grounds of the palace, stands an hotel for travelers, with wretched outbuildings.

I met at the hotel an American family, which I had seen some years before on the western shore of the Mississippi. Now, as then, we met with friendly sentiments. All parts of the world are coming nearer and nearer to each other. Human beings also; thanks to steam, and to the influence of mind!

I wished to take hence a little boat to Isola Madre— a half-hour's rowing from Isola Bella—and for this purpose went down to the shore where a number of gondolas lay side by side. A gentleman with black whiskers and mustache, rushed forward, saying that he would assist me in making a bargain with the boatman. He assisted me so far, that the little trip would cost me seven francs, and two vigorous rowers prepared themselves, with great importance, to receive me on board their gondola.

"Seven francs is the tariff-price," asserted they and the dark-complexioned man.

"Very well!" said I, "take your pleasure with them then. For my part, I prefer returning by steamer to Palanza and taking a boat thence!" And I very quietly turned back towards the palace.

But now came first one and then another from the boats, running after me. "Signora, will you have a boatman?" "A boatman, Signora? Here is one! There is one!—Take that, Signora. He will row you for four francs—nay, for two francs and a half. Take him; I will answer for him!" "Take me, Signora! I will row you as far as you like for three francs!" This last speaker was an elderly boatman, with a remarkably frank, and good countenance, of the strong Italian stamp. I nodded assent, and stepped into his boat, a large, good gondola, not without being followed by the angry glances of the dark-complexioned, helpful gentleman and his men; but we were soon out on the calm lake.

It was a warm, sunny day; the lake lay like a mirror, and the passage across was calm and smooth as it.

"Are you married, Francisco?" inquired I, from my boatman,—who propelled the boat with the oars, standing, bending himself forward the while.

"No, unmarried, Signora."

"Indeed! But it is now time for you to be thinking about it, Francisco!"

"The time is past, Signora; it is now too late. But though I have never been married, yet I have been and still am the father of a family."

"How so?"

"When my mother died, she left me four little girls to provide for. The bringing up of these four "*povere ragazzi*," and the marrying of them, has given me something to do in my life, and as you may believe, not so easy either. And now I have the youngest still left,—and thus the time has gone, and I have not had leisure to think about getting married myself—and now I am too old!"

Honest Francisco evidently did not think how beautiful was this short unpretending autobiography; he looked pious, and full of peace, and seemed quite satisfied with his four *ragazzi*.

As we approached the steps which ascend to Isola Madre, I saw that the stone girdle which surrounds the green island was fastened by a door; but scarcely had we touched the land at the foot of the steps, before the door was opened by a young man, who welcomed the solitary stranger with evident pleasure. He was the young warder of this little earthly paradise,—for Isola Madre is an actual little paradise, where a number of beautiful and rare plants have been collected from many countries of the world, and grouped here with such beautiful art, that you merely seem conscious of the loveliness of nature. Aloes, which blossom every century, grow here with the pine trees of the north. One wanders through the most charming groves of laurels and camelias; cedars stretch forth their shadowy branches over the soft, flowery turf; tea-trees grow amongst roses; along the stone wall shines out the bright amaranthus; lemon and orange blossoms diffuse their fragrance from lofty espaliers, and outside the wall, upon the rocks, grow colossal cacti, which give a tropical character to the scene. I recognized many plants which I had seen in America and Cuba. Doves cooed, and golden pheasants marched along the shadowy alleys of verdant growths, with their splendid blossoms and berries. Whichever way I looked, there was something beautiful and uncommon, and every thing as perfectly well-kept, and as fresh, as if in an eternal spring. My young attendant seemed amused by my delight over the plants, and my knowledge of many of them. He made me a bouquet of the most beautiful flowers.

But the young son of Adam found it, however, wearisome in this paradise, because he dwelt there alone, without Eve, and without visitors. When I asked him whether the time did not sometimes seem long in this solitude, the whole year round,

"*Ah securo!*" replied he. "Nobody comes here; all the strangers go to Isola Bella. If one were married, however, one could live here very pleasantly; but *il Conte* will only have unmarried servants!" And he sighed.

Nightingales, by numbers, sing here in the spring, whilst the camelias are in blossom, and the roses fill the air with their perfume. What a residence this for the honeymoon! I wonder that no rich Englishman has thought of it for his bridal tour.

The castle, or residence, on Isola Madre, is uninhabited, and does not seem intended for a place of abode; yet it has some large and handsome rooms, which afford far more extensive and more beautiful views, than can be had from Isola Bella.

The island lies nearly in the centre of the lake, and has been the largest cultivated, as it is also the largest of the Borromean islands, whence its name,—Isola Madre. The island of St. Giovanni is merely grass-ground and some vineyards. Isola dei Piscatori is wholly covered with small and ugly fishermen's huts.

It is a current saying, that when one has seen Isola Bella, one has also seen Isola Madre. A great mistake, this! Isola Bella is an earthly work of art, which leaves the heart cold. Isola Madre is an earthly Eden, like that which all happy, loving hearts, possess within themselves,—a miniature image of the first paradise, where all was beautiful, and all was good.

My respectable Francesco rowed me back to Palanza, and, after we had parted with mutual cordiality, I went out to visit the grand promenade—for even Palanza has such a one—along the shore of the lake.

The evening was lovely and tranquil. I took my seat on a stone bench, under a shady beech, a little way apart from the road. Just opposite, on the other side of the road, a poor blind man was also seated, under a tree. When he heard the approaching steps of promenaders, he stretched forth his hat, repeating the while a monotonous prayer, in which I could only hear distinctly the name of Maria. And now one crowd of evening promenaders went by after another, —ladies in crinoline, as stately as ostriches, and gentlemen with cigars in their mouths,—but all passed the blind man; not one of them listened to his prayer. There now comes up a smartly-dressed servant-girl, following her young mistress, who has a mantilla over her pretty head, and a little boy by the hand. They reach the spot where the blind man sits; he puts forth his hat, and mutters his prayer; the servant-girl puts her hand into her pocket—now he will assuredly have an alms! No, the girl lets her hand remain in her pockets, and they pass by. Now the loud trotting of horses is heard, and three handsome equipages drive along in succession. On the high-driving box of the foremost, are seated a young man and a handsome, more elderly lady; she it is who holds the reins, and drives the grandly-trotting horses,—a proud sight; they also drive past without taking any notice of the beggar. And hundreds pass by, but not a single one of them all gives a look at the blind man. It is really distressing to see, in a country where, according to the religious avowal, alms-giving belongs to the first duty of the Christian. It is true that the beggar's voice and form of prayer are not very attractive, but he is old and feeble, and he is blind; he cannot behold the sun, and the unspeakable beauty of evening! It is now already late, the shadows are descending, and the gay promenaders become ever fewer and fewer. Now occurs a pause; the road is empty,—no, there now comes along a lad of about twelve, in a leathern apron,—evidently a poor man's child; he is whistling carelessly, and has already passed the blind man, when he hastily checks himself, stops, looks around him, and pulls out his little purse; it seems very meagre and light, but it contains, nevertheless, a farthing for the blind man! Thanks, good lad! say I, *in petto*, and the blind man and I go, each consoled, homeward, on our own side of the road.

I have, to-day, made an excursion by steamboat to Tessin—the Italian Switzerland, the southern shore of which is washed by the waters of Lago Maggiore—to see its capital,—Lucarno,—and the banks of the lake on this side.

Lucarno lies on the shore of the lake, with a background of verdant wooded heights, directly exposed to the midday sun,—a beautiful place of sojourn for the winter, but fearfully hot in summer. The green mountains, with their white houses and churches, in particular the church of Sta. Maria del Sasso,—the ascent to which, in zig-zags up the mountain, is marked by fourteen little chapels or stations,—affords a beautiful view. Plane-trees, lemons, and oranges, grow around the city. The people have an Italian look, speak Italian, and are said to be separated into very strongly dissimilar classes, or, more properly speaking, castes. No one would observe here that Tessin is one of the states of the Swiss confederation. Its people have not the best reputation.

Lago Maggiore reminds me somewhat of the lake of Lucerne, although that has more variety and grandeur. Yet here one sees the snowy heads of Simplon, Cima di Jazi, and the Strelhorn, now and then glance forth from above the lower Alpine chain around the northwestern side of the lake. The day was warm and sunny, and the air seemed to me oppressive.

As far as the so-much-praised Italian sky is concerned, I cannot, as yet, see that it is more beautiful than that of Switzerland; or even that of Sweden on fine days. But perhaps I am not now in a proper state to understand Italian beauty. The journey to Monte Rosa and across the Simplon, have left behind an affection of the chest and a fatigue which somewhat depress me. And now—it is evening and dark out of doors, and I write in the endeavor to dispel certain feelings which, like birds of twilight, are very apt to appear at this time of day—especially in the autumn—and make me, as it were, afraid of the life and the labor of my solitary journey! I will not listen to the rustling of their nocturnal wings; I know indeed, after all, that in the morning I shall feel my courage returned. And such needs especially to be the case in the morning when I have before me a probably laborious day's journey to Turin. I shall not, however, remain any length of time there; but, on the present occasion, proceed to the valleys of the Waldenses, and, somewhat later, pay my visit to the Capital of Piedmont.

I take my leave of Lago Maggiore without regret, although I see all its beauty. But the beauty of lakes, their fresh-water life, have something empty and circumscribed, which is not sufficient for me. I require a view over a vast extent, across which mists and clouds speed in their wild career, and cast down their wandering shadows, or—over the vast, free, briny ocean, where ships come and go; that—Good night!

LA TORRE, *September* 20*th.*—I am in the valleys of the Waldenses, in the oldest home and hearth of evangelical Protestantism on the earth! How entirely it agrees with me! It seems to me now, as if I had slept ever since my arrival in Italy, had slept on Lago Maggiore, on Isola Bella, in Turin, and had first awoke here, where the hills and the woods talk, where the rivers sing about the life of spiritual freedom—mine, thine, all of ours who come to freedom and to light in the Redeemer, Jesus Christ!

Besides, it is here so infinitely beautiful; one lovely

day, intoxicated as if with sunshine, succeeds another, gladdening the well-watered earth. The situation, too, of these valleys and their scenery, is glorious!

Extending from the southern ranges of the Cottian Alps, these valleys expand like a fan towards the plain of Piedmont, upon which they lie, between their mountain ridges, as upon a high terrace. The fertile heights and plains along the mountain ridges are covered with chestnut woods, which are just now laden with fruit, "the manna of the valleys," as it is called, because it furnishes food to the inhabitants of the valleys the whole year through, from the one harvest to the other. Lower down grows the mulberry-tree in great luxuriance, the maize, the vine, &c., intermixed with beautiful pasture-land, while through all these valleys rivers dance, and becks leap along, clearer and purer, it seems to me, than I have ever before seen elsewhere. Such are the rivers of Lucerne and Angrogna, and the wild Germanasco in the valley of San Martino. All proceed from sources in the Alps, and all contribute to swell, with their pure waters, the mighty Po, which leads them through Italy into the great ocean.

The valleys run out in rays from the mountains towards the plains, and as they open themselves into it, a view expands as grand almost as if over the sea, especially in the morning, when mists cover the plain, and the sun rises above this misty sea, over an extent of from one hundred and fifty to two hundred miles, and shines upon the blue mountain-chain of the Apennines, which bound the distant horizon in the States of Tuscany.

A mountain, by the name of Cavour, rises, like a rock-island, solitarily from this misty ocean in the midst of the plain. The beautiful, wooded valleys resemble a peaceful haven, from which one gazes forth upon the ocean, whose storms do not disturb its repose. Ah! but it has frequently been otherwise: these valleys were frequently, instead of calm havens, homes for bloody persecutions and strifes, yet were they at the same time glorious witnesses of the strength of faith and patience, of the victory of the light—of the light which shines in darkness. *Lux lucet in Tenebris*, has been, from the most ancient times, the motto in the church of the Waldenses; it surrounds the candlestick which is engraved on its seal.

How much have I liked and enjoyed since my arrival here, during my rambles in these lonely valleys, and in my intercourse with their inhabitants, as well peasants as of the more educated classes! Foremost amongst the latter, I must mention the evangelical preacher, M. Meille, minister of the new Waldenses church of Turin, but who, with his family, have their summer home in the valleys; a man of Italian grace, both in language and manner, who has the warmest affection for the dales-people and their doctrines, and the most beautiful gifts, both as a teacher and preacher; and Louise Appia, the superintendent of the girl-schools in the valleys, a noble, amiable woman, and a remarkable teacher. Upon the benches of her crowded schools, one sees the peasant's daughter and the descendant of the doges of Venice, sitting side by side, participant of the same learning, and the same affectionately earnest, maternal care. Through these estimable persons, I became acquainted with the latest history of the Waldenses and their present life.

Allow me, my R——, to sketch for thee here a few traits of this history, in the hope of creating in thy heart a desire to know more; because, whilst it affords an episode in the history of a Christian people, which ought to be known by all and repeated from father to child, from one generation to another, in evidence of God's providence over a faithful and heroic people, it embraces that of "the Israel of the Valleys," as the Waldenses deserve to be called.

But little, and that indefinite, is known of the first commencement of the Waldenses church, and the learned disagree at the present time about the origin of their name. That which is certain is, that from the earliest period, when the light of history begins to fall upon the region between Mont Cenis and Monte Viso, by the sources of the Po, it is spoken of as being inhabited by Christians, "who in many respects are separated in faith, ecclesiastical customs, and government," from that, which, under the power of the Pope, became dominant in the rest of Italy. The evangelical apostles extended their travels, very early, across the Cottian Alps, to convey the glad tidings of the Saviour to the shores of the Rhone and the Rhine.

Historians relate, that Christians of the Theban legion fled from persecutions on account of their faith, during the second century, to the foot of Monte Viso to the sources of the Po. In the fourth century, mention is made of a man, by name Vigilanti, who, after having vehemently protested against the worshiping of images and relics, with other abuses of the Romish church, was obliged to flee from Rome, and who found a place of refuge and friends, in a district between the Cottian Alps and the Adriatic sea. In the eighth century, the congregation of the valleys advanced into a clearer light, when Claudius, bishop of Turin, was said to blow upon the smouldering coals of Vigilanti's heresies, and he came forward in a written treatise against the abuses and usurpations of Rome, encouraging, at the same time, the congregations of Piedmont in their protest against them. He supports himself by the words of Origen, in his Commentary on the Gospel of St. Matthew: "If we even say, with Peter, 'Thou art Christ, the son of the living God!'—not through our own flesh and blood, but through the light of God in our heart, then will each one of us become a rock. Every one of Christ's disciples, who drinks the water which flows from that spiritual rock, may bear its name. These words, 'the gates of hell shall not prevail against this rock,' are applicable to the whole of the Apostles. All the followers of Christ derive their name from that spiritual rock," &c.

In the twelfth century, the people of the valleys are spoken of, in many Roman Catholic writings, as a disbelieving people, who deny the right of Popes and Cardinals, translate and circulate the Holy Scriptures, and send out apostles to preach the gospel in opposition to the doctrine of the Roman Church. The Waldenses were said to be a people of shepherds and husbandmen; but against their morals no charges whatever were made. The most highly esteemed writers bear the fullest testimony to the innocence and sobriety of their life.

Their priests were called *Barbes*,* from the word *Barba*, which, in their language, is used to indicate an elderly, venerable man, and which is used at the present day for the oldest person in the congregations, and principally for elderly and esteemed men. "*Bou soir Barba*," said Louise Appia, when, during our rambles in the valley, we met an elderly peasant.

The oldest translation existing of the New Testament, is in the language of the Waldenses, called Romaunt, or *Lingua Rustica Romana*.

These Barbes were educated for some years in solitude, amidst earnest studies, at a place called Pra del Tor, in the depth of the mountains in the valley of Angrogna. There they studied the Bible, the human heart, and nature; because they were to become physicians for the body as well as for the soul. At the close of this course of study, they passed a couple of years in still deeper solitude, and tradition says that pious women also lived in a similar solitude, rigidly separated from the world.

Thus prepared, these young men went out, two and two, an elder and a younger man, to convey the Gospel to various parts of the world. Sometimes they traveled in the guise of hawkers—there still exist in the old language naïve songs on this subject—and, as such, often gained access to high-born ladies, to whom they sold pearls and other ornaments. "But when, by means of these, they had awakened their attention,"

---

* They were governed by these, as by their elders.—*Author's Note.*

—relates one author accusingly, "they then say that they have a still more costly pearl; a yet far more precious ornament in their store, and when any one desired to see it, they would bring forth the Holy Scriptures, and speak of that which they contain, according to their faith, so as to inspire a desire to purchase the book—and in this way they attract souls from us to their apostatized sect."

The Waldenses lived for a long time untroubled, amidst the defense of their mountains, their remote situation, and their pure, simple manners. They cultivated their fields, practiced a pure Christianity, and received the Holy Communion of bread and wine, conformably with the usage of the most ancient church. An author favorable to them says: "There is scarcely a woman to be found amongst them who cannot, as well as any man, read the whole text of the Scripture in their everyday tongue. They teach the pure doctrine, and exhort to a holy life."

In the eleventh century, a kind of poetical prose poem, called "*La Noble Leçon*," testifies to the moral life and doctrines of the Waldenses. The church of the Waldenses had at that time founded flourishing colonies in Apulia and Calabria. They had connections with Dauphine and Provence, and are brethren in faith with the Albigenses, afterwards so cruelly persecuted.

But the little light which shone in darkness, began now to spread abroad too strong a brightness. The popedom, terrified at this, threatened the congregations with the excommunication if they did not conform to the customs and statutes of the Romish church. To which they replied, "Death rather than the mass!" On this a bloody persecution commenced against them. "Wherefore?" inquired the Waldenses; "we merely follow the usages and laws which we have inherited from our fathers since the time of the Apostles!" The reply to this was imprisonment, and the most cruel executions. These were carried on with such fury in Calabria, that the flourishing congregation there was soon extirpated.

They who were saved from the massacre, fled to the mountains of the Waldenses, within which the whole church of the Waldenses was soon confined. But in nearly every succeeding century, they were visited even here by the persecutions of the Roman Catholic church, and by its hired servants, soldiers athirst for blood and plunder. History has no scenes more cruel, neither has it any more heroic than those which occurred, and which again and again were repeated in these valleys. There is not here a single rock or river which has not been dyed with the blood of martyrs. But they suffered cheerfully, heroically; they encouraged each other to die rather than to swerve from their own and their fathers' faith. I will give, from many individual traits, merely the following:

One man, during the fifteenth century, was offered either within three days to accept the Romish doctrine, or to be burned alive. He was in prison when that sentence was passed, and his wife then desired to speak with him "as she had something of importance to his best interests to say to him." They, not doubting but that she would endeavor to persuade him to abjure his faith, admitted her into the prison. Great then became the anger and astonishment of the attendants when they heard her encourage her husband "to continue firm to the end." "Do not be uneasy about any thing which belongs to this world," continued the heroic woman; "do not think about leaving me a deserted widow, because, by God's mercy, I will accompany thee to death. Do not think about the sufferings of death—for they are soon over!" And she prayed so earnestly to be permitted to die at the same pile with her husband, that they finally granted her prayer.

During the cruel progress of the Marquis Pianezza through the valleys, the wife and daughters of the brave Janavel fell into his power. The Marquis sent word to him that if he would not renounce his heresy, his wife and daughters should be burned alive. Janavel replied that he "would endure the most cruel torture rather than abjure his religion; that if the Marquis burned his wife and daughters, the flames could, after all, merely destroy their bodies, but that he commended their souls to the hand of God, even as his own."

A young girl having fled with her old grandfather from a troop of murderous soldiers which roamed about the valleys, found refuge in one of the caves high amongst the mountains, of which many such are to be found in these valleys. One night, when, as was her custom, she stole forth to collect chestnuts for herself and the old man, she was discovered by the soldiers, and tracked to her retreat. They killed the old man, and were about to seize upon the young girl, when she, seeing no escape between dishonor and death, boldly chose the latter, and breaking loose from the hands of the soldiers, threw herself head foremost from the rock down into the stream which flowed below—"and was killed," says simply the old historian Gilly. Tradition adds that she sung her favorite hymn as she was carried down the stream.

Similar scenes were repeated, century after century, in one valley after another. But the violence of persecution converted by degrees the peaceful people into warriors. They rose up against their oppressors; they fought with them, and the victories of the little band were often remarkable, over an enemy far superior to them in numbers. These victories, and the weariness of fruitless persecution, obtained for the Waldenses at length a long period of rest, during which they again were able to cultivate their desolated fields, and to maintain their divine service. For although some of their priests permitted themselves to be seduced into apostasy—at least outwardly, by being present at the Catholic mass—yet a considerable number of the people neve. swerved from their faith. God had intrusted to them "the light which shines in darkness," and they knew that they must maintain and defend it to the last drop of their blood. The consciousness of this appears with extraordinary clearness in the expressions which are presented of their leaders and Barbes.

Thus, till the time when the great Protestant movement took place in Germany and Switzerland. The Waldenses in the depths of their valleys heard mention made by their returning Barbes, of Zwingli, of

Luther, of Martin Bucer, and Œcolampadius. And full of joy they sent to the latter, as being the nearest to them this greeting:—

"The Christians of Provence* to Œcolampadius, health!

"As we have understood that the Almighty God has filled you with His Holy Spirit, therefore, we turn to you, assured that God's spirit will enlighten us through your council in many things, which are concealed from us by our ignorance and weakness. You may know that we, poor shepherds of this little flock, have during more than four hundred years suffered the cruelest persecutions, neither at the same time without evident signs of Christ's mercy. In all important points we hold with you, and ever since the time of the Apostles, has our faith been the same. But through our fault, or through the weakness of our souls, we do not understand the Scriptures so well as you, and therefore, we come to you for guidance and edification."

The reformers replied with encouraging and strengthening words. The Barbes of the Waldenses convened a synod in the valleys, on the 12th of September, and beheld with joy various representatives of the Reformation present there.†

---

* This expression, as well as the language of the Waldenses, shows us a near relationship, and perhaps, also, union with the French Albigenses. Because now, and already in *La Noble Leçcon*, is the language of the Waldenses, a French dialect.—*Author's Note.*

† On this occasion it was determined that the whole of the Bible should be translated into French from the original tongues. A Swiss, by name, Olivetan, who was acquainted with Hebrew

Shortly afterwards, in the year 1559, the most bloody persecution broke out against the Waldenses which had yet taken place in their valleys. The French government had left the valleys under the dominion of Savoy; and the young regent of Savoy, Emanuel Philibert, sent Count Della Trinita, and the Inquisitor-General Jacoma, to convert the people, or to baptize them in blood. In consequence of this, Auto da fes took place, and atrocities which make the blood run cold. One honest man, named Corbis, a member of the commission, who had been sent to the valleys on this business, gave up his post because he could no longer be the witness of these horrors.

Whilst the Waldenses fought against their oppressors, or were bleeding under their hands, they continued to present incessantly the most deeply submissive prayers to their Duke, whom they could not believe, desired that they should be so treated, because they had always been obedient subjects, and had always worshiped God according to the teaching of their fathers and of the most ancient church.

During these wars, two men especially distinguished themselves amongst the Waldenses, "Jahel and Janavel," who often performed miracles of bravery. At length they two fell before the sword. Just above

---

and Greek, accomplished the work in two years and a half. The poor Waldenses contributed two hundred crowns in gold towards the cost of printing this work. This translation of the Bible became an evangelical bond between them and their brethren in the faith in Switzerland. Calvin said, on this subject, "The French Reformation is now in its stronghold, and will not more be driven thence!"—*Author's Note.*

the now peaceful town of La Torre, lay a fortified tower, whence issued troops to devastate the valleys, and carry the inhabitants to prison. It seemed as if the little flock could not long stand against these desolating persecutions.

Holland, England, and the whole of Protestant Europe, raised a protest against the treatment which the Waldenses received. Then came the year 1655, which brought with it the foulest misdeeds against the people of the valleys. On promise of perfect amnesty and freedom of faith, signed by the Duke of Savoy, the people laid down their arms. On which followed a perfect raid and plundering, by the banditti of the Popedom. Great numbers of the poor people were killed, and the rest cast into many of the prisons of Piedmont. It was computed that fourteen thousand, both of men and women, were imprisoned. Many of the clergy were led to death, and met it with the courage of martyrs.

On the fame of the Waldenses, martyrdom being noised abroad, the powers of Protestant Europe again raised their voices, and that with such effect, that the prisons of the Waldenses were opened, but only with the sentence of perpetual banishment.

It was in the winter of the year 1656, when they were obliged to fly across the Alps into a foreign land. They had been miserably fed in prison, most of them were ill or insufficiently clothed. Hundreds of them died of fatigue, hunger, and cold, in the snow, on their journey across the Alps. Those, however, who reached Switzerland, were received with open arms by their brethren in the faith, in Geneva, Zürich,

Basle, Neufchâtel. They were fed, clothed, and well-cared for. They received gifts of habitations and fields, as well in Wurtemburg as in Switzerland. The Catholics took possession of the valleys of the Waldenses; dwelt in their homes, sowed and reaped the harvests of their fields.

The people of the valleys now lived in foreign countries, amongst their friends, who did all to make them comfortable, and forget the past and the old native land.

But that people could not forget. In Switzerland and in Germany, the Waldenses lived by the labor of their hands, leading exemplary lives amongst their foreign brethren, but listening with indifference to their offer of substantial dwellings, answering little, but silently longing for their valleys, their chestnut woods, their clear mountain streams. The little light which shone there so brightly amidst the bloody night of persecution, burned feebly in peaceful but foreign abodes. Their longings grew into action Whether it was a secret feeling, that they were called to testify of the most ancient faith and doctrine, in the place where they built their earliest temple, or whether it was something of that instinct which leads the eagle and the bird of passage back to their former nest, certain it is, that troops of the exiled people, attempted again and again to force their way into their former habitations.

The year 1687 saw four hundred people, secretly assembled on the shore at Lausanne, ready to betake themselves across the lake to Savoy. But the Bernese government—at that time powerful in Switzerland—

discovered their intentions and drove them back. The following year, a troop of from six to seven hundred, assembled on the valley of the Rhone, in order thence to endeavor to force their way to their mountains. It was now evident that a more mature plan was in operation. They had sent messengers before hand, to spy out the way to their valleys, and to prepare the brethren who still lingered there, for their arrival, and they had already received from them encouraging answers.

But the plan of the poor, home-sick exiles, was again discovered, and the French commandant at Aigle, in the Rhone valley, counseled them—yet with great humanity and good will—to abandon their undertaking. He consoled them at the same time by a discourse on the text, "Fear not, little flock; for it is your Father's pleasure to give you the kingdom." And whilst the dejected wanderers went to pitch again their tents in a foreign land, Providence was preparing the man and the means which should carry out their attempt to victory.

This man was Henri Arnaud. He was born in Dauphine, and was early destined, by his parents, for the priest's office. He studied for this purpose, but the spirit and the necessity of the times caused him to abandon this career for that of the soldier. He took service under the Prince of Orange, afterwards king of England; distinguished himself especially in military tactics, was appointed captain, and received many proofs of the princely favor. He afterwards abandoned, likewise, the service of war, resumed his clerical studies, and was consecrated as priest in the still remaining little congregation at La Torre. For by means of certain concessions to the Catholic requirements, such as being present at the Catholic mass, a small number of Waldenses remained quietly there in the valleys. Thus Henri Arnaud became closely united with the people of the valleys, and prepared to be their deliverer.

His name is found already amongst the leaders in the unfortunate attempt of the six hundred, just mentioned, in the valley of the Rhone. Two years later, we meet with him as the principal person in a new attempt, but this time with greater means. Arnaud had secretly turned to the Prince of Orange, and even to other Protestant Princes, with entreaties for support. This was granted, and Arnaud obtained means for the accomplishment of an attempt, which, nevertheless, according to human reasoning, was wild, even to insanity, and could not succeed. But Henri Arnaud was illumined by "the inner light;" this alone, and the power of his faith and spirit, put him in a condition to carry out that heroic undertaking which afterwards was designated as *La glorieuse rentré.*

Arnaud was forty-six years old when he became the leader of the Waldenses flock, which gathered around for the reconquering of the valleys. His portrait, taken at this time, presents a handsome, manly countenance, with an aquiline nose, a piercing glance, and a mouth, the lines of which show the firmness of an inflexible will. Beneath the priest's gown and band, gleams forth the costume of the warrior.

Such a man alone could accomplish such a work.

Well might it be sung of the little Waldenses flock, who, under the leadership of Henri Arnaud, went forth, in August, 1689, to reconquer their valleys, as it was of Gustavus Adolphus and the Swedes in Germany. "Be not dismayed, thou little flock!"—for it consisted but of nine hundred men, little acquainted with military tactics, whilst there lay, in the Piedmontese valleys, of French and Savoyan troops, twenty-two thousand men.

At nine o'clock at night, the little band was assembled on the shore of Lake Leman, at Nyon, in order to cross for the shore of Savoy. Here they fell on their knees, whilst Arnaud invoked aloud the blessing of God on their undertaking. The passage of the lake was made happily. During the whole night, and the first day, they proceeded through the mountain pass, in heavy rain; but nevertheless, in the evening, they returned thanks to God who had permitted their advance to be made so far successfully. Henri Arnaud has himself kept a diary of his march through the most inaccessible and dangerous pass, which they chose in order to escape observation. We cannot follow them through it.

Twelve days after their landing on the shore of Savoy, they again beheld their valleys. The troop had now diminished to seven hundred; but they were possessed of a firm confidence, and an unwavering courage. In the beautiful valley of Lucerne, after having put to flight two hundred soldiers of Savoy, they were able, upon a hill by the clear waters of the river Pelice, to listen to a sermon from Pastor Montoux; after which, they bound themselves to each other, by a solemn oath, which Arnaud read aloud. Its opening words are as follows: "When God, by his divine grace, leads us again into the hereditary land of our fathers, in order that we may there again establish the pure worship of God according to our holy religion, we promise the pastors, leaders, and other men, in the presence of the living God, and as truly as we desire our own souls' salvation, not to separate one from another as long as God gives us life, even though our numbers should diminish to three or four."

Amongst various other items in the oath, we find one against plundering, and particularly against plundering the wounded or dead of the enemy. The leaders also bind themselves to punish every one severely who shall swear or take God's holy name in vain. The leaders swear fidelity to the soldiers, and the soldiers to their leaders. And all vow, before our Lord and Saviour, Jesus Christ, if possible to liberate the brethren, and, together with them, establish his kingdom, and live for it until death.

Such is the oath which was afterwards called "The oath of Sibaud."

Soon after this, the little troop had to commence an uninterrupted fight with an enemy tenfold their own force. Arnaud, with his company, was driven, still fighting, from height to height, and finally from the valley of Lucerne, to the still wilder valley, and the bare rocks, of San Martino. Many men were lost in this march; the French soldiers in their company deserted, and the confidence even of the Waldenses began to waver. But Henri Arnaud wavered not.

"Let us take counsel from above!" said he, and strengthened his little band both by his courage and his prayers.

In the depth of the valley of San Martino, lies a rock, which is called "La Basiglia." It is a peaked rock, which terminates two mountain chains, running in diverse directions, but which meet at this point. Two rivers, flowing from the two valleys which they form, flow into each other at the foot of this peaked rock, and thence, united, form the rapid river Germanasco. The rock rears itself, with wood-covered terraces, as it were, three or four stories high, decreasing in size, upwards, and terminating in the form of a cone. Here Arnaud led his little band, now diminished to four hundred men, and here he intrenched himself, and built barracks and fortifications.

Some days later, he saw himself surrounded by French battalions. But when they attacked the people of Basiglia, they suffered such great loss, that this circumstance in connection with the severity of the season, for it was now the end of October, compelled the French commander to turn back and place his troops in winter quarters.

"Expect us again at Easter!" exclaimed the Frenchmen to the Waldenses in Basiglia, as they departed from the valley of San Martino.

Arnaud was now left in peace with his little band in his eyrie on the rock. But how were they to find food during the winter for four hundred men. Providence has cared for this. The Catholic population had, on the entrance of the Waldenses, fled from the valley, and a great portion of their harvest still remained buried under the fallen snow. The Waldenses found chestnuts, potatoes, and maize, in great quantities, and wine, butter, and other necessaries, were daily brought in by their foraging bands.

Every morning, and every evening, the warrior-priest, Arnaud, assembled his soldiers around him for prayer; every Sunday and Thursday, he preached to them, and they received from his hands the Holy Communion of bread and wine. At the same time he was endeavoring by all possible means, to fortify the rocky terraces of Basiglia, so as to be prepared for the tempest of the spring.

The enemy sent many embassies with the white flag of truce to negotiate. But the terms which were still offered to the Waldenses, were again—exile. They might as well have spoken to the rock of Basiglia, as offer such terms. Thus the winter passed on; the snow melted and Easter came. And with it, came again the host of the enemy into the valley of San Martino. A host of twenty thousand men—and at their head the French Marshal, Catinat—encamped themselves in the valley at the foot of La Basiglia.

A May day was decided upon for the storming of the rock stronghold. A troop of five hundred picked veterans under the conduct of the brave De Parat, were intrusted with the main attack, supported by the fire of seven thousand muskets. Catinat beheld, in the watch-fires around the camp at night, the *feux de joie* over the certain victory. But the Lord of Hosts willed it otherwise. The little troop of picked veterans were cut down by the brave garrison of Basiglia, its leader taken prisoner, and the enemy suffered so great a loss that the army withdrew as if struck with a panic terror. For every shot from the Basiglia had hit its man, whilst not a ball from the camp of the enemy touched a soldier behind the defenses of the rock. In the evening, Arnaud addressed his people, and those countenances, lately fierce and stern with the lust of war, were now bathed in tears.

Ten days afterwards, again the white flag showed itself before the Basiglia. Marshal Catinat admonished the Waldenses to surrender; he had commanded cannon to be placed upon the rocks on the other side of the valley, just opposite Basiglia, and they would be directed against its fastnesses. The Waldenses replied, " We will defend the soil of our fathers! Let your cannon thunder; our rocks will not tremble, and we—we will listen to the firing!"

But after some hours' firing, a breach was opened in the lower fortifications, and although twilight compelled the enemy to discontinue the attack, yet it was evident that it was only to be renewed the following morning, and that neither the stronghold of the Basiglia nor its people could long hold out. The French commander was also aware of the same fact, and sent word to the town of Pignirol, "that any who wished to see the Waldenses hanged two and two must make haste before the following morning to the valley of San Martino." He collected his troops and ordered watchfires to be lighted still closer around the rock-fastnesses of Basiglia, and their flames mingled through the night with the wild cries of derision, of fiendish joy, from the camp.

In the stronghold of Basiglia, all was hushed and

silent. The sun had set, but hundreds of fires on the cliffs, and in the valley, had changed the night into a dreary day, in the light of which the Waldenses could plainly read their own doom. They must either die, or save themselves by flight. But how fly? Sentinels and fires surrounded them, and watched every step.

"Let us pray!" said Arnaud. "For what shall we pray?" asked a mistrusting voice. "That the tempest may destroy our enemies!" exclaimed another. Arnaud represented to both that they evinced but little Christian disposition. "Let us," said he, "pray God to save us — in what way soever he may please!"

All lifted up their hands and voices in fervent prayer.

In the twilight of the evening a thick fog gathered on the mountains, and rolled down into the valley in such dense, impenetrable masses, as soon to conceal the enemy's watch-fires from the sight of the Waldenses, and to vail La Basiglia from that of the enemy. The Waldenses could now make their escape unobserved. Captain Poulat, a native of San Martino, on this offered himself as their guide by paths which were known to him, although difficult and dangerous, on the edge of the cliffs, along the precipice. The Waldenses took off their shoes, bound on their backs every thing which they could carry away with them, and amid deep silence, creeping upon hands and feet along the edge of the cliffs, followed their bold leader. A little incident had, however, very nearly betrayed their enterprise at the commencement. An iron kettle, which one of the fugitives was taking with him, slipped and rolled down the rocks. A French sentinel cried *Qui vive?* "But the kettle, luckily," writes Arnaud, speaking of it, "not being one of the talking kettles of Dodona, made no reply, and the sentinel did not repeat his question."

The paths were dangerous by which the Waldenses accomplished their nocturnal flight,—but, they succeeded in it.

When daylight again appeared, and the mists rose from the valleys, the enemy turned their blood-thirsty glances toward the eyrie of the Basiglia; but behold! the eagles had flown, and the fortress was empty. Not a trace remained of the warrior troop, and the thick mists which continued through the whole day to linger over the mountains, favored their flight through the rocky wilderness. "When we," relates Arnaud, "reached Majère, after having long sought for water in vain, the Lord took compassion on us, and sent us abundant rain."

In the mean time, the change in political relationships had all at once altered the condition of the Waldenses.

Victor Amadeus, of Savoy, entered into a confederacy with England and Germany against France, and sent messages of peace, and perfect amnesty, to the little warrior band of Waldenses, on condition that they should aid him in a war with France.

"You have," thus said the regent, "only one God and one Prince. Serve both faithfully. Hitherto we have been enemies; but henceforth we shall be friends. Others have been the occasion of your misfortunes.

But if you risk your lives for me then I will risk mine for you."

Nothing could be more cordial than this reconciliation between the Prince and the Waldenses in the commencement. The Waldenses gave the assurance of entire fidelity, as did also their friends in the faith of Provence and Dauphine. Their valleys were restored to them; the prisoners were set free, the exiles recalled. And from all quarters were seen Waldenses returning to their valleys, "like doves to the dovecote." The heroic Arnaud was raised to the rank of Colonel, and to the brave men of his troop were offered posts of honor in the Duke's army.

"The light which shines in darkness," shone again brightly in the valleys; the churches were re-established and attended with renewed zeal by the crowds of the now thanksgiving "Israel of the Valleys."

But a long time passed without the fair promise which had been made to the Waldenses being fulfilled; and still, to within a few years, they might ask themselves, "What will be the future of us and our children?" The Waldenses, it is true, had peace within their own valleys, but, out of them, they had no right of citizenship. Not one of them could hold office, or purchase houses or land in Piedmont, excepting in the valleys. The clergy and the aristocracy opposed every attempt to obtain civil freedom, and the Bishop of Pignirol, Monsignore Charvaz, declared openly, not many years since, "that he would give all he had to root them out."

But a powerful movement, as it were of a new spring, passed through the heart of Italy between the years of 1840 and 1848. Awakened by the noble Piedmontese, Gioberti, in his *Primato d'Italia*, it entered with new life into millions of souls. "A united and free Italy! A fraternal, free, and humanly-noble people!" was the cry which was heard from the Cottian Alps to the foot of Etna. In Piedmont, a very distinguished and liberal-minded man had already given the State an impulse towards independence and constitutional freedom. Carlo Alberto, at that time king, and Duke of Savoy, had early shown sympathy with this freedom. As king, he gave to his States *Il Statuto*, which secured this to them. During this time of general excitement, the Advocate Audifredi exclaimed one day, at a great public entertainment at Turin: "Twenty thousand of our brethren are now shut up in their valleys, deprived of their rights as fellow-citizens. They are industrious, moral, sensible, vigorous; they inspire their children with noble thoughts; they have sacrificed and suffered much and long for their freedom and their faith. Let us, in the common father-land, restore to them a mother; and, as brothers, give to them their share in the common social life. Long live the emancipation of the Waldenses!"

Vehement applause from the assembled guests replied to this exhortation.

Soon after this, the Marquis Roberto d'Azeglio headed a petition, the purport of which was, that the Waldenses should have the same rights as all other citizens of the State of Piedmont. And this petition, when represented to Carlo Alberto, was signed by six hundred citizens of note of all classes; amongst whom were several priests, but not a single bishop.

Shortly before this, Carlo Alberto had visited the valleys for the first time. The ostensible motive for this visit was the consecration of the Catholic church, which Monsignore Charvaz had built for the brethren of the Oblati order, very near the town of La Torre, at the entrance of the valleys of Lucerne and Angrogna, and on which occasion the presence of the king was desired. The Bishop of Pignerol, who had been the tutor of Carlo Alberto, hoped, by this means, to prepare a triumph for the Catholic church in the valleys. But it was quite otherwise.

The members of the government wished that the monarch should be accompanied, on this occasion, by a strong guard. But the king said, "I am in the valleys, amongst my people, and I will have no other guard but they." When the Waldenses heard these words, they at once hastened to prepare a guard of four thousand men who should meet and accompany the king.

On the appointed day, this guard presented a rather extraordinary and sometimes laughable aspect. A portion of them had arms, but a great number also had only sticks or umbrellas. And on more than one occasion, they were seen to put their weapons under their arms to take their hats off when the king rode by. But that which every one saw, and for which Carlo Alberto had both eyes to see, and a heart to appreciate, was the cordiality and the devotion with which the hearts of these honest men met him. This guard, which received him with such unanimous enthusiasm, and which remained standing quietly at a distance, when the king with bare head and a candle in his hand, entered with the procession into the church, and there performed his devotions, received him again with warmest cries of welcome when he returned from the church, and conveyed him thence as in triumph to the city of Lucerne, where he was to be entertained.

A great victory was won this day, and that was the heart of the king for the Waldenses. A beautiful stone fountain, near the Catholic church, testified of this, by the following inscription:

"*Carlo Alberto al popolo che l'accogliava con tanto affetto.*"

It was the 24th of September, 1844.

That which I have above related, and shall still relate, was told me by an eye-witness of both occurrences, M. Meille.

In 1847, Carlo Alberto gave to his States *Il Statuto*, the constitution, and in this transaction the Waldenses were also remembered and freed from much oppressive injustice. Still they had not, after all, obtained as yet perfect rights as fellow-citizens, and their position still remained uncertain and undefined. Nevertheless they were grateful, and hoped for the rest. It was on Friday, the 25th of February, 1848, when the news spread through the market of Lucerne, derived from the *Gazetta Piedmontese*, that Carlo Alberto granted to the Waldenses full emancipation, with the rights and immunities of all other subjects of the State.

It was market-day, and the market was crowded; but now all business was forgotten; people shouted aloud for joy; they pressed one another's hands, embraced, wept for joy. Old and young hastened away, to convey the glad tidings, each to his own valley and home. When night came the little town of La Torre was illuminated; even the Catholic convent lighted lamps in token of their sympathy in the joy of their brethren. And at all distances, upon the snow-covered mountains, even up to their very summits, bonfires played, changing the night into day. Many houses were also illuminated in Turin, the residences of the English and Prussian ambassadors amongst these. A movement of joy passed through the whole of Piedmont. On the 27th of February, deputations from all the provinces and communes of the realm, assembled on the Champs de Mars, outside Turin, to thank the king for the gift of the constitution, and also, by a general festival, to celebrate the new form of government. Six hundred Waldenses stood there, headed by ten of their pastors, as representatives of the population of the valleys.

The order in which the deputations should march into the city, was to be decided, it was said, by chance. But the noble Marquis d'Azeglio had arranged it otherwise. He himself, at the head of a small division of the central commission, approached the Waldenses, to whom he said:

"Waldenses! You have hitherto often been the last amongst us; to-day you shall be the first. Enter foremost of the corporations from the provinces, into Turin!"

The Waldenses bore a banner, upon the blue silk ground of which, might be read these words, worked in silver; "*Al Re Carlo Alberto, gli Waldensi recognoscenti!*" When they, with this banner, at the head of numerous corporations, marched across the Champs de Mars, and through the gates of Turin, a noble enthusiasm took possession of the assembled population. On all sides was heard the exclamation; "Long live the Waldenses, our brothers!" Handkerchiefs waved from every window, flags floated, flowers were thrown; people seized and shook their hands amidst congratulations and tears of joy. Catholic priests were even seen to hasten forth from the crowd, and embrace various of the new brethren. During the hours which followed, and until the corporations separated, were the Waldenses the object of the affectionate regard and homage of all. It was a festival of brethren, in which the youngest, long under-valued brother was now become the most beloved, the Benjamin of all. M. Meille retained a memory of this day, which even now overpowered his heart.

From this time, the Waldenses have not had the slightest occasion to complain of the government of Piedmont. Quite the reverse. Carlo Alberto's son, Victor Emanuel, steadfastly upholds the Constitution, the maintenance of which was his father's legacy to him; and his distinguished and, in all ways, progressive ministry, under the guidance of Cavour and Azeglio, interprets to the advantage of the Waldenses, every doubtful question of the Constitution. Cavour desires freedom of conscience on the ground of principle, and knows how to defend it with a steady hand. Hence he has, not long since, defended the Waldenses' project of building churches for their congregation in Turin and Genoa. In vain the Bishop of Pignerol, Monsignore Charvaz, fell on his knees before the king, beseeching of him not to permit it. The king replied, "What can I do? I must maintain the Constitution. The Waldenses are acting according to their rights." And Monsignore Charvaz, the most violent opponent of the Waldenses, resigned his office.

From the time of their *Glorieuse rentré* into their valleys, the Waldenses experienced manifold sympathy and support from foreign brethren of their faith. Above twenty schools have been established, a college built for the studies of the young, and a fund provided for the payment of teachers. The noble Scottish veteran, Colonel Beckwith, whose portrait I have seen in many houses, deserves, for his active interest in their behalf, and his rich gifts, especially to be designated the benefactor of the valleys. By these means, the Waldenses have been able, in many respects, to keep pace, in intelligence and humane institutions, with the development of the evangelical community. They are now able, in peace, to carry out the work which God confided to them,—that of testifying of the light and the gospel of truth amongst a people yet dwelling in darkness.

Monday, September 28th.—After five days of incessantly pouring rain, which I spent very agreeably at my good hotel, The Bear, in La Torre, in reading various works relative to the history of the valleys, and writing the foregoing little sketch, the sky cleared up yesterday afternoon, and I went out upon the handsome stone bridge over the Angrogna river, where I, with some other curious people, noticed how the little mountain-stream, which, a few days since, leaped in clear, silvery cascades, over rocks and stones, with water scarcely sufficient to drown a cat, now rolled along its waves like the very Rhone, pouring itself down, turbid and broad, from the hills, with a force which dashed huge stones together, and occasioned a noise as of dull thunder. I went down into the valley of Lucerne, enjoying the soft, fragrant air, gladdening myself with the fruitful earth, which was odorous as as a violet or a babe, still wet after a fragrant bath!

Whilst I have it in my memory, I will note down some peculiar marriage customs, which are universal in these valleys.

On the evening before the wedding-day, the bride invites all her young friends to visit her, and celebrates with them a kind of parting feast, not, however, like that of Jephthah's daughter, but a little merrier, and also accompanied with every kind of entertainment. On the wedding-day itself, the bridegroom comes to the bride's house, accompanied by his father and godfather,—the latter being his spokesman,—together with several others of his friends. The spokesman knocks at the closed door of the house. It is opened by the father of the family, who seems much astonished, and inquires, "what they may please to want?" The spokesman replies, that he wishes to beg for one of the daughters of the house as a wife for his godson, whom he presents. The father replies that the request is very flattering to him, and that this wish shall be gratified, hoping at the same time that it may be a cause of happiness to the two young people. He then goes in to his daughters, and brings out one of them, but not the right one. "Is this the one which your godson wishes for," inquires the father, as, with his daughter by the hand, he comes forth into the parlor. "This one," replied the spokesman, politely, "would certainly make my godson very happy, but—it is not she who is the object of his choice." The young girl, who, having been offered, is thus refused, then goes out with her father, who returns with another young maiden by the hand, and says, "This one is perhaps she who has taken your godson's fancy?" "This," replies the godfather, "will make some other man happy; but neither is it she whose hand we desire." The father retires, and comes in again, with a fresh one, who is complimented out of the room in the same way. If the father does not happen to have more than one daughter of his own, he will borrow some daughters for the occasion. "I myself," said the lively lady, laughing, who related this custom to me, "have many a time been offered and refused in the same way." Sometimes the father, if he be fond of a joke, will offer a young girl who is already betrothed, and whose lover is amongst the company present. He then steps forth with a protest against this attempt, or "mistake." At length, however, the right bride is brought forth, who is dressed, however, in her girlish attire. The father then asks, "Is this the right one?" "Yes," replies the godfather, "that is right!" On which the father answers, "Very good! I give her to you with honor and good repute, and I beseech of you, that you will maintain her with the same; and in particular that you will preserve her from *evil*," (*que vous la preservez de tort,*) a strong emphasis being given to the last word. The godfather receives her hand, and lays it in that of the bridegroom. He leads her to his father, who is the first to embrace and welcome her. The bride then goes out to dress herself in her bridal attire,—a black dress, with a light violet-gray apron. The more wealthy wear a white one. And upon her white Waldenses head dress, she places a garland of fresh flowers. During this time, the rest take their breakfast.

When the bride comes out again, she gives to every one present, a red and white rosette, which is fastened upon the breast; after which they all go to church. It is not until after the marriage ceremony, and in the church porch, as they come out of church, that the bridegroom places the wedding ring upon the bride's finger. The bridal procession then takes its way homeward. But at the first farm they come to on the way, the farmer's wife stands at the gate and prays the bridal company to enter her house and rest for a moment. "It will not take up much of your time," she says, "and it will give me great pleasure." It is impossible to say nay. The bridal company enter and find a table spread with every kind of dish and dainty. They eat and they drink, and they fill their handkerchiefs, and their pockets, with bread or pastry; return thanks, and compliments, take their leave, and again set out on their way home. But at the next farm house, comes a new invitation and a new entertainment. These invitations, which are called *des barrieres*, are renewed three or four times on the way. At length, however, they reach the bridal-house; where the mother meets the bride and hangs round her waist a little silver spoon, in token that her life as mistress of a family is now beginning. At the bride's house they dine, that is, if they can, and it is asserted that they always can do so on such days—what their digestive powers are, I cannot conceive! During dinner a pretty silver salver is sent round upon which gifts are laid for the young housekeeper. Healths are drunk, and speeches made. At these weddings there is a great deal of weeping. The bride meets again mother, father, sister, brother, and they think about parting, and they burst into tears.

"Ever since my fifteenth year," said the lively Mademoiselle Monastier, the daughter of the excellent historian of the Waldenses, in describing these things to me, "have I been at our weddings, and every time my eyes have wept out of sympathy with the weeping around me. One gets into the way of it."

Just now, whilst I am writing this, I hear a noise, and the talking of cheerful voices in the inn court. I go out into the gallery and see a wedding procession. But the marriage itself, the *barrieres,* and the weeping, are already over, and the bride, a very proper and rosy maiden, is just setting off with her young bridegroom, to Turin, where he is a manufacturer. The wedding party has breakfasted at the inn, and are about to step into their cabriolet. The bridal pair are surrounded by congratulating, hand-shaking, and kissing friends. Now they are in their carriage. The driver has a red and white rosette on his breast. *Forette Cocher!* cries an elderly gentleman, and all present join in a jubilant *Eviva la Sposa!* A right cheerful scene.

La Torre, *October* 10*th*.—"Salut!"—"Bonjour!"—"Buon giorno!"—"Buon Viaggio!"—"Bon voyage!"—"Ceria!"—"Jagro!"* were the salutations, which met me on all sides from the kindly people, as accompanied by Barba Legrain, I went to the hills of La Vacchiera, and Pra del Tor. They were addressed to me by people who came from the dwellings amongst the hills, with mules laden with sacks of chestnuts, apples, and such like, which they bartered for corn, and other articles, at the market of La Torre, which was not thronged with people. The third hay harvest was going forward in the valleys, and the people seemed cheerful; the day was sunny and warm.

I left the region of the chestnut groves and came to the birch woods, where also the beech and the hazel grow. By degrees, bushes took the place of trees; then bushes ceased, and on the heights of La Vacchiera, nothing grew but grass and ling. Arrived here, after four hours of gradual ascent, I obtained a full view of the wavy, gray, mountain chains, which separate in long rays, the valleys Pragela, San Martino, Angrogna, Lucerna, and Rora, even from the Alps of Dauphine to the Piedmontese plain. I saw in the north, the river Angrogna, which has its source in Mont Roux, and in the northwest the snow-covered heads of Monte Viso, and Pragela, rising above the gray mountain walls. On the south, lay the immense Piedmontese and Lombardic plains, cultivated like a garden, ex-

---

* Jagro is a salutation in the Piedmontese patois which signifies the same as "Allegro," Be merry! or, Mirth be to you! "Ceria!" is a similar salutation, but no one knows the origin of the word.—*Author's Note.*

tending to the Apennines which bounded the horizon. Down in the valleys at my feet, I saw the rivers rushing along; further off, I saw the river Pelice unite itself to the Cluson, and the two united carry the waters of the valleys to the Po. The mist which rested upon the Po, marked out its course. High above this shone "La Superga," with the Kings' graves upon its proud height; and to the west, close by the river, I could discern Turin. That was a view! The most complete which I had yet had of mountain and plain in this region. The Waldenses dwell in a perfect fastness of granite. It is redoubt after redoubt, with ditches and towers—but not the petty work of human hands!

With various kind and educated inhabitants of the valleys, I have now visited all such as are inhabited by an evangelical population. One portion, or the valleys of Fenestrille and Pragela, have a Catholic population established there from the time of the latest persecutions, which in part rooted out the original inhabitants, partly induced them, apparently at least, to adopt the usages of the Catholic church. That this is more apparent than real, is shown from the fact, that a few years back the Bishop of Pignerol established a severe search in these valleys after Bibles and New Testaments which the people had secretly preserved. He collected and burned—as trustworthy persons have informed me—many such.

The most beautiful and most fertile of the valleys is that of Angrogna. The cultivated heights ascend in terraces, carefully laid out, wherever the smallest turf is to be met with; fruit trees surround the farm houses. The valley of Lucerna is also beautiful and fertile, but is narrower than that of Angrogna. The valley of Rora derives its principal revenues from its stone-quarries. That which is most worthy of notice in the valley of San Martino, seems to me to be the rock of La Basiglia, as well as the large white and red block of marble over which rush the rapid water of the Germanasco. A very fragrant lavender grows wild upon the steep side of the valley, and is used by the inhabitants for the distillation of perfumed water.

The inhabitants of these valleys are, in a high degree, both a moral and a good-tempered people. The spirit of mutual helpfulness is one of their chief virtues. No one is sick, no woman gives birth to a child, without being visited by their female neighbors, who on such occasions always carry with them wheaten bread or flour for polenta, or oil for the night-lamp. Mlle. M. told me that she, more than once, has seen a housewife deprive herself of her portion of soup, in order that she might take it to a neighbor in want.

"I have myself done so," she said; "I know how it feels!"

The people are poor; the population, at the present time, amounts to about twenty-five thousand souls, but their great frugality prevents the existence of any bitter sense of poverty. Polenta and chestnuts are the principal food, and both are very palatable. Polenta is a kind of porridge made from maize, eaten with milk, and even in coffee and milk. Chestnuts are dried and smoked, and thus keep good the whole year round. Flesh meat is eaten very seldom. In the winter evenings several families will unite around one lamp, which, in order to save wood, they place in the cow-house. Here the women sit, and spin, or knit, and the men, tired with the day's work—felling and cutting wood—lie to rest on the straw, or talk. Occasionally some one reads aloud. Young men at these times go from house to house, and sit for a little while in the spinning-room, where they make acquaintance with the young girls. One troop sometimes chases out another, but for the most part in good fellowship.

As, in former times, this little people is governed by their pastors and elders. A moderator and his council keep watch over the pastor's economic stewardship of their congregations. Crimes very rarely occur which demand the interference of the judication. Marriages are frequent, and as the land and the means of sustenance have not increased in proportion to the increase of the population, a portion of the people have begun to emigrate, especially out of the community of San Giovanni. Near Santa Fe, in the Argentine republic of South America, a little community of Waldenses has established itself, and is beginning to flourish, and only a short time since requested from the mother-community that a pastor might be sent to them. The affection for, and the confidence which the people have in their pastors is often affecting.

During my residence here I have been the witness of three marriages. The first was one of that class which, as it seems to me, would have been better un-

done. A young ragged worker in the silk-factory*
married a young slatternly girl, also a worker in the
same factory. "Hunger who had married thirst!"
said Mrs. Fierze, speaking of them. The second marriage was that of a wealthy young man, with a girl
whom he had loved for seven years. She was not
however in the least pretty; rather the contrary, but
celebrated as being good and capable. He looked a
very excellent fellow. In marrying, the bride is commanded, in two several passages, to be submissive to
her husband. In Switzerland I believe this exhortation
is repeated three times. I wonder whether it does any
good. Of the third marriage I have already spoken.

As far as the creed of the Waldenses is concerned,
it has, since the time when a great visitation of the
plague carried away nearly all the pastors, been strongly influenced by the Swiss Reformed Church, from
which the Waldenses community after that time received the greater number of their new pastors. Some
customs in the church service of this community have
appeared to me peculiar, and I have been told that
they have existed from time immemorial. Thus, for
example, divine worship begins by the reading aloud
of the ten commandments. The pastor then adds: "In
the presence of this picture of what we ought to be, let
us acknowledge what we are!" The confession of sin
then follows, and is such that one can with one's whole
heart repeat it after the minister.

---

* The cultivation of silk is one of the pursuits of these villages. An Englishman, Mr. Fierze, married to a sister of Mr. Cobden, has established a large silk-factory in the valley of Lucerna.—*Author's Note.*

The form of baptism is here one of the most rational which I am yet acquainted with. The child is given up, as it were, to Christ. The church receives it in the place of Christ, and asks the father and the god-parents whether they will promise to watch over the child, so that it shall become instructed in and brought up conformably with the doctrines of Christ. The father and the god-parents answer "Yes," on which the priest says, "God give you grace to fulfill your vows!" After which he baptizes the child in the name of the "Father, of the Son, and of the Holy Spirit." On the confirmation of children the priest says: "These young Christains now come to confirm openly, and with full knowledge, the vows which were made for them in their baptism, in order that they may henceforth enjoy," and so on. One custom, also peculiar in this church, is the religious ceremony by which her elders are consecrated to their office, partly as justices of the peace, partly as religious instructors. Every pastor of a congregation, has around him a council of five or six elders or barbes. These are chosen for their life, and continue in their office so long as they are not unworthy of it, otherwise they can be displaced.

Near the high road through the valley of Lucerna, not far from La Torre, a handsome, newly-built church may be seen, with its two towers, around which thousands of swallows skim joyously. Over the door of this church, stands written in golden letters; "This is life eternal, to know the only true God, and Jesus Christ whom Thou hast sent." This is the latest built church in the valleys of the Waldenses. It will contain about one thousand persons.

I have mostly seen it filled on the Sunday; and the number of men on such occasions is greater than that of the women, which I have never before seen in any church. The people are well, but simply clad; all the women in white caps, with starched and crimped, projecting borders, which are becoming to the aged, but which make the young look old. The countenances are well-formed, the features refined, but with more of the French than the Italian character; eyes dark and deep, the expression mild, but grave. This congregation presents in exterior and manners, a strong contrast to the Catholics, at whose services I have this day been present. Here were mantillas and flowers; some were ragged and few serious. The preacher, in a fine parti-colored costume, preached on the sixth commandment. I did not understand much of his Italian patois, but yet sufficiently for me to hear that he was studious about picturesque effects, and that *le donne* should begin earnestly to make confession. The audience were evidently more amused than edified. They burst out more than once into involuntary laughter. The understanding between the Catholics and Waldenses, is no longer that of enemies; amongst some of the pastors of both parties it is friendly. The latest conspiracy against the Evangelicals, by a portion of the Catholic population, was put an end to by a Catholic priest. At La Torre the Catholic party is small, and confines its demonstrations to occasionally promenading around the market some image or other of a saint. The Waldenses look on without contempt, but with perfect indifference.

During my rambles in the valleys, and even often at night, I have heard sung a kind of pleasing melancholy ballad, with long concluding cadences, like those in our northern folk-songs. I have been told that these songs are called "Complaints," and that they have been sung in these valleys ever since the times of the persecutions. More than once have I heard these songs ascending out of the depths of the valleys with a most touching power and expression. To-day, while on a visit, which I paid to the descendants of Henri Arnaud—who now reside on a beautiful estate on the height, where formerly stood the tower of the enemy—I was able to hear two of these songs sung by two young women, servants of the house, who were called in for that purpose.

"On winter evenings, when we are alone," said Madame Peijrot, the daughter of Henri Arnaud's grandson, "I frequently let my maid, Margrete, sing to me some of these 'Complaints,' because she knows many of them; they have all their distinctive names." But Margrete was now shy, and would not sing unless the dairy-maid, Susanne, came and sung with her. Susanne, a stout and very handsome young woman, was called in, and after she had consulted some little time with Margrete, they sang, with remarkably pure and beautiful voices, a ballad of a prisoner, doomed to die for his faith. He was imprisoned in the tower. The spring came; the trees put forth their leaves; he perceived the scent of the violets; he heard the song of the nightingale, but '*he must go to die!*" Each verse began by a charming description of the life and beauty of the spring, and ended with the words, *et moi je vais mourir!*

Another ballad described the desolations caused by the persecution in the valleys. The husbandman sees his fields trampled down; "his walnut and chestnut trees burned down,—with what can he pay his taxes?" This lamentable ballad was full of power, simple and deeply bitter, and had long and dying cadences which resembled those in our northern folk-visor, yet have these a something still more melancholy in them. It amazes me that nobody has as yet noted down the words and music of these lamenting songs of the Waldenses. *Les Complaints* are an affecting memory of the tragical history of the valleys.

Arnaud's young descendants showed me the relics, which the family preserved with holy reverence; the silver-cup of the great ancestor, in which he dealt forth the wine when he administered the Holy Communion; his portrait, seal, &c. The eldest of the young girls bore in her handsome features a likeness to him. Mme. Peijrot's father, the old Arnaud, and last male descendant of his name, is a handsome old man, with snow-white hair, and it is beautiful to see him amongst the flock of blooming grand-children. The hill from which, in the old times, the peaceful valleys were fired upon and desolated, is now garlanded round with vines and fig-trees. Sleek, well-fed cattle, come home to the yard from labor, or from feeding in the valley.

After a month's residence in these valleys I am now about to leave them. I have had great enjoyment here, both from nature and from the people.

The families Pelligrini, Mallan, and Peijrot, Mrs. Fierze, (Cobden's amiable sister,) have given beauty to my visit. M. Meille, and Mlle. Appia have made it rich and instructive. How many lovely evenings have I not spent with this gifted young woman, and her little select troop of young girls! I have also to thank her for the acquaintance of two remarkable men, two elders of the valleys, Barbe David and Barbe Odin Barthelemi. We visited these Barbes in their homes. Both of them belong to the so-called Pietists of the valley, because they have had religious meetings among themselves, ever since two French evangelical pastors Neff and Blanc, preached here a *recueil*. But they have not separated themselves from the church of the Waldenses. Barbe David's wife was confined to her bed from a long, consuming sickness, and Louise Appia allowed three of her young girls, who were with us, to sing spiritual hymns to her. The sick woman joined in with a peaceful but beaming expression. The house was orderly and remarkably clean, but all the window panes were of paper, which whilst it admitted sufficient light excluded all view. Glass windows are a luxury rare in the valleys. The table was spread, and we were entertained with chestnuts and cider.

Several poor boys were brought up in the house of Barbe David, of whom his daughter was the teacher, and these children were maintained there by means provided by young M. Appia.

Both Barbes accompanied me back to my house at La Torre. Barbe David could not sufficiently admire and praise the ways of God, who caused that two persons from such far different lands and people, as he and I, should yet be able to recognize each other on our first meeting as brother and sister, and rejoice in the same truth and the same hope. This man's heart seemed to me to overflow with gratitude to God, and from the necessity to praise him. Barbe Odin was also a clear-headed thinker. On my inquiry "whether they, as Waldenses, would rather call themselves Evangelical-Catholics, than Protestants?" he replied, " Yes, Evangelical-Catholic! Protestant, what does it matter? Not much—one ought to be Evangelical!"

Barbe David mentioned that, some years before, an Italian youth of the Catholic faith came to the valleys, and excited attention, not merely on account of his unusually handsome person, but still more for the fervor and eloquence with which he poured forth himself in prayer and blessings over the people. Not a word of contention, or of a polemical character, came from the lips of the young preacher; words only of prayer to God and of love to man. Thus he appeared at some of the Waldenses congregations, and thus he vanished, nobody knowing whence he came or whither he went; neither was his name known to any one. His person and his voice were like those of an angel. "And yet he was a Catholic!" added Barbe David, thoughtfully, and as if wondering within himself, when he had with emotion related to us the account of the young man's appearance amongst them.

How entirely I could agree with Louise Appia, when she said, "We talk about converting Italy to the gospel, but do we indeed yet know what power

Italy contains within herself to convert us to a right evangelical disposition?"

Convert Italy to the gospel! Ah! Before that, the Protestant church, including that of the Waldenses, must become itself more evangelical. The bitter contentions which have long existed between some of the teachers of the valleys, the representatives on the one side of staunch orthodoxy, and on the other of too latitudinarian a rationalism — contentions, which every fully vitalized church must, to a certain degree, pass through—very clearly shows the necessity which exists of another new form of creed or formula of doctrine, than that which was drawn up more than three hundred years ago, shows,—before every thing else, the necessity of a deeper consciousness even of the signification and purport of a creed.

It also pleases me, that whilst most of the thinking people of the valleys take part either for or against the combatants—the latest cause of strife being the exclusion by the Synod of a young candidate from the priest's office, because he could not in every particular swear to the accepted formulary of faith,—Louise Appia, her brother, and some of the Barbes, withdrew themselves from the contest, do not even talk about it, but continue alone, by word and deed, to labor for God's kingdom. With these laborers it is that M. Meille joins himself in his beautiful, evangelical preaching, in his instruction of children, and in the religious periodical *La Buona Novella*, of which he is the editor, and which has now taken the place of the former newspaper, *L'Echo des Vallées*. I know more than one Catholic, who has been brought over to the Evangelical church, by *La Buona Novella*. The Waldenses church does infinitely much for Italy, as an evidence of the light which it possesses through the diffusion of the Holy Scriptures, and which is continually increasing, as in Piedmont so in Tuscany, and that above all from its really evangelical Christianity. The evidence of the life and the character is above every other. The gospel doctrine of grace has none higher, and the intellect requires it at which to kindle its light.

TURIN, *October 19th.*—I left the valleys amidst rain and cold; in rain and cold I came hither, and in rain and cold I am now sitting here. But I have good quarters in the *Pension Suisse*, and the best of all is, that, spite of a fatiguing journey through a country very little visited, lying between the valley of San Martino and Turin, I find myself perfectly well.

Traveling for hours on foot in pouring rain, arriving at night in cold quarters, in little miserable towns, where the filthiness exceeds all description; and where, instead of tea, you are presented with a sort of poisonous decoction from the apothecary, and are besides preyed upon by every kind of sharper;—that is the fate of the traveler every now and then, and he must take it in the bargain for all the good and beautiful which his life of travel affords him in other respects. One must be thankful, if one keeps one's life, health, and one's luggage; and so I am!

My first ramble in Turin—when the weather would allow me to ramble at all—was to the banks of the Po. The great river poured along its turbulent waters, broad, and of a dirty-brown, in long sweeps between green banks. Swollen with the rains and the floods of the smaller rivers, it is at this moment dangerous. The father of a family, who was going this morning in a little boat to his country-house, was drowned by the upsetting of his boat, which was driven by the violence of the stream against the bridge.

From this bridge, which extends, with its seven arches, between the city proper and its suburban portion, which is called *La Collina*, the view is really splendid. Far away, to the northwest, rises the pointed cupola of Monte Viso—very like a gigantic artichoke—from a chain of snow-covered Alps, at the feet of which lies Piedmont, as its proper name *Piedmonte* shows, and which separate Italy from the rest of Europe. The river Po, which has its source in the bosom of MonteViso, now looks like a dark and hideous tyrant, but its banks are lovely! On the green heights of La Collina, white palaces, country-houses, and churches shine out, and foremost amongst these, the Pantheon-like church Gran' Madre di Dio, built by Carlo Alberto. Wooded grounds surround the white buildings. Further south, rises La Superga, with a convent, and the family mausoleum of the Princes of Savoy, 2,500 feet above the sea, the largest building, it is said, which has ever been erected at this elevation, a colossal *Ex Voto*, raised to the Lord of Hosts, in the year 1706, by the King of Sardinia, Victor Amadeus, in memory of the victory which he obtained in that year, over a French army. Carlo Alberto rests there—he died 1849—after his unquiet life. At a greater distance below the height of

Superga, may be seen the union of the river Dora-riparia, with the Po, which now, with majestic force, speeds along over the plains of Piedmont and Lombardy. The Po has the dignity and the aspect of the great river. This point—that of the large bridge over the river—is the most beautiful I have yet discovered in Turin, which, for the rest, seems to me to be a city of but little architectural interest, and which has something of the American city's wearisome regularity. Streets cross one another in all directions, at right angles. One sees on all hands, handsome houses and outward prosperity. Beggars slink away ashamed into the twilight. Gens-d'armes march proudly along the streets, which are broad and stiff, multitudinous and long.

I have been told that Turin is not a perfectly Italian city, and that it does not possess a perfectly Italian life. Yet one sees bare-headed and bare-footed monks wandering along the streets, also great numbers of priests with broad hats and small legs. Here and there one sees a little girl with castanettes dancing *cachuca* to a circle of spectators, and another circle gathered round a comic female singer who is very bold in her behavior to the bystanders. Life exhibits itself in forms of bright contrast, and is not afraid of so exhibiting itself. This is the manner of the southern people. But without regarding the question of how much or how little of the theatrical life of Italy is possessed by Turin, I will speak of that which Turin, of that which Piedmont possesses at the present time of distinctive peculiar life, and which the rest of Italy has not—that life, by means of which, the state at the foot of the Alps has become the head of Italy, lawgiver, prophet, perhaps its Joshua. I will speak of Piedmont's young life of freedom, and of the men who have called it forth, and of those who are now leading it forward to development.

Already on my arrival in Turin, I met with an expression of this life in a folk's almanac, which was to be seen in the window of every bookseller; and on the title-page of which one read, under the banner of Sardinia and Savoy, the words: *La legge e equale per tutti*—the law is alike for all. The words referred to the last victory which had been won by the constitutional liberal party, by the abolition of a separate tribunal of justice for the priesthood, whereby the priests, like all other citizens were rendered amenable to the same civil law. That is a great victory in Piedmont, which is an entirely priestly-catholic country, and the liberal party of Turin have raised in commemoration thereof, a handsome obelisk upon one of the principal market-places of the city.

How, and whence comes the vernal wind, which at certain periods of time awakens the hearts of mankind and of nations to a consciousness of new power, for the acquisition of new objects and of a new future? Does it come like the spring-time to the earth, from an inner divine order and necessity? Or does it come in consequence of the use which free spirits have made of the divinely-conferred gifts of light and will, in unison with the summoning voice of God? I believe the latter. Because the spring-time of the earth always awakens the same flowers and the same birds' songs, which again die and return in the same succession.

The spring-time of humanity, on the contrary, always comes with something new; something beautiful or good, which no former occasion possessed; and we see—if we take a survey of the ages and of nations—that cultivation ascends, as it were, spirally. This is a very satisfactory position to recognize. It gives a desire both to live and to labor.

But what is human culture? That is the question. Is it a growth in splendor, such as many of the oriental states, Greece, and some of the later Italian republics, have presented it? Nay, then, we have not much to hope for in our future. Because we cannot expect to produce more brilliant events, greater men, warriors, statesmen, artists; actions more noble, or more beautiful works of art; and the people, and the states which have brought these forth, have nevertheless, after having flourished for a short time, passed in confusion and madness, or have sunk into spiritual inanity. What are we? What have we? What do we desire more than they? We who glance up admiringly at those works of art, which we could not equal, the Pyramids, the Parthenon, the Odyssey, the Pantheon, the Column of Trajan, La Divina Comedia, and the creations of Raphael, and Michael Angelo!—Let us speak it with humble joy—because the merit is only in a small degree ours—we love, however, we desire, however, something higher, something more! What? I will let Piedmont and the genius of young Italy, answer.

The whole of educated Europe, and also of America, knows *Il Prighione*, of Silvio Pelico, and also the heart-rending biographies of the prisoners in Spielberg. The very gentlest heart cannot, on reading these, prevent itself from feeling an emotion of hatred and vengeance against Austria. When the prisons of the Italian captives at length opened, their confessions testified before the world, of the sacred fire which burned and long had burned,—but as if under the earth, —in the heart of the Italian youth, for Italy's freedom and independence. They testified of that which secret societies and unions have labored for in Italy since the conclusion of the last century. They testified of this also,—that what the young patriots desired, was not alone the liberation of Italy from foreign domination. They dreamed of the unity of Italy, and of an ideal of its life, which they were not yet able clearly to comprehend, nor yet to give form or name to, but which caused their hearts to throb with noble desire. It was the attempt at revolution in Piedmont and Lombardy, in the year 1821, which first revealed the secret, holy fire. Austria soon quelled the outbreak. Its originators were executed, exiled, or confined in dark prisons. Amongst these last, was the gentle, laurel-crowned young poet of Francesça di Rimini,—Silvio Pelico.

Two young men were participators in this revolutionary attempt, who were later, with very dissimilar gifts and means, in very dissimilar ways, to cooperate in the continuation of the then unsuccessful and little-understood work of liberation. These were the priest Vincinzo Gioberti, and the Prince of Savoy-Carignan, Carlo Alberto. Both were Piedmontese. I shall here mention particularly these two, because, of all their cotemporaries, they have had the greatest influence upon the later fate of Piedmont and Italy,— the former by his writings,—the latter by his deeds,— and both by their character and disposition.

I will first speak of Carlo Alberto, because I have inquired much, and carefully examined into the life and disposition of this prince. I believe myself to have found in these the key to Piedmont's happy issue from the ill-starred Italian struggle for freedom, in the years 1848 and 1849. I have also heard much regarding him, both here and in Switzerland, from persons who knew him intimately. But the explanation which I sought, I found less in him, than in the circumstances and the persons whose work-tool he became.

His sympathies were, in the year 1821, entirely sincere, but indistinct, obscure, rather the inspirations of a warm and not ungenerous heart, than the result of insight and conviction. He had passed the greater part of his youth in Paris, Geneva, and many of the larger European cities: the rallying places of liberal opinions, and of their most gifted representatives. He loved the society of artists and literary men. When he returned to Turin, he attached himself to the young men who were enthusiastic for liberal opinions. He was himself young, ambitious, vain, open to influence. The prospect of his succeeding to the throne of Sardinia was at that time uncertain. He allowed himself to be easily persuaded to endeavor to become the prince of a large realm, of freedom, and Italy. The attempt was quashed in the beginning, and Carlo Alberto saved himself, by abandoning and renouncing his friends, and attaching himself to Carlo

Felice, at that time King of Piedmont, and to his despotic system of government.

When, in 1831, he ascended the throne of Piedmont, he first showed a trace, as it were, of his former sympathies, in some small reforms, but he soon stood forth as the most determined opponent of freedom, and united himself to the most reactionary party of the Jesuits, and the aristocracy. He persecuted the friends of reform,—imprisoned or banished them; even the noble Gioberti was compelled to become an exile. After this gloomy tendency had culminated in Carlo Alberto, in the year 1833, another phase of character presents itself, resembling that of his earlier youthful years, but now more matured, and from this he never again wholly swerved, although his inner life seemed to have remained a continual struggle between the Jesuits and the friends of freedom, or between Jesuitism and conscience.

Whether it were a reaction of his conscience, of his better self, or whether it were the pressure of the ever-increasing liberalism of the public spirit of Piedmont, united to his inborn vanity, which made him wish to be the first in any movement, certain it is, that Carlo Alberto, after the dark events of 1833, began to enter upon the path of these liberal reformers. He amended the laws, regulated the administration, encouraged arts and sciences, gave to his people various desired enfranchisements, and surrounded himself with a ministry of liberal-minded and distinguished men; amongst whom were the brothers D'Azeglio.

A dispute about imposts, insignificant in itself, brought Piedmont at this time into opposition with its old enemy, Austria, and the dispute growing every year more bitter, assumed, at length, large proportions. Carlo Alberto took, in this quarrel, still more and more openly, the part of Piedmont and Italy. This made him in a high degree popular. People began to talk about war with Austria, and a private letter of the king was made public in what he wrote: "If Providence send us a war of liberation, I shall mount, with both my sons, and place myself at the head of it."

But at this moment, Italy demanded, above all things, internal reforms, free constitutions, and many and various were the claimants. But there was one voice which raised itself, which gathered all into one chorus, because that voice expressed the unconscious wishes of all, and gave the word which many sought to spell. It was the exiled Gioberti who gave this word, in his work on the moral and civil primates of Italy—*Primato morale e civile d'Italia.* This new primate should not be a military dominion, like the old Roman; it should not be one of the fine arts, like that of medieval Italy,—no, it should be, above all, a supremacy of human morality, beauty, and order, in which Italy, as a union of free states, should stand forth as an example amongst the people of the earth, and under a spiritual primate (the Pope), represent the kingdom of God upon earth. The means for this new formation were devised with a tact and practical insight, rare in Italy,—if still not free from error,—and with clearness and moderation. The style and composition of the work were those of the most perfect master, often of the inspired seer. The purest heart, the most fervent love of the native-land, breathed from every page.

The work, two thick volumes, was interdicted in every state of Italy, excepting Piedmont. Carlo Alberto received it with joy, and allowed its free circulation in his realm. Thence it spread—spite of the interdict—to all parts of Italy. The enthusiasm which it awakened, exceeds all description. Now, for the first time, the young, upward-striving Italy, perceived what she wished for, what she ought to be, and might be. For she believed fully and firmly that she could realize this beautiful vision of the future. *L'Italia fara da se!* (Italy will help herself!) became the favorite expression of the young Italy.

"Christian nations may sink, but they cannot die!" had Gioberti said. Young Italy felt herself full of vigorous, new-awakened life. She hailed Gioberti as her spiritual awakener, and when he, recalled from exile, set foot on his native soil, he was carried as in triumph from city to city, from province to province, by a unanimous, enthusiastic people. The old Roman soil had never seen a nobler triumph. It was that of the spirit and the word.

The spirit and the word continue now, in Italy herself, his work. Innumerable writings, large and small, presented variations of Gioberti's theme. Amongst these, the most important and influential, was the work of Count Cesare Balbo, *'Speranze d'Italia.* This thick volume, first printed at Paris, was afterwards reprinted at Florence, Turin, and Naples, and in a few years passed through five editions. Cesare Balbo, also a Piedmontese, of an old and aristocratic family, the friend of constitutional freedom, and the friend of Gioberti, but a perfectly independent thinker, dedicated to him his book, and taught the public first rightly to understand how Gioberti, in his work, separated himself from the blind Italian lovers and flatterers, who, "contented with proclaiming Italy as the renovator of all culture and civilization, the discoverer of Eastern Asia, and of America, mother of the great Romans, as well as Gregory VII., Marco Polo, Dante, Raphael, Michael Angelo, Columbus, Vico, Galileo, and Volta, exhume every day some unknown great man, and praise the shores, fields, cultivation, princes, priests, people, and governments, *tutti quanti*, besides the air, climate, situation—a very paradise!—before all men, so that it is evident that all is good, and people have nothing else to do, and ought to undertake nothing else than—to enjoy life."

Balbo cannot condemn with sufficient severity these false prophets, who pour out comfort for the lazy, encouragment to the vices, to the "*beato far niente*," and to that still far worse *far male*. Very different is Gioberti! If he be not always as full of masculine strength, as Dante and Alfiere, still it is his great merit, to have spoken with admirable wisdom and eloquence, on the future of the fatherland, of which so much has been said in other countries, and there has been so much silence in our own; to have spoken of this in so frank and large a manner, and with more moderation than any of his predecessors; and that, although priest and philosopher, to have spoken thereof in a more practical manner, than the few practical men and historians, who have touched the dangerous subject with doubtful hands. This made his book more than a book; it is an act which cannot do otherwise than serve the fatherland. The subject is now open. Others will follow, criticising, correcting, completing. I am merely one of those—God grant there be many!—who tread in Gioberti's foofsteps."

Balbo, agreeing with Gioberti in the moral ideal, and also in the question of an Italian confederation of states, such as are determined by nature and history,* yet separates from him in other questions. Although sincerely devoted to the Catholic Church, he will not have the Pope as President of the New Italy, and lays an exclusive weight upon Italy's independence of all foreign powers, as the condition on which the renewal of her inward independence is to be accomplished.

New works of Gioberti and Balbo, all eagerly received by the Italian public, developed both their points of view. The former was that of the priest, the latter that of the layman. But both were alike sincere lovers of Italian liberty and development. Gioberti, though a Catholic priest, was opposed to the Jesuits.

An extensive literary movement arose in the northern portion of Italy, which produced a literature which I will call the politico-patriotic. This might be said to have commenced with the Piedmontese Alfiere, who infused into his tragedies the magnanimous hatred which his powerful mind cherished against all oppression, especially foreign, and the love that he bore to

---

* These states, according to Gioberti, are "*Magna Grecia*," or the Neapolitan kingdom; "*Latien*," or Rome; "*Etrurien*," or Tuscany; "*Ligurien*," or Piedmont; "*Insubrien*," or Lombardy. The lesser states or powers of Italy to be collected or incorporated in these five larger ones.—*Author's Note.*

republican virtues. Cotemporary with Alfiere—that is to say, at the close of the last and the beginning of the present century—was Betta, also a Piedmontese, who wrote his *Storia d'Italia*, and awoke through it, a new love for the country, and new interest in its destiny The lucid and fervent manner in which he presented his facts, has made his work, in the best sense, popular.

After Gioberti's *Primato* and Balbo's *Speranze d'Italia*, a legion of young writers arose, as combatants for the freedom of their country. Tragedies and novels emulated each other in calling forth the great memories and virtues of the fatherland. Azeglio, Nicolini, Guerazzi, stand high amongst the authors of the present time in this respect. (Manzoni's *Promessi Sposi* is a charming novel, but it cannot be said to belong to the fatherland's literature of liberty, of which I am now speaking.) A number of poets and prose-writers united themselves to them, and the Princess Belgiogioso,—who, by her personal influence and wealth supported, unquestionably, the patriotic movement,—had their works printed in Paris, in a paper devoted to this purpose; for the censorship did not allow of their publication in the Italian States.

The hour came when this blossoming in the realm of word and spirit should produce its fruit. A circumstance now occurred which made it hastily ripen—alas, ripen too soon!

It was in 1843 that Gioberti's *Primato d'Italia* came out and made its round of Italy. In the year 1847 died Pope Gregory XVI., and the electoral-conclave came together to choose a new primate over the Catholic World.

"If the devils inspire the Cardinals,"—it is related that Cardinal Micara said to Abbé Lambruscini—"then one of us will be elected; but if the Holy Spirit rules the choice, good Mastai Feretti will be the Pope!"

When, shortly afterwards, Cardinal Mastai Feretti ascended the Papal throne as Pio Nono, and began his government by purely liberal acts of generosity—a magnanimous amnesty, together with the gifts of various rights and immunities which the people had wished for,—then of a truth people believed that the Holy Spirit had ruled the new election. Italy saw in Pio Nono that spiritual primate and liberator whom Gioberti had beheld in his enraptured vision. All Italy sang the praise of Pio Nono. Foreigners and princes sent greetings to him. There was a universal jubilee, a universal complimenting and festivity.

Pio Nono had given the firstlings of popular freedom, and of free constitution in his States. The temporal sovereigns of Italy could not do less if their people asked it from them. They did so, and now follows that which history and the world knows. The conceded rights were celebrated with great festivities; then came new demands, new concessions, and new festivities; then again demands for the fulfillment of promises, or for new concessions; then procrastination or denial from the princes, clamor on the part of the people, and by degrees, ever more and more uneasy relationships. The liberal party divided itself into two camps, and in these there were many sections. The moderates desired reform and freedom, but gradually, and with the maintenance of the religion of the church. Of the ultra-liberals there were also many shades of color, but they increased more and more under the banner of Mazzini, which—whether rightly or not—was called that of the red republicans. Both parties were united in demanding constitutional liberty for the people of Italy. And they demanded it by fair means or by foul. Constitutions were granted by the rulers, with good will by some, by compulsion from the greater number. Delirious rejoicings succeeded. On the 11th of February, 1848, was granted, or rather forced from the government, the Neapolitan constitution. That of Turin was given on the 4th of March; of Rome on the 14th of March; of Florence on the 17th of March. On the 18th of March began the insurrection in Milan; and on the 19th, Carlo Alberto ordered the Piedmontese army to assemble at Ticino. On the 23d, the King of little Piedmont, with its four and a half millions of souls, declared war, alone and without allies, against the powerful Emperor of Austria, sovereign over thirty-six millions.

Thus stood affairs in Italy in the spring of the year 1848.

I now return to Carlo Alberto. It was the insurrection in Lombardy, and the cry of the whole of Italy which caused him to open the war—the war of liberation. Piedmont possessed a brave and well-armed military force. This was known to all. The whole of Italy called upon Piedmont to place itself at the head in the war for the liberation of Italy from Austria. Piedmont did so chivalrously.

Carlo Alberto who at the prophetic exhortations of

Gioberti and Balbo, and at the flaming up of all Italy for freedom in every form, had readily given to his people *Il Statuto*—a constitution—placed himself of his own accord at the head of the Piedmontese army, which, united to auxiliary troops from all the States of Italy, should achieve its freedom from foreign domination. But although personally brave, Carlo Alberto was no military genius, and that he himself knew. But hope and joy were supreme at that moment. The king and people were one. The people believed in their king, were enthusiastic for the cause of liberty, and had a high degree of military spirit. Gray-headed men took up arms; boys escaped from their homes to fight against the Austrians; whole families of brothers were seen to leave their peaceful occupations to muster under the banner of Piedmont

With this brave army Carlo Alberto burst into Lombardy and went forward, for some time, from victory to victory. Austria however sent against him Radetzky, and the eighty-six-years-old commander soon cut short the career of victory. Then again the peculiar defects showed themselves, which lay in the depth of Carlo Alberto's character, and which had shown themselves during his whole life. His action became hesitating and undecided; now and then he made a brilliant military movement, but he did not carry it out, or he did it merely by halves; he delayed when he ought to have been active,—perhaps he might be also, as the Piedmontese assert,—ill-supported by the troops of the other States which seemed to be willing that Piedmont should fight for them all,—in short, spite of the bravery of the king and the Piedmontese army, and the many fine actions of the honest allies, the campaign soon became a retreat, sometimes a flight.

In August, 1848, Carlo Alberto saw himself necessitated to conclude a truce with Austria, which was nothing less than honorable to Piedmont.

But nevertheless, the prospects of the other Italian States were far worse. After an actual Bacchanalian of joy and freedom, in which these people forgot all moderation and sense, a time of blood-stained sorrow succeeded. The Pope and the Monarchs, driven back by the people's intoxication of freedom, relapsed into the old state, under shelter of the cannon of France and Austria. Naples, Rome, Florence, Milan, Venice, were all compelled within a few months to lay down their arms and submit themselves to their former rulers, mercy or no mercy. Nearly all the rights and immunities, which had been promised to the people, or which they had obtained for themselves, they were now compelled to resign. The free constitutions were withdrawn, or no more spoken of; "the people could not govern themselves; they had just proved it; they must be ruled and governed as formerly!"

The supporters of freedom and the patriots bled, were imprisoned, or they dispersed on all sides.

In one only of the Italian States, in Piedmont alone, the liberal movement did not go backwards. Carlo Alberto had given a constitution to his people; he alone, of all the Italian princes, did not retake that which he had given. Amidst raging war—amidst the bitterest opposition, he continued to allow its statutes to be carried out and to take effect. Piedmont obtained freedom of the press; freedom of election, &c., and every constitutional question was explained in a liberal spirit by the liberal-minded minister. It is true that the noble Gioberti was obliged to withdraw into voluntary exile, where he shortly afterwards died; and it is true also, that the council of reactionary men operated not unfrequently upon the acts of the king; but, upon the whole, he continued faithful to the course he had taken, and in which the most thoughtful and distinguished men of Piedmont kept him steadily by their counsel and activity.

A pleiad of such men had grown up around his throne, as is always the case at certain periods in the nations which Providence has destined for some important work. Cavour, though then quite young, had already drawn upon himself the attention of the thoughtful friends of the country, by his conduct as deputy, his keen insight and his unusual talents; and more than óne had predicted that this young man would sometime play an important part in the fortunes of Piedmont.

But I will now speak of Carlo Alberto.

He had made *fiasco* before the whole world, in the war with Austria. That was bitter to his self-love and to his love of his country. Ambition, thirst of revenge, the hope of recovering his lost laurels, from an enemy which was now disturbed in another quarter—by the insurrection in Hungary—and the warlike spirit existing in Piedmont, especially in its army, which, lately beaten by Austria, now again stood ready for battle with the old foe—all this drove Carlo Alberto to break suddenly the ignominious truce, and to burst in upon Lombardy, with an army of eighty thousand men. It was in March, 1849. But Radetzky, "the admirable old man," *l'amirable vecchio*, as Cesare Balbo and some of his enemies in Italy called him, was not long in making his appearance, and by a bold and hasty movement, opposed himself to Carlo Alberto, and drove him back to Novara. With death in his heart, Carlo Alberto prepared here for the fight, the unfortunate result of which he foresaw.

In three days, the new campaign was here ended between Radetzky and Carlo Alberto. The latter sought for death, through ten long hours on the battle field—but in vain. Not a ball hit him. In vain he and his two brave young sons performed miracles of personal bravery—the battle was lost. Radetzky won the victory wholly, perfectly. When twilight came, and put an end to the slaughter, Carlo Alberto collected around him his faithful followers, surrendered the crown of Piedmont to his eldest son, Victor Emanuel, commanded him faithfully to defend and carry out the constitution, *Il Statuto*, which he, Carlo Alberto, had given to Piedmont; and after this last testament, delivered on the field of battle, the king departed, under the shadow of night, accompanied by merely two persons, to voluntary exile, in order, far from the scene of his ruined honor, and of his humiliation, to hide his weary head, pray, and die.

A memory from the days of his youth attracted him to the laurel-groves of Oporto. The government and people of Portugal, met him with honor and festivity. But the star of his life was set; he knew it, and wished only to die. He was ill when he arrived at Oporto, lived there a few months, amidst prayers and severe penitential exercises, and died—within the year after his abdication.

But the star which was extinguished above his earthly career, was now first kindled into its highest glory over his memory, and he stands, at this moment, before his grateful people, in the splendor of a saint, whilst his struggle for liberty, and his last chivalric action, caused him to appear before Europe as a tragically heroic form. He was, however, as little like a saint as a hero or a great character. He was a man of noble impulses, but unequal, weak, and full of contradictions. Once having entered upon the path of liberty and reform, and being upheld there by the exulting shout of friends and of Europe, he could and would not again turn from it. But his inward struggle was often great between the Jesuits and the demands of freedom. Sincere piety—especially during the later years of his life—kept him from despair, and his chivalric sympathies, from the ignominy of a miserable position. But the struggle was more than he could bear; it undermined his health, both of body and soul; he became old before his time: he knew that he was not equal to the part, which the necessities of the time assigned to him. He wished to do that which was right, he loved that which was good, but he was governed by circumstances. He did not rule his age, but was ruled by it. The contradictions, the disharmony in his inward being, were also mirrored in his exterior. He was a tall man, of handsome proportions, but his demeanor wanted firmness and dignity. This is perceptible, even in the excellent picture of him in the Museum at Turin, painted by the French artist Vernet, and which represents him on horseback at a review. The eyes are large and beautiful, but have a fanatical melancholy glance; the lower part of the countenance is projecting, and not handsome; the chin retreats. It is, nevertheless, an exterior which is not insignificant; it is what we call "taking." His conversation, voice, and friendly manners, are said to have had an irresistible fascination. But the same man whom he to-day fascinated by his friendship, might the day afterwards receive a Uriah letter. The same king who showed himself so engaging to foreigners, was in his family often gloomy and strict, even to severity towards his children. He was devotedly loved by a wife, whom he yet deceived. His piety, nevertheless, was sincere, and during his latter years, assumed a still deeper character. He prayed much, fasted often, and his bed was like that of a capuchin monk. I know not if it were so, but it seems to me, that the prince, with his soul corroded by anguish, might yet amidst the laurel-groves of Oporto, have been refreshed by one grand peace-giving memory— the memory of that moment when he was wholly loyal to his better self, the moment of his abdication, when he gave himself as a sacrifice, to preserve the freedom and independence of his people. For it was this act which saved them.

The young, new king demanded peace from the old general and conqueror, Radetzky, and he obtained it, as well as his kingdom, for the sum of fifteen millions of francs. Radetzky esteemed, in the young prince and his people, the bravery of which he had seen proofs during the campaign. He was afraid of driving them to extremity; besides which, he was obliged to turn his forces towards Venice, where now the heroic Manin had excited the people to fight for freedom. Radetzky's moderation and mildness prevented, also, here, affairs coming to extremes; and by this means, Venice was preserved to Austria for the present.

And thus Italy had again peace,—a peace which gave life to Piedmont; to all the rest death!—But no! "Christian nations may sink, but not die!" Italy is not dead, it only sleeps the sleep of the trance, of weariness, and becomes more mature, the while, for a new awakening. It is impossible to doubt this, especially here, and in this time, when, in Piedmont, every thing breathes the life of the new day, and every thing is prepared to impart it, but in a manner different to its former one, and with a higher consciousness of freedom and right.

The noblest citizens and friends of Italy are united in this,—to attribute to the Italians themselves, rather than to foreign arms, the unfortunate results which followed the struggle for freedom in 1848. Want of unity, contentions between the states about trifles, about rank, about the capital, language, and so on, when they ought to have united themselves against the common enemy. The endeavors of foolish tribunes of the people to inflame the passions; weakness and fickleness in many leaders; treachery in some;—these opened Italy to the troops of the enemy, Many of Italy's noblest sons died for grief over the issue of the war; but many also bowed their heads to chastisement, whilst they kept their faith in a future better day.

"It will—it must come!" say they, "but Italy must ripen for it,—and she does spiritually ripen every day! The national, the *Italian* party, becomes stronger every day, under the pressure of the foreign power, and the hatred which it inspires; it ripens through the memory of the past error, of the bitter conflict, and from the taste which it has of freedom. This has been baptized in blood, but it must be so baptized that we may learn rightly to understand it and ourselves."

No one is more acute than the noble Count C. Balbo, in the detection of the errors of Italy and her blind flatterers, no one more hopeful for her future. In his excellent *Summario della Storia d'Italia*, a book which has already passed through ten editions, he considers that, from the struggle for freedom in the year 1848, a new period in the history of Italy, and a new development of her higher life, have begun, if Italy will only listen to the teachings of her misfortunes, and gather from her humiliations the fruit of self-knowledge. And it must be so. Her higher consciousness has awakened, and it cannot again die. The hour, the hour of resurrection must come, sooner or later. Thus speaks this noble friend of his country, who, a short time since, wrote the history of this latest struggle, although, with dimming eyes, he saw, spiritually, the future of Italy bright.

A great deal, it is evident, depends upon the conduct and progress of Piedmont. Its secure course along the path of law-restricted freedom has, in a great measure, annihilated the bandit freedom of the Mazzini party; and the inward and outward power of Piedmont increases daily, from the number of distinguished men who fly hither from the subjected states of Italy, and here find shelter, and a sphere of operation, and are thus able to labor for Italian freedom, whilst they themselves are maturing for it. The rôle of Piedmont at this moment, is that of the hero in the play—a great and hazardous mission; but God defends it, and wills its progress; and therefore he gives it a king, honest and brave, like Victor Emanuel; and a statesman such as M. de Cavour. Both allowed the banner of Italy to shine in unson with those of the allies, on the field of the Crimea, before the walls of Sebastopol. Piedmont did not raise that banner in vain.

October 21st.—Professor Melegari, one of Piedmont's exiled, but lately recalled and universally honored patriots, and who is an invaluable acquaintance of mine here, introduced me to-day to Count de Cavour, for I was unwilling to leave Turin without seeing the man who has awakened the lively sympathies of myself and many others in Sweden, by what the newspapers have taught us of his words and works.

We, Melegari and I, drove to the ministerial palace in pouring rain—it has poured with rain incessantly ever since I have been here. We passed through several large, handsome apartments furnished with silk, before we came to the cabinet of the minister. A couple of foreign ambassadors had just left as we entered. Cavour was seated at his writing-table, with his face turned towards the door.

I had been told that his exterior presented nothing very remarkable, and a young English lady had assured me that he looked very much as one might imagine Mr. Pickwick, in Dickens' Pickwick Papers; and I confess that, at the first glance, he reminded me more of an English red-complexioned country squire, who rides and hunts, eats good dinners, and takes life easily and gayly, than of a deep-minded statesman, who, with a secure glance and hand steers the vessel of the state towards its destined object, over the stormy political sea. But very soon was that countenance lit up for me; and the more I studied it, during my tolerably long conversation with Cavour, the more significant and agreeable it seemed to me. They who have painted Cavour's portrait, have not understood this countenance, nor the character of this head. It has a something almost square in it, but at the same time refined. The complexion is fresh and delicate, the forehead magnificent, open, with room in it for both lofty and broad ideas; the glance of the light blue eyes is clear, lively, and penetrative; the nose and the mouth remind me of those of Napoleon the Great, as does also the form of the countenance. They have the firmness and delicacy of outline. In the play of the muscles about the nose, there is something arch, and the smile has the graciousness of the south. The figure is not tall, but strong and well-built, and has something particularly solid and robust about it. The manners are calm, easy, very agreeable, and evince natural self-government,

It seemed to give Cavour pleasure to learn that even in Sweden, the affairs of Piedmont were a subject of interest; and that therefore his own words and actions were regarded with attention. From his expression, I perceived that he was perfectly acquainted with our form of government, and our mode of representation, which seemed to him to be "heavy machinery."

To my inquiries regarding Piedmont, and his views of its future, he replied so simply, so candidly and kindly, that it gave me great pleasure. It seemed to me, that with entire clearness and security he will conduct Piedmont upon a path from whence it cannot turn back; and, that he is not afraid of making pecuniary sacrifices for this cause.

"Piedmont," said he, "has long been like a vessel which, having run too close to the rocks, is prevented by that means from having the wind in her sails, and this impediment must be removed."

One of the means, therefore, which Cavour mentioned for this purpose, was the gigantic work now commenced; the tunnelling of Mont Cenis, which will open a speedy communication between Piedmont and the social culture and social life of the most developed cities of Europe. He presented me with a work on this undertaking. When I expressed my anticipations for the rest of Italy, from Piedmont's advance on the path of freedom, he assented thereto, but he expressed himself as a wary general and did not say much.

I asked him what would be the consequence in Piedmont of the chamber's rejection of the measures of the ministry?

"Then," replied he, "it must go out." "But," added he, as if half in thought, placing at the same time a letter-case straight on the table,—"even if the ministry should be compelled to resign from one cause or another—still it is my conviction that the present system would stand firm, and that the new ministry could not avoid carrying it out."

The manner and the tone in which these words were spoken, convinced me that in them Cavour expressed his innermost thought. The principle for which he labored was the important thing, not his own position.

When I told him that I had not seen any statesman who appeared so easily to bear the burden of state life, he smiled, as he replied:

"Oh, it only appears so; but behind in the depth are many cares, and it is not easy to preserve alight the sacred fire (*le feu sacré*)."

And yet the appearance is not here deceptive. Cavour, according to what I heard from more than one of his friends, bears comparatively easily his post, important and difficult as it is at this time, as President of the Council of Piedmont, and as the foremost leader of its destiny. The fact is, that he is possessed of a statesman nature, and executes his business as Mozart executed his symphonies or fugues, Raphael his pictures, without racking his brains or with much difficulty of any kind. He is in his realm a genius, and an artist, as they. But I will now bring my conversation with him to a close, or rather my recollection of it.

At parting, I laid upon his heart to bring about

more just laws for the women of Piedmont, who, as regards the right of inheritance now stand a long way behind the men. M. de Cavour laughed, half waggishly as at an expression called forth by a certain *esprit de corps*, but he spoke afterwards seriously of the difficulties which, in particular amongst an agricultural population, stood in the way of an equal right of inheritance—difficulties, which it rather surprised me to hear uttered by a great statesman. It pleased me likewise when he added, with the accent of conviction: "In any case equal right of inheritance will become law, sooner or later, amongst us. It exists in the spirit and the tendency of all our legislation, and besides—*it is right.*"

Those were words which it did me good to hear from a statesman and legislator. I left Cavour, with an extremely refreshing sense of his words and whole character.

"*Quelle jolie physionomie!*" exclaimed I involuntarily to M. Melegari, as I left the minister's apartment, whilst I recalled my own preconceptions before I entered it.

"*N'est ce pas?*" replied he, and we added as in emulation, "*que de finesse! que de clarté, que de fraicheur, que de fermeté!*"

I have heard, from persons who know M. de Cavour more intimately, that his happy temperament both of body and soul cannot however, save him from an annual attack of inflammation on the chest—probably at the close of the session of the chambers. He is then obliged to be repeatedly bled, and his friends are often in great anxiety about him. But his athletic nature soon overcomes the occasional disease, and his natural good-heartedness prevents him from entertaining bitterness towards political enemies.

"You make enemies in the chambers by your ironical smile!" said one of his friends to him one day, "one can see that you look down upon your opponents."

"What would you have?" replied Cavour. "It is stronger than I am;—and why do people say such stupid things to me?"

On one occasion he fought a duel, but it was with a man who had attacked his honor, and would not recall the charge before bullets were exchanged.

Cavour had great difficulty, as the son of a most highly unpopular man, in obtaining the public confidence, and many persons considering it purely impossible that he could do so, said of him, "If this young man were not laboring under an insurmountable burden of unpopularity, he would be the man which Piedmont requires." It was in the periodical *Il Resorgimento*, by means of which Count Balbo, and other patriots, led onward Piedmont into the right understanding of legitimate reform, that Cavour first exhibited his unusual qualities, especially in questions of political and national economy—his clear glance, and his logical mode of thought and power of representation. Afterwards he raised his voice in the chamber of deputies for the discontinuance of a separate judicial court for the clergy, as well as for several other constitutional reforms, with a power, which soon dispersed the mist of unpopularity from the young statesman, and caused it to be acknowledged what kind of man he was. Political advancement sought him; not he, it.

The Marquis d'Azeglio was President of the Council—an office which in Piedmont, unites two portfolios, that of foreign affairs, and finance—when he resolved to resign this post in favor of Cavour, whom he regarded as more suitable than himself for its important duties. He went up to the chamber and himself spoke for Cavour, and when his aim was accomplished and he returned home, he sent his carriage to fetch Cavour to his house for breakfast, in order to be the first who should announce to him his elevation to the post from which Azeglio had retired. This was in the year 1851.

From this time Cavour has continued to be the leader of the Piedmontese Cabinet, and is said to have made himself indispensable to his office. He steadily advances on the path of liberal reform, and it is a peculiarity which deserves to be remarked, that Cavour, from the very commencement of his political career, has remained ever faithful to the same principles. Those political views, both domestic and foreign, which he advocated as a young author, he still pursues and acts up to at the present time as the Prime Minister of Piedmont. When he was insisting that the constitution should be given without any delay to Piedmont, one of his friends said to him:

"You spoke some time ago of giving it in ten years, when Piedmont should have become ready for it."

"It must be done now," replied Cavour, "if not the revolution will get beforehand with us."

The chivalric course which Piedmont commenced

when, in order to support the revolution in Lombardy, it declared war against Austria, Cavour has ever since maintained with intrepid mind and steady glance, although frequently without the certainty of victory. When peace was again broken with Austria, in the spring of 1849, Cavour said to some one who represented to him his imprudence and danger:

"We must risk the game if we would maintain our self-respect. If we remain quiet with our miserable truce, we shall perish in our own mud; if we fall on the field of battle it will be in the blood of our enemies, and with the maintenance of honor."

Austria and other European powers opposed the right of Italy to have a national flag. But Piedmont had adopted the tricolor, which Italy raised in the insurrectionary year of 1848, and as this flag participated in the victories of the allied powers in the war against Russia, no one has ventured to oppose the right of the Italian flag to be raised amongst those of the independent nations. When later, at the Congress in Paris, Cavour appeared as the representative of the state of Sardinia, it appeared probable that he might be refused the same rank and suffrage as the representatives of the larger states. Cavour on this let it be understood that he should, in that case, leave the Congress and depart from Paris. This was not desired; and the worthy representative of brave little Sardinia sat and voted on equal terms with the rest.

The same heroic course of politics had led Cavour to carry through the opening of the subterranean-railway-communication of Mont Cenis, and to undertake the work in the name of the state, in order to have the power over its execution, and to apply for that purpose all the means which science and art are able to afford.

"We say," remarked he to a friend, with a fine smile, "that it will be ready in eight or ten years, but it may be twelve years or more, so that the thing be but done, and this great artery formed between Italy and the remainder of Europe!"

This magnificent undertaking—both of war and peace—has occasioned to Piedmont a very considerable national debt—"and," said lately a great banker of Geneva, M. Delarue, when speaking on the subject, "it would certainly be better to bear its own national debt and to advance, whilst means are prepared for its liquidation."

The railway through Mont Cenis is one of these means, a grand bond, but which will assuredly be honored in a grand manner.

Of late, several persons have said to Cavour, "Ought you not to pause, or to go on more slowly?" To which he has replied, "I have to guide a carriage with four horses down hill. When we have reached the level and begin to go up hill again, then—I will drive slowly!"

Cavour has continually met with many enemies, and much enmity during this progressive advance. They bring against him occasionally, in the chambers, the worst accusations. But they trouble him very little. He listens to them calmly, sometimes with a sardonic smile, sometimes with such a good-humored expression, as ought to disarm the opponents, if any thing be able to disarm party bitterness, especially in

Italy. But it may be disarmed or not; Cavour is alike calm. He may be seen wandering along the promenades, whistling carelessly and playing with his cane, kindly greeting his acquaintances, and with an appearance as if he had nothing else in the world to do, but to go out and look about him. Such ought a statesman to be—if he can. Work, it is said, has always been his pleasure, and at this time it is his only love. Not even slander has been able to attack his morals or his character. His friends speak warmly of the goodness of his heart. His enemies have never experienced his hatred.

October 23d.—I had, last Sunday, the pleasure of hearing the gospel proclaimed to great and small, in the beautiful, newly-erected Waldenses church of this place. It was, in the morning, to the Sunday-school children; in the afternoon, to the public; and both times by M. Meille, and in the Italian language, which seems made on purpose to be the interpreter of that which is the most beautiful and inward in life. The service was somewhat disturbed by the Catholics, who went about staring and wondering at what was going forward in the church. One old man walked round the pulpit, examining it and the preacher, as if he were gazing at a strange animal. It is not long since the most absurd stories about the Waldenses were current amongst the lower Catholic population in Piedmont, and it was believed that their faith had no connection at all with Christianity. It was not until after the emancipation of 1848, and since the Waldenses pastors have been able to preach freely, and to baptize, and to bury their dead openly amongst the Catholics, that these have begun to perceive with astonishment, that the Waldenses, as well as themselves, believe in God, in the Saviour, and the Holy Spirit. And the prejudiced daily diminish. The Holy Scriptures, especially the gospels and the epistles—which are therefore printed separately—are circulated more and more in Piedmont and the neighboring states. In most of the towns of Piedmont and also of Tuscany, small societies have been formed, which meet for general reading, meditation, and the singing of hymns. I was told this to-day by an Italian, Signor R., a member of the Waldenses church, who, during the time of the persecution, was confined several months in prison for his religious faith. An Italian nobleman, M. de Santis, formerly a Catholic priest, now ordained in the Waldenses church, is at the head of a separate branch of this church, which gives to laymen some of the duties of the priest's office.

It has rained so incessantly during my stay in this city that I have been compelled to give up many drives, and many acquaintances also, which would otherwise have been valuable to me. The two last days have, however, been tolerably fine, and I have, during them, looked about me in the city, in company with two young Norwegians who have been to me as young brothers and friends. The museum, with many good pictures, both ancient and modern, as well as *L'Armeria Reale*, has given me pleasure. It would be difficult to find a more picturesque and better arranged collection of ancient weapons and knight's armor, both on horse and foot, than that in the arsenal of Turin.

One institution, which I regret not to have seen, is that which a poor young girl, Rosa Govona, founded, with her young friends, poor like herself, by their united savings, for the education of indigent girls. The "Asylum delle Rosine," as this institution is called, now receives and gives a good education to 400 girls. Another excellent institution, *L'Albergo reale di virtu*, founded in 1851, by Victor Emanuel, receives pupils for all trades. The benevolent institutions of Turin, are said to have undergone great improvements of late years, and are now extremely well managed.

More than once during my rambles through the streets of Turin I have paused before the print-seller's windows to contemplate a countenance which has a maternal, almost heavenly, gentleness in its expression. It is the portrait of the lately deceased young Queen of Piedmont, the wife of Victor Emanuel, and the mother of his five children. She was, I have been assured, as affectionate and as good as the portrait indicates, gazing gently on the earth, in the pleasures of which her delicate health prevented her taking part. The King loved her tenderly, and likewise feared her, it is said, as lofty purity and virtue are sometimes feared by the less perfect. She was an angel of mercy, and her early removal has been regarded in Piedmont as a public misfortune. The former winter, when she sickened and died in Turin, the people would not indulge in any pleasure. The sorrow of the royal family was the sorrow of all.

Victor Emanuel is at this time one of the most popular and beloved of the European monarchs. He is faithful to his word, brave, good-humored, beloved by his people, and is inviolably faithful to the statutes of the constitution. His portrait represents him as a *bon-vivant*, and perhaps it does not do him injustice. It is said that he expresses his surprise at his father having so long delayed to give Piedmont its constitution. For his part, he finds it in the highest degree comfortable and convenient to be a constitutional monarch. He need not hold himself responsible for that which goes forward in the state, as it all belongs to the ministers.

It is said, that of the King's three sons, the eldest is a remarkably gifted and promising youth. The eldest of the daughters, the Princess Clotilde, now thirteen, is said to resemble her heavenly mother.

There is, in a park-like grove in Turin, a beautiful white marble statue, representing an elderly man, sitting as in calm conversation. The countenance is noble and regular, and the lofty forehead denotes a thinker. It is the figure of Count Cesare Balbo, the noble Piedmontese aristocrat, and friend of liberty, of whom I have already spoken. He liked to assemble around him in his house the promising young men of Piedmont, and many of these have to thank his conversation, as well as his writings, for their insight into the nature of true, constitutional liberty, and also for the acquirement of higher views regarding the means by which a noble, self-conscious, popular life, is to be obtained. It is only two years since he was living and teaching in Turin, surrounded by numerous friends and pupils.

One notability of another kind—I beg pardon for the great leap!—I am in duty bound to mention before I take my leave of Turin, because I have derived great pleasure from this member of the state—Grizzinis, as it is called. It is a kind of bread, long and slender, like willow-twigs, which is consumed in great quantities all over Piedmont. Although this extremely delicate bread consists, it is asserted, of nothing but the common dough of wheaten bread, of flour and water, which is drawn out into yard-long lengths, yet the making of it succeeds nowhere but in Piedmont. It has been attempted in all quarters, but in vain. Napoleon the Great, who took great delight in this bread, had bakers fetched from Piedmont to Paris, flour, and also water, but the self-willed grizzinis, would not bow itself to the ruler of France and Italy, and he was obliged to give up the attempt. It stays in Piedmont, and will not succeed anywhere else. People say that it exists in the air. In the mean time I will take some grizzinis with me to Sweden.

The 23*d.*—A bright day at last, and as bright, as beautiful, as sunny, as if there were not a cloud to be found in the world!

In the afternoon, I ascended the Capuchin hill, on the other side of the Po, in company with M. Meille, and my two young countrymen. The view from the top is of the most beautiful description. In the north the great Alpine ridge, with Monte Viso as the principal figure, and further off, Monte Rosa, Mont Blanc, and Simplon, which glance forth with snow-white crowns, a guard of ice-giants around the verdant, fertile plains of Piedmont, where the silk is spun and the orange ripens. Midway between north and west, the romantic and historically-celebrated valley of

Susa, opens itself between hills; and directly through the middle of the plain, winds the Po, eastward towards the Adriatic Sea, receiving on its course, a number of rivers and streams. An elderly monk was sitting in the Capuchin convent, by an open window, reading; the sun shone upon the handsome white-haired head, producing a peaceful picture.

"I sometimes look upon these monks with a feeling akin to envy," said M. Meille, with his melodious Italian voice, and melancholy expression—"What an enjoyment to be able thus to devote themselves at ease to quiet studies!"

But the life of the Christian preacher of the gospel is not a peaceful *sinecure;* it is a constant preaching with life and doctrine,—an actual following in the footsteps of Christ!

It was beautiful to see how a little cloud which concealed the summit of Monte Viso, raised itself by degrees, and became more and more transparent until it entirely vanished, and the beautifully formed cupola of Viso stood free against the bright evening sky. When we had seen the sunset from the Capuchin hill, we walked backwards and forwards on the great bridge whilst the after-glow ascended step by step, and spread a clear splendor over the heights we had just left.

The after-glow, "the second brightness," or rather the new crimson of morning, does it not now ascend over Piedmont? What does the young Italy desire? What are the ideas which exist in the minds of the noblest thinkers, and which Piedmont is endeavoring each day to bring into actual reality? Are they not those which lead the way in the highest moral development of all nobler nations, and which constitute the conditions of it; the equality of every individual in the eye of the law; the right of all to be trained to a free, self-conscious existence; the right of all to become co-operative in the constitution, and in the laws by which they are to be governed.

But beyond, or more properly speaking before, this consciousness of the claims of all, stands the duty of all to carry out the right, the just, and the good, on the life of the state, to be co-workers in the construction of the community—to build thereof a city of God, a Holy Priesthood, as the Apostle says: "in one word a kingdom of God upon earth." Thus have I understood the striving towards liberty in Italy at this moment. Is there any higher? The Pyramids, the Acropolis, the Pantheon, and the states which produced these by the labor of slaves—do they not sink down to mere pieces of art in comparison with this highest work of art of a free community, in which the smallest, as well as the greatest, is called to the same freedom, goodness and happiness; where every one lives for all, and all for every one!

I do not desire from thee, my R——, that thou shouldst take part in each cry for freedom, in each national movement, which is not sustained by the knowledge of the true purport of freedom. But when we see a people seeking freedom, and the right to establish itself upon the basis of the purest and highest human interests, then it is clear to me, that this people is prepared to pass from the period of its minority, and to become free as men who have attained to years of discretion, and it would grieve me if thou wast not of the same mind, if thou wouldst not give thy voice for the highest sacred right of this people!

Piedmont is at this moment a witness before the world, that what Italy desires it can also attain. Piedmont has taken the first step out of the realm of the ideal into that of reality, yet still adhering to the ideal. Can this path be pursued without Italy coming into conflict with the sole governing principle of the Roman Catholic church, that of a right over the human conscience and belief? I think not. No: Catholicism must be born again, must be regenerated in the source of the gospel, if it is to become a religious creed for an independent people possessed of political and civil liberty. This is evident to me, and — perhaps may arise more than one bloody recompense upon the people who persecuted with fire and sword the faithful professors of the gospel during centuries. Piedmont has liberated, has adopted its first witness, the Waldenses; Piedmont has perhaps, in so doing, obtained for herself full amnesty from the Supreme Judge. Be it so!

I can now leave Turin with a good conscience. I have seen Monte Viso and M. de Cavour; but how am I to leave it? That is the question. Tidings arrive daily of the devastation occasioned by the floods; bridges are washed away; railways broken up; nearly all communication is uncertain; the road from Turin to Genoa is said to be impassable, and it was to Genoa that I now intended to proceed. They speak of the possibility of reaching that place by going round by Novara, and this I shall attempt. My young country-woman, and my companion for the winter, in Rome, Jenny Lind has been waiting for me too long in Genoa already.

END OF VOL. I.

T. B. PETERSON & BROTHERS' PUBLICATIONS

The Books in this Catalogue are the Best and Latest Publications by the most Popular and Celebrated Writers in the World. They are also the most Readable and Entertaining Books published.

Suitable for the Parlor, Library, Sitting-Room, Railroad, Steamboat or Chamber Reading.

PUBLISHED AND FOR SALE BY

T. B. PETERSON & BROTHERS, Philadelphia.

Booksellers, News Agents, Pedlers, etc., will be Supplied at Low Rates.

Copies of any of Petersons' Publications, or any other work or works Advertised, Published, or Noticed by any one at all, in any place, will be sent by us, Free of Postage, on the receipt of the Price.

MRS. SOUTHWORTH'S WORKS.

The Two Sisters. This is Mrs. Southworth's last new work. Two vols., paper cover. Price $1.00; or bound in one volume, cloth, for $1.25.

The Three Beauties. Complete in two volumes, paper cover. Price One Dollar; or bound in one volume, cloth, for $1.25.

Vivia. The Secret of Power. Two volumes, paper cover. Price One Dollar; or one volume, cloth, for $1.25.

India. The Pearl of Pearl River. Two vols., paper cover. Price One Dollar; or bound in cloth, $1.25.

The Wife's Victory. Two volumes, paper cover. Price One Dollar; or bound in one volume, cloth, $1.25.

The Lost Heiress. Two volumes, paper cover. Price One Dollar; or bound in one volume, cloth, for $1.25.

The Missing Bride. Two volumes, paper cover. Price One Dollar; or bound in one volume, cloth, $1.25.

Retribution: A Tale of Passion. Two vols., paper cover. Price One Dollar; or in one vol., cloth, $1.25.

The Curse of Clifton. Two vols., paper cover. Price One Dollar; or bound in one volume, cloth, $1.25.

The Discarded Daughter. Two volumes, paper cover. Price One Dollar; or one volume, cloth, for $1.25.

The Deserted Wife. Two vols. paper cover. Price One Dollar; or bound in one vol., cloth, for $1.25.

The Belle of Washington. Two volumes, paper cover. Price One Dollar; or in cloth, for $1.25.

The Initials. A Love Story of Modern Life. Two vols., paper cover. Price $1.00; or in one volume cloth, $1.25.

The Dead Secret. Two volumes, paper cover. Price One Dollar; or bound in one volume, cloth, for $1.25.

Kate Aylesford. Two volumes, paper cover. Price One Dollar; or bound in one volume, cloth, for $1.25.

The whole of the above are also published in very fine style, bound in full Crimson, gilt edges, sides, backs, etc., making elegant presentation books. Price $2.00 a copy

JAS. A. MAITLAND'S GREAT WORKS.

Sartaroe. A Tale of Norway. Highly recommended by Washington Irving. Complete in two volumes, paper cover. Price One Dollar; or bound in one volume, cloth, for $1.25.

The Watchman. Complete in two large vols., paper cover. Price One Dollar; or in one volume, cloth, $1.25.

The Wanderer. Complete in two volumes, paper cover. Price One Dollar; or in one vol., cloth, for $1.25.

The Diary of an Old Doctor. Complete in two vols., paper cover. Price One Dollar; or in cloth, $1.25

The Lawyer's Story; or, The Orphan's Wrongs. Two vols., paper cover. Price One Dollar; or bound in one volume, cloth, for $1.25.

W. H. MAXWELL'S WOKS.

Stories of Waterloo. One of the best books in the English language. Complete in one large octave volume. Price Fifty cents.

Brian O'Lynn; or, Luck is Everything. Price 50 cents.

Wild Sports in the West. One volume. Price 50 cents.

MRS. CAROLINE LEE HENTZ'S WORKS.

The Lost Daughter; and Other Stories of the Heart. (Just published.) Two volumes, paper cover. Price One Dollar; or in one vol., cloth, for $1.25.

Planter's Northern Bride. Beautifully Illustrated. Two volumes, paper cover, 600 pages. Price One Dollar; or in one volume, cloth, for $1.25.

Linda. The Young Pilot of the Belle Creole. Two volumes, paper cover. Price One Dollar; or bound in one volume, cloth, for $1.25.

Robert Graham. The Sequel to, and Continuation of Linda. Two vols., paper cover. Price One Dollar; or bound in one volume, cloth, for $1.25.

Courtship and Marriage. Two volumes, paper cover. Price One Dollar, or one volume, cloth, for $1.25.

Rena; or, The Snow Bird. Two vols, paper cover. Price One Dollar; or in one vol., cloth, for $1.25.

Marcus Warland. Two volumes, paper cover. Price One Dollar; or bound in one volume, cloth, for $1.25.

Love after Marriage. Two vols, paper cover. Price One Dollar; or bound in one vol., cloth, for $1.25.

Eoline; or, Magnolia Vale. Two vols., paper cover. Price One Dollar; or in one vol., cloth, for $1.25.

The Banished Son. Two vols., paper cover. Price One Dollar; or bound in one vol., cloth, for $1.25.

Helen and Arthur. Two vols., paper cover. Price One Dollar; or bound in one vol., cloth, for $1.25.

The whole of the above are also published in a very fine style, bound in full Crimson, with gilt edges, full gilt sides, gilt backs, etc., making them the best book for presentation, at the price, published. Price of either one in this style, $2.00 a copy.

MISS PARDOE'S WORKS.

Confessions of a Pretty Woman. By Miss Pardoe. Complete in one large octavo volume. Price 50 cents.

The Jealous Wife. By Miss Pardoe. Complete in one large octavo volume. Price Fifty cents.

The Wife's Trials. By Miss Pardoe. Complete in one large octavo volume. Price Fifty cents.

The Rival Beauties. By Miss Pardoe. Complete in one large octavo volume. Price Fifty cents.

Romance of the Harem. By Miss Pardoe. Complete in one large octavo volume. Price Fifty cents.

The whole of the above Five works are also bound in cloth, gilt, in one large octavo volume. Price $2.50.

The Adopted Heir. By Miss Pardoe. Two vols., paper cover. Price $1.00; or in cloth, $1.25. (*In Press.*)

MRS. ANN S. STEPHENS' WORKS.

Mary Derwent. This is Mrs. Ann S. Stephens' last new work. Complete in two volumes, paper cover. Price One Dollar; or in one vol., cloth, $1.25.

Fashion and Famine. Two volumes, paper cover. Price One Dollar; or in one volume, cloth, for $1.25.

The Old Homestead. Two volumes, paper cover. Price One Dollar; or in one volume, cloth, for $1.25.

The Gipsy's Legacy; or, the Heiress of Greenhurst. Two volumes, paper cover. Price One Dollar; or in one volume, cloth, for $1.25.

COOK BOOKS. BEST IN THE WORLD.

Miss Leslie's New Cookery Book. Being the largest, best, and most complete Cook Book ever got up by Miss Leslie. Now first published. One volume. Price $1.25.

Mrs. Hale's New Cook Book. By Mrs. Sarah J. Hale. One volume, bound. Price One Dollar.

Miss Leslie's New Receipts for Cooking. Complete in one large volume, bound. Price One Dollar.

Widdifield's New Cook Book, or, Practical Receipts for the Housewife. Recommended by all. One volume, cloth. Price One Dollar.

MRS. HALE'S RECEIPTS.

Mrs. Hale's Receipts for the Million. Containing Four Thousand Five Hundred and Forty-five Receipts, Facts, Directions, and Knowledge for All, in the Useful, Ornamental, and Domestic Arts. Being a complete Family Director and Household Guide for the Million. By Mrs. Sarah J. Hale. One volume, 800 pages, strongly bound. Price, $1.25.

T. B. PETERSON & BROTHERS' PUBLICATIONS.

CHARLES LEVER'S WORKS.
All neatly done up in paper covers.

Charles O'Malley, Price 50 cents.	Arthur O'Leary,... Price 50 cents
Harry Lorrequer,..... 50 "	Knight of Gwynne,.. 50 "
Horace Templeton,... 50 "	Kate O'Donoghue,.... 50 "
Tom Burke of Ours, 50 "	Con Cregan, the Irish Gil Blas,..................... 50 "
Jack Hinton, the Guardsman,............... 50 "	Davenport Dunn, a Man of our Day,...... 50 "

A complete sett of the above will be sold, or sent to any one, to any place, *free of postage*, for $4.00.

LIBRARY EDITION.

THIS EDITION is complete in FOUR large octavo volumes, containing Charles O'Malley, Harry Lorrequer, Horace Templeton, Tom Burke of Ours, Arthur O'Leary, Jack Hinton the Guardsman, The Knight of Gwynne, Kate O'Donoghue, etc., handsomely printed, and bound in various styles, as follows:

Price of a sett in Black cloth,... $6.00
"   "   Scarlet cloth,.. 6.50
"   "   Law Library sheep,....................................... 7.00
"   "   Half Calf,.. 9.00
"   "   Half Calf, marbled edges, French,........................ 10.00
"   "   Half Calf, antique,....................................... 12.00

FINER EDITIONS.

Charles O'Malley, fine edition, one volume, cloth,.................. $1.50
"   "   Half calf,... 2.00
Harry Lorrequer, fine edition, one volume, cloth,................... 1.50
"   "   Half calf,... 2.00
Jack Hinton, fine edition, one volume, cloth....................... 1.50
"   "   Half calf,... 2.00
Valentine Vox, fine edition, one volume, cloth,.................... 1.50
"   "   Half calf,.. 2.00
"   "   cheap edition, paper cover,............................... 50
Ten Thousand a Year, fine edition, one volume, cloth,.............. 1.50
"   "   Half calf, ... 2.00
"   "   cheap edition, paper cover. Two volumes, ... 1.00
Diary of a Medical Student. By S. C. Warren, author of "Ten Thousand a Year." One volume, octavo,.................................. 50

HUMOROUS ILLUSTRATED WORKS.

Major Jones' Courtship and Travels. Beautifully illustrated. One volume, cloth. Price $1.25.

Major Jones' Scenes in Georgia. Full of beautiful illustrations. One volume, cloth. Price $1.25.

Sam Slick, the Clockmaker. By Judge Haliburton. Illustrated. Being the best funny work ever written by any one in this vein. Two vols., paper cover. Price One Dollar; or bound in one volume, cloth, for $1.25.

Simon Suggs' Adventures and Travels. Illustrated. One volume, cloth Price $1.25.

Humors of Falconbridge. Two volumes, paper cover Price One Dollar; or one vol. cloth, for $1.25.

Frank Forester's Sporting

Scenes & Characters. Illustrated. Two vols., cloth. Price $2.50.

Dow's Short Patent Sermons. First Series. By Dow, Jr. Containing 128 Sermons. Complete in one volume, cloth, for One Dollar or paper cover, 75 cents.

Dow's Short Patent Sermons. Second Series. By Dow, Jr. Containing 144 Sermons. Complete in one volume, cloth, for One Dollar; or paper cover, 75 cents.

Dow's Short Patent Sermons. Third Series. By Dow, Jr. Containing 116 Sermons. Complete in one volume, cloth, for One Dollar; or paper cover, 75 cents.

American Joe Miller. With 50 Illustrations One of the most humorous books in the world Price 25 cents

CHARLES DICKENS' WORKS.

Fourteen Different Editions in Octavo Form.

"PETERSON'S" are the only complete and uniform editions of Charles Dickens Works ever published in the world; they are printed from the original London Editions, and are the only editions published in this country. No library either public or private, can be complete without having in it a complete sett of the works of this, the greatest of all living authors. Every family should possess a sett of one of the editions. The cheap edition is complete in Sixteen Volumes paper cover; either or all of which can be had separately, as follows:

Little Dorrit,..........Price 50 cents.	Barnaby Rudge,...Price 50 cents
Pickwick Papers,........ 50 "	Old Curiosity Shop,.... 50 "
Dickens' New Stories, 50 "	Sketches by "Boz,"..... 50 "
Bleak House,.............. 50 "	Oliver Twist,............... 50 "
David Copperfield,...... 50 "	The Two Apprentices, 25 "
Dombey and Son,........ 50 "	Wreck of the Golden
Nicholas Nickleby,...... 50 "	Mary,........................... 25 "
Christmas Stories,...... 50 "	Perils of certain En-
Martin Chuzzlewit,.... 50 "	glish Prisoners,......... 25 '

A complete sett of the above Sixteen books, will be sold, or sent to any one, to any place, *free of postage*, for $6.00.

LIBRARY OCTAVO EDITION.
Published in Seven Different Styles.

This Edition is complete in SIX very large octavo volumes, with a Portrait of each of Charles Dickens, containing the whole of the above works, handsomely printed and bound in various styles.

Vol. 1 contains **Pickwick Papers and Curiosity Shop.**
" 2 do. **Oliver Twist, Sketches by "Boz," and Barnaby Rudge.**
" 3 do. **Nicholas Nickleby, and Martin Chuzzlewit.**
" 4 do. **David Copperfield, Dombey and Son, and Christmas Stories.**
" 5 do. **Bleak House, and Dickens' New Stories.**
" 6 do. **Little Dorrit. In two books—Poverty and Riches.**

Price of a sett, in Black cloth,.. $9.00
" Scarlet cloth, extra,... 10.00
" Law Library style,.. 11.00
" Half Turkey, or Half Calf,.................................... 13.00
" Half calf, marbled edges. French,......................... 14.50
" Half calf, real ancient antique,.............................. 18.00
' Half calf, full gilt backs, etc................................... 18.00

ILLUSTRATED OCTAVO EDITION.

THIS EDITION IS IN THIRTEEN VOLUMES, and is printed on very thick and fine white paper, and is profusely illustrated with all the original Illustrations by Cruikshank, Alfred Crowquill, Phiz, etc., from the original London editions, on copper, steel, and wood. Each volume contains a novel complete, and may be had in complete setts, beautifully bound in cloth, for Nineteen Dollars a sett; or any

T. B PETERSON & BROTHERS' PUBLICATIONS.

volume will be sold separately at One Dollar and Fifty cents each. The following are their respective names:

- Little Dorrit.
- Pickwick Papers.
- Barnaby Rudge.
- Old Curiosity Shop.
- Bleak House.
- David Copperfield.
- Dombey and Son.
- Nicholas Nickleby.
- Christmas Stories.
- Martin Chuzzlewit.
- Sketches by "Boz."
- Oliver Twist.
- Dickens' New Stories.

Price of a sett, in Black cloth, in Thirteen volumes,............................$19.
" " Full Law Library style,.. 25.00
" " Half calf, or half Turkey,..................................... 29.00
" " Half calf, marbled edges, French,........................... 32.00
" " Half calf, ancient antique,................................... 39.00
" " Half calf, full gilt backs, etc............................... 39.00

---◆◉▶---

DUODECIMO ILLUSTRATED EDITION.
Complete in Twenty-Five Volumes.

The Editions in Duodecimo form are beautifully Illustrated with over *Five Hundred Steel and Wood Illustrations*, from designs by Cruikshank, Phiz, Leech, Browne, Maclise, etc., illustrative of the best scenes in each work, making it the most beautiful and perfect edition in the world; and each work is also reprinted from the first original London editions that were issued by subscription in monthly numbers, and the volumes will be found, on examination, to be published on the finest and best of white paper.

This edition of Dickens' Works is now published complete, entire, and unabridged, in Twenty-five beautiful volumes, and supplies what has long been wanted, an edition that shall combine the advantages of portable size, large and readable type, and uniformity with other standard English authors.

This Duodecimo edition has been gotten up at an expense of over *Thirty-Five Thousand Dollars*, but the publishers trust that an appreciative public will repay them for the outlay, by a generous purchase of the volumes. All they ask is for the public to examine them, and they are confident they will exclaim, with one voice, that they are the handsomest and cheapest, and best illustrated Sett of Works ever published. This edition is sold in setts, in various styles of binding, or any work can be had separately, handsomely bound in cloth, in two volumes each. Price $2.50 a sett, as follows:

- Pickwick Papers.
- Nicholas Nickleby.
- David Copperfield.
- Oliver Twist.
- Bleak House.
- Little Dorrit.
- Dombey and Son.
- Sketches by "Boz."
- Barnaby Rudge.
- Martin Chuzzlewit.
- Old Curiosity Shop.
- Christmas Stories.
- Dickens' New Stories.

Price of a sett in Twenty-Five volumes, bound in Black cloth, gilt backs,....$35.00
" " Full Law Library style,... 40.00
" " Scarlet, full gilt, sides, edges, etc.,......................... 45.00
" " Half calf, ancient antique,.................................... 60.00
" " Half calf, full gilt back,..................................... 60.00
" " Full calf, ancient antique,.................................... 75.00
" " Full calf, gilt edges, backs, etc.,............................ 75.00

T. B. PETERSON & BROTHERS' PUBLICATIONS. 7

PEOPLE'S DUODECIMO EDITION.
Published in Eight Different Styles.

This Duodecimo edition is complete in Thirteen volumes, of near One Thousand pages each, with two illustrations to each volume, but is not printed on as thick or as fine paper as the Illustrated Edition, but contains all the *reading* matter that is in the Illustrated Edition, printed from large type, leaded. The volumes are sold separately or together, price One Dollar and Fifty cents each, neatly bound in cloth; or a complete sett of Thirteen volumes in this style will be sold for $19.00. Following are their names:

Little Dorrit.	Nicholas Nickleby.
Pickwick Papers.	Christmas Stories.
Martin Chuzzlewit.	Old Curiosity Shop.
Barnaby Rudge.	Sketches by "Boz."
Bleak House.	Oliver Twist.
David Copperfield.	Dickens' New Stories.
Dombey and Son.	

Price of a sett, in Black cloth,..$19.00
"   "   Full Law Library style,..24.00
"   "   Half calf, or half Turkey,.....................................26.00
"   "   Half calf, marbled edges, French,......................28.00
"   "   Half calf, ancient antique,..................................32.00
"   "   Half calf, full gilt backs,...................................32.00
"   "   Full calf, ancient antique,..................................40.00
"   "   Full calf, gilt edges, backs, etc........................40.00

ADVENTURES AND TRAVELS.

Harris's Explorations in South Africa. By Major Cornwallis Harris. This book is a rich treat. Two volumes, paper cover. Price $1.00; or in cloth, $1.25.

Wild Oats Sown Abroad; or, On and Off Soundings. Price 50 cents in paper cover; or cloth, gilt, 75 cents.

Don Quixotte.—Life and Adventures of Don Quixotte; and his Squire, Sancho Panza. Complete in two volumes, paper cover. Price $1.00.

Life and Adventures of Paul Periwinkle. Full of Illustrations. Price 50 cents.

EUGENE SUE'S GREAT NOVELS.

Illustrated Wandering Jew. With Eighty-seven large Illustrations. Two volumes. Price $1.00.

Mysteries of Paris; and Gerolstein, the Sequel to it. Two volumes, paper cover. Price $1.00.

First Love. A Story of the Heart. Price 25 cents.

Woman's Love. Illustrated. Price 25 cents.

Martin the Foundling. Beautifully Illustrated. Two volumes, paper cover. Price One Dollar.

The Man-of-War's-Man. Complete in one large octavo volume. Price 25 cents.

The Female Bluebeard. One volume. Price 25 cents.

Raoul de Surville. One volume. Price 25 cents. (*In Press.*)

GEORGE LIPPARD'S WORKS.

Legends of the American Revolution; or, Washington and his Generals. Two vols. Price $1.00.

The Quaker City; or, The Monks of Monk Hall. Two volumes, paper cover. Price One Dollar.

Paul Ardenheim; the Monk of Wissahikon. Two volumes, paper cover. Price One Dollar.

Blanche of Brandywine. A Revolutionary Romance. Two volumes, paper cover. Price One Dollar.

The Nazarene. One vol. Price 50 cents.

Legends of Mexico. One volume. Price 25 cents.

The Lady of Albarone; or, The Poison Goblet. Two volumes, paper cover. Price One Dollar; or bound in one volume, cloth, for $1.25. (*In Press.*)

New York; Its Upper Ten and Lower Million. One volume. Price 50 cents.

T. B. PETERSON & BROTHERS' PUBLICATIONS

ALEXANDRE DUMAS' WORKS.

Count of Monte-Cristo. By Alexandre Dumas. Complete and unabridged edition. Beautifully Illustrated. Two volumes, paper cover. Price $1.00; or in cloth, $1.25.

Edmond Dantes. Being a Sequel to Dumas' celebrated novel of the "Count of Monte-Cristo." 1 vol. 50 cts.

The Three Guardsmen. By Alexandre Dumas. Complete in one large volume. Price 75 cents.

Twenty Years After. A Sequel to the "Three Guardsmen." One volume. Price 75 cents.

Bragelonne; the Son of Athos: being the continuation of the "Three Guardsmen," and "Twenty Years After." One volume. 75 cents.

The Iron Mask. Being the continuation and conclusion of the "Three Guardsmen." Two vols. Price $1.00.

Louise La Valliere; or, The Second Series and End of the "Iron Mask." Two volumes. Price $1.00.

The Memoirs of a Physician. Beautifully Illustrated. Two vols. Price One Dollar.

The Queen's Necklace. A Sequel to the "Memoirs of a Physician." Two volumes. Price One Dollar.

Six Years Later; or, The Taking of the Bastile. A Continuation of "The Queen's Necklace." 2 vols. $1.00.

Countess of Charny; or, The Fall of the French Monarchy. A Sequel to Six Years Later. Two vols. $1.00.

The Memoirs of a Marquis. Complete in two vols. Price $1.00

Diana of Meridor; or, France in the Sixteenth Century. Two volumes. Price One Dollar.

The Iron Hand; or, The Knight of Mauleon. Beautifully Illustrated. One volume. Price 50 cents.

The Forty-Five Guardsmen. Beautifully Illustrated. One volume. Price 75 cents.

Fernande; or, The Fallen Angel. A Story of life in Paris. One volume. Price Fifty cents.

Thousand and One Phantoms. Complete in one vol. 50 cts.

George; or, The Planter of the Isle of France. One vol. Price Fifty cents.

Genevieve; or, The Chevalier of Maison Rouge. One volume. Illustrated. Price 50 cents.

Sketches in France. One volume. Price 50 cents.

Isabel of Bavaria. One volume. Price 50 cents.

Felina de Chambure; or, The Female Fiend. 50 cents.

Andree de Taverney; or, The Second Series and End of the Countess of Charny. Two vols. $1.00. (*In Press.*)

The Conscript Soldier. A Tale of the Empire. Two volumes, paper cover. Price $1.00; or bound in one volume, cloth, for $1.25. (*In Press.*)

The Corsican Brothers. 25 cents. (*In Press.*)

EMERSON BENNETT'S WORKS.

The Border Rover. Two large vols., paper cover. Price One Dollar; or in one volume, cloth, for $1.25.

Pioneer's Daughter; and the Unknown Countess. Complete in one volume. Price 50 cents.

Clara Moreland. Price 50 cents; or cloth, gilt, $1.00.

Viola. Price 50 cents; or in cloth, gilt. 75 cents.

The Forged Will. Price 50 cents, or cloth, gilt, $1.00.

Ellen Norbury. 50 cents; or one vol., cloth, $1.00.

Bride of the Wilderness. 50 cents.; or in cloth, 75 cents.

Kate Clarendon. 50 cents; or in cloth, gilt, 75 cents.

Heiress of Bellefonte; and Walde-Warren. 50 cents.

HARRY COCKTON'S WORKS.

Valentine Vox, the Ventriloquist. One vol., paper cover, 50 cts; or a finer edition in cloth, for $1.50.

Sylvester Sound, the Somnambulist. Illustrated. Complete in one large octavo volume. Price 50 cents.

The Sisters. By Henry Cockton, author of "Valentine Vox, the Ventriloquist." Price 50 cents.

The Steward. By Henry Cockton. Price 50 cents.

Percy Effingham. By Henry Cockton. Price 50 cents.

T. B. PETERSON & BROTHERS' PUBLICATIONS.

HUMOROUS AMERICAN WORKS.
With Original Illustrations by Darley and Others.
Done up in Illuminated Covers.

Major Jones' Courtship. With Thirteen Illustrations, from designs by Darley. Price 50 cents.

Drama in Pokerville. By J. M. Field. With Illustrations by Darley. Price Fifty cents.

Louisiana Swamp Doctor. By author of "Cupping on the Sternum." Illustrated by Darley. 50 cents.

Charcoal Sketches. By Joseph C. Neal. With Illustrations. 50 cents.

Yankee Amongst the Mermaids. By W. E. Burton. With Illustrations by Darley. Price 50 cents.

Misfortunes of Peter Faber. By Joseph C. Neal. With Illustrations by Darley. Price Fifty cents.

Major Jones' Sketches of Travel. With Eight Illustrations, from designs by Darley. Price Fifty cents.

Western Scenes; or, Life on the Prairie. By the author of "Major Jones' Courtship." 50 cents.

Quarter Race in Kentucky. By W. T. Porter, Esq. With Illustrations by Darley. Price Fifty cents.

Sol. Smith's Theatrical Apprenticeship. Illustrated by Darley. Price Fifty Cents.

Yankee Yarns and Yankee Letters. By Sam Slick, alias Judge Haliburton. Price 50 cents.

Life and Adventures of Col. Vanderbomb. By author of "Wild Western Scenes," etc. Price 50 cents.

Big Bear of Arkansas. Edited by Wm. T. Porter. With Illustrations by Darley. Price Fifty cents.

Major Jones' Chronicles of Pineville. With Illustrations by Darley. Price Fifty cents.

Life and Adventures of Percival Maberry. By J. H. Ingraham. Price Fifty cents.

Frank Forester's Quorndon Hounds. By H. W. Herbert, Esq. With Illustrations. Price 50 cents.

Pickings from the "Picayune." With Illustrations by Darley. Price Fifty cents.

Frank Forester's Shooting Box. With Illustrations by Darley. Price Fifty cents

Peter Ploddy. By author of "Charcoal Sketches." With Illustrations by Darley. Price Fifty cents.

Streaks of Squatter Life. By the author "Major Jones' Courtship." Illustrated by Darley. 50 cents.

Simon Suggs.—Adventures of Captain Simon Suggs. Illustrated by Darley. Price 50 cents.

Stray Subjects Arrested and Bound Over. With Illustrations by Darley. Price Fifty cents.

Frank Forester's Deer Stalkers. With Illustrations. 50 cents.

Adventures of Captain Farrago. By Hon. H. H. Brackenridge. With Illustrations. Price Fifty cents.

Widow Rugby's Husband. By author of "Simon Suggs." With Illustrations. Price Fifty cents.

Major O'Regan's Adventures. By Hon. H. H. Brackenridge. With Illustrations by Darley. 50 cents.

Theatrical Journey-Work & Anecdotal Recollections of Sol. Smith, Esq. 50 cents.

Polly Peablossom's Wedding. By the author of "Major Jones' Courtship." Price Fifty cents.

Frank Forester's Warwick Woodlands. With beautiful Illustrations, illuminated. 50 cents.

New Orleans Sketch Book. By "Stahl." With Illustrations by Darley. Price Fifty cents.

The Charms of Paris; or, Sketches of Travel and Adventures by Night and Day. 50 cents. (*In Press.*)

C. J. PETERSON'S WORKS.

Kate Aylesford. A Love Story. Two vols., paper cover. Price One Dollar; or bound in one vol., cloth, for $1.25

Cruising in the Last War. First and Second Series. Being the complete work. By Charles J. Peterson. Price 50 cents.

The Valley Farm; or, The Autobiography of an Orphan. A Companion to Jane Eyre. Price 25 cents.

Grace Dudley; or, Arnold at Saratoga. Price 25 cents.

Mabel; or, Darkness and Dawn. Two vols., paper cover. Price One Dollar or bound in cloth, $1.25 (*In Press*)

MRS. GREY'S POPULAR NOVELS.
Price Twenty-Five Cents each.

Gipsy's Daughter.
Lena Cameron.
Belle of the Family.
Sybil Lennard.
Duke and Cousin.
The Little Wife.
Manœuvring Mother.
Baronet's Daughters.
Young Prima Donna.
Old Dower House.
Alice Seymour.
Hyacinthe. [50 cents.
Passion & Principle.
Mary Seaham. 50 cents.

D'ISRAELI'S POPULAR NOVELS.
With a Portrait of D'Israeli in each volume.

Vivian Grey. One large volume, octavo. Price 50 cents.
Venetia; or, Lord Byron and his Daughter. Price 50 cents.
Henrietta Temple. A Love Story. Price 50 cents.
The Young Duke. One octavo volume. Price 38 cents.
Contarini Fleming. An Autobiography. Price 38 cents.
Miriam Alroy. A Romance of the 12th Century. Price 38 cents.

MISS ELLEN PICKERING'S WORKS.
Price Twenty-Five Cents each.

Orphan Niece.
Kate Walsingham.
Who Shall be Heir?
The Secret Foe.
The Expectant.
The Fright.
Quiet Husband.
The Heiress.
Poor Cousin.
Ellen Wareham.
Nan Darrel.
Prince and Pedlar.
Merchant's Daughter.
The Squire.
Agnes Serle.
The Grumbler. 50 cts.

FRANK FAIRLEGH'S WORKS.

Frank Fairlegh; or, Scenes in the Life of a Private Pupil. By Frank E. Smedley, Esq. Illustrated. Paper cover. Price 50 cents.
Lewis Arundel. By author of "Frank Fairlegh." Illustrated. One volume, paper cover. Price 75 cents.
Harry Racket Scapegrace. By author of "Frank Fairlegh." Complete in one volume. Paper cover. Price 50 cents.
Lorrimer Littlegood. By author of "Frank Fairlegh." Complete in two volumes paper cover. Price $1.00; or bound in one volume, cloth, for $1.25. (*In Press.*)
Harry Coverdale's Courtship, and All that Came of It. Now first published Entire and Unabridged. Illustrated. Two volumes, paper cover. Price One Dollar; or bound in one volume, cloth, $1.25. (*In Press.*)

CAPTAIN MARRYATT'S WORKS.
Price Twenty-Five Cents each.

Jacob Faithful.
Phantom Ship.
King's Own.
Snarleyow.
Midshipman Easy.
The Naval Officer.
Newton Forster.
Rattlin, the Reefer.
Japhet Search Father.
Pacha of many Tales.
Pirate & Three Cutters.
Percival Keene. 50 cts.
Poor Jack. 50 cents.
Sea King. 50 cents.
Peter Simple. 50 cents.
Valerie. 50 cents.

REYNOLDS' GREAT ROMANCES.

Mysteries of the Court of London. Complete in two large volumes, paper cover. Price $1.00.

Rose Foster; or, "The Second Series of the Mysteries of the Court of London." 3 vols., paper cover. $1.50.

Caroline of Brunswick; or, the "Third Series of the Mysteries of the Court of London." Two vols., paper cover. Price One Dollar.

Venetia Trelawney; being the "Fourth Series, or final conclusion of the Mysteries of the Court of London." Two volumes, paper cover. Price One Dollar.

Lord Saxondale; or, The Court of Queen Victoria. Two vols., paper cover. Price One Dollar.

Count Christoval. The "Sequel to Lord Saxondale." Two volumes, paper cover. Price One Dollar.

Rosa Lambert; or, The Memoirs of an Unfortunate Woman. Two vols., paper cover. Price One Dollar.

Mary Price; or, The Adventures of a Servant-Maid. Two vols., paper cover. Price One Dollar.

Eustace Quentin. A "Sequel to Mary Price." Two volumes, paper cover. Price One Dollar.

Joseph Wilmot; or, The Memoirs of a Man-Servant. Two volumes, paper cover. Price One Dollar.

The Banker's Daughter. A Sequel to "Joseph Wilmot." Two vols., paper cover. Price One Dollar.

Kenneth. A Romance of the Highlands. Two volumes, paper cover. Price One Dollar.

The Rye-House Plot; or, Ruth, the Conspirator's Daughter. Two vols., paper cover. Price $1.00.

The Opera Dancer; or, The Mysteries of London Life. Complete in one octavo volume. Price 50 cents.

The Ruined Gamester. With Illustrations. Complete in one large octavo volume. Price Fifty cents.

Wallace the Hero of Scotland. Beautifully Illustrated with Thirty-eight plates. Price Fifty cents.

The Child of Waterloo; or, The Horrors of the Battle Field. Complete in one octavo volume. 50 cents.

The Discarded Queen. One volume. Price 50 cents.

Lucrezia Mirano; or, The Countess and the Page. Complete in one large volume. Price 50 cents.

Ciprina; or, The Secrets of a Picture Gallery. Complete in one large volume. Price 50 cents.

The Necromancer. A Romance of the Times of Henry the Eighth. Two volumes. Price One Dollar.

Robert Bruce: the Hero King of Scotland, with his Portrait. One volume. Price Fifty cents.

Isabella Vincent; or, The Two Orphans. One volume, paper cover. Price 50 cents.

Vivian Bertram; or, A Wife's Honor. A Sequel to "Isabella Vincent." One vol., paper cover. 50 cents.

The Countess of Lascelles. The Continuation to "Vivian Bertram." One vol., paper cover. 50 cents.

Duke of Marchmont. Being the Conclusion of "The Countess of Lascelles." One vol., paper cover. 50 cts.

Gipsy Chief. Beautifully Illustrated Complete in one large octavo volume Price Fifty cents.

Pickwick Abroad. A Companion to the " Pickwick Papers" by "Boz." One volume. Price Fifty cents.

Queen Joanna; or, the Mysteries of the Court of Naples. Illustrated. 50 cents.

The Soldier's Wife. Beautifully Illustrated. Complete in one volume. Price Fifty cents.

May Middleton; or, The History of a Fortune. Complete in one volume. Price Fifty cents.

Massacre of Glencoe. Beautifully Illustrated. Complete in one volume. Price Fifty cents.

The Loves of the Harem. Price 50 cents.

Ellen Percy; or, The Memoirs of an Actress. Price 50 cents.

Agnes Evelyn; or, Beauty and Pleasure. Price 50 cents.

The Parricide. Beautifully Illustrated. Price 50 cents.

Life in Paris. Handsomely Illustrated. Price 50 cents.

Edgar Montrose. One volume. Price 25 cents.

J. F. SMITH'S BEST WORKS.

The Usurer's Victim. By J. F. Smith, Esq. Complete in one large volume. Price 50 cents.

Adelaide Waldgrave; or, The Trials of a Governess. Complete in one large volume. Price 50 cents.

12 T. B. PETERSON & BROTHERS' PUBLICATIONS

AINSWORTH'S BEST WORKS.

Life of Jack Sheppard, the most noted burglar, robber, and jail breaker that ever lived. Illustrated. 50 cents.

The Tower of London. With over One Hundred splendid Engravings. Two volumes. Price $1.00.

The Miser's Daughter. Complete in two large vols. Price $1.00.

Pictorial Life & Adventures of Guy Fawkes. Bloody Tower, etc. Illustrated. Price 50 cents.

The Pictorial Old St. Paul's. A Tale of the Plague and the Fire. Illustrated. Price 50 cents.

The Star Chamber. Illustrated. Price 50 cents.

Mysteries of the Court of Queen Anne. Price 50 cents.

Mysteries of the Court of the Stuarts. Price 50 cents.

Windsor Castle. One volume. Price 50 cents.

The Pictorial Newgate Calendar; or, The Chronicles of Crime. Beautifully Illustrated. 50 cents.

Life of Henry Thomas, the Western Burglar and Murderer. Full of Plates. One volume. Price 25 cents.

Pictorial Life & Adventures of Dick Turpin, the Burglar, Murderer, etc. One vol. Price 25 cents.

Life and Adventures of the Desperadoes of the New World. Illustrated. 1 vol. 25 cents.

Life of Ninon De L'Enclos With her Letters on Love, Courtship & Marriage. Illustrated. 1 vol. 25 cts.

Pictorial Life and Adventures of Davy Crockett. One volume. Price 50 cents.

Grace O'Malley—Her Life & Adventures. Price 38 cents.

Life & Adventures of Arthur Spring. Price 25 cents.

T. S. ARTHUR'S BEST WORKS.
Price Twenty-Five Cents each.

The Lady at Home.
Year after Marriage.
Cecilia Howard.
Orphan Children.
Love in High Life.
Debtor's Daughter.
Love in a Cottage.
Mary Moreton.
The Divorced Wife.

The Two Brides.
Agnes, or Possessed.
Lucy Sandford.
The Banker's Wife.
The Two Merchants.
Insubordination.
Trial and Triumph.
The Iron Rule.
Pride and Prudence.

GREEN'S WORKS ON GAMBLING.

Gambling Exposed; a full Exposition of all the various Arts, Mysteries, and Miseries of Gambling. By J. H. Green, the Reformed Gambler. Complete in two volumes, paper cover, Price One Dollar; or one volume, cloth, gilt, $1.25.

The Reformed Gambler; or, The Autobiography of the Reformed Gambler, J. H. Green. Written by Himself. Complete in two volumes, paper cover. Price One Dollar; or in one vol. cloth, gilt, for $1.25. (*In Press.*)

The Gambler's Life; or, The Autobiography of the Life, Adventures, and Personal Experience of Jonathan H. Green. Written by Himself. With a Steel Portrait of the Author, and other Illustrative Engravings. Two vols., paper cover. Price One Dollar; or one volume, cloth, gilt, $1.25.

Secret Band of Brothers. Compiled by J. H. Green. Beautifully Illustrated from original designs, by Darley and Croome. Two volumes, paper cover. Price One Dollar; or in one vol., cloth, gilt, for $1.25. (*In Press.*)

LIEBIG'S WORKS ON CHEMISTRY.

Agricultural Chemistry. Complete in one volume. Price 25 cents.

Animal Chemistry. Complete in one volume. Price 25 cents.

Letters on Chemistry.

The Potato Disease.

Chemistry and Physics in relation to Physiology and Pathology

The above Five works of Professor Liebig are also published complete in one large octavo volume, bound. Price $1.50. The three last works are only published in 1st bound volume.

T B. PETERSON & BROTHERS' PUBLICATIONS 13

WORKS BY THE BEST AUTHORS.

The Quaker Soldier; or, The British in Philadelphia. By a noted Judge Two vols., paper cover. Price One Dollar; or in one vol., cloth, for $1.25

Currer Lyle; or, The Autobiography of Louise Reeder. Written by Herself, and containing her Portrait on Steel. Two vols., paper cover. Price One Dollar; or bound in one volume cloth, for $1.25.

Life and Beauties of Fanny Fern. Complete in two volumes, paper cover, price $1.00; or bound in one volume, cloth, for $1.25.

Corinne; or, Italy. By Madame De Stael. Translated expressly for this edition. The poetical passages by L. E. L. Two vols., complete in one. Price Fifty cents.

The Roman Traitor. By H. W. Herbert. Two vols., paper cover. Price $1.00; or one vol., cloth, $1.25.

Flirtations in America; or, High Life in New York. Complete in one volume. Price 50 cents.

The Pride of Life. By author of "Henpecked Husband." 2 vols., paper cover. Price $1.00; or bound in one volume, cloth, for $1.25.

The Cabin and Parlor. By J. Thornton Randolph. Price 50 cents in paper; or bound in cloth for $1.00.

Life in the South. An Antidote to "Uncle Tom's Cabin." Illustrated by Darley. Price 50 cents.

Mysteries of Three Cities; Boston, New York, and Philadelphia By A. J. H. Duganne. One vol. 50 cts.

Red Indians of Newfoundland. An Illustrated Indian Story. By author of "Prairie Bird." 50 cts.

The Greatest Plague of Life; or, The Adventures of a Lady in Search of a Good Servant. Price 50 cents.

Ned Musgrave; or, The most Unfortunate Man in the World. By Theodore Hook. One volume. 50 cents.

Llorente's History of the Inquisition in Spain. Complete in one large octavo volume. 50 cents

Genevra; or, The History of a Portrait. By one of the most prominent Writers in America. One vol. 50 cts

Abbey of Innismoyle. By Grace Kennedy. Price 25 cents.

Father Clement. By author of "Dunallen." Price 50 cents.

The Fortune Hunter. By Mrs. Mowatt. Price 38 cents.

Romish Confessional. By M. Michelet. Price 50 cents.

Whitehall; or, The Times of Oliver Cromwell. Complete in one volume. Illustrated. Price 50 cents.

Whitefriars; or, The Days of Charles the Second. Complete in one volume. Illustrated. Price 50 cents (*In Press.*)

USEFUL BOOKS FOR EVERYBODY.

The Lady's Work-Table Book. Full of plates. Beautifully bound in one volume in crimson cloth, gilt. Price One Dollar.

Lardner's One Thousand and Ten Things Worth Knowing; to which is added Employment to All; or a Hundred Ways to make and keep Money. Price 25 cents.

Pocket Library of Useful Knowledge. A work that all should own. Price 50 cents.

Gentlemen's Science of Etiquette; and Guide to Society. By Count D'Orsay. With his Portrait. Price 25 cents.

Ladies' Science of Etiquette; and complete Hand-Book of the Toilet. By Countess De Calabrella. 25 cents.

The Complete Kitchen and Fruit Gardener. A work that all that have a garden should own Price 25 cents.

The Complete Florist; or, Flower Gardener. The best work on the subject ever published. Price 25 cents.

Knowlson's Complete Farrier, or Horse Doctor. All that own a horse should possess this book. Price 25 cents.

Knowlson's Complete Cattle; or, Cow Doctor. Whoever owns a cow should have this book. 25 cts

Arthur's Receipts for Putting up Fruits & Vegetables in Summer to Keep. 12½ cts.

DR. HOLLICK'S WORKS.

Hollick's Anatomy and Physiology; with a large Dissected Plate of the Human Figure. $1.25.

Dr. Hollick's Family Physician. A Pocket Guide for Everybody. Price 25 cents.

WORKS BY THE MOST POPULAR AUTHORS.

Robert Oaklands; or, The Outcast Orphan. By Leitch Ritchie, author of "Robber of the Rhine." Price 25 cts.

Moredun. A Tale of 1210. By Sir Walter Scott, Bart., author of "Waverly," "Ivanhoe," etc. Price 50 cents.

The Two Cousins. By P. Hamilton Myers, author of "Bell Brandon," etc. One vol., cloth. Price $1.00.

Courtenay Hall. A True Tale of Virginia Life. By James T. Randolph, Esq. One volume, cloth. Price $1.00.

Wilfred Montressor; or, New York Life Exposed; or the Exposition of the Secret Order of the Seven. Illustrated with 87 Illustrative Engravings. Two volumes. Price $1.00.

Salathiel. By Rev. George Croly. Price 50 cents.

Aristocracy; or, Life among the Upper Ten. Price 50 cents.

Henry Clay's Portrait. By Nagle. Size 22 by 30 in. Price $1.00 a copy. Originally sold at $5.00 a copy.

The Miser's Heir. By P. H. Myers. Price 50 cents in paper cover; or 75 cents in cloth gilt.

Tom Racquet; and His Three Maiden Aunts. Price 50 cents.

The Two Lovers. A Domestic Story. Price 50 cents.

Arrah Neil. A Novel. By G. P. R. James. Price 50 cents.

Sketches in Ireland. By W. M. Thackeray. Price 50 cents.

The Coquette. One of the best books ever written. Price 50 cents.

The Orphan Sisters. A beautiful book. Price 38 cents.

Victims of Amusements. By Martha Clark. Suitable for Sunday Schools. One volume, cloth. 38 cts.

GEORGE SAND'S WORKS.

Consuelo. By George Sand. Translated from the French, by Fayette Robinson. Complete and unabridged. One volume. Price Fifty cents.

Countess of Rudolstadt. The Sequel to "Consuelo." Translated from the original French. Only Complete and unabridged edition. One volume. Price 50 cents.

Indiana. By author of "Consuelo," etc. A very bewitching and interesting work. Two vols., paper cover. Price $1.00; or in one vol., cloth, for $1.25.

First and True Love. By George Sand, author of "Consuelo," "Indiana," etc. Illustrated. Price 50 cents.

The Corsair. A Venetian Tale. Price 25 cents.

CHRISTY & WOOD'S SONG BOOKS.

No music is so generally esteemed, or songs so frequently sung and listened to with so much delight, as is the music and the songs of the Ethiopian Minstrels. They have commenced a new epoch in Music, and the best works relating to them are those mentioned below. Each Book contains near Seventy Songs.

Christy & Wood's Song Book. Illustrated. Price 12½ cents.

The Meledeon Song Book. Price 12½ cents.

The Plantation Melodies. Price 12½ cents.

The Ethiopian Song Book. Price 12½ cents.

The Serenaders' Song Book. Price 12½ cents.

Christy and White's Complete Ethiopian Melodies, containing the whole of these five song books, are beautifully bound in one large volume, cloth, gilt back. Price Seventy-five cents a copy only.

REV. CHAS. WADSWORTH'S SERMONS.

America's Mission. A Thanksgiving Discourse. By Rev. Charles Wadsworth. Complete in one large volume. Price 25 cents.

Thankfulness and Character. Two Discourses. By Rev. Charles Wadsworth. Price 25 cents.

Politics in Religion. A Thanksgiving Sermon. By Rev. Charles Wadsworth. Price 12½ cents.

SIR E. L. BULWER'S NOVELS.

Falkland. A Novel. One vol., octavo. Price 25 cents.

The Roue; or, The Hazards of Women. Price 25 cents.

The Oxonians. A Sequel to "The Roue." Price 25 cents.

Calderon, the Courtier. By Sir E. L. Bulwer. Price 12½ cents.

PETERSON'S MAGAZINE

Best and Cheapest in the World for Ladies!

This popular monthly will be greatly improved for 1861. It has a circulation of nearly 100,000: *or ten times as much as any other two dollar Magazine.* It contains about 1000 pages of double column reading matter yearly; from 25 to 30 Steel Plates and about 800 Wood Engravings: *which is proportionately more than any periodical, at any price, gives.* The newspapers, very generally pronounce it *superior in many respects,* to the three dollar Magazines. Subscribe for it, and

SAVE A DOLLAR.

The stories in "Peterson" are conceded to be *the best published anywhere.* The editors are Mrs. Ann S. Stephens, author of "Mary Derwent," "Fashion and Famine;" and Charles J. Peterson, author of "The Old Stone Mansion," "Kate Aylesford," "The Valley Farm," etc., etc.; and they are assisted by Frank Lee Benedict, the author of "Susy L.'s Diary," by T. S. Arthur, E. L. Chandler Moulton, Mehitable Holyoke, Virginia F. Townsend, Mary A. Denison, Ella Rodman, Clara Augusta, Gabrielle Lee, H. C. Gardner, Mary W. Janvrin, Carry Stanley, Caroline E. Fairfield, Ellen Ashton, Clara Moreton, E. Dewees, A. L. Otis, and all the most popular female writers of America. There will be given in 1861, several

ORIGINAL COPYRIGHT NOVELETS:

Equal in merit, at least, to those for which this Magazine has already attained such celebrity, and superior to those to be found anywhere else. Morality and virtue are always inculcated. *Clergymen recommend this Magazine particularly for families in which there are daughters.* Its pictorial embellishments are also unrivalled. Its

SUPERB MEZZOTINTS and other STEEL ENGRAVINGS

Excel those in any other Magazine, and one at least is given in every number.

COLORED FASHION PLATES IN ADVANCE.

☞ IT IS THE ONLY MAGAZINE WHOSE FASHION PLATES CAN BE RELIED ON. ☜

Each number contains a Fashion Plate, engraved on steel, and colored; also, a dozen or more New Styles, engraved on wood; also, a Pattern, from which a Dress, Mantilla, or Child's Costume can be cut, without the aid of a mantua-maker—so each Number, in this way, will SAVE A YEAR'S SUBSCRIPTION. The Paris, London, Philadelphia and New York Fashions are described, at length, each month. Engravings of new styles of Caps, Bonnets, Head-Dresses, Mantillas. Cloaks, Capes, Under-Garments, &c., &c., given in great profusion in every number. ☞ Also, a Plate of CHILDREN'S FASHIONS EVERY MONTH.

COLORED EMBROIDERY PATTERNS.

The Work-Table-Department of this Magazine is WHOLLY UNRIVALLED. It is edited by Mrs. Jane Weaver, who continually furnishes beautiful Original Patterns. Every Number contains a dozen or more patterns in every variety of Fancy work; Crochet, Embroidery, Knitting. Bead-work, Shell-work, Hair-work, Wax Flowers, Stained Glass, Leather-work, Painting, Photographs. &c., &c.: *with full descriptions.* Every Number will contain a SUPERB COLORED PATTERN for SLIPPER, PURSE, CHAIR SEAT, HANDKERCHIEF, EMBROIDERY, COLLAR AND CUFF, or some other useful, or ornamental article: and each of these would cost at a retail store, Fifty cents. *These can be had in no other American Magazine.*

RECEIPTS FOR THE TABLE, TOILETTE, SICK ROOM, &C., &C.

Will be given in every Number. ☞ A PIECE OF NEW AND FASHIONABLE MUSIC WILL APPEAR EACH MONTH. Also, articles on the Flower Garden, and Horticulture generally; and Hints on all *matters interesting to Ladies.*

TERMS—ALWAYS IN ADVANCE:

One Copy for One Year, $2.00	Eight Copies, One Year, $10.00
Three Copies for One Year, 5.00	Twelve Copies, One Year, 15.00
Five Copies for One Year, 7.50	Sixteen Copies, One Year, 20.00

PREMIUMS FOR GETTING UP CLUBS.—Three, Five, Eight, Twelve, or Sixteen copies make a Club. To every person getting up a Club of Three, and remitting Five Dollars; or a Club of Five, and remitting Seven Dollars and a Half; or a Club of Eight, and remitting Ten Dollars; we will send *gratis,* our splendid MEZZOTINT or an ALBUM, at the choice of the person getting up the Club. To every person getting up a Club of Twelve, and remitting Fifteen Dollars; we will send either an extra copy of the Magazine for 1861, or the Mezzotint or Album, as the remitter may prefer. To every person getting up a Club of Sixteen, and remitting Twenty Dollars, we will send the Mezzotint or Album, *and also an extra copy for* 1861.

CHARLES J. PETERSON,
306 Chestnut Street, Philadelphia.

☞ All Postmasters constituted Agents. A Specimen sent when desired.

www.ingramcontent.com/pod-product-compliance
Lightning Source LLC
Chambersburg PA
CBHW051849300426
44117CB00006B/327